The Dutch-American Experience

Robert P. and Joan Swieringa (1995)

The Dutch-American Experience

Essays in Honor of
Robert P. Swierenga

Edited by

Hans Krabbendam
and
Larry J. Wagenaar

VU Uitgeverij
Amsterdam 2000

VU Studies on Protestant History, Publication Series of the Historisch Documentatiecentrum voor het Nederlands Protestantisme (1800-heden) Vrije Universiteit Amsterdam.
General Editors: Prof. Dr. J. de Bruijn and Prof. Dr. G.J. Schutte.

1 *Bunyan in England and Abroad.* Edited by M. van Os and G.J. Schutte (1990)
   ISBN 90-6256-911-0
2 *Sharing the Reformed Tradition: The Dutch – North American Exchange, 1846-1996.* Edited by George Harinck and Hans Krabbendam (1996)
   ISBN 90-5383-519-9
3 *Kuyper Reconsidered: Aspects of his Life and Work.* Edited by Cornelis van der Kooi and Jan de Bruijn (1999)
   ISBN 90-5383-640-3
4 *Breaches and Bridges: Reformed Subcultures in the Netherlands, Germany, and the United States.* Edited by George Harinck and Hans Krabbendam (2000)
   ISBN 90-5383-695-0
5 *The Dutch-American Experience. Essays in Honor of Robert P. Swierenga.* Edited by Hans Krabbendam and Larry J. Wagenaar (2000)
   ISBN 90-5383-702-7

ISBN 90-5383-702-7

© VU Uitgeverij, Amsterdam, 2000

Cover: Neroc, Amsterdam
Printed by: Ridderprint, Ridderkerk
Type: Hans Seijlhouwer, Amsterdam

Contents

Section 3: Immigrant Mobility

Section 4: Dutch-American Religion

Section 5: Portrait Gallery

Acknowledgments

The editors like to thank the following institutions which contributed to the publication of this volume: the Van Raalte Institute at Hope College, Holland, Michigan, the Joint Archives of Holland, Holland Michigan, the Dutch-American Historical Commission, the Historical Documentation Center for Dutch Protestantism (1800 to the present day) at the Vrije Universiteit Amsterdam, the Netherlands, the Roosevelt Study Center, Middelburg, the Netherlands, and the Nederlands Emigratie Fonds. Moreover, we would like to thank Dr. Jeanne M. Jacobson who rendered a valuable service in copy-editing the manuscript, Mr. Hans Seijlhouwer for his care in the lay out of the volume, and Mrs. Lori Trethewey and Mrs. Leontien Joosse who assisted in meeting secretarial needs to complete our efforts.

SECTION 1

ROBERT P. SWIERENGA AND THE DUTCH AMERICAN EXPERIENCE

The Dutch-American Immigrant Experience of Robert P. Swierenga

Hans Krabbendam and Larry J. Wagenaar

Graafschap, Overisel, and Vriesland, villages of the Dutch immigrant concentration in Michigan all possessed a monumental, historical white church of one of the major Dutch Reformed denominations. These buildings, dating from the 1860s, lost their original function or were torn down because they no longer met requirements of contemporary church life. The church of the founder of the Holland colony, Albertus Van Raalte still stands as a visible, yet lonely, permanent reminder of the strongly religious past of the Dutch immigrant settlements. More transient phenomena such as festivals, parades, lectures, exhibits, memorials, concerts, and other public events also commemorate the Dutch immigrant experience in the United States. A lasting legacy of the Dutch American experience has been created by the publications of historian Robert P. Swierenga which document and analyze this important ethnic tradition.

Swierenga's Commitment

Though Robert P. Swierenga was born into a second-generation Dutch-American family in Chicago's West Side, received his education in its Christian school system through Timothy Christian High-school and Calvin College, and briefly taught at Calvin after he earned his Ph.D. in American history at the University of Iowa, his primary research interest was not the Dutch landverhuizers. He earned his reputation in agricultural and economic history, and made his name as a pioneer in the frontier of new quantitative history, while never losing sight of the qualitative sources. A 1976 Fulbright Fellowship in the Netherlands physically reconnected him with the land of his forebears. Recurrent returns enabled him to build a network of Dutch-American scholarly contacts, resulting in a growing group of colleagues and Dutch students for whom he became an example of an engaged and yet scholarly researcher.

Robert Swierenga's expertise is by no means restricted to the field of immigration history, as one of his first students Harry S. Stout explains in the first essay, but his influence is best felt in immigration research. While he schooled generations of students at Kent State University in Kent, Ohio, and provided them with tools, textbooks, and topics, his "school" of graduates counted a number of students of immigration. His fundamental fieldwork enabled him to transcend the common contrasts between city and countryside, innovative and traditional methods, secular and Christian topics, outside behavior and interior convictions, details and generalizations, the common man and the elite leaders, Dutch and American perspectives. In the following essays, colleagues and students alike show their debt to Robert Swierenga by connecting their specialized questions to his broad perspectives.

Four Themes
The editors selected four themes out of Swierenga's work as focus points: the relationship between worldview and immigration (why did or didn't people emigrate?); the trek itself (how did they move and to what destinations? In which phases and how definitive?); the religious setting (how did the church influence them and they influence the church?); and the role of the individual (how did individual immigrants experience and shape the Dutch-American community)? His productive output of databases, articles, and books inspired students and colleagues to participate in these research projects. His eagerness to share and stimulate, to compare notes and revise theories, has helped to build a circle of scholars who aim not at glorifying the Dutch in America, but describe and analyze the characteristics of this group in comparison with their fellow Americans and fellow Dutchmen. The chronological order within each section and the variety of subjects result in a – albeit far from complete – representative survey of the Dutch immigrant experience.

Immigration history reveals not only the demographic trends, but also the crises in a nation's culture and the strength of human imagination. Would departure bring advancement? How would life in the new world compare to life in the old? What would happen with family relations? How did the immigrants and their descendants evaluate the decision to emigrate? The editors are aware of the existence of a rich ethnic literature, but chose to concentrate on the historical background. Yet, the relationship between history and literature can be intimate as author and literature professor James C. Schaap illustrates in his essay. Scholarly exploration of Dutch immigrant history helps us to understand the narratives circulating among the descendants and the writers working with ethnic subjects. Schaap attributes great importance to the historian's tales, which supply the indispensable elements to create fiction by providing settings, plots, and characters. The contributions offer a rich pallet of these features.

Immigration and Ideology
The setting and plot of the story of immigration is often simplified to the adven-

tures of people fleeing for food and faith. Few Dutch immigrants fit the category of refugees. Robert Swierenga always emphasized the rational character of Dutch emigration and searched for convictions behind the enormous data file of countable features. Four contributions explore the role that ideas and ideals played in the immigration phenomenon and deal with the relationship of church and state, the persistence of communal goals in agricultural communities, the internal tension in the Social Democratic worldview, and the gender and class characteristics of the emigration movement to the US compared to the migration to the Dutch East Indies.

Provoked by the statement that protests against the established church easily spilled over to protest against the state and subsequently led to emigration, Hans Krabbendam re-examines the motivation of the first wave of Seceder emigrants. Why did some leave and other stay, while they all shared the same criticism of the *Hervormde Kerk*? Differences in opinion about the ideal relationship between church and state in the Netherlands and the other constitutional arrangement in the US shaped the will to move. Though the assumptions were not always explicitly and precisely articulated, those who more or less propagated in practice or principle a separation of church and state were inclined to emigrate, while those who set their hopes of a Christian state guarding the church decided to stay. So, even among a rather homogeneous group of Seceders, variations in their worldview guided the willingness to emigrate. Later on, the importance of this issue declined, when the Neo-Calvinists successfully participated in the Dutch political culture.

Communal features in the worldview of Dutch Calvinist farmers assisted them to keep tenure of their land and secure expansion of their settlements. This enabled the Dutch agricultural communities to survive the recurrent economic crises. A feeling of responsibility, rather than a special attachment to the land, was crucial and led to a stable settlement. Geographer Janel M. Curry compares this communal orientation in three rural Dutch American communities.

The Socialist subculture in the Netherlands was well developed and many laborers left for the US. The records of individuals who most often settled in urban America reveal that they had not come to start a revolution, but to improve their standard of living. Pieter Stokvis notes a tension in their Socialist worldview. While the Socialist immigrants before the 1917 Russian Revolution could still foster hopes that in the United States the most advanced phase of capitalism would mean the first chance for the workers' revolution, the next generation knew better. If they maintained a Socialist outlook, they had to join other ethnic groups, mostly Germans, for lack of a substantial Dutch socialist network. A general conclusion is that a worldview that did not match with American ideals had little chance to survive. Their Socialist worldview worked against organized continuation.

Suzanne M. Sinke explores a more general level of worldview, the change in cultural boundaries between the sexes, by comparing the ideals of Dutch immigrants in the US with those in the colony of the Dutch East Indies. In short, the women (and men) moving to the Indies generally belonged to the upper class, and confirmed their status and gender division. Those coming to the US abandoned the older class distinctions and developed broadened gender roles, allowing married women to also work outside the home. The confrontation with other races in the East Indies strengthened gender roles, while in the West it undermined them.

Immigrant Mobility
Swierenga's comprehensive overview of Dutch immigrants includes close scrutiny of their transport and travel. He discovered the careful planning and efficient traveling of the immigrants. The transatlantic crossing was certainly impressive and a marker, but mobility had more impact on the immigrant experience. Three contributions examine the influence of the Civil War in opening new destinations, the shift from rural to urban settlements, the assimilative role of social mobility, and the more global movements of migrants after World War II.

Brian W. Beltman retrieves the story of the Dutch who left their Pella enclave during the Civil War. Some joined the Union army as recruits, others fled conscription in the same army. Two groups sought their way to the west coast. Their dramatic adventure showed how difficult it was to start a new community, even in a coherent group that helped to broaden their horizon. When the war ended they returned, which showed the strength of the Dutch-American magnet in the Midwest, but also functioned as a stepping stone for the move to the western part of Iowa.

The immigrant experience of Dutch Catholics reveals two other mobility aspects. Different geographical and social mobility patterns stimulated intermarriage and accelerated the assimilation process of Dutch Catholics. Yda Schreuder explains why the Roman Catholic hierarchy decided to concentrate their flock in the cities because they could not provide pastoral care in the rural areas and feared anti-Catholic reactions. The short frontier phase of the Dutch Catholics in Wisconsin was quickly followed by the urbanization and industrialization phase, where farm hands occupied jobs in industry and service. These Dutch Catholics were part of the general movement towards the city, where they also could advance their social position. Schreuder discovered that social mobility advanced intermarriage. Both geographical and social mobility, advanced by the Catholic clergy, led to quick assimilation, while most of the Dutch Calvinists kept Americanization at a distance.

After World War II the Dutch government and the pre-war emigration societies had to reach a compromise in channeling the migration, as Henk van Stekelenburg describes.[1] Private farmers' organizations took the lead in mobilizing and organizing potential emigrants. The Dutch government was interested in emigration as a means to reduce unemployment, while the private societies focused especially on the small farmers solving their problems, and guiding the process. The initial agricultural stimulus faded and new factors added to the complexity of emigration. The American Walter-Pastore Acts tripled the quota for Dutch, in order to prepare a place for the repatriation of Dutch citizens from Indonesia. The *Noord-Brabanders* reflected the change in background of the emigrants to more urban origins. Emigration had ceased to be a regional movement, both in terms of the earlier agricultural stream and in terms of the international migration.

Dutch-American Religion

The 1857 split in the original Dutch Reformed Church in the United States was and continues to be a significant issue in Dutch-American immigration history. Swierenga contributed to the ongoing debate about the origin of the Christian Reformed Church (CRC) by comparing a number of variables and reconstructing the procedures. The break did not diminish, but rather increased the role of the church in immigrant life.

Donald A. Luidens and Roger J. Nemeth follow a quantitative path to determine how the subsequent waves of Dutch immigrants shaped the regional concentration and composition of the Reformed Church in America (RCA). The Midwestern branch came into existence through the first two waves of immigration up till the 1880s, while the immigrants in the period 1890-1920 meant a strong injection of the Eastern section of the church. The present spread of the RCA was a result of the nineteenth century Dutch immigration, not only their sheer numbers but also their clustering which built a strong church with a regional base. This enabled the RCA to become part of the mainline denominations.

Richard H. Harms deals with the institutional growth of the CRC. How could a small splinter develop into a viable denomination? He shows that though the CRC in the nineteenth century had a reputation of strict adherence to the traditional Dordt Church Order, it in fact was searching for strategies to survive as a church community. It accepted ministers and congregations previously affiliated with other denominations. When unification with an small orthodox Presbyterian denomination failed to materialize because of the language and the use of hymns, the CRC tried to join the mother church in the Netherlands. The *Christelijk Gereformeerde Kerk*'s rejection of the CRC partnership was a blessing in disguise and helped the CRC to prepare for independence. In the meantime, *De Wachter* played a crucial role in lining up arguments justifying the CRC's existence and molding more unity. The movement for Christian day schools built a strong identity, while the agreement to establish a seminary solved the problem of continuity and meant de facto a decision to become an American denomination.

The result of Harms' analysis is that the strict image of the CRC vis-à-vis the RCA did not mean it had a clear program of action. The shape of the denomination resulted from the dead ends reached in some strategies to overcome its extreme vulnerability and the new openings which helped it become truly independent. It would be a useful research project to determine whether the recent developments of the churches seceding from the CRC have any parallels with the early search of the CRC to find its own place and organization.

Portrait Gallery
Easy access to the versatility of the Dutch immigrant experience provide a representation series of individual portraits. Most Dutch immigrant leaders were ministers, but apart from them descriptions of an average *landverhuizer* and an exceptional Dutch-American belong in this gallery, while their female relatives would have been added had they left sufficient sources. These portraits supply the characters for the tales of history.

Lammert J. Hulst played his role in continuing the old life in the United States. He wanted to maintain the Seceder way of life, not only by resisting the anglicization of Reformed church life in the United States, but also the Neo-Calvinist offensive started by Abraham Kuyper and spreading in Christian Reformed circles of the day. James D. Bratt explains how the anti-change pastor was still accepted because of his authority supported by a committed pastoral role. He provided clear standards, personal comfort and attention. His was a personal authority as a patriarch. Hulst's presence in the midst of the magnet, the big city Grand Rapids, drew many newcomers from the northern provinces in the Netherlands to him and when he exchanged the RCA for the CRC in 1876 they moved with him. In this phase of almost two decades, Hulst was a beacon when especially northern Dutchmen streamed to Grand Rapids. But the dynamics of changing geography and changing culture undermined his position. Fit for local leadership, he did not grow to a larger regional leader. He was too closely linked to one of the factions to be accepted by the larger CRC crowd.

The Rev. Egbert Winter personally connected the various regions of Dutch-American and he also encountered their internal divisions, as Earl Wm. Kennedy shows. Born in a typical Seceder environment in Groningen, his family emigrated with the first wave of Seceder landverhuizers to Holland, Michigan. After his training as a pastor in New Brunswick, he served RCA churches in the East before he accepted calls to Pella at the end of the Civil War. From there he served the next wave of Dutch settlements further west, in Sioux County, Iowa, and the Dakotas.

George Harinck found in the life story of theologian Geerhardus Vos the key to his question why Abraham Kuyper chose to address a Presbyterian audience at Princeton instead of the concentration of Dutch immigrants in the Midwest. Vos introduced the ideas and person of Kuyper to B.B. Warfield as an ally in his struggle to defend the orthodoxy of the Presbyterian church. Vos' own move to Princeton Seminary was caused by the restrictive atmosphere of the Theological School in Grand Rapids. His position and his contribution to theology shows that orthodox scholars in different countries struggled with the same issues and used various traditions to find answers to questions about the relationship between faith and reason.

The Pieter Groustra story reveals the experiences of an average Dutch immigrant. Based on a long series of letters to Friesland, Annemieke Galema, a specialist of the emigration movement from that region in the period 1880-1920, shows how they received their information in the Netherlands. Their departure, journey, and reception in Chicago, where they worked in the Pullman factory, made them a prototype of the Dutch immigrant of that period. They took a calculated risk, clung to their religious feelings, maintained strong family ties, sent positive reports back home, worked hard, and enjoyed a high standard of living compared to his relatives in the Netherlands, and gradually felt he was an American.

Of course, there were many more Dutch Americans than those living in the midwestern enclaves. Hendrik Willem Van Loon is the "other Dutch American" far removed from his fellow country men of the Reformed bent and with little sympathy for them, but enormously popular as best selling author, populizer of history, and critic of culture. While living and working in the United States and Europe for a period of 40 years, working his *Stories* of Mankind, the Bible, America, of Rembrandt and so on, he became a true cosmopolite. He absorbed the American atmosphere and recreated this in his popular histories as Cornelis A. van Minnen shows. Working mainly in the New York area, Van Loon had no connections or a warm relationship with the midwestern Dutch immigrant communities. In a 1924 article published in *De Amsterdammer* he described the midwestern Dutch in pejorative terms and loathed them for their "backwardness" and servility towards their religious leaders. In his view this group of fellow Dutch immigrants belonged in the worst category of prejudiced primitive provincials in the United States.[2] On their part they ignored him and his publications. Van Loon's life offers a very different Dutch immigrant experience. But let us turn to the first of the portraits, one of the master: Robert P. Swierenga.

Notes

1. On May 28, 1999 Henk van Stekelenburg died just a few weeks after the completion of this article. This was his last article. "I enjoyed doing this for Robert who became a true friend," he wrote in the cover letter. His book on post World War II emigration was published posthumously as *De grote trek. Emigratie vanuit Noord-Brabant naar Noord-Amerika, 1940-1963* (Tilburg: Zuidelijk Historisch Contact, 2000).
2. Hendrik Willem Van Loon, "Brieven uit Amerika," *De Amsterdammer*, 24 March 1924.

Robert P. Swierenga, Historian and Teacher: An Appreciation

Harry S. Stout

Few, if any, contemporary American historians have achieved the breadth of Robert P. Swierenga's scholarly oeuvre. In a career spanning thirty-five years and still very much in high gear, Professor Swierenga has published definitive works of scholarship in such diverse fields as econometrics, the history of agriculture and the frontier, immigration historiography and Dutch immigration in particular, quantitative methods and social scientific theory, and American religious history. To fourteen major books he has added over 125 scholarly articles, and served as founding member of the Social Science History Association and long-time editor of its journal *Social Science History*.

In an age of increasing specialization, diversity is worthy of note, and can be traced, in part, to Swierenga's graduate training and early teaching experience at Calvin College. When Swierenga began his graduate training at the University of Iowa in 1961, he entered a program quickly gaining national prominence for its pathbreaking approaches to historical study. In the hands of now-legendary mentors like Samuel P. Hayes, Alan Bogue, or William Aydelotte, Iowa graduate students were trained to concentrate as much on method and research design – terms borrowed from the social sciences – as on particular topics or chronologies. Every subject in every time period requires an appropriate research design that will simultaneously allow a project to stand on its own legs and, at the same time, contribute to a broader fund of theoretical knowledge. In contrast to "Progressive" historians, who stressed the transience and presentism of all history, Iowa historians continued to believe in something like an objective body of truth that was recoverable through proper attention to detail and method. These were lessons that have followed Swierenga throughout his career and have enabled him to confront such a variety of programs and chronological periods in original and arresting fashion.

Though raised a "city boy" in the ethnic neighborhoods of Chicago, Illinois, Swierenga's interests at Iowa shifted to frontier and economic history. In the early 1960s, long before historical ecology became fashionable in "environmental studies" programs, Swierenga was engaging its principal interpretive themes and methodologies. In addition to the influence of his graduate mentors, Swierenga early came under the intellectual spell of the idiosyncratic University of Kansas environmental historian James C. Malin (1893-1979). Years later Swierenga would edit many of Malin's inaccessible writings. From Malin he inherited a methodology of social history that proclaimed the "possibility of objective history, within the limits of human knowledge." In opposition to "new historians" such as Carl Becker or Charles Beard, who saw all history-writing as merely personal constructions of reality, Malin argued that history could be objective if done within strict, empirical, behaviorist restraints. This meant doing history "from the bottom up" in carefully controlled, statistically measurable local case studies. From Malin and his own Iowa mentors, Swierenga learned early that systematic sampling, counting, aggregation of individual level data, and replicable research designs would restore the necessary degree of objectivity to historical study. The key was amassing sufficient numbers of sample "cohorts" or communities for comparative study.

Swierenga would take this objectivist or "behavioral" methodology to his own research on land speculation on the frontier through a broad sampling of agricultural communities in frontier Iowa. His design required a dogged pursuit of data with little immediate payoff – a trademark of Swierenga scholarship ever since. Earlier scholars, intimidated by mountains of aggregate data, and ignorant of the computer, routinely ignored the sources Swierenga eagerly ransacked for his "new" economic history of the frontier. The result would be history in a new key, the notes of which would not be fully appreciated until the following decade.

Upon completing his dissertation in 1965, Swierenga returned to his alma mater, Calvin College, as a freshly minted assistant professor of American History. At that time, Calvin was peopled almost exclusively by children of the (Dutch) Christian Reformed Church. Most of the faculty were, like Swierenga, Calvin graduates themselves. Required courses on the history of Calvinism, Calvin's *Institutes*, and the Bible insured that the school would inculcate students with a "world and life view" modeled very much on the Dutch Reformed model of Abraham Kuyper and the Free University of Amsterdam. As well, Calvin cemented loyalties to Dutch ethnicity that would become almost co-important with religion. Before the term would become popular, Calvin epitomized a truly "ethnoreligious" institution. In time this insularity would be questioned, and efforts put forward to recruit a diverse student body, but for Swierenga, Calvin College remained a model of how a Christian citizen could be "in" the United States without being "of" the United States.

As in most small liberal arts colleges, Calvin's faculty were not specialized, and all American historians were expected to teach courses in American history and "Western civilization," a "core" course required of all students. Calvin could offer no luxury of specialization, no time off for preparation of courses (not to mention research and writing). Waiting for him in his first year were preparations in Western Civilization, American history surveys, and an upper division course on the American West. Soon he would add a senior seminar on historical method. With textbooks and monographs at his elbow, he plunged into the new subject matters far removed from his research interests in agricultural history. At the end of his first year he surfaced with notes for over a hundred lectures. Something of Swierenga's versatility was nurtured in these years as he alternated courses on American history, the history of the Frontier, and quantitative methods with course lectures on ancient Mesopotamia, the Middle Ages, and the Reformation. In retrospect, this too would contribute to his diversity in ways a junior appointment at a research university could never have done.

In addition, Swierenga was blessed with an abundance of energy. Nights were meant for work, not sleep. When not attending to teaching and his own research, he devoted substantial amounts of time to his budding family and to the local Christian Reformed Church. Music was never far from his experience, bred in his childhood and later bequeathed to his own children. At an early morning (compulsory) chapel service at which he was invited to preach, Calvin students were stunned awake one morning when Swierenga suddenly interrupted the opening hymn by standing up and announcing to all present: "I'm not satisfied with the singing; let's pick it up!" The idea that music might become a part of one's inner spiritual life was not a notion that had occurred to most undergraduates – especially at 8:00 in the morning! But it was an enduring dimension of Swierenga's faith and recreation.

Though his stay at Calvin was brief, his influence was enduring. Many of his students went on to receive Ph.D.'s and achieve distinction in the profession. Together with his colleague Herbert Brinks, Swierenga took an active interest in building a Dutch American archive at Calvin. In the course of exploring the new archive he discovered a microfilmed copy of the original Netherlands government emigration lists for all Dutch provinces in the years 1847 to 1877. Such discoveries are the stuff of which historians' dreams are made. The detective in each of us discovers unknown materials as a thrilling call to action. It would take Swierenga another decade to make good on his discovery, but make good he would.

Before Swierenga could turn to other fields, the frontier beckoned. In all, he would prepare two massively researched monographs and a score of articles that would establish his reputation as the finest "young" agricultural historian in the country. The first monograph, *Pioneers and Profits*, was published in 1968. That book would lead to his appointment in American Economic History at Kent State University in the same year. At Kent State he was also given responsibility for an entirely new doctoral qualifying field in historical theory and methods. The lessons learned at Iowa would now be passed on to a rising generation of graduate students hungry for new ways to write history from the bottom up. Civil rights and the rise of "Black History" (a preeminent field at Kent State under the direction of August Meier and Elliott Rudwick), convinced many graduate students that the profession's preference for intellectual history was "elitist" and irrelevant to the lives of ordinary men and women. How, we asked, can we "listen to the inarticulate?" This was a question Swierenga knew how to answer: through exhaustive analysis of aggregate data in which thousands of ordinary people left the only marks for historians to recover. Soon Swierenga's seminar would be the most popular graduate seminar in the department. Students working in European history, early American history, recent American history, and even European history, all found in Swierenga's introduction to social scientific research designs and quantitative methods the tools we needed to write a "new" history.

In 1970, while deeply immersed in his analysis of Iowa land records, Swierenga edited a graduate text on *Quantification in American History: Theory and Research*. The reader immediately established itself as a classic in the field and spread the new methods of quantification to graduate seminars across the country. Of course Swierenga was not the only scholar working these vineyards, and indeed, the text itself was a distillation of other works produced by other quantitative scholars. The great contribution of his reader was to make the field as a whole available, when before it had to be extracted from scores of often esoteric books and articles. The reader featured a general discussion of "quantification and the computer," followed by five broad areas of research in which quantitative methods had already made significant inroads: content analysis, econometrics, popular voting behavior, and the "New Social History." Less about methods and statistical analysis (indeed there was none of this), the book focused on possibilities and futures.

At the time of *Quantification*'s appearance in 1970, tensions were running high in the profession between "traditionalists," who emphasized the artistic and narrative nature of the craft, and "quantifiers," who emphasized the scientific and analytical nature of the craft. To the extent that most of the quantifiers were also economic and social historians, the divisions also represented a division between "elite" intellectual historians on the one hand and "egalitarian" social historians on the other.

Although clearly in the quantifiers camp, Swierenga was a traditionalist by nature and not given to polemical extremes. To the extent that the new social history was driven by present day political or ideological agendas he was not interested. Anachronism was no more useful to the profession than elitism. Nor, Swierenga argued, were quantitative methods an end in themselves to be admired for their mathematical precision; they were simply instruments that existed, ironically, not to tame the past in the interests of the present but to recapture its pastness – its differentness. Far from shackling the past to the interests and fads of the present he saw in social scientific methodology exactly the opposite capability – the capacity to be surprised at how different the past was from anything we imagined. What excited Swierenga were the differences between past and present, not the similarities. Only in light of these, he reasoned, can the historian leave partisanship behind and find equal humanity in all the actors, the elites and the ordinary people, the winners and the losers.

Swierenga's traditionalist preoccupation with quantitative methods for the sake of the past would be seen even more clearly in his second (and last) major exploration of frontier history. Published in 1976 as *Acres for Cents*, the work employed quantitative methods to explore at ground level delinquent tax auctions in nineteenth-century Iowa. Earlier historians, lacking any empirical grounding, had interpreted these auctions through presentist assumptions grounded in "Turnerian" interpretive categories. Central to these studies was the notion of the frontier as a democratizing institution. When confronted with the widespread incidence of land auctions, scholars had unthinkingly assumed that these bidding wars were won by poor frontier speculators attempting to get a stake on the American frontier. In time, the theory went, these speculators became established farmers themselves, creating a "democratizing" effect that built the democratic agricultural communities of the future.

The problem with this interpretation, Swierenga sensed, was its anachronism and lack of any empirical grounding. But to establish such a grounding would again require the sort of Herculean research that had produced *Pioneers and Profits*. Over a period of years, punctuated by frequent trips to local court houses throughout seventeen Iowa counties, Swierenga scoured pages of tax sale certificates, tax lists, redemption certificates, property sales, and delinquent tax lists. Hundreds of pages of documents were photocopied or microfilmed and later coded and "punched" onto primitive "IBM" (Hollerith) cards for statistical correlation and multiple regression analyses.

The picture that emerged from this exhaustive research was contrary to the prevailing stereotypes. The past, it turned out on close empirical analysis, was different. The key actors in tax purchases were not indigent farmers but nonresident speculators from Eastern syndicates and prosperous local farmers who used tax auctions as a moneylending mechanism to circumvent usury laws. Instead of being a "democratizing" institution, tax auctions allowed rich farmers or speculators to allow lands to be sold for taxes for short-term capital accumulation and then later to redeem the farm liens within the grace period.

When Swierenga moved to Kent State he intended to immerse himself in major research projects and graduate education. But history would intervene and profoundly shift the priorities and preoccupations of the rising star. Soon after the appearance of *Quantification in American History*, tragedy struck the Kent State Campus – and the nation. On a bright sunny day in early May 1970, four students were shot dead by an occupying force of Ohio National Guardsmen deployed on Kent's campus. Suddenly academic debates over Vietnam and campus demonstrations crashed to their denouement in one mindless act of cruelty and murder. Swierenga was sitting in his Bowman Hall office when the violence erupted only a hillside away from his comfortable setting. One of the slain students had been a student in his undergraduate seminar. Swierenga's life – and all those associated with the tragedy – would never again be quite the same.

It is a truism of American historiography that intense social strain produces revivals of cultural identity and calls for a return to core values. Yet historians themselves are seldom the subjects of such crises. Swierenga and his colleagues at Kent State were. No sooner was martial law declared on Kent's campus then all present were thrust into a present where courses, grades, and degrees no longer mattered as they once did. Cries for "dialogue" and "community" abounded. In place of the "I lecture, you listen" model of graduate education that prevailed in the past, faculty members increasingly involved graduate students in university governance and decision-making. Allowances were made for absences due to involvement in the peace movement or the civil rights movement. Concerns over "sexism" and "male chauvinism" – still relatively new protest terms in university discourse – led to the creation of Women's Studies programs alongside the just created "Afro-Am" Centers. In history departments, dissertations on social history and women's history gained new legitimacy and unprecedented importance, hinting at the triumph of "gender studies" that twenty years later show no signs of abating. The existential question all members of the Kent community faced, some for the first time, was how do we restore community to a place in which one's own peacemakers made war? Or, more personally, what is *my* responsibility outside of the classroom as well as inside?

In Swierenga's case the answer was two-fold, personal and academic. Personally the tragedy prompted a reassertion of his Reformed Protestant convictions in open dialogue with university undergraduates, graduates, and faculty. In an address to the local InterVarsity chapter, published after classes resumed in the Fall of 1970, he called for a Christian response to the shootings that transcended reflexive national loyalties and traditional academic concerns. He wrote:

Conditions are no better this fall. The war continues, depersonalization and polarization increase, humanistic attempts to improve societal ills are bankrupt and political man increasingly obliterates spiritual man. What are Christians to do? It is time, I believe, to recognize that God expects His followers on the campus to engage in an active ministry of intercession, proclamation, and reconciliation. We cannot sit idly on the sidelines. And we cannot remain paralyzed as we were last spring.

Years later, in reflecting on these days, Swierenga would say "the 1970s was the most stimulating decade of my life, and my faith deepened as never before or since."

Although more active than ever with campus ministries and faith-based courses in a newly-created Experimental College at Kent, Swierenga never lost his scholarly focus. To complement his personal engagement with religion, he would shift his scholarly focus from economics and the natural environment to ethnicity and immigration. Implicit in this scholarly redirection was the sense that new Americas needed to be discovered in the mind as much as the continent, and the old "melting pot" monolith dismantled. This brought him at last back to the breathtaking discoveries at Calvin College's archives, and to Dutch immigration. With his core list of 21,000 immigrants, he began to build an enormous data file from additional sources. First came ship passenger manifests collected by U.S. customs agents beginning in 1820. By 1983 Swierenga had identified more than 55,000 names from 1,000 reels of microfilm dutifully borrowed from the National Archives through Kent State's cooperative interlibrary loan staff. Finally, and most ambitiously, Swierenga abstracted Dutch-born immigrants and their children from the U.S. Federal Population Census manuscripts of 1850, 1860, and 1870. With these three major data anchors in place Swierenga was able to employ computer capabilities to "link" these lists by name and trace Dutch emigrants from their home provinces in the Netherlands, through their arrival in American ports, to their destination of choice in the United States. Along the way he could provide information on the age, gender, occupation, and social status of all his subjects. Never before or since has such an ambitious immigrant linkage project been undertaken.

The first hint of the historical significance of this vast data collection project came in 1982 in the form of a computerized printout of Dutch emigration lists derived and translated from original Dutch records rather than the imperfect and woefully incomplete U.S. Customs lists that scholars previously had to rely upon for aggregate data. Published as *Dutch Emigrants to the United States, South Africa, South America, and Southeast Asia, 1835-1880: An Alphabetical Listing by Household Heads and Independent Persons*, the work included information on name, sex, age, occupation, religion, economic status, tax assessment class, household size, and motive for immigration. Prior to this work, nothing so complete had been compiled for persons of Dutch origin.

Besides serving the wider profession and Dutch American community, the data in the computer listing represented the raw materials of Swierenga's own ongoing research published in a staggering array of monographs, edited books, and scholarly articles. Seldom is there a greater testimony to patience and sheer determination. The research data, years in the making, represented a gold mine of almost infinite wealth which, after years of savings, would yield a career's worth of dividends.

In 1982 the Dutch government assigned Swierenga major responsibility for organizing, and later publishing, an international symposium, held in Amsterdam, June 1-4, 1982. The papers presented were co-edited by Swierenga and published later that year as *A Bilateral Bicentennial: A History of Dutch-American Relations 1782-1982*. The work is a tour de force in American diplomatic and international studies. Major scholars from R.R. Palmer to Lawrence S. Kaplan, Frank Freidel, and Michael Kammen all contributed original essays. Swierenga himself published an overview of his vast research in an essay entitled "Exodus Netherlands, Promised Land America: Dutch Immigration and Settlement in the United States."

Throughout the 1980s Swierenga moved from the international history of Dutch emigration to the immigrant experience itself on American shores. In 1985 he edited a major book of essays entitled *The Dutch in America*. Again he recruited a "who's who" of distinguished immigration scholars to explore such diverse subjects as religion and immigration, labor and immigration, ethnic clustering and immigration, and mobility and immigration. Himself expert in all of these areas, Swierenga contributed the single most important essay in the collection, an overview entitled "Dutch Immigration Patterns in the Nineteenth and Twentieth Centuries." In that article he was able to empirically demonstrate that neither "push" factors nor "pull" factors contributed significantly to Netherlanders' attraction to America. In fact, relatively few Netherlanders left the tolerant and comfortable boundaries of their local "gemeenten," but those who did exerted a disproportionate influence on their "host" American society, from colonial origins on the east coast to the successful midwestern enclaves in the nineteenth century.

Though Swierenga's own immigrant roots lay in the "secessionist" Christian Reformed Church, with strong ethnic enclaves in Chicago, Grand Rapids, and Iowa, he would select an entirely different group for his next major monograph: Dutch American Jews. Later Swierenga would recall his upbringing in Cicero where he and his family developed close friendships with neighboring Jews. This interest carried over into his research and led to a major work, published in 1994, *The Forerunners: Dutch Jewry in the North American Diaspora*. This work – the first history of Dutch Jews in the United States – marks a major addition to scholarship on immigration, but even more on American Judaism. Although always a relatively small proportion of the American population in absolute numbers, Jews have been a major presence from their first arrival in the colonial period. Yet hardly any attention had been paid to the Dutch Jews before Swierenga. Where earlier treatments focused on Sephardic and Ashkenazic Jews from Germany, Russia, and Iberia, Swierenga uncovered another distinct tradition that initially resisted assimilation into the larger Jewish American community. Most were Orthodox and repudiated the Reform tendencies of German Jews, and many retained their native Dutch language and customs. Only after the Civil War, when German Jews arrived in overwhelming numbers, would the Dutch mark their transition to Reform and begin to blend into the German Jewish community.

Whether writing about Jews, Catholics, or Reformed Protestants, Swierenga found the fact of cultural persistence important for reasons that go far beyond the

Dutch immigration experience. In the background of Dutch immigration looms a question destined to dominate the 1970s: pluralism and the retention of ethnic identity. Were American immigrants "blended," whether willingly or unwillingly, into one hybrid culture of "Americans," or was America rather a mosaic of distinct colors and parts, forever hyphenating "American" with "Irish" or "Black" or "Asian"? For scholarly and personal reasons, Swierenga had no doubt where to line up on this issue – with the forces of pluralism and cultural retention. When Swierenga turned to consider the Dutch, he rejected the old line of argument. Above all, he insisted, American immigrants retained intense loyalties and associations with the "mother land." One characteristic of the immigrants that Swierenga would come back to in much of his writings on the Dutch was their dogged resistance to assimilation. In contrast to many other ethnic groups – including the Germans, French, and English – the Dutch "remain a self-conscious ethnic group after many generations in America."

The search for the significance of ethnic identity in American history led to major works on the subject of ethnicity and politics. By this time at Iowa, Swierenga wrote an essay on the election of 1860 that examined the "ethnic vote" for or against Lincoln in the Iowa elections. In typical fashion Swierenga ignored the conventional wisdom, which assumed that "ethnics" voted Democratic, and looked at ground level data, using the computer to analyze electoral data in several Iowa counties. His findings showed conclusively that "contrary to all expectations, over 80 percent of the new [Dutch] voters cast Whig ballots." Swierenga's essay on the Lincoln election would later serve as the nucleus for an edited book of essays entitled *Beyond the Civil War Synthesis: Political Essays of the Civil War Era* (1975). Instead of using class and region variables, this collection demonstrated through roll call analyses and micro-community studies a "reorientation of American political studies" from class and region to ethnicity and religion.

Little did Swierenga realize when writing that essay that he was anticipating arguments that would revolutionize the study of nineteenth-century American political history in the 1970s and 80s. A wave of scholarly electoral "case studies" employed the computer to ask who voted in elections, how they voted, and what variables best predicted voter preference. In place of static models of economic determinism that presumed voters behaved according to their socioeconomic status, these new "ethnocultural" studies discovered, as had Swierenga earlier, that in election after election religion and ethnicity were better predictors than class or region in predicting voter behavior.

At a national conference on religion and politics held at Wheaton College (Illinois) in 1988, Swierenga had the satisfaction of presenting an overview of the ethnocultural studies he had done so much to encourage a decade earlier. All of these electoral studies demonstrated that "religion was the key variable in voting behavior until at least the Great Depression." By arraying religious and ethnic traditions alongside a "pietistic-liturgical" continuum, Swierenga was able to correlate liturgical traditions with Democratic votes and pietistic traditions with Whig, and later Republican, votes.

One year later Swierenga reissued his ethnocultural paper at a seminal symposium of Soviet and American historians convened in Moscow in 1989. The time was momentous. Glasnost was in the air. Religious services were held in Red Square for the first time since the Revolution. Talk in East Germany was obsessed with bringing down the wall. Most of the thoroughly disillusioned Soviet historians present at the symposium openly scoffed at Marxism, often over the objections of some American historians still holding on to the old orthodoxy! In this environment of dashed pasts and hopeful new beginnings, Swierenga's paper became the cause celebre of the entire conference. When rendered in Russian through a skilled team of simultaneous translators, his "Ethnoreligious Political Behavior" had an electrifying effect. All those present (including this writer) could not fail to notice how riveted the Soviet scholars were by its subject matter. The reasons were not hard to decipher. Ethnocultural analysis presented Russian scholars with a model of political behavior that bypassed class in just the ways they were attempting to do in the Soviet Union and East Germany. And ethnicity, in all its power to form and deform, was conspicuous in breakaway Soviet republics and a newly assertive Orthodox Church. The subsequent – and often bitter – history of post-Soviet ethnic wars and "cleansings" confirms all too powerfully the prescience of the ethnocultural explanatory model that Swierenga presented to these scholars for the first time.

One question that remains open from Swierenga's pioneering forays into "ethnocultural" history is the issue of how to separate out the hyphenated ethnic-religious variable and examine religion on its own terms. This would constitute a major agenda for Swierenga's most recent scholarship and push him from political and ethnic history to American religious history.

In 1991, Swierenga co-edited (with a former Calvin student, Philip VanderMeer), a major collection of essays entitled *Belief and Behavior: Essays in the New Religious History*. The work represented a powerful exhibit of cutting-edge scholarship, not unlike the impact of *Quantification in American History* twenty years earlier. Consistent with his own research proclivities, Swierenga chose to showcase local, grassroots studies of religious behavior from all the major religious traditions, including Protestant, Catholic, and Jew. The chronology was similarly inclusive, spanning the seventeenth to the twentieth centuries. Together the essays embodied the contours of a "new religious history" that moved the profession "from theology as the pronouncement of theologians to religious belief systems, from an examination of the religious lives of some members to an analysis of the role of religion in the lives of many men and women, and from a consideration of churches as narrow religious institutions to an awareness of their broad social-political significance."

In 1996 Swierenga retired from Kent State but not from an active career in scholarship. He accepted a research appointment from Hope College as the Albertus C. Van Raalte Research Professor at the A.C. Van Raalte Institute devoted to the study of the Dutch in America. Although a dedicated teacher and mentor to scores of graduate students, scholarship remained his first love and that to which he has happily returned at the peak of his career. His likens his new post to a "permanent sabbatical."

Since moving to Hope College, Swierenga's interests in Dutch immigration and religion have yielded impressive results. In *Family Quarrels in the Dutch Reformed Churches in the Nineteenth Century*, co-authored by Swierenga and Elton Bruins, Swierenga continues the theme of behaviors grounded in beliefs with a magisterial summation of the theological debates and issues that divided Reformed Dutch immigrants from first nineteenth-century settlements to the present. The key issues revolved around what might be termed an assimilationist "Americanist" wing of the Dutch Reformed communities versus a "sterner" Calvinist and isolationist wing who resisted assimilation and Americanization. These issues, Swierenga demonstrates, live on in the 1990s as the new ecumenical issues of female ordination and homosexuality threaten once again to fracture consensus and issue new splits. Many of these themes are given fuller treatment in his forthcoming *Faith and Family: Dutch Immigration and Settlement in the United States, 1820-1920.*

Swierenga's career as teacher and scholar, viewed as a whole, warrants several generalizations. First, some observations of Swierenga as teacher. Swierenga never claimed to love undergraduate survey courses, and his move to Hope College was at least partially motivated by his desire to pursue full-time scholarship. But he was an extraordinary teacher with a life-long influence on many of his students. Anyone with any experience in college education recognizes that teaching is not, in the first place, mesmerizing lectures, nor is it performance and entertainment. In its essence, teaching is a call to personal attention, and this Swierenga evidenced to distinction. Decades later, his first Calvin students would recall the influence he exerted on their careers by the sheer fact of his caring. The same was no less true of Kent State students culturally and spiritually adrift following the shootings of 1970.

At the graduate level, Swierenga was simply superb. To appreciate Swierenga as mentor one must go beyond the relatively sterile environs of his office in Bowman Hall to his self-constructed study in the basement of his house, located four blocks from campus. That is where the real learning and study took place. There he welcomed graduate students into his home and invited us to discuss their research, often for hours at a time. Routinely he invited us to dinner, where conversations would continue to late in the night, often with coffee and dessert supplied by his wife – and loyal word processor – Joan.

In all, Swierenga would direct nineteen masters theses at Kent State and twenty-three doctoral dissertations. As well he would sit on the doctoral committees of scores more students, often advising them on method and theory. Many of the scholars trained by Swierenga occupy important teaching and research positions in international settings – a placement record unrivaled for relatively new Ph.D. programs such as Kent State's.

And what of scholarship? In summarizing thirty-five years of ongoing scholarship, we have already noted the great breadth of Swierenga's interests from the environment to immigration, to ethnicity, and religion. The interesting pattern here is the way in which Swierenga evidenced an almost mystical knack for hitting on each of these scholarly waves at their crest. No sooner did new fields or problems come to the attention of the profession, then Swierenga was there at the foundation. The 1970s can fairly be described in American historiography as the time when quantification took off. So too immigration and ethnicity in the 1980s and, most recently, an unprecedented interest in American religion today, both past and present.

Swierenga's uncanny (and surely unintended) sense of timing goes some distance in accounting for another remarkable facet of his career: released time for research and writing. Throughout his time at Kent State, he was blessed with two Fullbright Fellowships for work in the Netherlands in 1976 and 1985. Through Kent State's Office of Research and Sponsored Programs he enjoyed an additional (and unprecedented) nine semester-long fellowships in twenty-eight years, together with a sabbatical.

Are there common threads running through Swierenga's bewildering and intimidating mastery of so many fields and centuries? At least two constants characterize his work. First is literary style. As stylist, Swierenga learned to make the most of social scientific history writing. Though numbers and tables are not ordinarily the stuff of great narrative, Swierenga turned his subjects into vignettes and stories of compelling drama. A constant in his career is his love of clear, expressive prose. The same urge to avoid the false note in music followed his writing career. Swierenga has always sought to be specific and accurate, to make each sentence as real as possible.

A second constant in Swierenga's writings is a conviction that careful empirical research is the best route to "objective" (within human constraints) history, and that empirical research is best directed at understanding *public* behavior. Although hardly insensitive to the New Social History and its recovery of the private sphere in human experience, Swierenga's metier has always been between the public and the measurable. Exactly *how* do people behave: As investors? As migrants? As voters? As "believers"?

Anyone who has had the privilege of working with Swierenga soon learns the lessons of exhaustive and meticulous research, patience spanning years of data collecting without deferred payoffs, and unending curiosity. The essays in this volume bear out these lessons by their diversity and rich empirical grounding. In a small way they pay tribute to his remarkable career, and more, his remarkable dedication to mentoring the rising generation with collegiality, and the immense goodwill that remains as inspirational as his books and lectures.

To Take A Crown

James C. Schaap

You have to know what it meant to go to town in those days. You have to know that the twenty-minute trip from a rented farm place outside of Maurice, Iowa, all the way in to the bustling village of Orange City, the county seat, was an event poor farm families ritually undertook only for weekly Sunday worship. Almost every-one had an automobile of some sort, so going to town didn't mean hitching up the horses, who undoubtedly needed a Sabbath of their own after a week in the fields that May. Nonetheless, you'd have to know that sixty years ago nobody except the rich and the silly just ran into town on a whim.

Going to town was an excursion that usually followed thoughtful planning, almost a holiday. Church was a necessity, but buying essentials – wheat and flour and sugar and dry goods – was an occasional requirement that often became a singular joy, the only outing a poor family ever took that didn't end with the singing of the Doxology.

You have to understand that going to town was the highlight of the week, if not month. For a child – a girl especially – the farm was a wonderful place for solitary wistfulness, all day in the richly silent company of cats. But a farm meant work. Lots of it. Going to town meant hundreds of people, men and women on wooden sidewalks chatting away as if life weren't all that difficult, the whole place in a plenitude of novel aromas – fresh bakery, the cottony clean smell of dry goods, the dank fleshy-ness of the butcher shop.

I say you have to understand what going to town really meant to a poor farm girl in 1940, even if Orange City, at best, was only a thousand recently planted Dutch-American souls on the broad Iowa grasslands. To an unmarried young woman from the farm, life blossomed on village streets where smart young men with mannered smiles courted comely young women who knew exactly how to hold their heads when they sauntered past the shops.

Fashion began there – the only bib overalls were on little kids and bumpkin farmers. People sang together and did plays and spoke the English language almost exclusively. Ball teams took to real diamonds, not just cow-pied pasture land, and all kinds of people gathered to watch Orange City guys duel Sioux Center's finest or Rock Valley's. Going to town meant leaving behind, at least for an afternoon, both the isolation and the drudging daily regimen of the farm.

You've got to know all of that to understand a story I'd like to write someday. The culture has to be set before the narrative will admit the imagination of the reader. Humanity emerges from typescript only in proportion to the story's ability to bring the reader to that time and place. Set adrift from its historical moorings, the story will not only have little appeal, it will have little drama. That's why I say you have to understand what going to town meant to a farm girl back then – spring, 1940 – when the story, a real story, occurred.

And you have to know her, too, the young girl I'm speaking of. I have to recreate the her she was then from my knowledge of the woman herself, from what I've come to understand about her, knowing her as I have for more than a quarter of a century. Her story is central to this story.

You need to understand what going to town meant to her, and not just going to town for an afternoon, but going to town actually to live there, to leave the farm. You have to understand what that opportunity meant to this particular farm girl, a young woman, the oldest of six children, who had already buried her father. You have to understand what it must have felt like to stop "working out," playing handmaid to some neighboring farm wife – doing the family's cooking, washing, ironing, cleaning house; you have to understand what it must have been like to end the isolation of that kind of job, too, the one she had to take when her father died. Going to town for this young woman meant claiming a life of her own.

She was a grade-schooler when her father died. It was mid-Depression, and Franklin Delano Roosevelt's New Deal had not as yet woven a safety net for poor families who suddenly found themselves so tragically bereft. There were deacons to be sure, but no social workers, no welfare, no food stamps. All they had was the pluck that could be generated by desperation.

When he died, she was in the eighth grade and she had to leave school. For the rest of her life she would judge that loss her handicap. Wherever she would go, she would remember that there were ideas about nationhood and culture, art and literature, science and math, that she would never know, because when he died her formal education became a luxury the family couldn't afford – especially not a girl. She had to work. Economic necessity made her leaving school and getting a job non-negotiable.

The woman at the heart of the story is someone I'll call Albertina Mellema, even though the historical record readily offers her real name. She stands as tall as she ever did – nearly six feet – and still holds the beauty that once set her apart from other poor farm girls who made their way into town in the late Thirties. Today she's eighty years old. Her face is thin, her hair silver, but her features carry a sense of that stunning darkness so characteristic of her family, a swarthiness the family attributes to a spot of Hispanic blood from the time of Philip II in the Netherlands. In 1940, in a town of blondes, she must have been remarkable.

She still looks markedly aristocratic. Perhaps it's her height, or her deep set eyes or the rim of heavy eyebrows that puts drama in her face. If the caricature Dutch girl is apple-cheeked and heavy shouldered, she has none of that. She worries almost excessively about her weight, even though she is regally slim. She is no slave to fashion – nor has she ever been. She believes in good taste – buy once, buy well. What she wears is invariably classic in line and color.

When she'd come to town in those days, people must have noticed her. The powers-that-be – Orange City's bourgeois, those folks who'd attained the education Albertina never could – must have spotted her in church or seen her at the grocery, because once, before she'd even moved to town, they asked her to serve tea for them. Her presence was requested by a woman's club, a group of patrician wives who thought to color their dreary, Iowa plains existence by reading and discussing books of interest to a national culture that must have seemed, back then, thousands of miles away from the far corner of a state known, if at all, for hogs and corn.

The women gathered at club member's homes for discussions and delights, and it was their custom to choose some needy girl, some impoverished immigrant maybe, to serve them their repasts. But the chosen had to be pretty. She had to grace their conversation. Today, such largesse seems vulgar – plucking pretty poor girls from their squalor, decking them in stiffly starched aprons to act as chamber maids for a dozen prissy women tipping their tea cups to chat about Edna Ferber or John Steinbeck.

Albertina Mellema was one of those young ladies graciously chosen for the honor of servanthood at the Orange City Ladies Reading Club. Albertina Mellema, whose father had died, who'd been forced to "work out of the home" because the family needed money; Albertina Mellema, that beautiful young woman, tall and willowy, darkly-featured, has the look of someone, well, southern European – maybe even Jewish, they might have said. You must have seen her in town? She's strikingly beautiful. Why don't we ask the Mellema girl? That's it, then, eh? – this Albertina Mellema. It's settled then. Next time, Albertina Mellema. Now who will ask her?

I can hear the conversation.

When I first heard that story, I wanted to spit in those tea cups. I wanted to unearth those women – all of them already dead – and explain that what they considered their grace was little more than self-righteousness. Not only was Albertina Mellema a showpiece, something human they could admire like good silver, their deep concern for poor girls gave them leave to admire their own compassion concurrently. Your grace, I would have told them, was in fact a curse.

But Albertina Mellema, I know, didn't see her servanthood to them in that way at all – didn't then, and doesn't now. To her, serving the Reading Club was her debut into polite society, an opportunity to touch a world so unlike her own that to be a doorkeeper was a privilege. The women reading Sinclair Lewis were symbols to her, symbols just as real as the Mall of America to some Honduran illegal straightening motel rooms in Bloomington.

Today, when she talks of the Reading Club, her chin rises. Those women were everything she was confident she could never be. Simply to be in the filmy grace of their presence – those women who could say such smart things, such beautiful things – simply to be in the same house was everything those women thought it would be for the poor and beautiful when they chose Albertina Mellema. It takes some history to understand that trade-off, but you have to know to enter the story. I need the history to bring the story to life. I need to make it real.

But the Reading Club is not the story I'd like to write. There's more.

When Albertina Mellema moved to town, she was not dreaming of wealth. In fact, by moving she'd already reached the goal she'd set before her: she was going to work in the dime store on Main Street, going to say hello to every customer, going to live in life itself. Making money was a given; everything she would make in that store – with the exception of her own room-and-board – would be coursed back to the family she needed to support.

It wasn't the money that made her heart glad when she moved to Orange City. It was "clerking," as she describes it today; it was checking out the goods her customers chose from the shelves. To be able to stand behind the counter and greet every last person – even the lawyers and the judges and those distinguished teachers from the academy – simply to be able to serve those people was the actualization of a dream. To be downtown Orange City, Iowa, every day, in the buzz of human activity, to circulate in that social swirl seemed itself rhapsodic to a young woman who'd been too often unceremoniously swiped by cows' tails.

I think you have to know all of that to understand what was at stake.

Finally, we come to the story. I've had to set time and character. I've had to dress the narrative in costume of the era, plant its humanity in time and place.

But while the story is true, the wrappings must be drawn from my imagination. I've done the best I could to bring myself and you into the setting – northwest Iowa, a rural, ethnic and religious community, eighteen months from Pearl Harbor.

But where the facts end, the imagination must fuel the narrative. While I know Mrs. Mellema well, I don't claim to have found my way into every shadowed corner of her soul – nor would I want to. With her, as with so much else, I'm left to color the sketch on my own because she's not told me every last detail. Were I to go to her now and ask her to recollect the events of the story in as much detail as she could, she'd refuse. She wouldn't want me writing about her. She wouldn't want me saying what I've already said. So I've got to make things up, create a virtual world around the anecdote I'd like to write. But even what I imagine requires history, the memorabilia of that time and place.

It's time to sketch a scene.

When Dena Vander Wel and Rietje Kok came into the store, they'd done it so quietly that Albertina hadn't even remembered hearing the bell. It was embarrassing too, that she hadn't heard them, because when they came to the counter, Albertina was down on her knees on the floor with a whisk broom, trying to get the space behind the counter clean for once. She'd not heard them, she was down in a squat with her backside poking their way, and only when she'd turned back toward the register did she see them, suddenly, so suddenly that the dustpan nearly dropped from her hand.

"I'm sorry," she said quickly. "I'm so sorry – I never heard you."

The two women looked at each other, smiling graciously.

"I hope you haven't been waiting long," she said. "I was trying to get things cleaned up a bit – "

"We just came in," Mrs. Vander Wel said, winking.

Odd thing – winking, Albertina thought. "Can I help you?" she said.

"We've got some news," Mrs. Kok said, and then the two of them – educated women, too – looked at each other and giggled like schoolgirls.

"We've got some news," Mrs. Vander Wel said, "and it's about you."

She had not dared to hope. Simon Abma had mentioned it, teasingly, after church on Sunday, once they were a full block away from the north door. He'd whispered it as if, behind them, the Lord was in His holy temple and all the earth should keep silence about such silliness. Simon said it was what he'd heard, and that lots of people were going to vote for her, and how it would really be something if it happened. It was in the air, he'd said, and everybody said it was going to happen because everyone liked her, too. She was kind and never bossy or moody. "You, Tina," he'd said. "You're the one." That's what he'd told her.

She looked up at the women at the counter. It couldn't be anything else. "Some news about me?" she said.

Mrs. Vander Wel threw her shoulders back, stood straight as a soldier, dropped the giggle, but kept the smile. "We are here from the Chamber," she said, "and we're here to tell you that you" – she nodded – "that you have been elected to be this year's Tulip Festival Queen."

She really hadn't dreamed about what Simon had said because it seemed farther away from her own possibilities than marrying the mayor. She wasn't even from Orange City, after all. She was a farm girl, and she was Christian Reformed, not Dutch Reformed, and who did she know? I mean, she couldn't claim a family in town. She was a boarder at Mrs. Rowenhorst's, and she wasn't anything really, anything at all.

"You're not happy?" Mrs. Kok said. "Tina, you were elected – people chose you."

"I don't think I can," she told them.

Mrs. Vander Wel looked non-plussed. "Why?" she said.

"What would I say?" she said. "What would I wear?"

"We make your costume, you know," Mrs. Kok said. "It's beautiful, and it's from the province of Friesland, where your people come from."

There were no words and there were all kinds of words. "I don't know what my mother will say," she told them, even though once the words had tumbled out she thought they were foolish. She put a hand to her lips and another on the register to steady herself. "What I mean is, I don't know what she'll say, but why me?"

"People voted for you," Mrs. Kok said. "People chose you. That's why. Out of the all the girls in town, you were picked. We voted."

"What did I do?" she said. "How come?"

"Don't ask why, dear," Rietje said. "We're here to say," and then she looked at Mrs. Vander Wel, "that you've been chosen Tulip Queen." She raised her chin proudly. "And both of us are so happy," she went on. "You'll make a beautiful queen – won't she, Margaret?"

Mrs. Vander Wel nudged Mrs. Kok. "As we were walking up, Tina – and this is the truth – as we were coming to the store, we both said that you would make such a beautiful Queen."

Albertina wanted to hide. She wanted to run and hide. "I can't do it," she said. "I just can't do it. I really can't."

"You will," Mrs. Vander Wel said, reaching for her hand. "Listen to me – you will, and it will be the best thing that ever happened – and it will be the best thing for Orange City, too." She nodded reassuringly. "We're not taking no for an answer, are we?" she said, looking at Mrs. Vander Wel. Once more, the two of them giggled like the school girls who came into the store every afternoon.

Albertina Mellema didn't remember ever having been touched before by someone like Mrs. Vander Wel. It wasn't just a pat on the arm either. She could feel the woman's hand squeezing. "You'll have to help me," she told the ladies. "You'll have to help me with everything – I don't know what to do."

"All you have to do is look as beautiful as you are," Mrs. Kok told her, and she reached across the counter, actually reached right over the desk and hugged her, took her in her arms and held her there for a moment. "We're so proud of you," she said. "Really – both of us are so thrilled. We think you are the perfect choice."

History suggests that not all of Orange City's finest shared Mrs. Kok's feelings about the choice of Tulip Queen that year. I've done what I could to interview people who remember May, 1940, but no one remembers the nature of the conflict. There was a conflict, however. The man who wrote the history of Orange City's Tulip Festivals says that in 1941 the method by which the queen was chosen was significantly altered.

I would like to know why the choice of Albertina Mellema as the Orange City

Tulip Queen occasioned a reappraisal of the voting procedures. Maybe things were changed because Albertina was from Maurice, not Orange City. Maybe those in the know rather appreciated her serving them tea, but would rather have kept her in the kitchen in a bibbed apron; she was, after all, poor and uneducated. Perhaps one of their daughters didn't get the crown. Maybe Albertina's being Christian Reformed had something to do with the way the powers-that-be redid the whole system the next year, since the Christian Reformed were far less excited about the trumpery of Tulip Festivals and klompen dancers, far more self-righteous about selling one's soul for a silly parade. Perhaps I'd like to believe Miss Mellema was a victim of prejudice because such a scenario might satisfy my own. But we'll need some historian to figure it out – why did the whole system change the next year?

I know this much. Why things changed doesn't matter to the story I've always wanted to write, a story I've been laggard in sketching.

Scene two.

"But what would your father say?" her mother said when she brought the news. All the way to the farm she knew her first reaction would be the exact question she'd heard – "what would your father say?" All the way out there, she'd had time to think up an answer, so sure she was that her mother would say exactly what she had.

"Dad would say, do it," she told her mother. "Dad would be proud, Mother," she insisted. "Dad would think it was the best thing ever."

"I'm not so sure that's true," her mother said.

They were sitting on the porch. Si Abma had brought her out to the farm in his Ford. The weather was dreary, but remarkably warm for April, and he stood there in the yard, leaning up against the car, looking away into the barren fields.

"Dad would proud of me," Albertina insisted.

"That he would," her mother told her, "but that he would like the idea of your parading up in front of people like some showy woman, everyone eyeing you, everybody looking at you the way they will – that I don't think he'd like at all, Tina. Not his daughter. Seems vain, don't you think?" her mother said. "Does it strike you as vain?"

"It's an honor—"

"To stand up in front of people and look pretty?" her mother said.

"Off all the girls in the Orange City – "

"You're the one they want to look at?" her mother said. "Is that true?"

"I'm going to be the Queen."

"Don't say it as if it's already decided," her mother said.

What made it difficult to talk to her mother was that her mother would never look into her eyes. They could sit and talk and talk, even about important things, and her mother would never address her, as if she were afraid.

Just as she'd been afraid to give her husband the insulin. "I don't think I can do that," she'd told Tina years before. "I don't have the wherewithal. You'll have to do it for me."

So Albertina, an eighth grader, had administered the needle to her father time and time again as he slowly wasted away in those last months of his life.

"I just don't know what to say," her mother said.

Just a sign, any sign of anything less than disapproval, Tina thought.

Her mother lifted her head and looked across the yard, where Si was standing. "Just you and the boy in that car?" she said.

"He's my friend, Mother."

"Just the two of you?" she said.

"He gave me a ride," she told her mother. "He was nice enough to give me a ride so I could talk to you."

"You be careful," she told her daughter. She raised her coffee up to her lips, but didn't drink. "Don't dishonor your parents – your father." Meanly, even angrily, she took a sip of coffee and looked down at her hands in silence.

"It's okay then?" she asked.

Her mother pulled on her skirt and straightened her apron. "I didn't say it was okay," she said. "I didn't say I would like it, did I? – and I don't think you should believe that your father would like it either. He was a God-fearing man, and the idea of his oldest daughter on display in front of all of those people."

"Mother," she scolded.

"I don't think he would have liked that. I knew him, you know – he was my husband for nearly twenty years." She pulled a handkerchief from her dress.

"I have to go," Albertina said. "Simon has to be back to work."

"It will be getting dark soon," her mother said, pulling a hand from her lap and shooing her daughter as she might have shooed a cat. "I don't want you in a car at night with a boy, not just any boy," she said. "You have to be careful, Albertina – I don't know if, with everything that happened, I really prepared you for what you must know about men – "

"Mother, it's Si Abma – from church. You know his parents."

Her mother looked at the car suspiciously. "I hope it's not me who has to make your costume," she said.

"No, no," she said. "It's already being planned."

Nothing. No more words.

"It's okay then?" Albertina said.

"It's not okay," her mother told her, and then, looked into her daughter's eyes. "But to say I'm not proud of you would be wrong, too. It's a good thing, I guess," she said, looking away. "I don't know what your father would say either. He'd be proud – sure, he would, but he wouldn't like it, you up there in front like some show horse. He wouldn't like that, mind you. So don't go thinking that he'd be all smiles either, see." And then she nodded.

The nod – that was what Albertina was looking for. Just the nod. When she left the porch, she glanced back at her mother and smiled.

"So?" Si said when they were back in the car.

"It's okay," she said. "It's not okay either, but it's okay."

He turned the Ford around in the yard and headed for the gravel road. "Do I have this right?" he said. "It's not okay, but it's okay?"

Albertina nodded discreetly.

"Women," Si said.

Character is in silhouette, setting is at least partially drawn, and conflict has begun to emerge. What we need is a complication, something to tie Miss Mellema's life up in knots.

By definition, what we need is an antagonist, the villainous force. But life experience teaches that hero/villain conflicts are often simplistic, if for no other reason than so rarely encountered. Black hats and white hats dramatize conflict vividly, but simplistically. In the great battles of life, the bad guys are rarely the monsters we'd like to make them; and this 1940s story, as Albertina herself tells it, is no exception.

What she told me makes the complication clear. It's the preacher who ties her life up in knots.

He's one of the town's true intellectuals, as preachers often were back then. Even though he's not just come from the Netherlands himself, the education required for him to become a dominee included lots of doctrine and history that kept him close to his ethnic roots. He's preached in the Dutch language ever since he first stepped into the pulpit, and in his weekly sermon preparations he's had to consider much broader concerns than those which have faced Albertina Mellema, clerking at the dime store.

History tells us also that this villain has a doctorate. He's studied more than the average dominee in rural Iowa churches, and he knows it. He's a learned preacher, and he carries his experience and calling with unquestioned confidence. He thinks of himself—as most preachers did—as the leader of the flock, as the "undershepherd" only because Jesus Christ himself was the only true and good shepherd. When he walks to get his mail, his swallow-tail coat symbolizes both his righteousness and power.

What do I know of what actually happened? I know what she told me. She didn't say where it happened, how firmly he spoke to her, how generously he lugged in the weight of his office, or how gently he questioned the depth of her commitment to the Lord. All I know for sure is what she told me — that the preacher at First Orange City CRC wanted to speak to her, the newly elected Tulip Festival Queen, and what specifically he asked her to do.

Let's assume that the preacher knows Holy Writ as well as personal decorum. He understands that his visiting this beautiful young woman in the house where she boards would have been inappropriate. Not only that, through the spacious front windows of Orange City homes, more than a few local residents might have jumped to the worst conclusions should they have seen him entering that boarding house alone. The apostle Paul made it clear that such visits should always be undertaken in the company of a fellow believer. So let's create the third scene with three characters – Albertina, the preacher, and a man we'll call Elder Vander Veen because there is no less doubt about his being Dutch than being male.

Scene Three, and I've dispensed with the small talk, even though I'm sure there must have been some when this scene actually occurred. The Dutch can be brusque and blunt, to be sure, especially in the cause of righteousness; but the dominee is a learned man and not without his charm, even if he has a burden.

Albertina is sitting on a chair she's not at all proud of, but at least she's sitting on it so the Dominee can't see the stain that was already there when she moved into the room. She'd thought about going to a sale some Saturday and picking up something cheap to replace it, but then she'd have to ask the landlord, who would be sure to be hurt by her disapproval. Now she wished she had just gone ahead and done it.

The Dominee and Elder Vander Veen sit on the love seat, the tapestry draping over it scrunching up behind them. That they had come to visit didn't surprise her, however; she knew this wasn't huisbezoek. *He'd mentioned wanting to speak to her, and in her mind there was no question why he'd come. He wasn't happy to have a Tulip Queen from his First CRC.*

"There's this matter of your being Queen," Dominee says. Elder Vander Veen nods silently. "Tulip Queen," Dominee repeats, as if the phrase itself is burdensome. "Is that what it is called?"

Albertina nods. She keeps her hands folded in her lap. She's taken off her apron in anticipation of their visit, checked her hair and rubbed off some of the lipstick she'd worn at the store. It's dark in the room, and she's sure that they won't notice anyway, but she knows there is already enough offense.

"Our people," he says, meaning the Christian Reformed, "have not been taken with the whole business, you know." He doesn't lift the last word as if to make the sentence a question. It is, therefore, a statement of fact. "And while it is indeed an honor—," and then he muffles a slight cough, as if it's hard for him to admit that much, "and even though it is an honor to have been chosen before the other young women, we want to talk about your participation."

Albertina has not yet spoken, but then, that's not unusual.

"We want to bring up some things you might consider as you decide what you're going to do," he says.

The Dominee is not harsh or overpowering. His strategy is to affect the young woman with reason because he knows that Adam, without will, was not Adam at all. He wants willful consent, not indignant or even blind submission. Because he is convinced that reason, not to mention compassion as well as decorum, is on his side in the question he wants her to face.

"We want to remind you that in Europe there is war – that Poland is already gone, like Czechoslovakia before it, that Denmark and Norway have been attacked, and that now – do you know about this, Albertina? – and that now, France, Belgium, Luxembourg, and even the Netherlands – even the Netherlands is under siege?" He stopped for a moment. "Are you aware of what is happening in Holland?"

Of course, Holland was of little relevance to her. She'd been born in America, and even though she spoke Dutch fluently, she didn't consider the Netherlands anything more significant to her than Belgium or France. It was all so far away. There was, after all, the dime store and her room in town. Life was here in Orange City.

"Did you know, Albertina, that as we speak the Germans have flattened Rotterdam?" the Dominee said.

She shook her head. She had no image of this place called Rotterdam anyway. What did she care, really, about Rotterdam?

"Did you know that as we speak our brothers and sisters in the Lord are dying in defense of their homeland? – people who read the Bible in the same language and sing the same Psalms?"

She did know and she didn't. She'd heard some talk in the store – you could hear it if you wanted to listen. Men spoke to each other in more reverent tones, with more gravity lately. There was less lightness in town, less sport. Somewhere, something was happening, she knew, something that even Si worried about. There was talk of war.

"Elder Vander Veen and I," the Dominee said, "we have come to speak to you about that – about war – "

"We're not at war," she said, then pulled her hand to her mouth as if shocked by her own impetuousness.

"No, you're right," the Dominee said.

"And it's not our war to fight," she told him. She wouldn't have said that unless she'd not heard important people say as much in the store. She'd heard them talk about the trenches in Europe during the last war, and how this one wasn't their fight, just like that one hadn't been theirs.

"Time will tell," the Dominee said.

Elder Vander Veen looked at the preacher strangely.

"But that's not at issue," the Dominee said. "What is at issue is your participation."

The dress was nearly finished. She'd seen it. She'd fitted it already, and it was beautiful. Mrs. Langstraat, the very best seamstress in town, was working day and night to get it finished. It looked perfectly wonderful on her.

"They chose me," she said. "It's not as if I wanted to be chosen. It's not as if I tried for it," she said.

"We don't fault your being chosen," the Dominee said. "We don't fault that at all – and both Elder Vander Veen – and indeed the entire congregation – is happy for you. And proud of you, too."

She looked for even the slightest trace of a lie in his eyes.

"But we've not always felt strongly about this Tulip Time," he said. "I admit that, personally, I would not want my daughter in your position, even though I would be proud," he said. "But that you were selected – it speaks well of you, of your character."

Albertina didn't know whether to be proud or angry.

"But that is not at issue – isn't that right, Elder Vander Veen?" the preacher said.

Vander Veen nodded again.

"The issue is whether any of us – all of us in this town – should be celebrating when there is war, not only in Europe either – for that's the excuse that many have given, you know: 'it is not our war, the war in Europe' – that's what is said. But now the war has even come to the Netherlands." He raised his hands as if the entire cosmos had been thrown into chaos. "How can we sing when Holland burns?"

"I am not from Holland," she said.

The Dominee nodded. "But you are," he said. "You are more of Holland than of America – "

"I've never seen Holland," she said.

Once more, he nodded. "These are our brothers and sisters in Christ," he said. "These are our family, and the Germans are destroying everything." Then he moved forward, sat at the edge of his seat, the tapestry sinking behind him. "You remember, of course, Psalm 137 – 'By the Rivers of Babylon we sat and wept when we remembered Zion.' The people of God were asked to sing their songs, and what they felt in their hearts was nothing but darkness." And then, "You remember, Albertina?"

"I know the Psalm," she said.

The preacher brought both hands together widely at the fingertips. "Elder Vander Veen and I – we believe that if you tell all of them, all of the people who are making all this silliness for Tulip Time – if you tell all of them that you can't take this position now because of the suffering in the old country and the war in Europe, then, Albertina, then you will be doing the right thing. You will be doing what the Lord wants."

Albertina rubbed her fingers in her lap but said nothing.

The preacher – the Dominee – asked her to give up the crown for the sake of the war in Europe. That's complication.

The conflict has now been revealed. What's left is the climax – Albertina's decision. I won't sketch out that scene – not right now. It occurred in a place and time which she never told me, if in fact she remembers making a decision at all. Perhaps there wasn't even a moment at which she decided which of the two roads she'd choose. Perhaps the opportunity to be queen was simply too great for someone who'd never known celebrity and admiration. However she measured her own response to what the Preacher had said, what's clear is that she didn't give up the crown. That's why I began all of this by saying you have to understand what it meant for her to go to town back then. The reader has to understand how compelling the crown had to be. That one week in May, 1940, she ruled Orange City as queen.

Someday maybe I'll come back to the sketches I've outlined and try to write that story. Now, only I know the incident I've described – and now you do too, the readers of this collection of historical essays.

This May, sixty years later, on the list of former Orange City Tulip Festival Queens, you will find Albertina's real name written elegantly behind the year "1940." The dress she wore not very long after the Nazis began a five-year occupation of Holland is hanging, like a revered surplice, in a local museum.

When tens of thousands of people come to Orange City for the Tulip Festival 2000, no one will consider what went on in the heart and soul of the Tulip Queen in May, 1940. No one will be reminded of the story she told me years later because, I suppose, she never quite forgot. Amid the klocking sounds of the klompen dancers, the swishing brooms of the street scrubbers, with the sonorous chords of the street organ ringing through the frivolity, with the smell of hot *sassajes* in the air and the sweet delight of *poffertjes*, no one, aside from you and me, will think of what she might have felt the year she stood before the crowd and accepted their generous appreciation, this young and beautiful farm girl who'd lost her father before he was fifty. No one will know the story in the heart of the girl blessed by the gracious favor of an approving town, but saddened too by guilt created by the power of the church, and a war that came home to her for the first time the night the dominee visited, but would soon enough affect every Orange City citizen, despite the spring-time frivolity.

To remind those who watch the parades this year of that story – those who might care – might well be worse than a weekend of thundershowers. After all, we need our joy, our festivals, our days of thanksgiving, our hours of praise. We need to celebrate, to laugh and to sing. Sometimes, more than we know or do, we need to dance in the streets.

But we also need the stories of how we've lived, what we've suffered, and how we've survived. We need to consider our toughest questions, our stickiest quibbles, and our most profound crises.

I for one think Albertina's story worth remembering, not as some sober reminder of the darkness of our lives, but as a model of how all of us confront dilemmas not unlike the conflict created in the heart of a Tulip Queen. Those issues, drawn from the well of a particular time and place, are never far from any of us. Was she a citizen of a small Iowa town or a citizen of the world? Was her joy to be slain for a war thousands of miles away? Why should she suffer for the dying in the Netherlands? Where is our joy? Where do we find our happiness?

Those questions all of us ask, no matter how far we live from Rotterdam or Orange City.

Albertina Mellema chose a crown, but not without having to remember, decades later, the visit of a dominee concerned for a world far away from the tulip-lined streets of Orange City, but a world from which no Tulip Queen can ever quite escape.

Four years later, the man to whom this Albertina Mellema had become engaged, stepped out of a landing craft at Normandy and was killed instantly by German defenses.

There is no relationship between the crown and the suffering, no cause/effect; but it remains the calling of the storyteller to remember, to piece things together, to pull narrative out of fact, to sing a melody created by the sometimes discordant notes of our lives.

This story has come to me specifically because my wife and I have a clock in our bedroom, the clock the woman I've named Albertina Mellema took home from the jewelry store in trade for the engagement ring she stopped wearing when it was clear there was no mistake about what had happened to the GI she had promised to marry. We have that clock because Albertina is my wife's mother. My children's grandmother kept the crown, but kept the story, too. She's the one who told me.

For reasons I've never understood, I have, for years, found myself telling stories like this one, and I know very well that in order to get it right I've got to know certain things and so does the listener/reader. To understand what made my mother-in-law accept the crown when the weight of the church and the fires of battle raging in the old country had been placed on her graceful shoulders, one has to know something about history.

There are many reasons why history is important, and I'm confident that other contributors to this book will make those reasons come alive.

But after more than two decades of writing, this storyteller has come to understand the importance of history in character, in setting, and in plot – within, in other words, the very elements of fiction. For that reason, this storyteller, throughout what writing days the Lord will give him, will be deeply grateful to the work of Professor Robert Swierenga.

Bibliography of Scholarly Publications of Robert P. Swierenga

BOOKS

2000

Faith and Family: Dutch Immigration and settlement in the United States, 1820-1920 (New York: Holmes & Meier, 2000).

1999

Family Quarrels in the Dutch Reformed Churches of the Nineteenth Century (with Elton Bruins) (Grand Rapids: Eerdmans, 1999).

1994

The Forerunners: Dutch Jewry in the North American Diaspora (Detroit: Wayne State University Press, 1994).

1976

Acres for Cents: Delinquent Tax Auctions in Frontier Iowa (Westport, CT: Greenwood Press, 1976).

1968

Pioneers and Profits: Land Speculation on the Iowa Frontier (Ames: Iowa State University Press, 1968).

BOOK IN PROGRESS

The Groninger Hoek: The Dutch on Chicago's West Side.

EDITED BOOKS

2000

For Food and Faith: Dutch Immigration to America, 1846-1960. The Holland Museum Sesquicentennial Lectures (Holland, MI, 2000).

Robert P. Swieringa and Larry J. Wagenaar, eds., *Dutch Enterprise: Alive and Well in North America* (Holland, MI, 2000).

1998
The Sesquicentennial of Dutch Immigration: 150 Years of Ethnic Heritage (with Larry Wagenaar) (Holland, MI: Joint Archives of Holland, 1998).

1991
Belief and Behavior: Essays in the New Religious History (with Philip R. VanderMeer) (New Brunswick: Rutgers University Press, 1991).

1985
The Dutch in America: Immigration, Settlement, and Cultural Change (New Brunswick: Rutgers University Press, 1985).

Jacob Van Hinte, *Netherlanders in America: A Study of Emigration and Settlement in the 19th and 20th Centuries in the United States of America*, 2 volumes. Robert P. Swierenga, general editor, Adriaan De Wit (Grand Rapids: Baker Book House, 1985).

1984
History and Ecology: James C. Malin's Studies of the Grassland (Lincoln: University of Nebraska Press, 1984).

Ethnic History (Special Issue of *Ethnic Forum*), 4 (Spring 1984).

1982
A Bilateral Bicentennial: A History of Dutch-American Relations, 1782-1982 (with J.W. Schulte Nordholt) (New York: Octagon Books, 1982).

1975
Beyond the Civil War Synthesis: Political Essays of the Civil War Era (Westport, CT: Greenwood Press, 1975).

1970
Quantification in American History: Theory and Research (New York: Atheneum, 1970).

COMPILATIONS
1987
Dutch Households in U.S. Population Censuses: 1850, 1860, 1870: An Alphabetical Listing by Family Heads and Singles (Wilmington, DE: Scholarly Resources, 1987) 3 vols.

1983
Dutch Immigrants in U.S. Ship Passenger Manifests, 1820-1880: An Alphabetical Listing by Household Heads and Independent Persons (Wilmington, DE: Schol-

arly Resources, 1983) 2 vols.

Dutch Emigrants to the United States, South Africa, South America, and Southeast Asia, 1835-1880: An Alphabetical Listing by Household Heads and Independent Persons (Wilmington, DE: Scholarly Resources, 1983).

ARTICLES IN PRESS

"The Church and Dutch Reformed Colonization in Argentina: A Worst Case Scenario," *Documentatieblad voor de Geschiedenis van de Nederlandse Zending en Overzeese Kerken.*

ARTICLES PUBLISHED

2000

"Stellingwerff's *Amsterdamse Emigranten* and Pella History," in Robert P. Swieringa and Larry J. Wagenaar, eds., *Dutch Enterprise: Alive and Well in North America* (Holland, MI, 2000), 17-21.

"True Brothers: The Netherlandic Origins of the Christian Reformed Church in North America, 1857-1880,"in George Harinck and Hans Krabbendam, eds., *Bridges and bridges: Reformed Subcultures in the Netherlands, Germany, and the United States* (Amsterdam: VU University Press, 2000), 61-83.

"'By the Sweat of our Brow:' Economic Aspects of the Dutch Immigration to Michigan," in Robert P. Swierenga, ed., *For Food and Faith: Dutch Immigration to America, 1846-1960.* The Holland Museum Sesquicentennial Lectures (Holland, MI, 2000).

1999

"Van Raalte and Scholte: A Soured Relationships and Personal Rivalry," *Origins* 17.1 (1999): 21-35. Also in *The Sesquicentennial of Dutch Immigration: 150 Years of Ethnic Heritage* (Holland, MI: Joint Archives of Holland and A.C. Van Raalte Institute, Hope College, 1997): 29-45.

"H. P. Scholte," *American National Biography*, 24 vols. (Cary, NC: Oxford University Press, 1999), 19: 420-421.

"A. C. Van Raalte," *American National Biography*, 24 vols. (Cary, NC: Oxford University Press, 1999), 22: 234-236.

1998

"'Better Prospects for Work:' Van Raalte's Holland Colony and its Connections to Grand Rapids," *Grand River Valley History* 15 (1998): 14-22.

"From Colony to City: Holland's First Twenty-Five Years," *Origins* 16.2 (1998): 11-16.

"The Little White Church: Historiographical Revisions on Religion in Rural America," in Ronald Wells, ed., *History and the Christian Historian* (Grand Rapids, MI: Eerdmans, 1998), 159-177.

"Decisions, Decisions: Turning Points in the Founding of Holland," *Michigan Historical Review* 24 (Spring 1998): 48-72.

1997

"'God's Building:' Holland Colony of Van Raalte Celebrates 150 Years," *DIS-Magazine* [Dutch International Society Nederland] 1 (1997): 36-39.

"The Little White Church: Religion in Rural America," *Agricultural History* 71 (Fall 1997): 415-441.

"Going to America: Travel Routes of Zeeland Emigrants," *Nehalennia: Bulletin van de Werkgroep Historie en Archeologie*, 114, theme number 11 (1997), "Zeeuwse emigratie naar Amerika, 1840-1920," 19-30.

"Dutch in America: The Settlement of People from the Netherlands in the United States," in *Encyclopedia USA*, v. 24 (1997): 139-147 (Reprint of "The Dutch," in *Harvard Encyclopedia of American Ethnic Groups*, 1980).

1996

"Cruzamiento Internacional de Registros de Inmigrantes Holandeses en Los Estados Unidos en el Siglo XIX" [International Record Linkage of Dutch Immigrants in the United States in the Nineteenth Century], *Estudios Migratorios Latinoamercanos* 33 (Agost 1996): 357-383.

"Calvinists in the Second City: The Dutch Reformed of Chicago's West Side," in Gerard Dekker, Donald A. Luidens, and Rodger R. Rice, eds., *Rethinking Secularization: Reformed Reactions to Modernity* (Washington, DC: University Press of America, 1997), 45-61.

"'Pioneers for Jesus Christ': Dutch Protestant Colonization in North America as an Act of Faith," in George Harinck and Hans Krabbendam, eds., *Sharing the Reformed Tradition: The Dutch-North American Exchange, 1846-1996* (Amsterdam: VU University Press, 1996), 35-55.

"Promoting Ethnic Pride: The Dutch-American Social Clubs of Chicago," *Origins* 14.2 (1996): 30-37.

"The Low Countries," in Robert W. Taylor, ed., *Peopling Indiana: The Ethnic Experience*, 2 vols., (Indianapolis: Indiana Historical Society, 1996), 1:102-23.

1995

"Religious Diversity and Cultural Localism: The Dutch in Cleveland, 1840-1990," *Northwest Ohio Quarterly* 67 (Summer 1995): 1-29.

"Netherlanders in Chicago," in *The Dutch in Chicago, 1870-1995* (Chicago: Consulate-General of the Netherland in Chicago, 1995), 5-16. (Reprinted in abridged form in *De Nieuwe Amsterdammer* 5 (November 1995): 11.

1994

"Dutch in Indianapolis," in Robert G. Barrow, ed., *Encyclopedia of Indianapolis* (Indianapolis: Indiana Historical Society, 1994), 516-17.

"'Odyssey of Woe': The Voyage of the Immigrant Ship *April* from Amsterdam to New Castle, 1817-1818," *Pennsylvania Magazine of History and Biography* 118 (October 1994): 303-323.

"Agrarian Capitalism in the Countryside: The North American Debates," in Herman Diederiks, J. Thomas Lindblad, and Boudien de Vries, eds., *Het platteland in een veranderende wereld* (Hilversum: Verloren, 1994), 79-86.

"The Journey Across: Dutch Transatlantic Emigrant Passage to the United States, 1820-1880," in Rosemarijn Hoefte and Johanna C. Kardux, eds., *Connecting Cultures: The Netherlands in Five Centuries of Transatlantic Exchange* (Amsterdam: Free University Press, 1994), 101-134.

"Thomas Corwin Donalson (1843-1898)," in Charles Phillips and Alan Axelrod, eds., *Encyclopedia of the American West* (New York: Macmillan, 1995).

"Samuel Myer Isaacs: The Dutch Rabbi of New York City," *American Jewish Archives* 44 (Fall/Winter 1992): 604-21. (Expanded version of *Origins* article of 1992.)

1993

"The Delayed Transition from Folk to Labor Migration: The Netherlands, 1880-1920," *International Migration Review* 27 (Summer 1993): 406-424.

"Identifying and Using Historical Materials: View from the Classroom" (with Jane A. Rosenberg) in Charles D'Aniello, ed., *Teaching Bibliographic Skills in History: A Sourcebook for Historians and Librarians* (Westport, CT: Greenwood Press, 1993), 51-68.

"Captain De Groot's Account of the Tragic Voyage of the *April*, Amsterdam to New Castle, 1817-1818," *The Palatine Emigrant* 18 (March 1993): 82-91.

"A Partial Passenger List of the Dutch ship *April*, to New Castle, Delaware, June, 1817," *The Palatine Emigrant* 18 (March 1993): 76-81.

"Samuel Myer Isaacs: The Dutch Rabbi of New York City," *Origins* 10.1 (1992): 16-21 (condensed version). Reprinted in *The Windmill*, U.S. Edition, 35 (April 23, 1993), 13; 36 (May 7, 1993), 13; 36 (May 24, 1993), 13. Reprinted again in *JWB Magazine*, New Year Number, September 9, 1993, Second Section, 1-7.

1991

"A Dutch Carpenter's 'America Letter' from New York, *New York History* 72 (October 1991): 421-438.

The Dutch Transplanting in the Upper Middle West, Inaugural Address, Society for the Study of Regional and Local History, (Marshall, MN: Southwest State University, 1991), 1-20.

"Jews First, Dutch Second, Americans Third: Dutch JewishSettlement and Life in the United States in the Nineteenth Century," in Rob Kroes and Henk-Otto Neuschäfer, eds., *The Dutch in North America: Their Immigration and Cultural Continuity* (Amsterdam: VU University Press, 1991), 391-409.

"List Upon List: The Ship Passenger Records and Immigration Research," *Journal of American Ethnic History* 10 (Spring 1991): 42-53.

"Religion and Immigration Behavior: The Dutch Experience" in Philip R. VanderMeer and Robert P. Swierenga, eds., *Belief & Behavior: Essays in the New Religious History* (New Brunswick, NJ: Rutgers University Press, 1991), 164-188. Reprinted in revised form under the title, "The Religious Factor in Immigration: The Dutch Experience," in Timothy Walch, ed., *Immigrant America: European Ethnicity in the United States* (New York: Garland Publishing, 1994), 119-140.

"Local Patterns of Dutch Migration to the United States in the Mid-Nineteenth Century," in Rudolph J. Vecoli and Suzanne M. Sinke, eds., *A Century of European Migrations, 1830-1930* (Urbana: University of Illinois Press, 1991), 134-157.

1990

"Protestant Immigration and Ethnicity in America," in Daniel G. Reid, ed., *The Dictionary of Christianity in America* (Downers Grove, IL: InterVarsity Press, 1990), 569-571.

"Jan Van Mekelenberg," in Daniel G. Reid, ed., *The Dictionary of Christianity in America*, (Downers Grove, IL: InterVarsity Press, 1990), 722-723.

"Peter Stuyvesant," in Daniel G. Reid, ed., *The Dictionary of Christianity in America* (Downers Grove, IL: InterVarsity Press, 1990), 1143-1144.

"Dutch Jewish Immigration and Religious Life in the Nineteenth Century," *American Jewish History* 79 (Fall 1990): 56-73.

"Historians and the Census: The Historiography of Census Research," *Annals of Iowa* 50 (Fall 1990): 650-673.

1989

"Religion and Political Behavior in the Nineteenth Century: Voting, Values, Cultures," in Mark A. Noll, ed., *Religion and American Politics* (New York: Oxford University Press, 1989), 146-171.

"The Settlement of the Old Northwest: Ethnic Pluralism in a Featureless Plain," *Journal of the Early Republic* 9 (Spring 1989): 73-105.

1988

"Samuel Pfrimmer Hays," in John Cannon, ed., *Dictionary of Historians* (Oxford: Basil Blackwell, 1988), 180-181.

"Under-Reporting of Dutch Immigration Statistics: A Recalculation," *International Migration Review* 21 (Winter 1988): 1596-1599.

"James C. Malin," in John R. Wunder, ed., *Historians of the American Frontier*

(Westport, CT: Greenwood Press, 1988), 384-407.

1987

"The Dutch in Cleveland," in John J. Grabowski and David Van Tassel, eds., *Encyclopedia of Cleveland History* (Bloomington: Indiana University Press, 1987), 351-352.

"Overseas Migration: A Mirror of Dutch Culture," *De Gids* 150 (February 1987): 152-155.

1986

"News from the Dutch Colony of Pella in North America, June 1854, *Annals of Iowa* 48 (Winter/Spring 1986): 155-158.

"The Dutch Transplanting in Michigan and the Midwest," The Clarence M. Burton Memorial Lecture (Ann Arbor: Historical Society of Michigan, 1986), 1-13.

"Dutch International Migration and Occupational Change: A Structural Analysis of Multinational Linked Files," in Ira A. Glazier and Luigi De Rosa, eds., *Migration Across Time and Nations: Population Mobility in Historical Contexts* (New York: Holmes & Meier, 1986), 95-124.

"Religion and Immigration Patterns: A Comparative Analysis of Dutch Protestants and Catholics, 1835-1880," *Journal of American Ethnic History* 5 (Spring 1986): 23-45. Reprinted in George E. Pozzetta, ed., *The Immigrant Religious Experience*, American Immigration and Ethnicity Series 19 (New York: Garland Publishing, 1991).

"The Malin Thesis of Grassland Adaptation and the New Rural History," in D.H. Akenson, ed., *Canadian Papers in Rural History* 5 (1986): 11-22.

1985

"Archival Materials and Manuscripts in the Netherlands on Immigration to the United States," in Lewis Hanke, ed., *Guide to the Study of United States History Outside the U.S., 1945-1980*, 6 vols. (Washington: American Historical Association, and Amherst: University of Massachusetts, 1985), 3:195-215.

"Dutch Immigration Patterns in the Nineteenth and Twentieth Centuries," in Robert P. Swierenga, ed., *The Dutch in America: Immigration, Settlement, and Cultural Change* (New Brunswick, NJ: Rutgers University Press, 1985), 15-42.

1984

"Historians and Computers: Has the Love Affair Gone Sour?" *OAH Newsletter* 12 (November 1984): Special Supplement, 2-3.

"Studying Dutch Immigration to the United States: New Methods and Concepts," *Ethnic Forum: Journal of Ethnic Studies and Ethnic Bibliography* 4 (Spring 1984): 8-20.

"Social Science History: An Appreciative Critique," in C. Thomas McIntire and Ronald A. Wells, eds., *History and Historical Understanding* (Grand Rapids, MI: Eerdmans, 1984), 93-102. Selected for abstracting in *The Philosopher's Index*, 1987.

"Bibliographic Instruction in Historical Methods Courses: Kent State University," *The History Teacher* 15 (May 1984): 391-396, 431-442.

1983

"Dutch International Labor Migration to North America in the Nineteenth Century," in Mark Boekelman and Herman Ganzevoort, eds., *Dutch Immigration to North America* (Toronto: Multicultural History Society of Ontario, 1983), 1-34.

"Catholic and Protestant Emigration from the Netherlands in the 19th Century: A Comparative Social Structural Analysis," *Tijdschrift voor Economische en Sociale Geografie* 74 (Spring 1983): 25-49 (with Yda Schreuder).

"Can History Survive Computers and Remain a Humanistic Discipline?," *Scope* (Scholarly Communication: Online Publishing and Education) 1 (November/December 1983): 39-40.

"History Online," *Network News Exchange* 9 (Fall 1983): 4-5.

"Rural Life and Agriculture: The New Rural History," in James B. Gardner, ed., *Ordinary People and Everyday Life: Perspectives in the New Social History* (Nashville, TN: American Association for State and Local History, 1983), 91-113.

"Quantitative Methods in Rural Landholding," *Journal of Interdisciplinary History* 13 (Spring 1983): 787-808. Also published as "Quantitative Methods in Rural Land Holding and Tenancy Studies," in Ivan D. Kovalchenko and Valery H. Tishkov, eds., *Quantitative Methods in Soviet and American Historiography* (Moscow: "Nauka" Publishing House, 1983), 82-108.

1982

"Exodus Netherlands, Promised Land America: Dutch Immigration and Settlement in the United States," in J. W. Schulte Nordholt and Robert P. Swierenga, eds., *A Bilateral Bicentennial: A History of Dutch-American Relations, 1782-1982* (Amsterdam: Meulenhoff International; New York: Octagon Books, 1982), 127-147.

"Catholic Emigration from the Southern Provinces in the Netherlands in the Nineteenth Century," Working Paper No. 27, Netherlands Interuniversity Demographic Institute, 1982 (with Yda Saueressig-Schreuder).

"Theoretical Perspectives on the New Rural History: From Environmentalism to Modernization" *Agricultural History* 56 (July 1982): 495-502.

"Het bestuderen van de Nederlandse emigratie naar de Verenigde Staten," *Jaarboek van het Centraal Bureau voor Genealogie* 36 (Den Haag: Centraal Bureau voor Genealogie, 1982), 252-268.

"A Denominational Schism from a Behavioral Perspective: The 1857 Dutch Reformed Separation," *The Reformed Review* 34 (Spring 1981): 172-185. Reprinted in *Canadian Journal of Netherlandic Studies* 3 (Fall 1981/Spring 1982): 49-57.

1981

"The New Rural History: Defining the Parameters," *Great Plains Quarterly* 1 (Fall 1981): 211-223.

"Social Science History: A Critique and Appreciation," *Fides et Historia* 14 (Fall 1981): 42-51. Selected for abstracting in *Religion Index One: Periodicals*, 1987.

"Teaching Quantitative Methods in History: At a Crossroads," *Network News Exchange* (The Society for History Education) 6 (Fall 1981): 8-9.

"Dutch International Migration Statistics, 1820-1880: An Analysis of Linked Multinational Nominal Files," *International Migration Review* 15 (Fall 1981): 445-470.

1980

"The Anatomy of Migration: From Europe to the U.S. in the Nineteenth Century," in Val Greenwood and Frank Smith, eds., *Preserving our Heritage: Proceedings of the World Conference on Records,* 12 vols. (Salt Lake City, UT: The Genealogical Society of Utah, 1980) 4, Series 357, 1-15.

"Dutch Immigrant Demography, 1820-1880," *Journal of Family History* 5 (Winter 1980): 390-405. Selected by Council of Abstracting Services for summary in *Sociology Abstracts*.

"The Dutch," in Stephen Thernstrom, ed., *Harvard Encyclopedia of American Ethnic Groups* (Cambridge, MA: Harvard University Press, 1980), 284-295.

"Immigrant Data Files and Computer Mapping" in J. Raben and G. Marks, eds., *International Federation of Information Processing, Proceedings of the Dartmouth Conference on Data Bases in the Humanities and Social Sciences* (Amsterdam: North-Holland Publishing Company, 1980), 119-123.

"Local-Cosmopolitan Theory and Immigrant Religion: The Social Basis of the Antebellum Dutch Reformed Schism," *Journal of Social History* 14 (Fall 1980): 113-135. Selected by Council of Abstracting Services for summary in *Sociology Abstracts*.

"Ethnicity and American Agriculture," *Ohio History* 89 (Summer 1980): 323-344. Reprinted in George Pozzetta, ed., *Immigrants on the Land: Agriculture, Rural Life, and Small Towns.* American Immigration and Ethnicity vol. 4 (New York: Garland Publishing, 1991).

1979

"Dutch Immigration Historiography," *Immigration History Newsletter* 11.2 (November 1979): 1-5.

"The Dutch in America: An Overview," in Linda Pegman Doezema *Dutch Americans: A Guide to Manuscript Sources* (Detroit: Gale Publications, 1979), xi-xix.

"Physicians and Abortion Reform in the Nineteenth Century: Social Control as the New Orthodoxy," *Fides et Historia* 11 (Spring 1979): 51-59.

"The Causes of Dutch Emigration to America: An 1866 Account," *Michigana* 24 (May 1979): 56-61; (Summer 1979), 92-97.

"The New Rural Social History," *MISHAP* (Minnesota Social History Project Newsletter) 1 (January 1979): 1-20.

1978

"Behavioralism in Historical Research," in Dwight W. Hoover and John Koumoulides, eds., *Conspectus of History: Focus on Interpretations of History, Number V* (Muncie, IN: Ball State University, 1978), 75-88.

"Social Statistics and Historical Research: A Symbiosis," *The Ukrainian Historian*, 1-3 (57-59), (1978): 90-101.

"The Open University: Historical Data and the Social Sciences," *Urban History Yearbook, 1978* (Leicester, UK: Leicester University Press, 1978), 64-67.

1977

"Land Speculation and its Impact on American Economic Growth and Welfare: An Historical Review," *Western Historical Quarterly* 8 (July 1977): 283-302.

"Netherlanders in America: A Bicentennial Lecture," *D.I.S.* (Dutch Immigrant Society) *Magazine* 7 (March 1977): 18-21.

"Ethnicity in Historical Perspective," *Social Science* 52 (Winter 1977): 31-44. Selected by Council of Abstracting Services for Summary in *Sociological Abstracts*.

1976

"Netherlanders in America," in *The Americans and the Dutch* (Den Haag: USIA-The Hague, the Netherlands, 1976), 24-29.

"Socio-Economic Patterns of Migration from the Netherlands to the U.S. in the Nineteenth Century," in Paul Uselding, eds., *Research in Economic History: An Annual Compilation of Research* (Greenwich, CT: JAI Press, 1976), 298-333 (with Harry Stout).

1975

"Dutch Immigration in the Nineteenth Century, 1820-1877: A Quantitative Overview," *Indiana Social Studies Quarterly* 28 (Autumn 1975): 7-34 (with Harry Stout).

"Christian Perspectives for History," *International Scholarly Review* 1 (May 1975): 11-21.

"Absentee Ownership," *Dictionary of American History* (2nd ed. 1975).

1974

"The Equity Effects of Public Land Speculation: Large vs. Small Speculators," *Journal of Economic History* 34 (December 1974): 1008-1020.

"Computers and Comparative History," *Journal of Interdisciplinary History* 5 (Fall 1974): 257-286. Selected by Council of Abstracting Services for Summary in *Sociological Abstracts*.

"Acres for Cents: Delinquent Tax Auctions in Frontier Iowa," *Agricultural History* 48 (April 1974): 247-266.

"Computers and American History: The Impact of the 'New' Generation," *Journal of American History* 40 (March 1974): 1045-70, reprinted in D. Balasubramanian, ed., *Current Trends in American History* (Hyderabad, India: American Studies Research Center, 1977), 63-89.

"Tenant Farming in Iowa: A Comment," *Agricultural History* 48 (April 1974): 151-154.

1973

"Quantitative Historical Data and the Archivist," *Ohio Archivist* 4 (Fall 1973): 12-13.

"Towards the New Rural History: A Review Essay," *Historical Methods Newsletter* 6 (June 1973): 111-112.

1972

"Computerized Historical Research in the U.S.A.: A Survey and Evaluation," *Information Processing 71*, North-Holland Publishing Company (1972), 1435-1442.

1971

"Computerized Historical Research: Problems and Prospects," ACM 70 *Conference Proceedings* (New York, 1971).

"The Christian Historian, The University, and Student Unrest," *Fides et Historia* 3 (Spring 1971): 4-19.

"The 'Odious Tax Title' A Study in Nineteenth Century Legal History," *American Journal of Legal History* 15 (April 1971): 124-139.

"Ethnocultural Political Analysis: A New Approach in American Ethnic Studies," *Journal of American Studies* 5 (April 1971): 59-79.

1970

"Clio with Numbers," *The Chronicle* (of the Historical Society of Michigan) 6 (October 1970): 13-19.

"The Iowa Land Records Collection: Periscope to the Past," *Books at Iowa* 13 (November 1970): 25-30.

"Clio and Computers: A Survey of Computerized Research in History," *Computers and the Humanities* 5 (September 1970): 1-21.

"Land Speculation and Frontier Tax Assessments," *Agricultural History* 44 (July 1970): 253-266.

"The Tax Buyer as a Frontier Investor Type," *Explorations in Economic History* 12 (Spring 1970): 257-292.

1969

"The Fort Dodge (Iowa) Claim Club," 1855-1856," *Annals of Iowa* 39 (Winter 1969): 511-518.

1968

"Place of Refuge (Pella, Iowa)," *Annals of Iowa* 39 (Summer 1968): 321-357.

1967

"The Western Land Business: Easley and Willingham, Speculators," *Business History Review* 41 (Spring 1967): 1-20.

1966

"Calvin and the Council of Trent: A Reappraisal," *Reformed Journal* 16 (1966).

"Land Speculator 'Profits' Reconsidered: The Case of Central Iowa" *Journal of Economic History* 26 (March 1966): 1-28.

1965

"A Dutch Immigrant's View of Central Iowa," *Annals of Iowa*, 38 (Fall 1965): 81-118, and reprinted in Dorothy Schwieder, ed., *Patterns and Perspectives in Iowa History* (Ames: Iowa State University Press, 1973).

"The Ethnic Voter and the First Lincoln Election," *Civil War History* 11 (March 1965): 27-43; reprinted in Frederick C. Luebke, ed., *Ethnic Voters and the Election of Lincoln* (Lincoln: University of Nebraska Press, 1971), 229-250.

SECTION 2

IMMIGRATION AND IDEOLOGY

DE VEREENIGING

VAN

KERK EN STAAT

IN

NIEUW–ENGELAND,

BESCHOUWD

IN DERZELVER GEVOLGEN VOOR DE GODSDIENST
IN DE VEREENIGDE STATEN.

DOOR

een' Amerikaan.

UITGEGEVEN

DOOR

H. P. SCHOLTE, *V. D. M.*

TE AMSTERDAM, BIJ

HOOGKAMER & COMP.

N. Z. Voorburgwal, N°. 153.

1841.

Cover of the Dutch translation of Robert Baird's
l'Union de l'Église et de l'État dans la Nouvelle Angleterre (1837)

Emigration as Protest? Opinions About the Relation between Church and State as a Factor in the Dutch Emigration Movement

Hans Krabbendam

Among the millions of immigrants entering the United States many were religious dissenters. Their departure was sometimes an emergency measure to maintain their identity or merely to survive. For others it was a rejection of a corrupt society and an attempt to make a fresh start in a new world. Among the Dutch immigrants in the United States, the dissenting Seceders were a prominent group. Though religious considerations certainly motivated their departure, physical survival was not their main motive, nor was it their intention to make a clean slate. The rather sudden and visible exodus of Seceders was used by progressive opinion leaders as a leverage to press for political reforms in the mid-1840s. This paper re-examines the claim of historians who state that the emigration of the Seceders was an act of protest. It contends that rejection of Dutch institutions did not automatically lead to emigration. Since the great majority of Seceders did not leave, I would like to add another factor to the spectrum of emigration motives by exploring the role of ideas about the relation between church and state. The difference in these concepts explain why some Seceders left while others stayed. Moreover, this perspective reveals that the first cohort of emigrating Seceders rejected a too narrow interpretation of their actions, and transcended localism and religious nationalism.

Rejection of Dutch Society?
The 1840s was a decade full of protest in the Netherlands. The political system badly needed revision. Liberal politicians and journalists discussed many propositions and tried to move the King and parliament to pass more liberal legislation. Individual pamphleteers and journalists perceived the emigration movement as an effect of social unrest. Though some liberal spokesmen warned against inflated expectations of easy wealth in America, others used the departure of many countrymen to increase the pressure on the government for reform. The *Nieuwe Rotterdamsche Courant* warned that the emigration movement might swell if the authorities refused to relax their legislation and that this exodus would aggravate

the economic crisis. A liberal group in Amsterdam even considered, but failed to follow up, the publication of a weekly with the title *Landverhuizing* to build up pressure for political reforms.[1] Though other newspapers trivialized the value of the protest and pointed to the periodic migration caused by population pressure, the Seceder emigrants were adopted into the protest movement.[2] Was that a proper place for them to be?

At face value it makes sense to explain the eagerness of the Seceders to emigrate to the United States out of their rejection of the official Dutch institutions. Rejection of the corrupted *Hervormde Kerk* found a logical consequence in dissociation from the immoral Dutch society.[3] Dissolution of ties that bound a person to his environment, liberated him or her to embark on the adventure of emigration. The more ties were severed the higher were the chances for departure. This is a plausible explanation for the overrepresentation of the Seceders.

However, this statement is too general. The circle of Seceders was more complicated. Not every Seceder was charmed by the emigration movement. The influential minister Simon Van Velzen, for instance, was a staunch opponent of the *Hervormde Kerk*, but also opposed the colonization plans of his colleagues Hendrik P. Scholte and Albertus C. Van Raalte. When these leaders publicized their motives, Van Velzen hastened to distance himself from them in a letter to King William II, claiming to speak on behalf of "by far the majority of the Christian Seceders in this country."[4] He disputed the validity of their arguments for departure, though he agreed with their conclusion that the country was in disarray. He argued that poverty resulted from the lack of godliness, which made him appeal to the authorities: "I know that a sincere return of the Dutch people to the service and to the God of their fathers is to be expected only through the working of God's Spirit, but it is part of the office of government, who is God's servant, to maintain the Lord's law."[5] Van Velzen also wanted to sever the silver cords between church and state, but this did not mean that the state should cease to pay attention to religion. Despite his criticism of the state he remained a loyal citizen, as the Secretary of Religion Zuylen van Nyevelt noticed by complimenting him for his "feelings of devotion to law and order and proper submission and rejection of everything leading to disorder and agitation…"[6]

The combination of ideas about the relationship between church and state and expectations for the future determined the likelihood of emigration among the Seceders. Though the positions were far from fixed, it is possible to distinguish a continuum with two ends. One extreme, represented by Hendrik De Cock and his follower Simon Van Velzen, defended the validity of article 36 of the Belgic Confession charging the state with the responsibility of defending true religion and contending false religion. At the other extreme was Scholte, who advocated a complete separation of church and state. In between those two positions stood the brother-in-laws Anthony Brummelkamp and Van Raalte, who were more positive about the relationship between church and state, though they also rejected all financial interference.[7]

The father of the Secession, Hendrik De Cock, had set the pattern for Van Velzen by linking the moral decline to the persecution of the pious in the third decade of the nineteenth century. The neglect in maintaining the old Reformed faith affected the state deeply. The growing unbelief undermined the relationship between church and state. Far from denying the prerogatives of the state, De Cock hoped the government would help to restore the position of the old church, which had found a continuation in the Seceded churches. To realize his hope he appealed to the King to call a national synod.[8]

Simon Van Velzen did not attribute the departure of Van Raalte and Scholte to differences of opinion about the church-state relationship but to his colleagues' personal frustrations: lack of prestige for Scholte and Van Raalte's disappointment about the lack of freedom within the Seceded denomination. Van Velzen reflected: "[Scholte] had little influence left here in the Church. Most religious people did not regard him anymore. His ambition to become a man of influence in North America and the necessity to reduce his luxurious state seem to have moved him to make this decision. His refusal to be atoned caused his dismissal after his many heresies were revealed and he left from here. Most members who departed thence fostered the same feelings as Scholte. They were not fully united with the doctrine of our forms of unity, but lawless. A few loyal to the pure doctrine also left."[9] Van Velzen's opinion about Van Raalte sounded similar: "Here matters turned against him and his efforts failed."[10]

Van Velzen correctly saw that Scholte and Van Raalte had their disappointments, but so had he. He also suffered from the debates and factional conflicts. Yet, emigration was no option to him, not only because his side was victorious in the internal strife, but also because he did not share his opponents' ideas about the proper relation between church and state, which motivated the latter group to join the emigration movement. No one is more responsible for developing this line of thought than Hendrik P. Scholte, the most learned and original mind among the Seceded ministers, who enjoyed great prestige in the provinces of Utrecht, Zuid-Holland, and Zeeland.

Scholte held the Royal family in high esteem, and King William II's ascension to the throne in 1840 renewed the personal connection. The new king knew Scholte from the Ten Days Campaign against Belgium in 1830 and even interrupted his grand tour in Utrecht in 1840 to greet the famous preacher with: "Bonjour, Mijnheer Scholte."[11] Scholte was the moving force behind the decision of many Seceders to request registration as a separate, new denomination. This official status meant a cessation of their claim to be the only heir to the Reformed tradition, but did not restore the official ties between their church and the state symbolized by the king.

Simultaneously Scholte paid attention to the international aspects of the revival and the idea of millennial thought.[12] His growing conviction that church and state must be separated was inspired by the American church historian Robert Baird, whose book convinced Scholte of the ideal situation in the United States.[13] Scholte translated Baird's history of the Puritans to reveal the harmful effects of intermingling church and state.[14] The consequence of this turn in Scholte's thinking was that the state lost significance compared to the Kingdom of God and increasingly became its opponent, despite its divine origin. This did not mean that Scholte abstained from all involvement in politics; far from that, he became engrossed in political issues and once in the United States, he actively campaigned in election time. Yet his persuasion that church and state had their own territory brought him into conflict with his coreligionists, who either believed that the church would redeem the state or that the state could be made Christian.

Scholte found a biblical justification in the gospel according to St. Matthew in the text urging believers to seek first the Kingdom of God and the warnings to flee when persecutions would break out. Scholte considered the bleak social circumstances forebodings of the end of times. His expectation of divine judgment on Europe in general and the Netherlands in particular was confirmed by the ecclesiastical struggle and economic disasters. Despite the inevitability of eschatological events, he charged the authorities with the responsibility for obstructing the obedience of the people to God's law, by hampering their ways of earning a living. Though the same authorities had ended the persecution of Seceders after 1841, Scholte realized the state still had the capacity to engage in such persecution. It was more than a growing disappointment with the government that made Scholte decide to leave. In his *New Year's Present*, a farewell address to people and king at his departure in early 1847 he confessed: "The Netherlands are not yet lost beyond salvation, but it seems that those who govern this nation, lack the brains or the ability to seize the proper instruments. We consider this situation a judgment of God for the sins of the nation."[15]

Scholte's fundamental ideas about the church, rather than his increasing frustration with the state as adversary, loosened his ties to the Netherlands. He did not condemn the constitution of the Netherlands until shortly before his departure, but he criticized its application. Scholte envisaged the limitations of the developing church structure in the Seceded churches, which blocked his ideal of an informal church of true believers. He resisted the efforts to reintroduce the Canons of Dordt as the church order, not only for functional reasons, but also because he rejected its mingling of church and state. The current pressing problems were sufficient evidence for his belief that a blending of church and state caused all kinds of disasters.[16] The old fatherland was lost. Perhaps Scholte's German family roots and his upbringing in the Restored Evangelical Lutheran Church made him more aware than his colleagues of different options for church and state relations.

The different positions about the proper relationship between church and state became visible when the various Seceded congregations considered the desirability of requesting official recognition by the state. Van Raalte, Brummelkamp and the majority of the Seceders followed Scholte in his request for recognition. At face value, this action seemed to contradict their ideal of separation, but he defended his request by asserting the separation of ecclesiastical and civic existence. Official recognition did not necessarily mean giving up the claim of being a true continuation of the Reformed Church of the Dutch Republic.[17]

Looking back in 1862, Van Raalte regretted this drive for recognition, but whatever his remorse, the practical effect was that it loosened the ties that bound the Seceders to the Netherlands, since a new denomination meant a discontinuity with the past.[18] Another factor which relaxed the ties to the Netherlands was that the Seceders could not forge a strong alliance with the orthodox part of the *Hervormde Kerk*. After the wave of emigration in the late 1840s and the decision to establish an ecclesiastical center in Kampen by starting a seminary, self-confidence and uniformity among the Seceders increased. In practice they accepted the separation between church and state and revealed this by requesting that the government cease subsidizing any church.[19]

Attachment to Church and Nation
Among the orthodox Calvinists the ties between church and state were strong. Some implicitly felt that intimate relationship; others explicitly formulated it. Both criticized the Seceders for not reforming the church or the state, but abandoning them. Guillaume Groen Van Prinsterer was the most prolific representative of the orthodox protestants with clear ideas of church-state relations in the theocratic vein: the state had to obey God's laws. He rejected the alleged neutrality of the liberal state and wished to restore the responsibility of the state to protect the *Hervormde Kerk*. Though he upheld the institutional separation between church and state, and granted other sects freedom of worship, he maintained the moral and spiritual relation. The state was the instrument that linked Christianity and culture. Modernist leaders in the *Hervormde Kerk* disagreed with Groen's confessional emphasis, but supported the view that the state had to (financially) support the civilization process, in which the church was an important instrument.[20] Groen saw the emigration as a sign that the Secession had reached a dead end. He regretted the departure of many kindred spirits. He ridiculed Scholte's plea for complete separation of church and state, frowning "that all states were from the devil, with the exception of old Israel."[21] In a letter to two unidentified Seceded ministers in August 1847 Groen indicated their shortcomings: they rejected the *Hervormde Kerk*, they started new congregations and they unintentionally assisted their adversaries by requesting official recognition and consequently abandoning their claim to continue the true Reformed tradition. For him, these facts explained the decline of the Seceders: they had removed the best forces from the *Hervormde Kerk*

and spilled their energy in futilities "and now, in a state of desperation, [they] seek a solution in North America."[22]

This destination was far from appealing to the lawyer Groen. The American political system did not attract him. His friend H.J. Koenen understood him well, but feared Groen's ideals could not be realized. Referring to Groen's famous lectures on unbelief and revolution, Koenen wrote "It seems rather that the principles followed in North America will penetrate even further. Your lectures are a forceful and eloquent protest, but whether it preaches a practical doctrine of the state in our time, is dubitable..."[23] America represented the opposite side of the principles defended by Groen.

Apart from this principled rejection of the American system, other orthodox Calvinist leaders raised practical objections against separation of church and state. The philanthropist Ottho Gerhard Heldring lamented when he heard Scholte's plans for departure and revealed the emotional bonding with the fatherland: "...what can we do with such a little people?... In North America only the poor will find a place. Scholte will become unhappy."[24] Though Heldring did not develop a precise framework about the relation between church and state, it is clear he was very much attached to the nation as such, and therefore he labored hard to match the interests of the government with the needs of the people. He was committed to caring for the poor and weak and tried hard to find solutions for them on Dutch soil, either in the Anna Paulownapolder or in the colonies. The destination of Scholte and Van Raalte was too far removed and relatively few people would benefit from their plans. Heldring's aim was to organize relief, and therefore the setting of a new society in a unspoiled environment was no option to him. He believed in building the state and the economy from which the common man and woman would benefit.[25] Whether principled or practical, the positions of Groen and Heldring offered strong antidotes against the emigration fever.

Among the common Seceders also the positions concerning state and church determined their willingness to emigrate. Those who requested and usually received official recognition expected equal treatment by the government, such as subsidies of preacher salaries and of their seminary. However, this wish met with no sympathy from the government. Disappointment concerning this unjust treatment by the government encouraged the desire to depart. The arguments in a letter to King William II by the consistory of the Seceders in Middelharnis, which disbanded a congregation because the majority had decided to emigrate, illustrates the seriousness of this feeling. Their motivation to leave "...was predominantly [caused] by the extraordinarily pressing circumstances of many of your subjects, but especially of the Christian Seceded congregations, who were forced in order to practice their religion without judicial persecution to comply with the taking away of the rights, which the constitution grants to all other denominations; they desire to go to another country where they share equal rights with all inhabitants."[26]

A similar tension between the church and the state caused orthodox Mennonites to emigrate. Refusing to submit to worldliness, a group of seventeen Mennonites from the Frisian congregation of Balk left in the spring of 1853 to settle in Indiana. Their main motive was their refusal to bear arms in service of the fatherland. These orthodox Anabaptists settled close to the Mennonite colonies at Goshen, Indiana, and continued their own worship services until they joined the Amish at the turn of the century.[27]

Rejection of Localism and Religious Nationalism
The Seceder emigrants praised the freedom in the United States exultantly and appreciated the opportunities to control their own churches and schools. They accepted the American Constitution and as soon as they were allowed, took the oath as citizens. For them, the official separation of church and state worked much better than the situation in the Netherlands. They needed no encouragement to embrace America's civil religion and enthusiastically participated in praising the principles of the American Revolution on the Fourth of July celebrations. An early witness of this event in the town of Zeeland reported: "Dominie Van der Meulen celebrated it with us in a religious fashion. Next he described the flourishing growth and rise of these United States, their glorious Declaration of Independence, their difficult fight under brave George Washington who persevered so brilliantly and brought the struggle to a glorious conclusion... Hearty prayers of thanksgiving were sent up to the great Ruler of peoples and of states..."[28]

Some unique letters from farmer Jannes Van de Luijster, emigrant leader from Borssele and founder of Zeeland, Michigan, reveal the spiritual line of thought, which liberated these people from too close an identification of God's plans with the Dutch nation, as a Dutch version of Israel. Van de Luijster defended the legitimacy of his departure against friends who criticized his decision. He agreed with them that God had poured out his Spirit in Europe, but claimed that Europe had subsequently proved itself unworthy. The light of God's revelation moved away to America. He saw abundant evidence for this movement: many men proclaimed God's truth and translated His Word. The gold rush was led by God to attract many unbelievers to California where they heard his word. Public morality was enforced. Van de Luijster did not dispute that his Dutch friends lived in Jerusalem, but warned that this city was abandoned by God. From his reading of scripture he concluded that God's blessing was not tied to a territory. Children of God who moved away carried his blessing with them. He strongly objected to his friend's identification of America with Babel. In turn he contrasted the situation of the Jews in the Babylonian exile with the circumstances of the colony: they were captives, we are free; they had poverty, we have abundance; they hung their harps in the willows, we have the opportunity to praise God publicly. He believed that sooner or later the others would follow him to America or other places, since God's grace for the Netherlands was past.[29] This openness to broader horizons marked all immigrant leaders among the Seceders. Their publications justifying their departure all refer to global developments in which they felt they were participating.

Conclusion

The plausible hypothesis that a conflict with the church automatically led to a rejection of the state is unjustified, at least for the majority of Seceders. A careful analysis of the ideas about the relationship between church and state shows that those who defended an intimate bond opposed emigration and vice versa. Though many emigrants were not aware of this argument, they were influenced by it nonetheless. Those who considered their Seceded churches, whether belonging to the Seceded denomination or not, as the only true continuation of the Reformed Church of the Dutch Republic, rarely left the country. Those who did, usually had a broader, cosmopolitan perspective, based on their religious insights.

Once in America, the Dutch Seceders easily adapted to the new arrangements between church and state. Since the group migration initially led to homogeneous settlements, the Dutch seized the opportunity to organize their own local society. The combination of official separation of church and state and the public presence of religion made them feel comfortable. This is not to say that the Seceders acted upon carefully developed theoretical ideas. But the broader expectations of the world certainly helped them to let the old world go. Later in the century, when the political system in the Netherlands was democratized, the Seceders entered politics and after joining forces with the rising Abraham Kuyper developed a political philosophy and became a formidable political power. The later waves of Dutch immigrants exported those ideas to the Dutch settlements in the Midwest.

Robert Swierenga's objective "number-crunching" in combination with his subjective empathy with the religious worldview of many immigrants secured a balanced portrait of this phenomenon, which both avoided a philiopietistic admiration and a reduction to functionalism. His immigration research not only generated a wealth of data, it also proved a reliable basis for further inquiry, which encouraged a detailed investigation of the connection between ideas and action.

Notes

1   *Nieuwe Rotterdamsche Courant,* 4 May 1847; G. Groen Van Prinsterer, *Brieven van J.A. Wormser,* 2 vols. (Amsterdam: Höveker, 1874-1876) 1:91 (19 December 1846).
2   P.R.D. Stokvis, *De Nederlandse trek naar Amerika 1846-1847* (Leiden: Universitaire Pers Leiden, 1977), 113-120.
3   Piet Hein Burmanje, "The Dutch Calvinist Press and the Social-Religious Development of Dutch Immigrants in the United States, 1850-1885" (M.A. Thesis, University of Amsterdam, 1988). See also Robert P. Swierenga, "'Pioneers for Jesus Christ': The Dutch Protestant Colonization in North America as an Act of Faith," in George Harinck and Hans Krabbendam, eds.,

Sharing the Reformed Tradition: The Dutch-North American Exchange, 1846-1996 (Amsterdam: VU University Press, 1996), 40: "Leaving the fatherland was another expression of social protest and it logically followed from the initial decision to separate from the national church." He refers to L.H. Mulder, "De afscheiding sociaal-wetenschappelijk benaderd," in A. de Groot en P.L. Schram, eds., *Aspecten van de Afscheiding* (Franeker: Wever, 1984), 83-104.

4   F.L. Bos, *Archiefstukken betreffende de Afscheiding van 1834*, 4 vols. (Kampen: Kok, 1946) 4:482.

5   Ibid., 483.

6   Ibid., 484-485.

7   M. Te Velde, *Anthony Brummelkamp (1811-1888)* (Barneveld: De Vuurbaak, 1988), 345-348.

8   W.C. Baartman put me on this track with his unpublished thesis "Kerk en staat bij H. de Cock en H.P. Scholte," 13-34. See also Jasper Vree, "Van Separatie naar Integratie. De afgescheidenen en hun kerk in de Nederlandse samenleving (1834-1892)," in Reender Kranenborg and Wessel Stoker, eds., *Religies en (on)gelijkheid in een plurale samenleving* (Leuven/Apeldoorn: Garant, 1995), 161-176.

9   A note by Van Velzen in the records of the Christelijk Afgescheiden Gemeente at Amsterdam, quoted by C. Smits, "De Afscheiding bewaard (De strijd van ds. S. van Velzen te Amsterdam)," in D. Deddens en J. Kamphuis, eds., *Afscheiding - wederkeer. Opstellen over de Afscheiding van 1834* (Barneveld: De Vuurbaak, 1984), 215.

10 H. Reenders, "Albertus C. van Raalte als leider van Overijsselse Afgescheidenen 1836-1846," in Freerk Pereboom e.a., eds., *Van scheurmakers, onruststokers en geheime opruijers: De Afscheiding in Overijssel* (Kampen: IJsselakademie, 1984), n.369.

11 *Van 's Heeren wegen. De Afscheiding van 1834 op 10, 11 en 12 october 1934 te Utrecht herdacht* (Kampen: Kok [1934]), 18.

12 L. Oostendorp, *H.P. Scholte: Leader of the Secession of 1834 and founder of Pella* (Franeker: Wever, 1964), 135-137.

13 Ibid., 140.

14 Robert Baird, *De Vereeniging van Kerk en Staat in Nieuw Engeland beschouwd in derzelver gevolgen voor de godsdienst in de Vereenigde Staten* (Amsterdam: Hoogkamer, 1841), vi. The original version was published in French in 1837.

15 H.P. Scholte, *Nieuwejaarsgeschenk aan Nederland. Een ernstig woord aan vorst en volk* (Amsterdam: Hoogkamer, 1847), 5.

16 Oostendorp, *Scholte*, 150-152.

17 F.L. Bos, *Kruisdominees. Verhalen uit Afgescheiden kringen* (Kampen: Kok, [1982]), 68-74 illustrates the nuances among the "Kruisgezinden" by W.C. Wust's experiences. He refused to explicitly denounce the Hervormde Kerk as false, and emigrated shortly thereafter in 1848. See also H. Florijn, *De Ledeboerianen. Een onderzoek naar de plaats, invloed en denkbeelden van hun voorgangers tot 1907* (Houten: Den Hertog, 1992), 34, 127: The Ledeboerianen shied away from all political involvement.

18 *Kompleete uitgave van de officieële stukken betreffende den uitgang uit het Nederl. Herv. Kerkgenootschap* (Kampen 1863) letter Van Raalte to Simon Van Velzen 1862; see also Reenders, "Van Raalte," 146-149.

19 Vree, "Van separatie naar integratie," 161-176.

20 J.Th. de Visser, *Kerk en staat*, 3 vols. (Leiden: Sijthoff, 1927) 3:318, 332. R. Kuiper, "Pro en contra de christelijke staat. Antirevolutionaire denkbeelden omtrent idee en ideaal van de christelijke staat omstreeks het midden van de 19e eeuw," *Radix* 16 (1990): 66-82; A.Th. Van Deursen, "Groen van Prinsterer over kerk en staat," *Radix* 24 (1998) 166-175; J.A. Bornewasser, "Twee eeuwen kerk en staat. Een veelledige confrontatie met de moderniteit," in J. De Bruijn e.a., red., *Geen heersende kerk, geen heersende staat. De verhouding tussen kerken en staat 1796-1996* (Zoetermeer: Meinema, 1998), 29-60. See also the article of J. Vree in the same volume.

21 G. Groen Van Prinsterer, *Ongeloof en revolutie. Een reeks historische voorlezingen* (Leiden: Luchtmans, 1847), 53.

22 *Groen van Prinsterer Schriftelijke nalatenschap. Zesde deel. Briefwisseling vijfde deel 1827-1869.*
    Bewerkt door drs. J.L. van Essen. Rijks Geschiedkundige Publicatiën Grote Serie 175 (Den
    Haag: Martinus Nijhoff, 1980), 159 (25 August 1847).

23 H.J Koenen responded on the receipt of Groen's *Ongeloof en Revolutie* on 31 August 1847. *Groen*
    van Prinsterer Schriftelijke nalatenschap. Derde deel. Briefwisseling tweede deel 1833-1848.
    Bewerkt door dr. C. Gerretson en dr. A. Goslinga. Rijks Geschiedkundige Publicatiën Grote
    Serie 114 (Den Haag: Martinus Nijhoff, 1964), 810-811.

24 Letter to Groen, 30 September 1846, ibid., 746-747.

25 H. Reenders, *Alternatieve zending. Ottho Gerhard Heldring (1804-1876) en de verbreiding van*
    het christendom in Nederlands-Indië (Kampen: Kok, 1991), 86-97. Heldring was not consistent
    in his fears, because he also expressed his anxiety that the wealthy would emigrate leaving the
    poor behind, Reenders, *Alternatieve zending,* 88 n19. In 1849 Heldring admitted Scholte and
    Van Raalte had made the right choice (p.89).

26 Letter 30 April 1847, quoted in C. Smits, *De afscheiding van 1834. Zevende deel, Classes Rotter-*
    dam en Leiden (Dordrecht: Van den Tol, 1986), 112.

27 Jacob Van Hinte, *Netherlanders in America: A Study of Emigration and Settlement in the 19th*
    and 20th Centuries in the United States of America, Robert P. Swierenga, general editor, Adriaan
    de Wit, chief translator (Grand Rapids: Baker Book House, 1985), 167-173.

28 This speech by the Rev. Cornelius Van der Meulen at Zeeland, Michigan on July 4, 1849 was
    reported by Hendrik Van Eyck. Henry S. Lucas, ed., *Dutch Immigrant Memoirs and Related*
    Writings, 2 vols (repr.; Grand Rapids, MI: Eerdmans, 1997) 1:478. See also Hans Krabbendam,
    "Forgotten Founding Father: Cornelius VanderMeulen as Immigrant Leader," *Documentatieblad*
    zendingsgeschiedenis en overzeese kerkgeschiedenis 5.2 (Fall 1998): 1-23.

29 Jannes Van de Luijster to A. De Muijnck, 27 February 1855, private collection.

Dutch Reformed Worldview and Agricultural Communities in the Midwest

Janel M. Curry

Recently a new or renewed interest in culture in general, and religion in particular, has arisen among those who study rural places. Robert Swierenga used his presidential address to the Agricultural History Society to call for the addition of the long-neglected religious variable in research on agriculture. He stated that the religious worldviews of various communities may emerge as the interpretive key to understanding rural agriculture, subsuming other variables such as class, gender, and race.[1] Worldview, as defined by Clifford Geertz, is a community's picture of the way things are, their concept of nature, of self, and of society. It is a comprehensive idea of how the world is ordered and provides an interpretative framework for all kinds of human actions.[2] Iain Wallace claims that one would expect to find local differences in forms of action among relatively similar cultures but with different religious perspectives because these religious perspectives – worldviews – give rise to differing societal philosophies. An example of these differences is the contrast between Catholic and Protestant social philosophies with differing emphases on organic versus individualistic conceptions of society. These differences find expression in attitudes toward regional disparity, healthcare policy as well as other aspects of economic life that find expression in rural areas.[3]

This study attempts to use the concept of worldview in the understanding the development of Dutch agricultural settlement in the Midwest. The analysis involves a synthesis of three different but complementary empirical studies of rural Dutch Communities. These studies include an historical land ownership study near Pella, Iowa, a study of the development of a marsh into the Dutch settlement of Hollandale, Minnesota, and a study of the present-day worldviews and agricultural systems among Dutch Reformed farmers in Hull, Iowa (Figure 1).

The Dutch communities of this study are part of the larger mosaic of ethnic/religious communities that make up the Midwest and upon which the prosperous agricultural economy of the region has been built. Thousands of these communities, whose study has been the focus of much research, were settled as church-centered ethnic colonies. Within the agrarian culture of the region, sociologists,

Figure 1: The location of the Three Study Sites.

rural historians, and geographers have consistently identified community-wide social patterns affecting farming.[4] These influence capitalization of the farm enterprise, the extent to which a farm is commercialized, land tenure change patterns, and farmers' risk-reduction strategies.[5] These in turn affect the ability of communities to reproduce themselves. A study of historic land ownership change in the Dutch community of Pella, Iowa bring to light some of the community-wide patterns that may be typical of Dutch settlement areas.

Pella Land Tenure Study

To discern a Dutch "type" related to agricultural land tenure, changes in land tenure were examined for four sections of land in South Central Iowa from settlement in the 1840s to the early 1980s.[6] These sections were part of an ethnically Dutch area of settlement. County deed records that contained data on land transactions formed the basis of the study and included information on land prices; types of transactions, such as intrafamilial sales, inheritances, or foreclosures; types of buyers and sellers such as private, corporate, or governmental; residence of buyers and sellers; and relationships among buyers and sellers. These data were supplemented by cemetery records and by family and oral histories. Changes in these aspects of land tenure were compared with county and regional data in order to differentiate what trends are part of general patterns and what was unique to this Dutch community.

Land prices, an essential part of tenure change, showed similar trends over time at all scales (state, county, four sections), showing evidence that land prices have been largely controlled by factors outside the local community (macro-scale factors). Land use patterns followed similar large-scale trends, responding to government programs and general economic and social trends in farming. In contrast, the overall pattern of landownership change in the study area was affected by both macro and micro social factors. As has been seen elsewhere,[7] transfers of acres increased within one or two years of high-yield years. Crop prices did not have the same effect on land transfers as did crop yields. However, a rise in land prices did follow the increase in land transfers, again often delayed by a year or two. Thus high yields preceded an upswing of acreage transfers, which in turn prompted a rise in land prices.

Although macrosocial phenomena such as crop yields and farm prices seemed to affect acreage transfers, microsocial phenomena, especially family-generation change, also shaped the pattern of transfers. After initial settlement of the study area in the early 1850s, eras of generational transfers appeared to be the primary force behind land transfer cycles. Peak time periods in acreage transfer, occurring approximately every thirty years, involved generational transitions, while non-family transfers dominated in times of low activity. Others have also recognized the existence of such cycles that are influenced by local characteristics:[8]

The structure of landownership – acquisition, use, and disposal of farmland – is conditioned by the life cycle of owners. This means as farmland owners age, a larger proportion of the total farmland base is potentially available for transfer to new owners in the near term than if the median age of agricultural landowner is, say 45. The timing and intensity of land turnovers are influenced by present landowner age structure and have obvious consequences for the structure of landownership more generally.[9]

The sub-elements of this family life cycle pattern become reflects of the characteristics of the community "type." The Dutch had unique inheritance characteristics of both Yankee and Yeoman farmers – Midwest community types as defined by Salamon.[10] The Yankee farmer viewed farming as a business and had no obsession with passing on land to the next generation as a farm unit. The Dutch farm owners in the study area shared this trait, perhaps due to the fact that many who settled in the area were not farmers in the Netherlands. Very few inheritances occurred before the next generation was in their fifties. Families also followed the practice of "partible" inheritance where land was divided among heirs.[11]

Within the seven families for which the most complete data existed, cycles and patterns of farm enterprise development and transfers were consistent. Among them, few pre-death transfers took place. Evidently the offspring of these Dutch settlers had to enter farming by purchasing their own land, or farm as tenants on the parents' farms. Many offspring chose other professions altogether since the Dutch emphasized education, upward mobility, and movement to non-farm occupations.

The Dutch settlers in the area also exhibited traits of the German Yeoman Farmers as described by Salamon[12] – strong community attachments with little out-migration, endogamy, and ethnically homogenous communities. Evidently the Dutch combined these two value systems by developing local industry and business, thus emphasizing both upward mobility away from the farm and maintenance of a generally homogenous community – the town of Pella.[13] These characteristics have made the area less dependent on farming today, and the entrepreneurial spirit has led to the development of several family owned manufacturing companies that do business in the international market.

Persistence of land holding, subject to much rhetoric, may also be very culturally determined. Persistence was low within the study area. Less than one percent of the land has remained within the same family from 1850 to the present (twenty acres) and this passed from uncle to nephew rather than directly. An analysis of fifty-year time blocks, each spanning two generations in the family life cycles, showed surprising similarity in lack of persistence. Only about twenty percent of the land stayed in one family for each of the two fifty-year blocks of time (1850-1899 and 1900-1949). Most land passed among two to three owners within each fifty-year time period. This pattern in another example of non-yeoman behavior that may have been tied to upward mobility.[14]

Often we have conceptualized the problems of agriculture on the individual level and assumed the individual as the main building block of society. This study points to a different assumption – the existence of social wholes. These community-wide systems are formed by the interaction of history, external economic pressure, and religious worldviews that lead to unique life-cycle patterns over more than a century (Figure 2). In times of economic stability the cycle is maintained, but in times of economic stress, such as World War I and the Depression, the cycle is disrupted by larger forces. Each ethnic/religious community may be unique in its response to economic change and policy change because of coincidence with community cycles.

Reformed Religious Worldviews

The patterns seen in the Pella, Iowa study cannot be fully understood without an exploration of the religious worldview elements that underlie Dutch agricultural communities. These worldview elements, grounded in a theological perspective, lead to the unique combination of upward mobility and resulting low individual family persistence on the land, yet little out-migration from the community as a whole. A study of rural farm groups in Iowa, including a Dutch Christian Reformed group in Hull tested the hypothesis that distinct worldviews existed and were grounded in common, metaphysical perspectives that are associated, in turn, with specific religious traditions. A key worldview element was the conceptualization of society along a range of emphasis from individualistic to communal.[15] Communal, in the context of this study, is not to be confused with associational involvement. Associational involvement refers to an individual's participation in institutional or congregational activities; by contrast, communal involvement entails primary-group interaction at the level of family and friends.[16] The individualistic-communal scale addressed the question, How do I think of myself? Do I think of myself as an autonomous, independent person, or do I see myself principally as part of a network of human relationships.

This range in societal conception has been linked to larger societal visions that include the perceived relationship between humans and nature, and contrasting views on farming. In a historical study on New England, Cronon[17] attempted to show the relationships among communal orientation, property rights, and the perception of the environment and use of its resources. Berkes and Feeny[18] argued for similar connections. They questioned Hardin's assumption of individual interest and competition in his classic work, "The Tragedy of the Commons," and argued instead for the possibility that society is grounded in cooperative, communal action. Their focus of concern was resource management and the often overlooked informal rule-making of communities. They began with the assumption

Figure 2: Farm Life Cycles.

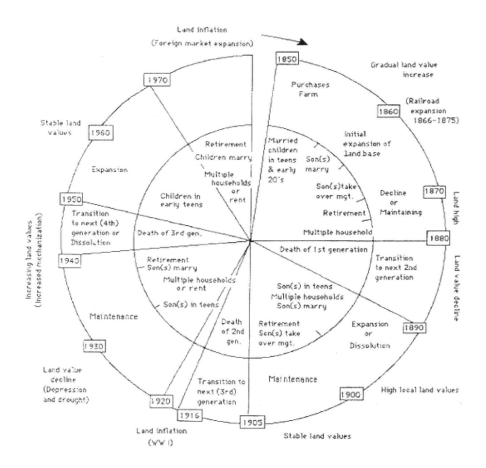

that actions are constrained by the community. They further argued that community-oriented management takes the long view and is more sustainable.

The work of Salamon[19] points to other factors that may be connected to communal orientation in her typography of Yankee and yeoman farmers. Among communities described as "Yankee" she found emphases on farms as businesses, and on geographic and economic mobility. Communities of German "yeoman" farmers emphasized continuity: efforts were made to keep the farm in the family and strong community attachment was evident. Cronon would argue that this represented a difference in economic orientation. Yankee farmers, on the whole, were capitalistic in orientation, which resulted in the further commodification of land and its resources, with an emphasis on individual, exclusive, property rights. Beus and Dunlap[20] have linked many of these same elements to the two major agricultural paradigms in the literature. Conventional agriculture included emphasizing farming as a business, farm specialization, world markets, the advantages of technology and science, and competition. In contrast, alternative agriculture emphasized farming as a way of life, farm diversification, domestic markets, skepticism toward science and technology, and cooperation among farmers and between farmers and consumers.

As Robert Swierenga[21] has pointed out, none of these studies, or other similar ones, have directly addressed the question of the underlying worldviews (the values that hold the social world together) that form the basis for these differences, called the "domain of commitment" by Murphy and Pilotta.[22] The study of a group of farmers among the Dutch Reformed community of Hull, Iowa, who were compared to others of different ethnic/religious heritages, attempted to address the question of the underlying, community-wide theological and value commitments and the inter-relationships among the previously discussed components of community worldviews.

Hull, Iowa Case Study

The Dutch Reformed of Hull, Iowa are located in the open country of northwest Iowa (Figure 1). The farms of the Dutch Reformed community of Hull in this study had extensive areas of corn and beans, as well as livestock. Some farms maintained hay, pasture, and a variety of livestock including sheep, cattle, hogs, and dairy cows. Hull, and most of Sioux County, Iowa, was settled after 1869[23] and the colonists were largely descended from persons who left the state Reformed church in the Netherlands due to its perceived doctrinal and moral laxity.[24]

The Dutch Christian Reformed vision of society is communal in comparison to other ethnic groups in the area.[25] A group of farmers and spouses were asked to respond to a story that presented a situation where a farmer was faced with selling his farm due to development pressures. However, the farmer knew that if he did so the whole community would follow because he was the largest farmer and rented the acreages of others, which helped sustain the community. His turmoil over the decision focuses on the knowledge that, as the largest landowner, he will affect the entire community with his decision. The responses to this narrative ranged from a very individualistic perspective among other ethnic/religious groups in the area to the recognition of embeddedness in community structures. Examples of the two extremes are illustrated by the following two comments: "He's going to eventually sell and move on, do whatever he wants with it," and "is it the right decision for all people in the community who are looking up to you?"

The Dutch group response to the narrative focused on the community as a whole. Participants spoke of the desire of people in Hull to stay in the community. They spoke critically about the heirs of this farmer, who would probably value money over the preservation of the community. Discussants also referred to the respect this farmer surely must have enjoyed in the community for putting the community's needs first. Similarly, responses to the most basic problem facing agriculture followed suite. More individualistic groups than Hull, Iowa identified problems of low prices, costs of labor and the reduced profit margin. Reasons for this reduced profitability ranged from government regulation to corporate farming. The farmers of Hull also identified low profit margin as a problem, but made connections to the larger community. Low hog prices were connected to low teacher salaries, church funds, and to their effect on local businesses. Overall, comments reflected much more a sense of how local community structure tied to agriculture or concern for small businesses, churches, and schools.

The origin of this communal perspective if found in Reformed theology. It is reflected in the worldviews expressed among the Hull Christian Reformed farmers and spouses, as well as the lack of out-migration in the Pella study. Both communities were originally settled by immigrants from the Netherlands who emphasized separation for the preservation of purity.[26] These Seceders wanted to create a religious ethnic island where their followers could practice their religion.[27] John Calvin, the major source of Reformed theology and tradition, emphasized bringing all things, secular and sacred, into proper order.[28] This meant building a society where particular rules governing the conduct of life could be obeyed literally, such as keeping the Sabbath.[29] Later immigrants to Hull were influenced by the thought of Abraham Kuyper, a late nineteenth century Reformed thinker in the Netherlands. Kuyper believed that Christians and non-Christians understood the world in radically different ways.[30] The natural working out of this idea led to Kuyper's call for the development of independent Christian centers of higher education. In addition, Christian schools, Christian labor associations, and Christian agriculture societies, etc., have developed out of this vision.[31] This emphasis on separation is reflected in the landscape of Dutch communities. Van Den Ban found that Dutch farmers were reluctant to leave their community and more willing to pay a considerably higher price for a nearby farm than other farmers.[32] The Reformed communal vision has lead to economically varied and institutionally rich communities built up under the desire to build a society that lives under the laws of God and institutions that are founded on Christian principles, but not controlled by the church. As a result of this worldview, the Dutch Reformed settlement region, of which Hull is part, continues to expand its borders and influence. This expressed worldview corresponds closely to the community-wide social patterns found in Pella land tenure study.

The communal vision of the Dutch Reformed included the clear incorporation of nature. Many Christian traditions put an emphasis on Christ as the personal savior of individual humans and heaven as their ultimate destiny. Such a perspective often precludes these traditions from integrating the earth and the natural environmental into their worldview as anything other than a backdrop on which human history takes place.[33] The Dutch Reformed expressed a very Calvinistic interpretation of the future – the concept of the continuity between this present material existence and some future perfected state that will be established when Christ returns. Members of the Dutch Reformed group expressed the belief that they expect Christ to one day restore nature as well as humans to their pre-edenic state. As one individual stated, there is a

connection between this life and the life hereafter...we've begun our eternal life...the opening chapter...what we do now has a direct link to our enjoyment of life eternal...The whole thing of stewardship, is certainly part of now and, or a part of eternity. The comparison between the seed and the fullgrown tree and our body and our resurrection body – there's a connection, but still, you wouldn't believe that a huge oak tree could come from a little tiny acorn. And I don't think you can even begin to fathom what the life hereafter will be, if you think of our cells, now, as the seed.

The Dutch emphasized an additional Calvinistic perspective – that of the relationship between obedience to God's laws (most clearly expressed in the Ten Commandments) and blessing, or financial success. This belief left them with a strong internal locus of control but rooted in obedience to God's laws. Furthermore, these participants expressed the belief that disobedience had a direct effect upon nature. One individual told about the lack of birds during the 1980s, something he attributed to the state of society rather than to direct actions of humans such as pesticide use. Living the communal vision out correctly, according to the laws of God, included the correct treatment and view of nature.

The communal worldview of Hull, Iowa was closely tied to an alternative agriculture paradigm. The Dutch Reformed expressed a strong commitment to family farms as well as suspicion of technology as the solution to problems. In addition, comments supported an alternative perspective, from concern over pesticides, to farming as a way of life, to non-monetary values associated with farming.

Why the communitarian/alternative agriculture connection? What seems to be key is that the Reformed worldview emphasizes the commitment of one's whole life to a religious worldview. It is a non-dualistic perspective, and one necessitating a certain level of "separateness" from society as a whole. For example, in a study in Wisconsin, Van Den Ban noted that a Calvinistic farmer saw himself as the steward of God on the farm the Lord had given him. Thus even the decision to adopt a new farm practice was sacred.[34] As is often said among Kuyperian Reformed people – all of life is religion.

Societal Vision on the Landscape
Lyson and Welsh, in their research on Midwestern agriculture, found connections among agricultural system, social context and nature. They found that the range of crops grown in a county is an indicator that can distinguish conventional agricultural systems from sustainable agricultural systems that are more oriented toward the inherent link between production, society, and the environment. They claim that counties having farmers who structure their operations to remain flexible and better able to grow a variety of crops as markets dictate do not conform to the organizational assumptions of the neoclassical economic paradigm.[35]

Lyson and Welsh were not able to connect farm systems with actual metaphysical worldviews. This study begins to draw those connections. Township-level farm data showed that while acreages of different kinds of crops are similar among a variety of ethnic groups in the area around Hull, Iowa, the diversity and number of animals per acre in a representative Dutch Reformed township is greater. This pattern may reflect both an alternative agricultural vision and the related farm intensification necessitated by the desire of so many to stay and share in the local communal vision.

Other evidence of the Dutch worldview can also be discerned on the landscape through analyzing farm size trends. The Dutch Reformed township has historically had smaller farm than the surrounding townships dominated by other groups. While the 1960s and 1970s brought dramatic changes in farm size to the Midwest, a representative Dutch Reformed township near Hull defied the trend toward extensive expansion of farm holdings. Their largest increases in farm size were in the 1960s – twenty seven percent – only to slow in the 1970s to ten percent. When compared to German Lutherans and Quaker townships within the same landscape region, the Dutch Reformed township consistently had the smaller farms (Figure 3).[36] Between 1982 and 1992, Sioux County farm size increases continued at the relatively low rate of about ten percent.[37] Likewise, Sioux County saw the lowest decreases in farm population of all the study areas during the 1980s (19%).[38] The area is known for its intense competition for land and expanding Dutch settlement boundaries, both the result of the desire of many to stay in the community. The physical landscape with

Figure 3: Comparison of Farm Size Trends.

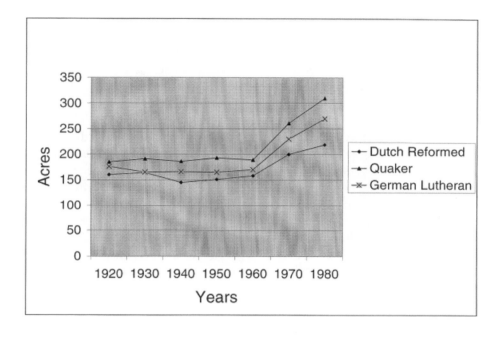

its dense settlement pattern is the visible reflection of this underlying worldview.

Settlement Expansion and Communal Vision

The Pella landownership study pointed toward the existence of a Dutch land tenure "type." Commitment to community was strong but not to farming itself, thus resulting in an acceptance of upward mobility away from the farm, yet the maintenance of a generally homogenous community. The end result was land remaining in Dutch hands, though not within a particular family. Community boundaries dominated over family boundaries. The study of the Dutch farmers of Hull, Iowa provided insight into the worldview that underlies such land tenure patterns. A communally-oriented worldviews leads to a strong desire to stay in the area. Combined with upward mobility, this results in an economically diverse local town economy as well as in competition for land. Smaller than expected farm sizes are the outcome. This communal worldview, as well as a Reformed perspective on nature, are in turn tied to agricultural paradigms with the Dutch Reformed farmers expressing support for an alternative agricultural paradigm. Concrete expressions of these elements are seen in both the smaller farm sizes and the higher levels of livestock diversity on the farms in comparison to other nearby groups. The Dutch Reformed worldview and its expressions on the landscape, taken together, ultimately lead to a tendency of Dutch Reformed agricultural communities to maintain their ethnic and religious homogeneity and to extend their boundaries over time. The third study, of the historic development of Hollandale, Minnesota, illustrates this tendency.

Hollandale's Expanding Dutch Settlement

The settlement of Hollandale, Minnesota is unique in that it came late for the region, beginning in the 1920s.[39] Located in southeastern Minnesota's Freeborn County, Hollandale is on what was in the past known as Rice Lake Marsh. This marsh of about 15,000 acres covered parts of four townships and stretched from Lake Geneva in the northwest to the Cedar River, 19 miles to the southeast. Rice Lake was in the middle of this acreage and the entire area was originally covered by three to ten feet of water. In the 1920s the boundaries of the Rice Lake Marsh became the boundaries of the Dutch community of Hollandale with an economy based on vegetable farming. Drained and developed by the Payne Investment Company, beginning in 1919, the company decided to offer its land for sale exclusively to Dutch settlers. They did so by advertising in Dutch Midwest communities and hired Dutch-American promoters and agricultural specialists to work with new farmers. The company invited a committee from the Dutch Reformed Churches of Sioux County to look at the land and offered them five acres in the planned town for a church and parsonage. The committee was impressed with the development and with the plan to sell only to Dutch Reformed people. Thus the company recognized that the worldview of the Dutch Reformed community, which would bring the traits needed to establish a strong farming economy, also required a church-centered life as well as religious homogeneity.

The first settlers arrived in 1922 and by the end of 1923, the business section of the town of Hollandale was completed. The project was a success. About 40 farms representing 1400 acres had been sold by 1926. The two main townships of the development, Geneva and Riceland, had increased in population 180 and 80 percent respectively. They became the only townships in the county outside the city of Albert Lea to have populations over 1000. The settlement was one of high density because of the intensity and the agriculture and corresponding small farm size – 20 acre celery farms. Potatoes and onions were also important crops over the years.

In September of 1926, at the height of the development's success, seven inches of rain fell on Freeborn County in a 24 hour period. Celery, potato and onion fields were flooded. Low onion prices added to the disaster. Excessive rains continued in 1927 and 1928. Banks began to foreclose and the twenty acre farms soon folded. The winters of 1928 and 1929 were extremely hard. Livestock starved. Credit was shut off and many farmers defaulted to the Payne Investment Company and then the company defaulted on its loans.

By 1929, at the beginning of the Great Depression, the company had gone into receivership. As a result the west section of the land that remained unsold was organized into Hollandale Farms, Inc. Another new corporation, Maple Island Farms, was created out of the east side unit (Figure 4). Maple Island Farms decided to liquidate its holdings in 1941-42 and did so through transfers of 1200 acres in 26 sales. The other major landholder within the former marsh, the McMillan Company, also sold to private individuals between 1940 and 1960.

A 1983 map of land ownership by people with Dutch family names shows the impact of these companies on the cultural landscape of this region (Figure 5). Because Maple Island Farms and McMillan Company did not sell exclusively to Dutch farmers, these areas show non-Dutch ownership. The tract west of Hollandale, sold during the time of initial development of the marsh, remains strongly Dutch. This area forms the core out of which Dutch land ownership has continued to expand – into the eastern tracts of the former Maple Island Farms and McMillan Companies as well as to outside the original marsh development region. In spite of the economic hardships that came initially after the settlement of Hollandale, the community survived with Dutch ownership of land persisting and expanding beyond the region of the original swamp. This expansion is the spatial outcome of the Dutch Reformed worldview mediated through social structures.

Conclusions
This study attempted to distill the elements of a Dutch Midwestern rural agricultural community type through the synthesis of three separate but complementary

Figure 4: Rice Lake Marsh Ownership after Initial Dutch Settlement – 1935.

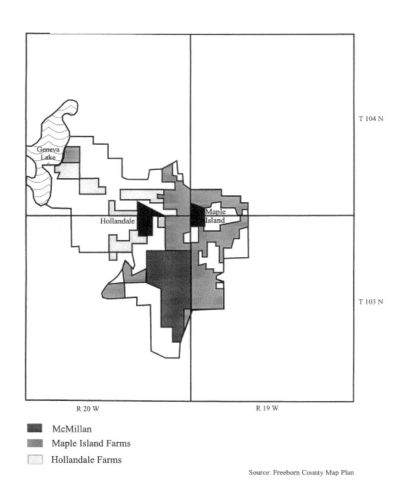

Figure 5: Expanding Dutch Ownership in Hollandale, Minnesota Sixty Years After Settlement-1983.

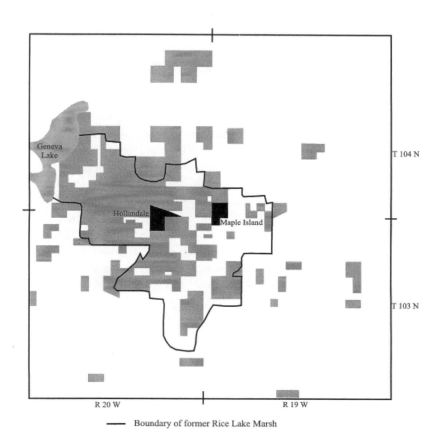

Boundary of former Rice Lake Marsh

Source: Freeborn County, Minnesota Land Atlas and Plat Book   Rockford Map Publishers, Inc., Rockford, Ill. 1983

studies of rural Dutch communities. These studies have been on Reformed Dutch communities. Such communities are to be distinguished from Catholic Dutch communities that experience much higher levels of assimilation, inter-marriage, and rural to urban migration. This assimilation is partially due to the emphasis on Catholic unity within the church.[40] In addition, Dutch Catholics exhibit less institutional completeness, a measure of the number of organizations or institutions that a group maintains, than Dutch Reformed communities. These organizations and institutions act as integrating forces and include the number of churches, schools, newspapers and welfare organizations. In fact, the more organized the group, the greater the flow of assimilation in the direction of that group rather than toward the larger society.[41] The Dutch Reformed communities have continued to expand their boundaries while the Catholic Dutch communities have become assimilated into the larger society and the larger Catholic community.

Understanding this Dutch community type gives insight into how community-wide religious worldviews provide the basis for particular values that impact rural life. These values in turn affect institutional and societal structures, leading to particular spatial outcomes and historical patterns (Figure 6). Ultimately these outcomes and patterns are the expression of the most basic worldview elements of the community. Mediated through social structures, Dutch communities' worldview had outcomes of both generational land tenure cycles and spatial expansion of Dutch settlement boundaries. Both of these outcomes are key to any group's ability to survive on the rural landscape.

Figure 6: Idealized Dutch Midwestern Agricultural Settlement Type.

Theological Viewpoint	Value Perspective	Societal Structures	Outcomes
Christian and non-Christians understand the world in radically different ways	Communal conceptualization of society	High community persistence	Expanding settlement boundaries
	Homogeneous community		
Separation for sake of Purity	Institutionally rich: Christian schools, farm organizations, etc.		
All callings are sacred	Upward mobility persistence	Low land tenure	Generational land ownership cycles
Non-dualistic: build a Society that brings all Things into proper Order	Alternative Agriculture:	— Partible inheritance	
	— Diversity	— Few pre-death transfers	
	— Way of life		
	— Community		
All of life is religion	— Co-operation	Economically varied and diverse community	
	— Domestic markets		
Obedience to God's Law connected to Blessing	— Suspicion of technology diversity	High livestock	
Continuity between present and future earth	Stewardship:		
	— Integration of nature into worldview	Small farm size	
	— Obedience includes correct treatment of nature		
	— Care of nature for the sake of humans and nature		

Notes

1. Robert P. Swierenga, "The Little White Church: Religion in Rural America," *Agricultural History* 71 (1997): 441.
2. Henk Aay and Sander Griffioen "Introduction," in H. Aay and S.Griffioen, eds., *Geography and Worldview* (Lanham, MY: University Press of America, 1998), xii.
3. Iain Wallace, "A Christian Reading of the Global Economy," in Aay and Griffioen, eds., *Geography and Worldview,* 46.
4. Swierenga, "The Little White Church"; Sonya Salamon, *Prairie Patrimony: Family, Farming, and Community in the Midwest* (Chapel Hill, NC: University of North Carolina Press, 1992). Robert C. Ostergren, "The Immigrant church as a Symbol of Community and Place on the Landscape of the American Upper Midwest," *Great Plains Quarterly* 1 (1981): 224-238. John Rice, "The Role of Culture and Community in Frontier Prairie Farming," *Journal of Historical Geography* 3 (1977): 155-175.
5. Sonya Salamon and Karen Davis-Brown, "Middle-Range Farmers Persisting Through the Agricultural Crisis," *Rural Sociology* 51 (1986): 503-512.
6. Janel M. Curry-Roper and John Bowles "Local Factors in Land Tenure Change Patterns," *Geographical Review* 81 (1991): 443-456.
7. John Bennett, *Of Time and the Enterprise* (Minneapolis: University of Minnesota Press, 1982), 236.
8. Charles P. Loomis and C. Horace Hamilton, "Family Life Cycle Analysis," *Social Forces* 15 (December 1936): 225-231. Sonya Salamon and Shirley M. O'Reilly, "Family Land and Developmental Cycles Among Illinois Farmers," *Rural Sociology* 44 (Fall 1979): 525-542.
9. Charles C. Geisler, Nelson L. Bills, Jack R. Kloppenburg, Jr., and William F. Waters, "The Structure of Agricultural Landownership in the United States, 1946 and 1978," *Search: Agriculture* Number 26 (Cornell University Agricultural Experiment Station, 1983), 6.
10. Sonya Salamon, "Ethnic Communities and the Structure of Agriculture," *Rural Sociology* 50 (Fall 1985): 326.
11. Sonya Salamon, "Ethnic Differences in Farm Family Land Transfers," *Rural Sociology* 45 (Summer 1980): 291.
12. Ibid.
13. Richard L. Doyle, "Wealth Mobility in Pella, Iowa 1947-1925," in Robert P. Swierenga, ed., *The Dutch in America: Immigration, Settlement, and Cultural Change* (New Brunswick, NJ: Rutgers University Press, 1985), 156-171. See examples in Elaine M. Bjorklund, "Ideology and Culture Exemplified in Southwestern Michigan," *Annals of the Association of American Geographers* 54 (June 1964): 227-241 and Gordon W. Kirk, Jr. and Carolyn Tyirin Kirk, "Migration, Mobility and the Transformation of the Occupational Structure in an Immigrant Community: Holland, Michigan, 1850-1880," *Journal of Social History* 7 (Winter 1974): 142-164.
14. Jan L. Flora and John M. Stitz, "Ethnicity, Persistence, and Capitalization of Agriculture in the Great Plains during the Settlement Period: Wheat Production and Risk Avoidance," *Rural Sociology* 50 (1985): 349.
15. Robert N. Bellah, R. Madsen, W.M. Sullivan, A. Swidler, and S.M. Tipton, *Habits of the Heart* (Berkeley: University of California Press, 1985).
16. Wade C. Roof, "Concepts and Indicators of Religious Commitment: A Critical Review," in Robert Wuthnow, ed., *The Religious Dimension* (New York: Academic Press, 1979): 17-45.
17. William Cronon, *Changes in the Land: Indians, Colonists, and the Ecology of New England* (New York: Hill and Wang, 1983).
18. Fikret Berkes and David Feeny, "Paradigms Lost: Changing Views on the Use of Common Property Resources," *Alternatives* 17 (1990):48-55.
19. Salamon, "Ethnic Communities."
20. Curtic E. Beus and Riley E. Dunlap, "Conventional Versus Alternative Agriculture: The Paradigmatic Roots of the Debate," *Rural Sociology* 55 (1990): 590-616.

21. Swierenga, "The Little White Church."

22. John W. Murphy, JohnW. and Joseph J. Pilotta, "Community Based Research: A New Strategy for Policy Analysis," *Humboldt Journal of Social Relations* 11 (1984): 23-24.

23. G. Nelson Nieuwenhuis, *Siouxland: A History of Sioux County, Iowa* (Orange City, IA: Pluim Publishing Incorporated, 1983), 61

24. Michael L. Yoder, "Anabaptists and Calvinists Four Centuries Later: An Iowa Case Study," *The Mennonite Quarterly Review* 67 (1993): 50.

25. Janel M. Curry-Roper, "Community-Level Worldviews and the Sustainability of Agriculture," in Tim Rickard, Brian Ilbery, and Quentin Chiotti, eds., *Agricultural Restructuring and Sustainability: A Geographical Perspective* (Wallingford, UK: CAB International, 1997), 101-115; Janel M. Curry-Roper, "Worldview and Agriculture: A Study of Two Reformed Communities in Iowa," in D. Luidens, C. Smidt, and H. Stoffels, eds., *Signs of Vitality in Reformed Communities* (Lanham, MD: University Press of America, 1998), 17-32.

26. James D. Bratt, *Dutch Calvinism in Modern America: A History of a Conservative Subculture* (Grand Rapids, MI: Eerdmans, 1984), 29.

27. Henry Aay, "The Making of an Ethnic Island: Initial Settlement Patterns of Netherlanders in West Michigan," *The Great Lakes Geographer* 2 (1995): 61-76, 62.

28. Barbara. N. Gingerich, "Property and the Gospel: Two Reformation Perspectives," *Mennonite Quarterly Review* 59 (1985): 265.

29. Elaine M. Bjorklund, "Ideology and Culture Exemplified in Southwestern Michigan," *Annals of the Association of American Geographers* 54 (June): 228.

30. Henry Stob, "Observations on the Concept of Antithesis," in Peter De Klerk and R.R. De Ridder, eds., *Perspectives on the Christian Reformed Church: Studies in Its History, Theology, and Ecumenicity* (Grand Rapids, MI: Baker Book House, 1983), 253.

31. Stob, "Observations," 256; John L. Paterson, "Stewardship: Theory and Practice in a Canadian Christian Farmers Organization," (Expanded Version of a Paper Presented at the Annual Meeting of the Association of American Geographers, Portland, Oregon, April 1987).

32. Anne W. Van Den Ban, "Locality Group Differences in the Adoption of New Farm Practices," *Rural Sociology* 25 (1960): 314.

33. Janel M. Curry-Roper, "Contemporary Christian Eschatologies and Their Relation to Environmental Stewardship," *The Professional Geographer* 42 (1990): 157-169.

34. Van Den Ban, "Locality Group," 316.

35. Thomas A. Lyson and Rick Welsh, "The Production Function, Crop Diversity, and the Debate Between Conventional and Sustainable Agriculture," *Rural Sociology* 58 (1993): 433.

36. Iowa State Assessor, *Annual Farm Census. Township Data* (Ames: Iowa State University 1917-1980).

37. United States Department of Commerce. Bureau of the Census, *1982 Census of Agriculture*. Volume 1, Geographic Areas Series. Part 15: Iowa: State and County Data. Table 4 (1984), United States Department of Commerce. Bureau of the Census. *1992 Census of Agriculture*. Volume 1, Geographic Areas Series. Part 15: Iowa: State and County Data. Table 4 (1994).

38. "Iowa Farm Population Drop," *Des Moines Rgister* (19 July 1992): J1-2.

39. Janel M. Curry-Roper and Carol Veldman Rudie, "Hollandale: The Evolution of a Dutch Farming Community," *Focus* 40.3 (1990): 13-18.

40. Yda Schreuder, *Dutch Catholic Immigrant Settlement in Wisconsin, 1850-1905* (New York: Garland, 1989).

41. Joanne G. Van Dijk, "Ethnic Identity Retention and Social Support: A Comparative Analysis of First Generation Elderly Dutch-Canadian Catholics and Calvinists," (M.A. Thesis, University of Guelph, Ontario, 1990); idem, "Ethnicity, Aging, and Support Among Dutch Canadians: A Study of Community in Two Generations of Catholics and Calvinists," (Ph.D. Thesis, McMater University, Hamilton, Ontario, 1996), idem, "Ethnic Persistence Among Dutch-Canadian Catholics and Calvinists," *Canadian Ethnic Studies* 30 (1998): 23-49.

Cover of the Dutch Children's book *Pietje Bell in Amerika* (1929)

Socialist Immigrants and the American Dream[1]

Pieter R.D. Stokvis

In several ways the religious and ideological segmentation of Dutch society, known as "pillarization", has left an imprint upon immigration history and historiography. Together with Robert Swierenga I have been inclined to focus on Calvinist immigrants from the Netherlands. The late Henk van Stekelenburg felt challenged to devote his research to the neglected field of Catholic immigration. Socialist immigrants, however, have not received much attention. In fact, they seem to have left so few traces, that one may wonder whether there were any socialist immigrants from the Netherlands. They appear like a lost tribe! Appearances may well be deceptive as the occupational composition of Dutch immigrants suggests. More than half of Dutch immigrants between 1880 and 1920 were classified as laborers and as the labor movement was gaining momentum in that period, some of them must have been socialists of some kind. To what extent did they voice their opinions and keep their convictions? How may their low profile be explained? For an explanation I will look at individual cases of socialist immigrants in America who may be classified as loners, dissidents within the ethnic community of Dutch Calvinists and last, but not least genuine socialist immigrants from the Low Countries.

Their life stories tell us about their interpretation of the American Dream. The term "American Dream" refers both to collective values and ideals in general and to the American key value of individual material success in particular. It is a moral framework or ideological construction which encourages people to work hard hoping their endeavors will be rewarded.[2] As "the common man's utopia" America seemed to promise European immigrants political, religious and economic freedom and social equality.[3] Until the Russian Revolution of 1917 many socialists viewed America as the land of the future where the capitalist mode of production and the inherent contradiction of capital and labor were most advanced. They expected a dialectical turn-about in America which to their surprise took place in backward Russia inspiring the dream of a communist revolution.[4] Individual life stories will show the impact of socialist and communist dreams in relation to the American dream, but first a quick survey of the Dutch language press will illustrate the low profile of Dutch-speaking socialist immigrants.

The Dutch Language Press

Looking for Dutch-language periodicals sympathetic to the labor movement or socialist ideals I managed to trace a few short lived periodicals.[5] The about equal number of Danish immigrants accounted for ten socialist periodicals and had a stake in thirty-seven Scandinavian ones catering for Swedes and Norwegians as well. If they wished, Danes could choose in the course of time from forty-four Swedish and four Norwegian radical newspapers. In the 1890s about ten leftist Scandinavian periodicals circulated and between 1900 and 1920 about fifteen.[6] So compared with the Danes Dutch immigrants obviously did not engage in producing a radical press in their own language. All the same there was no shortage of Dutch language newspapers. Starting with *De Sheboygan Nieuwsbode* of 1849 at least a hundred Dutch-language periodicals appeared in the United States until the Second World-War. Between 1880 and 1930 *Ayer's directory* mentions 56 periodicals. The majority appeared in Michigan (28) and a substantial number in Iowa (8), Illinois (7) and New Jersey (4). As to politics 8 were Republican and 6 Democratic, 2 changed loyalties, 1 was prohibitionist, 1 populist, 1 socialist, 14 religious and 23 independent with religious undertones. The number of periodicals published simultaneously doubled during the immigration wave of 1880-1893 and remained close to 20 declining somewhat in the 1920s. The average circulation climbed from over 1,000 copies in the 1880s to 2,000 in the 1890s and 3,000 to 5,000 in the first three decades of the twentieth century. This was, however, mainly due to the huge circulation figures of church periodicals. The highest circulation figures of secular periodicals were 9,009 in 1928 for the (Flemish) *Gazette van Detroit*, 7,506 in 1924 for the (Flemish) *Gazette van Moline*, 7,400 in 1905 for the *Grondwet*, published in Holland, Michigan, 6,500 in 1920 for the *Hollandsche Amerikaan*, published in Kalamazoo, Michigan and 5,780 in 1928 for *De Volksvriend* of Orange City, Iowa. Continuity of publication was not lacking; 7 periodicals of 1880 were still going strong in 1930 and 27 appeared for more than ten years at least. The publication of new periodicals reached a peak in the decades before and after 1900, when immigration was highest and the communities not yet shaken by the Americanization agitation of World-War One. According to Ayer's directory 7 new periodicals appeared in the 1880s, 12 in each decade before and after 1900, still 10 in 1910-1919, but only 4 in the following decade, when immigration came to a halt and Americanization progressed.

Reformist, labor and radical periodicals were few. Of some only the names survive. *De Christen Werkman*, which appeared in Grand Rapids from 1892 till 1894, propagated the ideas of the American Christian Workmen's Union: Patrimonium.

Likewise in Grand Rapids in 1892 *Het Volksblad* circulated under the auspices of The Dutch Cabinetmakers Union. It was "devoted to the interests of working classes." A genuine reformist periodical was the modernist Protestant *Stemmen uit de Vrije Hollandsche Gemeente te Grand Rapids.* Socialist periodicals were rare and short-lived. In the election year 1908 a socialist weekly *De Volksstem* circulated in Grand Rapids and in 1914 *Voorwaarts* was published in Holland, Michigan. There seems to have been another socialist paper *Nieuw Nederland* (1911-1912) in the industrial city of Paterson, New Jersey.[7] The apparent low profile of a Dutch-language radical press does not mean that there were not any immigrant Dutch radicals. As a matter of fact some individuals of Dutch parentage played an important part in American labor, socialist and pacifist movements.

Labor Leaders and Calvinist Radicals

The founder and leader of the American Federation of Labor (1886), Samuel Gompers (1850-1924), was of Dutch-Jewish descent.[8] His father, a cigar maker, had moved from Amsterdam to London, where Samuel was born. In 1863 the family settled in New York. Samuel joined the Cigar makers Union the following year which inaugurated a long career as a moderate trade unionist. In his autobiography he refers to his knowledge of the Dutch language and to Dutch customs. "With thorough-going Dutch cleanliness" the children were regularly scrubbed in the tub. House-keeping in general bore the mark of Dutch traditions: "My parents were both Hollanders born in Amsterdam. Our home preserved many of the customs of the Dutch community from which mother and father came. In our big room was a large fire place, in which mother had a Dutch oven… All mother's cooking utensils were of the squat, substantial Dutch make, necessary for the old-fashioned Dutch cooking that nourished us youngsters three times a day. We had plenty of dishes – an unusual possession in our neighborhood. These mother brought to this country."[9]

One of his more radical opponents was the Sephardic Dutch Jew, Daniel DeLeon (1852-1914). He was born in Curacao where his father was an army surgeon. After some secondary education in Hildesheim and Amsterdam, DeLeon settled in New York in 1874 where he got a law degree in 1878. In 1888 he joined the Knights of Labor and in 1899 the Socialist Labor Party, which dated from 1877. Since 1892 editor of the weekly *The People*, he rose to prominence as a revolutionary theorist. In practical politics he achieved little, because his doctrinaire authoritarian leadership and failure to cooperate with organized labor kept the party small, if not sectarian.[10]

The labor leaders Samuel Gompers and Daniel DeLeon were not rooted in a Dutch-American immigrant community as were the ministers and political activists Abraham Muste and Pierre Van Paassen. The life story of Abraham J. Muste (1885-1967) illustrates the impact of Calvinism on the Dutch immigrant community and in spite of his non-conformism on Muste's personal choices as well. In 1891 his family moved from Zierikzee to Grand Rapids. As a minister in New York he preached the "social gospel" and joined the pacifist "Fellowship of Reconciliation." After World War I he became involved with Trokskyism and unionism until he found a way back to religiously inspired pacifism in 1936, which he professed until his death.[11] According to Muste's autobiography Dutch immigrants were much appreciated because of their sober, religious way of life, their industry and anti-union sentiments. "The church, especially in the first years, when our life was mainly lived within the Dutch community was the center of social life and culture, as well as of worship and religious training ... The Hollanders settled in the Middle West in the decades before World War I, formed a fairly numerous group in Grand Rapids... With the rarest of exceptions every Dutch family belonged to a church, the Reformed or Christian Reformed, to which it had belonged in the old country. The services and the preaching were all in Dutch. In the larger population in Grand Rapids the Dutch constituted a lower stratum."[12] Less radical than Abraham Muste was Pierre Van Paassen (1895-1968) who moved from Gorcum to Canada in 1914 with his parents and from Canada to the United States in 1923. Although trained as a minister he did not climb the pulpit after his demobilization from the Canadian army, but instead took up journalism. As such he gained some fame as a ardent proponent of Zionism and opponent of national-socialism.[13] The persons mentioned so far became active as trade-unionist, political agitator, radical militant and progressive journalist in the United States. So the question remains how immigrants who had been active socialists in the Netherlands, fared after arrival in the United States. The only way to answer this question is to explore some life-stories.

Socialist Immigrants From the Low Countries
The first socialist from the Low Countries who wrote about his immigrant experience, is Pol De Witte (1848-1929) from Ghent. This tailor was a member of the First International. The bloody suppression of the Parisian Commune in 1871, the quarrels between followers of Marx and Bakunin in 1872 and lost strikes in Ghent shocked his faith in a socialist future. In March 1873 he left for America with faint ideas of founding a communist settlement. In New York, his host, the Dutch tailor Pasman, familiarized him with the American way of life: "For sure, no man is more publicly respected and admired here than the man who manages to gather a lot of dollars, no matter how... The dollar is the God for whom one kneels in worship." Pol wondered disenchanted: "Was this the free, democratic republic which was held in such high esteem in Europe? And the laws, are they not equal for everybody, in a people's republic where male suffrage reigns?" On his question whether negroes were liked, he got the following answer: "Liked? They are hated, for they are not admitted in trams, theatres, nowhere. They are hired for the most dirty, heavy and low-payed jobs." In one respect workers and immigrants were better off in America: their meals were abundant according to European standards! When

Pol questioned the visitors of a Flemish tavern about the difference between Republicans and Democrats, they replied unanimously that all politicians were swindlers and money-grubbers. Pol's exposition about communism fell on deaf ears and was cut short by Pasman as an impossible dream. German comrades, however, confirmed his socialist beliefs: "I firmly believed that things in America would collapse, and that what had failed in Paris in 1871, had more chance of succeeding here. My new friends from one of the German sections of the International of which I had become a member, thought so too." Looking for jobs he browsed the advertisements in the *New York Herald Tribune* and the *New Yorker Staatszeitung*, but due to an economic depression employment was low and therefore he returned to Antwerp in January 1875.[14]

Louis Van Koert, a member of the Social-Democratic Association lead by the former Lutheran minister Ferdinand Domela Nieuwenhuis, crossed the ocean twenty years later, in 1893, leaving his wife and children and a pregnant girl friend behind. In letters to Domela Nieuwenhuis he reported in detail about his personal affairs, the condition of the working classes and the labor movement.[15] He spent most of his time working in the building-trade with like-minded compatriots in Chicago and Grand Rapids. His friends were members of a German trade-union of painters. To his disappointment no more than a thousand people showed up for the commemoration and unveiling of a monument for the Haymarket Martyrs, anarchists accused of bombing and hanged in Chicago on November 11, 1886. Socialist mass meetings in his home-town in Den Haag drew more people! The common practice of electoral fraud and ballot rigging confirmed that elections and parliamentary democracy were a sham: "The bourgeoisie in America is much more domineering than in Europe and the police is all-powerful." The revolutionary potential of the people was not tapped, because effective organization was lacking. "The passion for money corrupts everybody. Everything makes way for the dollar. That is, in my opinion, the main reason for the lack or weakness of organized socialism in America." The better organized unions did not foster class-consciousness, divided by trade and ethnic origin and led by corrupt officials. German unionists with whom Louis Van Koert was familiar, for instance drunk a lot and argued loudly, but were afraid to act. In Grand Rapids he spoke up at a public meeting of the "Christian Workmen's Union: Patrimonium" and started a socialist debating club which became a chapter of the Socialist Labor Party in 1894. Most members were at odds with the dominant reformed churches or came from the (Unitarian) Free Congregation whose minister preached the social gospel. Van Koert wrote that in order to make socialist converts in Grand Rapids one had to oil the rusty Dutch heads, struggle against a church and ministers "more vile than the catholic ones" and challenge the "damned lying religious periodicals."

Van Koert's efforts to start such a challenging paper never materialized. A printer in New York, possibly connected with *Der Anarchist*, told him about the corrupt behavior of a fellow party-member Von Barnekow who corresponded with Domela Nieuwenhuis and wrote some articles for *Recht voor Allen*. This Freiherr Hans von Barnekow (1855-1930) was a shady German aristocrat who became a member of the Social-Democratic Association and hastily emigrated in 1891 to evade the consequences of his fraudulent schemes. Shunned by socialists in America who received information from Dutch comrades he turned in vain to the Netherlands consul-general asking for money in exchange for information about Dutch socialists. Until his remigration in 1910 he earned a living writing for German-language journals and doing odd jobs.[16]

A more savory acquaintance of Louis van Koert, Hendrik Jan Van Steenis (1862-1939), spent the latter half of the 1890s in the United States. In New York he attended editorial meetings of *Der Anarchist: Anarchistisch-Communistisches Organ*, a German-language periodical which was also read by Dutch kindred spirits in Chicago, Grand Rapids and Holland. In travel notes from America published in the *Anarchist* which circulated in his home-town Den Haag, he expressed his regrets seeing that even anarchists, just like other immigrants, were keen to adopt the American way of life and have their share of prosperity. He had to admit, however, that the impressive technological and organizational progress in the New World also benefited the working classes.[17]

Van Steenis, Van Koert and Von Barnekow had been active in the Social-Democratic Association just like a number of Frisian fellow immigrants. When rural laborers in Het Bildt (Friesland) formed a Social-Democratic Union called *Broedertrouw* (1889-1892) and engaged in a long lasting strike, emigrant comrades in Chicago and other places associated in *Hulpbetoon* offered financial support. As the strike petered out in 1891, many disappointed activists joined their overseas comrades in the latter half of the 1890s when the American economy was expanding again. One of the strike leaders, Jan Stap (1859-1908), crossed the ocean in 1896.[18]

Another activist, Tjeerd Stienstra (1859-1935), left the same year for strictly personal reasons: an unhappy marriage. With his teenaged son he joined his brother Tjibbe who had settled in Paterson in 1895. There he met other, mainly Frisian, socialists like Jan Stap. In Paterson, Grand Rapids and other centers these socialist immigrants had started chapters of Association of Socialists, the anti-parliamentarian and syndicalist successor of the Social-Democratic Association. Besides they were active in American Unions and the Socialist Labor Party. Political developments in the Netherlands were scrutinized, especially the Hogerhuis-case in 1896 involving three brothers in Friesland – fellow socialists – accused of armed and violent robbery and convicted on dubious grounds. Because Tjeerd declined the request to return to the Netherlands and testify as witness for the defence, former comrades tended to give him the cold shoulder. First still active in the Socialist Labor Party and prospering as a tailor in Little Falls he found his own way in

America. Upon his return to Paterson he refuted revolutionary socialism and embraced the idea of land nationalization.[19] His younger brother Klaas Stienstra (1871-1929) who had earned some fame as socially committed playwright in Friesland, lost his revolutionary zeal in America. He came to Paterson in 1900 with his mother and worked his way up from tailor to shopkeeper. He married a Frisian immigrant daughter in 1904 and took part in a non-political Frisian cultural and literary circle.[20]

The tendency among immigrants to abandon socialism as a consequence of economic success or to improve their chances of succeeding seems to have been wide spread and was reinforced by the Americanization movement during the First World War. In 1922 G. Elferink, a former textile worker from Twente, wrote to the Dutch emigration historian Jacob Van Hinte, that he had tried in vain to start a socialist association in Rochester, New York. A *Domela Nieuwenhuisclub* for mutual aid was short-lived. According to Elferink material prosperity had lead to spiritual corruption or 'mouldy minds'.[21] The socialist temperance advocate N.A. De Vries noted to his regret that his former comrades had become bourgeois in America: "Many who still felt the need to struggle for ideals, were drawn into the whirlpool of moneymakers and drowned. I talked with them, good Dutch socialist veterans who have lost all their ideals after arrival. Leaning back in a plush armchair they point out their gains. They counter my reproaches by saying: 'Didn't we always suffer and struggle to gain a good house, a car, the opportunity to see something of the world and to offer the children a better education?'"[22]

One socialist immigrant eventually became a successful entrepreneur. By opening a grocery store in Greenville, Michigan in 1934 Hendrik Meijer (1883-1964) laid the foundation for "Thrifty Acres", a chain of cheap department stores. The third of seven children Hendrik was born in Hengelo where the machine factory of Stork employed his father. After his school days were over, he was hired as an apprentice spinner by the textile factory of Stork in 1896. In spite of his anarchist conviction, in military service (1903-1906) he learned to appreciate order and discipline and enjoyed outdoor life. He was a member of the choir of Free Socialists where he met his future wife Gezina Mantel (1888-1978). The Mantel family were ardent followers of Domela Nieuwenhuis, collaborators of the periodical *Recht door Zee*, teetotalers, vegetarians and neo-malthusians. Because Hendrik saw no way of improving his lot in the Netherlands he considered trying his luck in Germany or America. After ample deliberation he left in 1907 with a sister and his father who had become deaf and had lost an eye while working in Stork's machine factory. His alcohol-addicted mother and his future bride remained behind. Aboard ship he read poetry about freedom, but what freedom meant in America he still had to find out: about the statue of liberty he wrote to Gezina "I don't know what it means." In his letters to Gezina who had to wait five years, he reported his experiences. Because they travelled second class and not steerage as most poor immigrants, they were allowed to disembark speedily without degrading inspection and took the train to Holland, Michigan. Life in this town of wooden, detached houses was different from life in Hengelo: "Nobody walks the streets on Sunday... Everybody (except me) sits in one of the 20 to 25 churches." He was amazed at the ease with which workers moved from one job to another. The socialist association – possibly a chapter of the Socialist Labor Party – which Hendrik joined in Holland, was more inclined to pragmatic socialism or economic action (syndicalism) than to the anarchism which Hendrik favored. So Hendrik and some anarchist (Free Socialist) comrades started their own meetings. A typical meeting drew perhaps a dozen young men and began with the singing of the revolutionary French anthem *La Marseillaise* in translation. A meeting to commemorate the Haymarket Martyrs only brought in a donation of two dollars for the Anarchist-Communist Congress! The efforts to keep a socialist newspaper *De Volksstem* going stranded on differences of opinion between moderate English-speaking supporters of Eugene V. Debs and anarchist immigrants such as Hendrik believing in revolutionary rhetorics. After trying his luck in a number of trades wandering from place to place he finally settled as a barber in Greenville in 1912 and had Gezina join him there. The date of their wedding on November 11, the anniversary of the Haymarket executions, was a last echo of their revolutionary past.[23] Once married and settled Hendrik Meijer who was also a Freemason and sympathized with the syndicalist Industrial Workers of the World, just like Klaas Stienstra kept his socialist ideals indoors. Their public silence about socialism may also be due to the life cycle, for those who remained active like Hendrik Jan van Steenis and Gerrit Roorda were only birds of passage in America.

Gerrit Roorda was born in the South-East of Friesland in 1890. His father was a school teacher and freethinker. With a colleague carpenter Gerrit moved to the German industrial center of the Ruhr in 1906, because earnings were better there. In 1910 he decided to follow his older brother Tjerk who had joined an uncle in Orange City, Iowa in 1891. In Iowa he switched from one Frisian employer to another. Finally he entered the employment of an American carpenter to learn American procedures and to master the language. Just like Hendrik Meijer in Michigan he found out in Iowa: "Who ever is walking the street during church hours immediately risks a bad reputation." When the minister of the Dutch church in Sheldon thundered about Freemasons and unions, Gerrit decided that their ideals appealed to him. In 1917 he joined the lodge and in 1918 he became a "wobbly," that is a member of the Industrial Workers of the World. He appreciated the equality or rather informality found in the lodge: "Everybody called each other by their first name regardless of their rank and station." Both Freemasons and wobblies had pacifism or anti-militarist leaning and were therefore considered pro-German. The Dutch (often confused with "Deutsch" = German) in Iowa were lumped together with Germans anyway, because they were anti-British since the

Boer War, listened to Dutch sermons and refused to admit an American flag in God's house. Gerrit's brother-in-law was dragged out of his bed by a mob to nail an American flag on the church door. Elsewhere a patriotic mob set fire to a Dutch church. Radicalized by these happenings and a forced enlistment in the American army he returned to the Netherlands in 1919 as a fervent partisan of the Russian Revolution.[24]

How would he have fared, had he stayed? Would he have settled and adjusted his ideological outlooks on equality and freedom? After all he too hoped to get ahead in America. It seems that most socialist immigrants who stayed, tended to interpret equality according to American ideology as equal opportunity and freedom as freedom to move and improve one's position. That image of freedom also appealed to the socially committed school teacher and writer Christiaan F. van Abcoude (1880-1960). The money he earned with his bestseller *Pietje Bell* (1914) enabled him to leave for America after his demobilization in 1916 and salute the Statue of Liberty, an occasion he describes in a sequel about *Pietje Bell in America*.[25]

A Dutch immigrant who never changed his ideological outlook, but remained a wobbly all his life, was Nicolaas Steelink (1890-1989). In his fascinating autobiography "Journey in Dreamland" he tells about his life until imprisonment in San Quentin in 1920.[26] After his father's death his strong-willed mother kept the family going by keeping a grocery shop, doing laundry, moving house every six months, using family connections and taking in lodgers. One lodger, a tailor, who became a family friend, instilled in him socialist ideas and later invited him to come to Seattle. Not satisfied with the clerical work he did since 1903 he booked a second class passage to America in 1912. In vain a fellow passenger, the son of a banker, gave him the well-meant advice to forget about socialism if he wanted to get ahead. Once arrived in Seattle he moved around from one job to another. Planting hops he was fired by the Dutch foreman, because he did not show up in the Dutch church of Moxee Valley. He had his mother and sister join him, when he found better-paid clerical work in Los Angeles in 1914. There he found a circle of idealistic friends – pacifists, socialists and wobblies – and experienced the wave of chauvinistic outrages during the war and its aftermath. Suspected of German sympathies because of his pacifist stand he was arrested in 1917. In reaction he promptly joined the wobblies and was thus confronted with harassing federal agents, intimidating local policemen, infiltrating agents provocateurs and assaults from the American Legion acting as right-wing vigilantes. Federal and state legislation against "criminal syndicalism" condoned the lynching of some prominent "fellow-workers" and enabled the conviction of Nicolaas Steelink as a wobbly. Both he and his Russian-born wife Fannia remained staunch liberals. Upon his death at a great age in Tucson he was honored as a labor and soccer organizer. Unlike many fellow Dutch socialist immigrants he did not forget or kept silent about socialism to get ahead, nor did he return to the Netherlands disappointed by the American dream.

Conclusion

Among the immigrants from the Low Countries who were working class, were most certainly a good many socialists. As an ethnic group they did not figure prominently in the American labor movement. Small wonder, for they did not come to change American society, but to improve their individual lot. When they settled in Dutch-American communities, the church as dominant institution compelled them to shun atheistic socialism and organized labor. Those who resisted or lived elsewhere and remained active, often read German-language periodicals and joined German or American organizations such as the iww.

Anyway, many immigrants argued that their ideals of freedom and equality were realized as chances to profit from economic freedom and improve their social position. They traded their socialist dream of a better society for the American dream of a better life for themselves and their children. If one may generalize from a few life stories, the fact that those who married and became self-employed, forgot about socialism, is revealing. Feeling at home and middle-class in America they embraced the materialistic version of the American Dream.

Two immigrants bore the brunt of the Red Scare in 1917-1919. Nicolaas Steelink who was married, remained an active member of the iww. The bachelor Gerrit Roorda returned to the Netherlands to follow the communist dream. Nicolaas' journey in dreamland ended in prison, stigmatized for life, but in essence he remained loyal to an idealistic version of the American Dream.

Notes

1. This article elaborates upon two earlier studies: Pieter R.D. Stokvis, "Socialistische immigranten in de Verenigde Staten: vrijheid versus gelijkheid," *Groniek* 96 (1986): 102-116 and idem, "Dutch-Speaking Peoples," in Dirk Hoerder and Chr. Harzig, eds., *The Immigrant Labor Press in North America 1840s-1970: An Annotated Bibliography* (New York: Greenwood Press, 1987) 3:263-281.
2. Robert Wuthnow, *Poor Richard's Principle: Recovering the American Dream Through the Moral Dimension of Work, Business, and Money* (Princeton: Princeton University Press, 1996), 4.
3. M.L. Hansen, *The Atlantic Migration 1607-1860* (Cambridge, MA: Harvard University Press, 1945), 146-171.
4. Marianne M. Mooijweer, *De Amerikaanse droom van Frederik van Eeden* (Amsterdam: De Bataafsche Leeuw, 1996), 11-14.
5. Stokvis, "Dutch-Speaking Peoples," 263-281.
6. Dirk Hoerder, "An Internationally Mobile Working Class and Its Press in North America: A Survey," in Hoerder and Harzig, eds., *Immigrant Labor Press*, 1-47, in particular 28.
7. *N.W. Ayer and Son's Directory, Newspapers and Periodicals* (Philadelphia 1880-1930). The most recent historical and bibliographical surveys are: Conrad Bult, "Dutch-American Newspapers: Their History and Role," in Robert P. Swierenga, ed., *The Dutch in America: Immigration, Settlement, and Cultural Change* (New Brunswick, NJ: Rutgers University Press, 1985), 273-293 and H. Edelman, *The Dutch Language Press in America* (Nieuwkoop: De Graaf Publishers, 1986).

8. *Dictionary of American Biography* (New York: Scribner, 1946) 7:369-373.
9. Samuel Gompers, *Seventy Years of Life and Labor* (New York: Dutton, 1957), 46-48.
10. *Dictionary of American Biography* (New York: Scribner, 1946) 5:222-224.
11. J.A. Ooiman Robinson, *Abraham Went Out: A Biography of A.J. Muste* (Philadelphia: Temple University Press, 1981).
12. N. Hentoff, *The Essays of A.J. Muste* (New York: Clarion, 1970), 5, 27-28.
13. Pierre van Paassen, *Days of Our Years* (London: [s.n.] 1939).
14. Pol De Witte, *Alles is omgekeerd. Hoe de werklieden leefden (1848-1918)* (Leuven: Kritak, 1986), 159-167, 187, 193.
15. Jan Gielkes and Bert Altena were so kind to send me the relevant part in typescript of their book *Ferdinand Domela Nieuwenhuis. De briefwisseling met geestverwanten buiten Nederland 1878-1896* (Amsterdam: Internationaal Instituut voor Sociale Geschiedenis, 2000).
16. H.J. Scheffer, *Henry Tindal. Een ongewoon heer met ongewone besognes* (Bussum: Unieboek, 1976), 95-106.
17. J.M. Welcker, *Heren en arbeiders in de vroege Nederlandse arbeidersbeweging 1870-1914* (Amsterdam: Van Gennep, 1978), 455-466.
18. Johan Frieswijk, "De beweging van Broedertrouw op Het Bildt (1889-1892)," *Jaarboek Arbeidersbeweging 1978* (Nijmegen: SUN, 1978), 83-139.
19. Johan Frieswijk, "Een Socialistisch Propagandist in Revolutionaire Jaren, Biografie van Tjeerd Stienstra (1859-1935)," *Tijdschrift voor Sociale Geschiedenis* 6 (oktober 1976): 219-256.
20. Gj. Jelsma, "Twa revolusjonaire toanielskriuwers ut de ein fan de foarige ieu," *It Beeaken* 5/6 (1979): 291-310.
21. Jacob Van Hinte, *Nederlanders in Amerika. Een studie over landverhuizers en volksplanters in de 19de en 20ste eeuw in de Verenigde Staten van Amerika,* 2 vols. (Groningen: Noordhoff, 1928) 2:466.
22. N.A. de Vries, *De Nieuwe Wereld. Amerika 1923* (Groningen: Wolters, 1924), 115.
23. H.G. Meijer, *Thrifty Years: The Life of Hendrik Meijer* (Grand Rapids: Eerdmans, 1984), 5-94.
24. K. Huisman, *It libben fan Gerrit Roorda* (Leeuwarden: Alternatyf/De Tille [1973]), 1-113.
25. H. van Gelder, *'t Is een bijzonder kind, dat is ie. Kinderboekenschrijvers van toen* (Bussum: Unieboek, 1980), 11-23; Chr.F. van Abcoude, *Pietje Bell in Amerika* (Alkmaar: Kluitman, 1929).
26. Nicolaas Steelink, *Reis in Droomland* (Sittard: Baalprodukties, 1998). The original English-language manuscript is deposited at the International Institute for Social History in Amsterdam.

Unidentified Dutch Immigrant Woman (Hope College
Collection of the Joint Archives of Holland).

Transnational Visions of Gender and Class in Dutch Migration

Suzanne M. Sinke

In 1993 Robert Swierenga published an article in *International Migration Review* describing the demographic patterns of migration from the Netherlands in the period 1880 to 1920. He outlined the centrality of the United States as a destination for rural migrants, especially farm laborers. Many of this group came in family units early in the period, though this later became a pattern in which single individuals were more prominent. Still, families tended to make up the majority of migrants to the United States, in contrast to the pattern for the Dutch colonies, where singles often dominated. Further, those who went to the Dutch colonies had greater wealth on average than the U.S.-bound, and were more likely to come from urban areas. In short, the colonial migrants tended to be "ambitious sons of urban middle-class families."[1] This essay explores the ramifications of some of those patterns by contrasting ideals of gender and class in the Netherlands with those which developed among migrants in the United States and in the Dutch East Indies.

Dutch Gender Roles Around 1900

In the Netherlands, ideals about gender and class were in flux at the turn of the century. As of the early 1880s there were significantly different patterns between rural, farm-laboring groups and those of the urban bourgeoisie. One of the most salient differences was their understanding of separate spheres. For those engaged in farm labor, and even for those operating small farms, the sense of women as belonging only in the home was rarely an economic possibility, and it tended to have a distinct and sometimes negative connotation of class snobbery. On the large farms of sea clay regions, the *boerin* [mistress of the farm] might "play the lady," but more often she supervised household, garden, small animal care, and perhaps dairy, including production of a large variety of products.[2] For the farm workers of the same area, who were much more likely to migrate, a woman who did not take an active role in earning and home production was extremely unusual.

Workers' budgets, collected to assist in law-making, illustrated the monetary bind of many farm workers' wives, who were hired along with their spouses. Women in rural areas, particularly widows, tended to work in jobs which paid well below a rate which would make adequate child care possible, meaning they had to leave infants with only slightly older children or very elderly women, or to bring them to the fields and leave them largely unattended.[3] As the government debated labor laws to "protect" women and children in various industries, notably those in which they competed with men for good wages, agricultural work consistently formed an exception.[4] Patterns of agricultural life, thus, were designed on the principle of gender complementarity in work outside the home and household production (whether for sale or consumption).[5] A man might ease his tasks through mechanization, or a woman through gaining more help, but both were crucial parts of the rural economy, and recognized this. Some rural women gained exposure to the realm of separate spheres through domestic service in urban areas, but even there the clear class differences did not encourage them to assume this as a lifestyle they could enjoy.

In contrast, the urban bourgeoisie of the late nineteenth century was firmly tied to the ideal of separate spheres. At the National Exhibition of Women's Work in 1898, Cornelie Huygens described how this ideology manifested itself in literature:

> If it is [a woman writer's] wish to depict Dutch family-life her heroines must necessarily be kept within the bounds and rules of our social institutions. And these rules, drawn with old-fashioned Dutch severity, strictly forbid a Dutch woman, especially of the higher classes, to move an inch outside her domestic sphere, rigidly fix and limit her daily occupations to housekeeping and philanthropy and anxiously screen her from every contagious influence, which might reach her through the faint echo of the great things done by women in political, literary and social matters in [other lands]....[6]

Huygens' sentiments hinted at the interest in women's social activism and a more public role, an interest which fueled the women's movement of this period. Other sections of the exhibition noted the increased role of women in child socialization.[7] Prescriptive literature on child raising in the late nineteenth century, with the exception of that coming from freethinkers and Neo-Calvinists, assumed mothers handled this task almost exclusively.[8] Families of means, even the petty bourgeoisie, thus, strove to maintain the ideal of the husband working outside the home for a family wage, while the wife managed home care and child rearing. In practice, women might be involved in a family business, particularly in shopkeeping, in social enhancement of the family's position through entertaining and making advantageous contacts, and in an increasing number of "public" fields which became associated with women, such as nursing and teaching. The "public" areas, however, tended to be limited to unmarried women. A series of Royal Decrees around the turn of the century placed bars on the employment of married women in most public service jobs, as well as limiting factory employment.[9]

Class Distinctions

What both rural and urban people shared, was a clear understanding of class and one's place in it. What people wore, how they spoke, how they interacted with others depended on *stand*, a term which encompassed shades of caste even in the late nineteenth century. In the Netherlands, people used titles and different forms of address to indicate one's place in the hierarchy. This was true not only for the nobility, but also to distinguish employers from employees, and the bourgeoisie from workers. Thus a worker had to address an employer with a formal title and with the formal form of you, whereas the employer would use the worker's first name and informal you.[10] Likewise clothing announced one's status, whether through expensive adornments for women or a formal coat for men. Lack of opportunities for washing and pressing also made the clothing of workers visibly different from those of the more affluent.[11] Though there was some attempt to break down these divisions, particularly through the civilization campaign underway at the end of the century, the distance was still great.

One of the most prevalent situations where those of different *standen* met was in the household, where servants interacted with employers. Bourgeois status required at least one servant, if not more. At the *Dienstboden-Congres* [Domestic Servant Congress] in 1898, speaker after speaker (who were almost without exception employers rather than servants) complained of the poor manners, lack of education, and brute characteristics of their servants.[12] For young women, however, service in an urban bourgeois household was one of the few opportunities for possible advancement. It allowed some to get out of rural areas, and in some cases even provided opportunities for marriage into urban areas, at times even into the petty bourgeoisie.[13] In the countryside, domestic service was often associated with field and garden work, thus eliminating the chance for training in a bourgeois lifestyle which some hoped would lead to higher things. Domestics in these areas sometimes complained that they were treated little better than slaves or animals by their employers.[14]

Coming out of this context, migrants going to the Indies or to the United States already had very different experiences of class and gender ideals. When they arrived in their new locations they encountered circumstances which then tested their visions, and pushed them to adapt those ideals in different ways.

Egalitarian America

Those who migrated to the United States tended to come from the farm laboring or small farming class up to the turn of the century. Thereafter, the migration stream included more urban workers, though chain migration still kept family links strong. The vision they presented of America was a land where *standen* did not exist, and where economic mobility was not only possible, but common. Immigrant letters stressed these themes in concrete ways: people eat meat three times a day, the children of farm laborers dress as well as the most prosperous farmers in the Netherlands, people of all backgrounds sit in the same locations, and deference to one's "betters" is not a general characteristic of life.[15] This did not mean that immigrants did not experience class divisions or economic difficulties. What it did mean was that on average, because of their experiences in the Netherlands prior to migration, they perceived class divisions in the United States as less hierarchical and more fluid. My comments in this section will concentrate on Dutch Protestant immigrants, for whom I have extensive research.

The absence of class distinctions was particularly notable for those who came from backgrounds in farm labor and remained in agriculture. In contrast to the generally shrinking opportunities for such work in the Netherlands, farm labor was in short supply in many areas of the United States. As Anje Nieveen Mulder succinctly stated about farming in Kansas in 1889: "…we have to work hard too for hired hands and domestics are not available. That is not the same as in the Netherlands. They earn good wages here."[16] Farm laborers, either men or women, could expect much better pay than in the Netherlands, and more importantly, opportunities to rise to the status of farmers themselves. Further, they received better treatment by their employers. The comment of one was typical: "[the female farm owner] treats me like one of her own children."[17] This had various manifestations, such as farm hands eating meals with their employers – not eating a lesser meal separately. Farm laborers were much less likely to wear "different" clothes or use different levels of formality in language. The lack of farm hands also contributed to the trend of relying upon machinery, turning away from labor intensive practices.

Opportunities for Women in the New World
For women from agricultural backgrounds, the changes were even more striking, because much of the work typically delegated to female servants in rural areas of the Netherlands either did not exist in the United States, or aspects of it changed hands. Lubbigje Schaapman tried to entice a friend to emigrate in 1911 by noting one of their neighbors was looking for a domestic, offering wages of twenty to twenty-five dollars a month: "…you would only have to cook and clean the house."[18] These monthly wages were closer to a half-year's wages in many parts of the Netherlands, and more over, the prospect of a domestic on a farm not working outside the house (in animal and garden care) was highly prized.[19] What this also meant, however, was that once people gained the status of farmers, they were less likely to be able to afford help, and that the help was less likely to handle the various tasks which would define a more striking class difference between employers and employees. The lack of hired hands and absence of class differences

were what differentiated the terms *"boer"* and "farmer" to a large degree.

For farm wives, however, many aspects of the Dutch gender division of agriculture did not disappear. Women fairly consistently reported doing tasks in the barns and gardens, and assisting at times in the fields, unless and until their children were old enough to handle these tasks. Men reported frequently, and women at times, of the "laziness" of American farm wives, who according to their observations would do little outside the home and who would sit in rocking chairs. It was a stereotype shared by other ethnic groups of the time.[20] For the immigrant generation in the United States class status depended on financial success, particularly property ownership, and was less coupled to gender role divisions of American society. Only much later, if at all, did this change. In an interview from the 1960s, for example, an elderly Dutch immigrant couple described their activities. The husband boasted his wife never engaged in "farm work." The wife added, "well, but" and then listed some of her typical tasks: milking the cows (up to a dozen), caring for the chickens, doing most of the gardening.[21] The shift of the meaning of "farm work" to field work along gender lines was also unusual, at least up until mid-century. Letters, pictures, and newspaper advertisements from the turn of the century included many examples of women involved in field work.

A similar kind of ideal applied to urban areas, where Dutch immigrants also identified success monetarily and evaluated American gender roles in derogatory terms. From the very beginning, immigrants got the word that those who anticipated social superiority based on education and occupation as in the Netherlands "will be trampled under foot."[22] The humble beginnings of the vast majority of the population meant that in the churches and other groups they founded, such individuals would also have opportunities for social recognition and advancement. Only as the group moved into subsequent generations did the desire for class ostentation begin to make inroads among Dutch Americans in a significant way.[23]

As in rural areas, however, the shift to more "American" class ideals did not presage a similar shift in gender ideology, though many young immigrant women tried to do so in urban areas. The older (and male) Dutch image of American women was negative. As one Dutch immigrant man stated: "The American woman is proud, lazy, dirty, and wasteful. If you acquired one with a $50,000 dowry, she would still be too expensive to keep."[24] For men the kind of shift in familial work patterns and patriarchal power which "American" embodied deserved strong opposition. Older women sometimes shared this view, and generally noted assisting with family business and applying a watchword of "frugality" to their household expenditures. Young single women often worked for wages and contributed most or all of these to the family budget. But this group also bore the brunt of sustained criticism for adopting individualism (as in keeping some of their earnings), freedom of mobility, and their desire for spouses who would share household tasks (like changing diapers).

The presence of an established Dutch presence in the United States also contributed to "new" gender roles. Descendants of the Dutch from the colonial era assisted the nineteenth and early twentieth century newcomers in a variety of ways, including encouragement to set up "Ladies' Aid" societies or other women's groups in their churches. They helped sponsor scholarships as educational opportunities opened, and provided an audience for women interested in teaching, mission and other developing professions. But the efforts of established Dutch Americans met opposition from men who ran many of the churches, particularly in Christian Reformed congregations. Church publications such as the *Gereformeerde Amerikaan* criticized separate women's activities in the older denominations, and some consistories would not allow representatives (often female) of women's organizations to speak to the congregation about forming women's groups. In other cases women's groups could not hold meetings without permission and an elder present. These measures postponed if it did not stem entirely further development of women's groups among the immigrant generation.

For Protestant immigrants to the United States in the late nineteenth and early twentieth centuries, then, their background at the lower end of the economic scale in the Netherlands contributed heavily to a rapid adjustment to more fluid class relations, and a positive evaluation of the loss of *standen*. The predominance of persons from rural areas early in the period contributed to much more conservatism in terms of gender roles, particularly the expectation that women would work in the barns and fields and not simply confine themselves to the home. Among those going to urban areas, it was young women who were the main exponents of something closer to an ideology of separate spheres and to an ideal of women not capable of hard work. This remained anathema to many of the immigrant generation.

Gender Positions in the Dutch East Indies
Those going to the East Indies, in striking contrast, had both a different vision of class and gender based on their experience in the Netherlands, and a different tangent of adaptation based on local conditions once they arrived. Unlike those who had comprised the migration to North America, those going to colonies were much more likely from an urban background, and the numbers of wealthy or middling among them were much higher.[25] The percentages of single individuals in the migration stream were also higher for those going to the East Indies. Even after the turn of the century, men were the majority of the single group, more than 65 percent in the period 1900-1920.[26] Migration to the colonies increased around the turn of the century generally. Up to 1870, nearly all of the male Dutch migrants had been in government service, and the few women who came tended to be spouses of this group. The opening up of more plantation agriculture, of the oil industry, and in general the extension of Dutch economic endeavors to newly acquired island areas provided a variety of relatively high ranking job opportu-

nities for men in the fin-de-siecle.[27] Immigrants from the Netherlands assumed the highest supervisory and administrative roles, while those of (at least partial) Dutch descent took intermediate positions, and non-European natives constituted the bulk of the work force. As the migration from the Netherlands increased, so did the proportion of European women in the population . As of 1900 there were 471 women to 1000 men born in Europe in the Dutch East Indies. By 1930 that ratio had dropped to a much less skewed 884 to 1000.[28]

Gender ideals in the colonies were in a period of flux at the turn of the century, yet not in the same way as in the Netherlands. Unlike the North American situation, the long period of Dutch political hegemony in the East Indies had created a very different kind of societal mix.

From the founding of the Dutch East India Company in the early 1600s, there were various regulations concerning marriage. In contrast to some colonial situations, the Dutch had generally condoned marriage of Dutch men (at least those of high status) to local women. In the early years of the Dutch East India Company this kind of marriage entailed giving up the chance of returning to the Netherlands for the man involved, because married men were forbidden to return.[29] Later, private companies used similar policies to encourage "settlers." In the plantation colonies of Sumatra's east coast from the late 1800s up until about 1920, for example, companies would only allow bachelors to come from the Netherlands, and would not allow them to marry for the first few years. As in the earlier colonial period, the companies would encourage men to live with a native housekeeper/concubine. This supposedly facilitated language acquisition and made it possible for the men to learn more about local customs quickly. Further, the companies assumed that Dutch women in these settings would be lonely and bored, and thus tend to interfere with a husband's activities.[30]

For many men, particularly those of the lower ranks in the military, marriage was not an option. Up until 1895 men in the military constituted about half of the European men in the East Indies, and among them, concubinage was widespread, even in shared barracks.[31] Concubinage for single Dutch men generally had been common, and was still accepted in newer colonies up to around 1920. In the most established and heavily populated regions of Java by 1900, however, the situation was changing, as several factors including the arrival of more women from Europe, added to pressure to be more "European" in order to gain socio-economic advancement.[32] Under colonial law if a Dutch man married a local woman, she automatically became "European." That, in addition to the adoption or legitimization of children from mixed relationships led to a very well established and fairly large group of "Europeans" whose civil status did not necessarily relate to skin color by the late nineteenth century.[33] Intermixing of male newcomers from the Netherlands with natives and with the resulting "Indo" group, thus, continued over the centuries. Yet by 1900 there was increasing prejudice against those of mixed background. Many "Indos" refused to do menial labor due to their status, yet they were barred from upper level positions in the civil service or other Dutch-operated businesses. The term "Indo" came to have negative connotations, and to be associated in particular with pauperism.[34] Those coming from the Netherlands generally tried to increase the class/racial differences, since this was to their advantage.

At the turn of the century, thus, newcomers from the Netherlands in the Dutch East Indies faced a situation where official civil classifications did not match the reality of racial discrimination, one where the newcomers, especially women, often tried to contribute to a sense of racial apartheid in order to enhance their own positions. Both men and women sought to uphold and expand a class system in which those from the Netherlands had the highest status. Status within the European group was embedded in military and civil service rank, and in rank on a plantation or other economic endeavor. These in turn were often related to one's position in the Netherlands, which allowed a person to obtain the jobs in the first place. Yet at the same time, all European-descended persons shared a "racial" status which placed them above others.

At the turn of the century, the "purity" of this racial status became increasingly important as a class indicator. Those from the Netherlands often encouraged such distinctions, adding to the class/racial divide. Part of this was in promoting the use of polite and high polite speech forms in Javanese, so that Europeans would be addressed as the equivalent of royalty. Those from the Netherlands also began taking a greater interest in having their children learn proper Dutch, rather than adopting the distinctive speech characteristics associated with those of mixed background. Those of native status were not expected (or even allowed according to some measures) to learn Dutch at all. Separate school systems for each group facilitated this. Wearing western clothing, which became almost compulsory for European-born women in older settled areas around the turn of the century, and which applied consistently to men in various positions, highlighted the native/European distinction. The Dutch in power also encouraged class differences with ceremonial settings where they embodied older feudal traditions.[35] A young Javanese noblewoman described what a friend had learned from being sent to a remote clerk's post: "He had learned wisdom there; namely, that one cannot serve a European official better than by creeping in the dust before him, and by never speaking a single word of Dutch in his presence."[36] Class thus had even greater importance than in the old country, and because it was linked to race, those from the Netherlands tended to stress this.

The gender role ideals of the East Indies also followed a very different pattern from those in North America. Married female migrants from the Netherlands in the East Indies generally had servants, often a number of them, who handled all food acquisition and preparation, cleaning, tending a garden, and child care.[37] To a much greater extent than in the Netherlands, these women had few productive roles in the home, and even fewer worked for wages outside it.[38] Rather, they concentrated on household management and status enhancement. The negative images of such women as notorious gossips, obsessed with conspicuous consumption and the smallest indications of status, came from trying to keep or to gain position in a world where such status within European circles could be the basis for economic advancement of the husband, and hence the family. The background of many European women, in middling or higher families, meant they were much more attuned to the older ideal of separate spheres, and to their role in that kind of arrangement.

Women working in productive tasks, which was standard for many native women, was seen as the sign of a less civilized society. H.E. Steinmetz's 1914 report, for example, indicated that one of the reasons for the lesser economic position of Javanese families compared to European ones, was the lack of strong family bonds, in part due to the extensive economic roles of women.[39] Separate legal structures applied to European and native women, and although *adat* or customary law generally gave women much greater economic power, women from Europe focused on things such as polygyny and lack of education among the native female population to underscore their "superior" status.[40] Overall, there was a distinct class and cultural division which Dutch women coming to the Indies for the most part tried to maintain if not enhance.

Conclusions

Both pre-migration ideals of class and gender, and the post-migration conditions contributed to the very different situations of the Dutch settlements in North America and the East Indies. The demography of the two streams of migration meant that those going to North America were more disposed to abandon older class ideals and to continue a gendered family ideal which allowed significant economic and/or productive contributions to the household by a married woman. Those going to the East Indies on the other hand, could not only stress their class background, but they could also enhance it in the new setting with racial overtones. Likewise, the gender separation which had characterized the upper class of the nineteenth century developed even further in the colonial setting, as it was imbued with a cultural superiority and a specific racial meaning. To what extent the demographic patterns of migration were a result of these kinds of developments, and to what extent the developments encouraged only certain types of migration I will not speculate. In any case, the meaning of "Dutch" to the two areas was very different, and class and gender ideals were a significant part of that difference. A more extended comparative study of Dutch migrants in other parts of the world, including South Africa and perhaps Brazil, could illuminate the dynamics of other settings, and perhaps provide a more concrete pattern for those studying the relationship of demographics and adaptation, one which could serve as a model for other migrant groups.

Notes

1. Robert P. Swierenga, "The Delayed Transition from Folk to Labor Migration: The Netherlands, 1880-1920," *International Migration Review* 27 (Summer 1993): 410.
2. The larger the farm, the less she did directly and the more she organized, but her responsibilities generally included 1) tending to the slaughter of pigs (and sometimes cows) and the subsequent preparation of smoked meat and sausages, 2) churning milk from the cows (and sometimes sheep) and sale of butter, 3) daily care and feeding of chickens, pigs, and calves, 4) storing of vegetables and fruit, especially large quantities of potatoes, green beans and cabbage, 5) preparing meals for family and staff, and 6) tending the garden. This list stems from Hilde Berg, "De positie van de boerin op het Hogeland, ca. 1880-1914," (Masters Thesis, Rijksuniversiteit Groningen, 1984). I chose this list from this work because the areas in the researcher's study included several major hotbeds of emigration.
3. Ali De Regt, "Vorming van een opvoedingstraditie: arbeiderskinderen rond 1900," *Amsterdams Sociologisch Tijdschrift* 5 (June 1978): 40-41; Lily E. Van Rijswijk-Clerkx, *Moeders, kinderen en kinderopvang* (Nijmegen: SUN, 1981), 133 .
4. For an overview of Dutch labor laws concerning women's work see Hettie A. Pott-Buter, *Facts and Fairy Tales about Female Labor, Family and Fertility* (Amsterdam: Amsterdam University Press, 1993), 233-236.
5. On the division of men's and women's work in rural areas see especially W.N. Schilstra, *Vrouwenarbeid in landbouw en industrie in Nederland* (1940; reprint, Nijmegen: SUN, 1976), 19-22.
6. Huygens initially used this for the Dutch section at the Chicago World's Fair in 1893. "Woman's Work in the Netherlands: Woman in Literature," Nationale Tentoonstelling van Vrouwenarbeid, 1898, Manuscript Collection, International Institute and Archive for the Women's Movement, Amsterdam.
7. Selections from G.M. Van der Wissel-Herderscheê and Egb. C. De Wijs-Van der Mandele, "Taak van Moeders," Nationale Tentoonstelling van Vrouwenarbeid, 1898, Collection, International Institute and Archive for the Women's Movement, Amsterdam.
8. Nelleke Bakker, *Kind en karakter. Nederlandse pedagogen over opvoeding in het gezin 1845-1925* (Amsterdam: Het Spinhuis, 1995), 239.
9. Pott-Buter, *Facts and Fairy Tales*, 249.
10. For background on language see my "Gender in Language and Life: A Dutch American Example," *Gender Issues* (Winter 1999): passim.
11. Kitty De Leeuw, *Kleding in Nederland 1813-1920* (Hilversum: Verloren, 1992), 409-412.
12. Jannie Poelstra, *Luiden van een andere beweging. Huishoudelijke arbeid in Nederland 1840-1920* (Amsterdam: Het Spinhuis, 1996), 216-217.
13. Ibid., 184-185.
14. See for example "Een woord aan de dames," *Groninger Courant*, 14 July 1872.
15. All of these themes appear in my book, *Dutch Immigrant Women in the United States, 1880-1920* (Urbana: University of Illinois Press, 2000), passim.
16. Anje Nieveen Mulder to Uncle [S. Smit], Stuttgart, Kansas, [end March 1889], Heritage Hall, Calvin College, Grand Rapids.
17. Teunis Van den Hoek to Parents et al., Junction Station [Englewood], Illinois, to Gourdriaan, Zuid Holland, 25 September 1866, reprinted and translated in Herbert J. Brinks, ed., *Dutch Immigrant Voices: Letters from the United States, 1850-1930* (Ithaca: Cornell University Press, 1995), 113.
18. Lubbigje Schaapman to Willamientje Beltman, [California, July 1911], Heritage Hall, Calvin College.
19. For women's wages in 1913 in the Netherlands see Anna Polak, "De arbeid der Vrouw," in C.M.

Werker-Beaujon, Clara Wichmann, and W.H.M. Werker, eds., *De Vrouw, de vrouwenbeweging en het vrouwenvraagstuk* (Amsterdam: Elsevier, 1914), 30-31.

20. On this, especially as espoused by Germans and some Scandinavians, see Jon Gjerde, *The Minds of the West: Ethnocultural Evolution in the Rural Middle West 1830-1917* (Chapel Hill: University of North Carolina Press, 1997), especially part 3.

21. Woman born in 1883 in Nijverdal, migrated with family in 1913 and settled in South Boardman, Michigan, later moving to Holland, Michigan, Tape 1010, Meertens Institute, Amsterdam.

22. Albertus C. Van Raalte to Abraham Kuyper, 4 July 1872, reprinted in Brinks, ed., *Voices*, 409.

23. See, for example, Jacob van Hinte, *Netherlanders in America: Colonization and Settlement in the United States in the Nineteenth and Twentieth Centuries*, general editor Robert P Swierenga, chief translator Adriaan de Wit (Groningen, 1928; Grand Rapids: Baker Book House 1985), 976.

24. Willem de Lange to H. Houck, Grand Rapids, Michigan, to Deventer, Overijssel, 4 October 1873, reprinted and translated in Brinks, ed., *Voices*, 414.

25. Swierenga, "Delayed Transition," 417-420.

26. Ibid., 415.

27. See Bernard H.M. Vlekke, *The Story of the Dutch East Indies* (Cambridge: Harvard University Press, 1945), 164; M.C. Ricklefs, *A History of Modern Indonesia since c. 1300* (Stanford: Stanford University Press, 1993), chapter 12.

28. Tessel Pollmann, "Bruidstraantjes. De koloniale roman, de njai en de apartheid," in Jeske Reijs, et al., *Vrouwen in de Nederlandse koloniën* (Nijmegen: SUN, 1986), 104.

29. Tineke Hellwig, *Adjustment and Discontent: Representations of Women in the Dutch East Indies* (Windsor, Ontario: Netherlandic Press, 1994), 11-14.

30. Nicole Lucas, "Trouwverbod, inlandse huishoudsters en Europese vrouwen: Het concubinaat in de planterswereld aan Sumatra's Oostkust 1860-1940," in Reijs et al., *Vrouwen*, passim.

31. Annemarie Cottaar and Wim Willems, *Indische Nederlanders. Een onderzoek naar beeldvorming* (The Hague: Moesson, 1984), 13; Frances Gouda, *Dutch Culture Overseas: Colonial Practice in the Netherlands Indies 1900-1942* (Amsterdam: Amsterdam University Press, 1995), 113.

32. Gouda, *Culture*, 112.

33. To make the situation more complex, the 1898 Civil Code revision revoked the citizenship of a Dutch woman if she married a native man. Such cases were rare, but highlighted that a woman's racial as well as social status depended on her husband in this context. Ideas of race also had to take into consideration other Asian immigrants to the region. In 1899 people of Japanese descent became "honorary Europeans" rather than the former "Foreign Oriental." The Chinese, however, remained in the other group, and faced specific restrictions on travel and living areas. Ibid., 163, 168; and Hellwig, *Adjustment*, 25.

34. Gouda, *Culture*, 112.

35. Ibid., 94-96.

36. Raden Adjeng Kartini, *Letters of a Javanese Princess* (1920; reprint, New York: Norton, 1964), 59.

37. Gouda, *Culture*, 158.

38. Elsbeth Locher-Scholten, "Door een gekeurde bril... Koloniale bronnen over vrouwenarbeid op Java in de negentiende en twintigste eeuw," in Reijs et al., *Vrouwen*, 48.

39. Ibid., 42.

40. On the vision of women's rights, see for example Kartini, *Letters*, passim. For an overview of *adat* see B. Ter Haar, *Adat Law in Indonesia* (New York: Institute of Pacific Relations, 1948).

SECTION 3

IMMIGRANT MOBILITY

PELLA DUTCH ROUTES TO AND FROM OREGON

Civil War Reverberations: Exodus and Return Among the Pella Dutch During the 1860s

Brian W. Beltman

Immigration, natural increase (births offset by deaths) and residential persistence favorably shaped demographic change during the first two decades of the development of the Dutch enclave in Marion County, Iowa. From 1847 to 1870, 2,713 Dutch immigrants settled in the Pella area. In 1850 the community, always including some non-Dutch, numbered 1,057 persons; by 1860 it had grown to 3,391, and in 1870 it totaled 4,975. Between 1850 and 1870 the population of the colony increased by 371 percent, more than tripling in the first decade and increasing again by almost half in the second. In addition, the decennial persistence rate – how many heads of households counted in one census were still present ten years later – for 1850-1860 was 77 percent and for 1860-1870 was 66 percent. These numbers suggest growth and constancy. Historian Richard Doyle, using a wealth of measurement criteria and statistical analysis, persuasively concludes that the Pella Dutch who came in 1847 and after to pursue "the promise of the American Dream" had that promise fulfilled. Doyle succinctly observed, "When these Dutch immigrants settled on the Iowa frontier, 'they fell with their nose in the butter.'"[1]

These ten-year snapshots that help characterize the Dutch enclave are instructive, but ten years is a long time and can mask significant intra-decade changes that may have great meaning and importance to individuals, families and an entire community. The path to the American Dream may be rocky, twisting, and hilly; it may even have detours. In this regard, one scholar questioned his social science colleagues who applied the new social history with it heavy dependence on large amounts of quantitative data over long periods to explain dominant trends of nineteenth-century America with the query "Have you forgotten the Civil War?"[2]

This question should be asked in any account of the Pella Dutch. Notably, Robert P. Swierenga did not overlook the Civil War in his social history analyses, for his first published article was on pre-war voting patterns among the Iowa Dutch. In addition, the standard studies of Kommer Van Stigt, Cyrenus Cole, Jacob Van Zee, Jacob Van Hinte, and Henry Lucas do not neglect to acknowledge the general conflict or the issues of slavery, shifting party allegiances, and union and secession, although their focus is usually on the perspective of local elites.[3] Beyond this, however, none of these scholars examined sizeable population movements that some of the Pella Dutch undertook during the 1860s largely as a consequence of the Civil War, an analysis rendered feasible by thorough use of the quantitative information contained in Swierenga's published census data of Dutch households in the United States.[4]

During the 1860s out-migration and repatriation emerged in a unique way among the Pella Dutch for the first time since the founding of the enclave in 1847. The exodus and return was neither intercontinental nor international, but rather internal. Its geographic course was consistent with military developments or larger population flows at work within the United States. Some of the migrants joined the nation's predominate westering impulse as well as its much more shadowy eastward retraction that involved travel by both land and sea. Relocating was a response of a minority faction within the enclave and was decidedly short-term. It arose in the context of special causation factors related to the Civil War, and some of it was shaped by wartime political action peculiar to Iowa. To some extent it also served as a dress rehearsal for subsequent "hiving" actions from the "mother colony" of Pella to other locations in 1870 and after. And its repatriation phase testified to the general vitality of the Pella colony, the magnetism of its ethnic identity, and the strength of its sense of community.

Pella's Participation in the Civil War
National developments degenerating into Civil War affected the regularity of life for some of the Pella Dutch, encroached upon their freedom, and ultimately forced a military or migratory response. Whichever the reaction, this led to the out-migration of over 210 persons from the colony, or 6.3 percent of the enclave's population in 1860. When armed conflict erupted in April 1861, some of the Pella Dutch were inexorably drawn into the fray. Within months a total of 75 men enlisted in the unionist cause, joined Iowa brigades and performed their military duty.[5] Ironically, these soldiers came from a community in which the majority of the Pella Dutch generally tended to focus not on national developments but on local and parochial affairs. As Robert Swierenga and others have shown, before, during and after the war they remained politically loyal to the Democratic Party. They were not attracted to the new Republican Party coalition that relied strongly on anti-slavery, pro-union interests but also included a wing of former Know-Nothings who championed nativism and prejudice against immigrants. To be sure, colony leader Henry P. Scholte shook the local political foundations of the enclave by abandoning his Democratic allegiance in 1859, switching to the Republicans and supporting Abraham Lincoln. He even served as an Iowa delegate to the Republican convention in Chicago that nominated Lincoln for president. Few of

the Pella rank and file, however, emulated the defection of the iconoclastic Scholte; they stayed firmly within the Democratic Party.[6]

Why, in such a political climate, did the Dutch-Americans rally militarily to the unionist cause? Perhaps a wartime psychology gripped some and aroused a volunteer spirit, but at least one very practical motivation was also at work for these immigrants not necessarily inspired by partisan-based patriotism nor familiar with the American tradition of a re-active militia. As with countless other places across the North, attractive incentives to volunteer soon emerged at the local and state levels in the form of "bounties" paid to individuals to join the army. In the case of Pella, Scholte translated his political support for Lincoln and the war effort into material support by offering each local volunteer a "soldier's plot of land" to be subdivided from property he owned just north of the village as an inducement to enlist. Thus, military duty carried entitlements to status and security associated with land ownership into the postwar years, which, in turn, encouraged some veterans to return to Pella. Scholte ultimately gave away 129 lots to Dutch and non-Dutch veterans.[7]

It is not my concern here to trace the individual or collective experiences of the seventy-five Dutch-American soldiers. From a list of Pella area combatants recorded in both Van Stigt's and Cole's works, I have gleaned the names of the soldiers of Dutch ethnicity. (See Appendix A.) Singled out among these are the eighteen men who were wounded and the eleven who died during the war. The hurrah of volunteerism did not usually envision casualties and fatalities. Most poignantly, Cole indicated that three young men were victims of war, not from battle related causes, but allegedly from homesickness, an observation that speaks volumes about the intensity of family life and the vibrancy of the community that these men missed so very much. Those three men included Cornelis Klyn, Cornelis De Zeeuw and Izaak Van der Meer.[8]

It is also worth observing that by joining the army these seventy-five men became the first population mass within the Pella colony to out-migrate in contrast to almost fifteen years of sustained immigration. Locational change because of wartime service implies by definition a temporary shift and anticipates a homecoming back to family and community, despite all the emotion attached to the departure and the uncertainty about the return. Did the Dutch-American soldiers repatriate to the enclave? A search of census records for 1870 reveals that of the 64 surviving Civil War veterans, at least 41, or 64 percent, returned to Pella where they resumed a civilian status and re-integrated into the socioeconomic life of the area.[9] Whether the war "Americanized" others to the extent that they chose a non-Dutch place of settlement can only remain speculative.

Escape From Civil War Conditions
Beyond this military cohort among the Pella Dutch, two other groups of local

residents departed and came back to the colony in time for reasons also stemming from the Civil War, but under different circumstances, for different reasons, with a different destination and in a different structural form. Totaling 138 persons, these civilian groups numerically exceeded the military volunteers by nearly two-fold. They out-migrated from a negative motivation to escape war's impact rather than a positive response to participate through enlistment. While the soldiers headed for military encampments and battlefields, the civilians proceeded for a place where war did not reach. The social composition of the civilian groups were almost entirely familial, not a soldierly assemblage of individual males. Hence the dynamics of the out-migrations of these two civilian groups and their ultimate repatriation was more complex and intricate and merits fuller examination.

Some of the Pella Dutch, independent thinkers by historical tradition and not fully acculturated into the American political culture where positions for or against something (anything) assumed burning significance, were unconvinced of the compelling urgency of the call to arms for the sake of unionism. This appeal particularly did not make sense to those who were not yet citizens of the United States – why fight in a foreign nation's internal dispute? These abstractions took on intensity when Lincoln, early in the war effort, made pleas for volunteers. Further developments complicated matters, for by 1863 Lincoln's army needed more manpower than voluntary service provided. Under the Enrollment Act of March 3, 1863, the president instituted a wartime draft in June that made all able-bodied single and married male citizens between ages twenty and forty-five eligible for conscription, albeit married men between 35 and 45 were to be drafted only after other enrollment pools were exhausted.[10] High volunteerism in Lake Prairie Township of Marion County exempted that area of the Pella colony from the draft and purchase of substitutes or payment of a $300 commutation fee was allowed, permitting some of the more prosperous residents to avoid conscription. In fact, some of the Pella Dutch generously assisted in buying exemptions for their ethnic neighbors and relatives in adjacent Mahaska County.[11] Nonetheless, other Dutch-Americans of more limited means or in township jurisdictions other than Lake Prairie Township remained under the threat of the draft. Moreover, since conscription legally applied only to citizens of the United States, some of the Pella Dutch who had never bothered with naturalization were exempt from military duty.

Alien status could reflect an act of choice or negligence, or it could be a consequence of the procedures of the Second Naturalization Act of 1795 that still controlled at mid-nineteenth century. Under that law, eligibility for citizenship was limited to males over age twenty-one. If they were household heads as well, all male family members gained citizenship status by default with the father. Children from families with female household heads or males under twenty-one who immigrated singly did not go through this kind of automatic, familial naturalization.[12] Thus, some men "slipped through a crack" in the process and remained aliens for many years unless they changed their status with formal naturalization in adulthood. Historian Richard Doyle determined that after 1850 never more than 8 percent of the male household heads held alien status in the Pella colony. He concluded that for 1860, 15 of 219 household heads, or 7 percent were not naturalized.[13] Still, Doyle admitted that local records were incomplete, so how many actually were aliens remains problematic and open to question.

This exceptional, even accidental convenience eventually engendered public resentment – should not those enjoying the landed bounty of Iowa as well as national freedoms also share in the maintenance and security of the central government amid the threat of disunion? On the other hand, some immigrants whose grandfathers and great-uncles were impressed into Napoleon's armies of conquest, some to die in Russia, had a decidedly different perspective on coercive recruitment and the "glory" of war. Indeed, some left the Netherlands to avoid military service. Moreover, non-Dutch Americans in the Skunk River Valley of southeastern Iowa (whose south fork flowed through Lake Prairie Township) earned that area notoriety as a stronghold for anti-war Democrats. In July 1861 supporters of this group held a convention in the area to denounce the Lincoln administration. Therefore, martial reluctance on the part of nearby Dutch-Americans made their defamation as Copperheads, a pejorative term applied to peace Democrats deemed "disloyal Northerners," easy for critics looking for targets to abuse. Some of the Dutch, however, held to their views for reasons far more cultural than partisan. Nevertheless, the matter became a political issue of serious dimension, and Governor Samuel Kirkwood simplistically but calculatingly resolved the divisiveness by proclaiming that all aliens in Iowa were to become citizens – and thus become eligible for the draft – or leave the state.[14]

Reasons to Dodge the Draft
Was this ultimatum not a restraint on freedom? Someone such as Cornelis Jongewaard may have thought so. Cornelis was one of the immigrant pioneers of the Pella community, arriving in 1847 as a single individual of nineteen. In 1852 or 1853 Cornelis continued to exhibit independent behavior among his Dutch neighbors by becoming one of only eight men in the ethnic colony to join the Gold Rush. In company with Leendert Van der Meer and Isaak De Vries of the Van der Meer clan discussed below, he traveled west over the Mormon-Oregon-California Trail to seek gold, either in California or in the Rogue River area of Oregon. Tragically, Isaak was murdered in Portland, but by 1856 Cornelis and Leendert were back in Pella, with the benefit of trail experience and perhaps a new appreciation of reality and human frailty, even if they did not attain wealth. By 1863 Cornelis was 35, married to Ellen S., had five children, and farmed 84 acres in Black Oak Township in Mahaska County valued at $1,000 in 1860; but, still independently minded, he had never seen the need to become a citizen. And he did worry about the draft, for in

August 1863 he wrote to a friend in the Netherlands, "Since the North as well as the South has already lost so many men and cannot readily get volunteers anymore, we daily expect the draft." He noted that Frederik Lakeman, a nearby neighbor who had immigrated in 1847 with him, "sold his property and went to Canada.... He was afraid of the draft because he is not married."[15]

Others had reason to share these concerns. Cornelis' younger brother Arie Jongewaard, who immigrated a year after Cornelis, was twenty-six in 1863 and married to Dirkje Van Rossum, who came to Pella in 1855 with her parents Gybert and Hendrika and brother Jan. The Jongewaard's had two children and farmed in Lake Prairie Township on land worth $500 in 1860, and, like Cornelis, Arie was not naturalized after fifteen years in the United States.[16]

Arie's brother-in-law Jan Van Rossum, twenty-four, was vulnerable to the draft if he was a citizen. In early 1864 he married Ellen Rijsdam, a daughter of Gerrit and Magdalena. The Rijsdam family of eight was among the 1847 colonizers to Pella, where they had prospered quickly. By the early 1850s they owned 320 acres in Lake Prairie Township, although in 1854 they sold that to purchase a general store in Pella. Jan Van Rossum, by marrying Ellen, became part of a prominent matrilineal family network in which the Civil War was creating serious disruptions. Ellen came to her marriage to Jan with a two-year-old child born in January 1862 whose father was Virgil Earp of the famous Earp family that lived in Marion County until 1864 before departing for California. Whether Ellen and Virgil ever married remains questionable, but he assumed no permanent family responsibility, for in July 1862 he signed up as a Union volunteer for the duration of the war.

Ellen's sister Adriana Rijsdam married Jan Van Blokland in late 1860. Jan, a son in the eight-member Andries Van Blokland family that immigrated in 1847, had boarded with the Arie Jongewaard household prior to his marriage. By 1863 he was twenty-nine, farmed thirty-six acres in Lake Prairie Township that he and his wife had bought from Gerrit Rijsdam, and was still not naturalized. Moreover, Jan's brother Teunis, six years his junior, died in the Civil War.

Finally, it also bears observing that Ellen and Adriana's brother Egidius Rijsdam volunteered for military duty in January 1862, but soon came to loathe the war. He deserted the army later that year and again in 1863, each time returning to Pella only to be arrested and sent back into service.[17]

Family Ties

As noted earlier, Izaak Van der Meer, like Teunis Van Blokland, was among the list of Civil War dead. His death impacted a large kinship network in the Pella area, for he was one of ten children in the family of Izaak Van der Meer.[18] Izaak the elder, a fisherman, and his wife Alida Van Den Bos emigrated from Zuid-Holland in 1849. Even then this family encompassed three generations, for the oldest daughter Jannetje was married to Izaak De Vries (the gold seeker later murdered in Portland)

and they had two children, although a daughter died at sea. During the 1850s some of Izaak and Alida's maturing children married, expanding the family connections. In 1850 Merte Van der Meer married Pieter Noteboom, the son of Arie and Neeltje who came from Zuid-Holland with seven children and arrived in Pella in 1848 after spending an interim winter in Buffalo, New York. Merte's sister Neeltje Van der Meer married Christiaan Nieuwendorp in 1854. Christiaan was part of the Hendrik Nieuwendorp family of eight that was among the Pella pioneers of 1847. In the late 1850s another Van der Meer daughter, Cornelia, married Johannes Klein, who as a single farmer also immigrated in 1847.

Meanwhile, in 1852 Izaak and Alida Van der Meer's oldest son Dirk married Cornelia Van den Bos and in 1856 Dirk's brother Leendert married Cornelia's sister Antje. These sisters were daughters of Cornelis and Otterzalina Van den Bos, who emigrated from Zuid-Holland on the same ship with the Van der Meers. Presumably Cornelis was not a brother to Alida (nee Van den Bos) Van der Meer.

Finally, during the 1850s Jannetje Van der Meer was twice widowed and married a third time, proof that quick reconstitution of family life was essential for survival in mid-nineteenth century rural society. To her union in 1860 with Luitje Mars, who immigrated singly in 1855, Jannetje brought one child from her first marriage to Izaak de Vries and a stepson and two children from her second marriage to Gerrit Ellerbroek. She and Luitje eventually had three children.

By 1860 Dirk Van der Meer and his brother Leendert and brother-in-law Dirk Van den Bos operated a sawmill in Marion County's Amsterdam Township, one of a half dozen saw services for the burgeoning Pella community. Dirk reported real estate property valued at $1,400 and declared his personal property to be worth $250. Leendert also valued his real estate at $1,400 and noted personal property of $250. By 1863 Dirk, thirty-five, and Cornelia had three children; Leendert, thirty-three, and Antje also had three children. Pieter and Merte Noteboom farmed 90 acres in Lake Prairie Township that had a cash value of $1,200. By 1863 Pieter was thirty-three, and the couple had eight children. Luitje, forty-two, and Jannetje Mars with seven children farmed in Black Oak Township on 230 acres valued at $1,824 and held $375 of personal property. Christiaan Nieuwendorp, thirty-four, was a laborer. He and Neeltje had three children, $50 of personal property, and real estate in Amsterdam Township worth $275. Finally, Johannes Klein, thirty-six, was also a laborer but lived in Pella. He and Cornelia, still childless in 1863, claimed no real estate and their personal property was worth only $25.

These multiple marriage unions and new family households created a consanguine and affinal network that formed a clannish group bonded by mutual familial, economic and cultural interests that offered greater security, prosperity, and identity. But the Civil War intervened and disrupted family life, not only when young Izaak Van der Meer joined the army but especially when his military legacy became a cherished memory. For according to family records, he died of sickness in a

Confederate prison camp on April 20, 1863, at the age of twenty-four. Another relative by marriage, Leendert Verhoef, a brother-in-law of Pieter and Merte Noteboom, was wounded during the war.[19] The Van der Meers were grievously touched by the war. Until that conflict came to an end, would other men in that kinship network, almost all of whom were in their thirties, be drawn into the war because of the draft and have to leave their families? Would they become wounded or have to die on battlefields, in field hospitals, or worse, in enemy prison camps? How many more must be put in harm's way?

Other Dutch families in Marion County surely experienced wartime stresses as well, but the historical record is less clear for some of them. For instance, Gerrit Jot, unlikely to be drafted at forty-five in 1863, may have remained a foreign-born alien since immigrating singly in 1849. He and his wife Seleke had three children, farmed 85 acres in Lake Prairie Township worth $1,200, and claimed $500 of personal property. Alexander and Regina Stoutenberg had two children, were tenant farmers in Lake Prairie Township, and reported $300 in personal property. Perhaps Alexander, thirty-four, was still not naturalized since he immigrated with his widowed mother and five sisters among the Pella pioneers of 1847. Teunis Burggraaf also arrived in 1847 with his parents Peter and Cornelia and four sisters, and by 1863 was twenty-one, married, and subject to the draft if naturalized. Barend Ten Broek, a cooper by trade, immigrated singly in 1847, but by 1863, when thirty-three, he and his wife Geertruida had three children and owned property in Lake Prairie Township worth $575. Cornelis Lakeman was another 1847 Pella pioneer, arriving as a single person with his brother Frederik, who, as noted above, later left for Canada because of the draft. In time Cornelis married, but his first wife died after they had a daughter. By 1863 Lakeman, now forty-seven, was remarried, his daughter was eight, and they farmed 20 acres in Black Oak Township valued at $200 and held personal property worth $370. At his age, military considerations were irrelevant; perhaps he too resented coercive citizenship.[20]

Cultural Tensions

A varied collection of wartime experiences and pressures created tensions for these Dutch-Americans. Living within a cultural milieu that grew intolerant and prejudicial of non-conforming non-citizens as well as those seeking to escape military service surely bore heavily upon them. One observer noted without elaboration that "various incidents took place during these four or five years which in many ways made life and contacts among them restless and miserable." Some may have incurred contempt from their own ethnic neighbors for any exception to the behavioral mainstream, although only the most churlish among their critics would have abused those families who had lost loved ones in the war. And these latter had their own private feelings about the cost of war. Thus, some Pella Dutch had reasons to put distance between themselves and an area where men were filling military quotas while others demanded compliance to wartime norms.[21] Rather than endure criticism, accept the obligations of citizenship, or attempt to exercise the costly options of hiring a substitute or paying the commutation fee, they chose to out-migrate from the Pella area. To be sure, no single cause can explain the complex motivations underlying the decision to migrate. Perhaps the lure of land elsewhere was at work on some, especially those with small property holdings, those who were tenants or laborers, or others who generally perceived meager opportunities in the Pella community. Perhaps too, migration was a choice of those least "Americanized" to the host political culture and most bound to embedded traditions and perceptions of their native culture.

Whatever the mix of push and pull factors, during the winter of 1863-1864, sixteen families, the great majority comprising inextricably linked family networks that included neighbors or friends, decided to leave Marion County and follow the overland route to Oregon. Janna Cornelia Jongewaard Bogaard, a daughter of Cornelis Jongewaard, wrote years later that her "father was between two fires ... enlistment in the army or an overland wagon trip across the Great Plains by ... the 'Oregon Trail' to the state of Oregon." A family acquaintance of the Van der Meer clan likewise observed in hindsight that "Being sincere believers in the admonition that "Ye who live by the sword, shall die by the sword, they ... migrated during the Civil [W]ar." In the Pacific Northwest no draft threatened, for the federal government, primarily owing to the high cost of transportation, never applied conscription to the states or territories west of the Rocky Mountains.[22]

All the adults of the group knew from experience as earlier transoceanic immigrants what migration across a long distance meant. Most of them made the former move as children or young adults and not as parents responsible for dependents. Although this may have biased their memory of moving with youthful naiveté, they were not novices in this process. Nor were they without the benefit of lessons learned and sage advice from the elder immigrants of their community. Additionally, the seriousness of the wartime context that placed a premium on life and death decisions surely sobered any mature participants who might have harbored unjustified expectations about migration. And within this framework, women, no less than men, undoubtedly understood the gravity of their judgments, for to stay meant husbands as well as older sons might be lost, families might be broken, and even survival might be threatened. But to migrate, of course, also posed enormous risks that none could afford to underestimate. If ultimate security, however, was available in a peaceful place far from the battlefield, relocation was a rational conclusion for people who had moved once before in search of a refuge. With the choice to relocate the group became a mobile and transient community. They were not fully abandoning their home community, where for most, relatives continued to reside, but they were leaving it as a band of kinsfolk and neighbors, homogeneous and cohesive, sharing ethnocultural ties and bound by unique issues of the Civil War.

They selected Cornelis Jongewaard, a veteran of the overland route, as the captain of their wagon train. Other family heads of the caravan included Leendert Van der Meer (another trail veteran), Dirk Van der Meer, Luitje Mars, Pieter Noteboom, Christiaan Nieuwendorp, Johannes Klein, Arie Jongewaard, Jan Van Rossum, Jan Van Blokland, Gerrit Rijsdam, Gerrit Jot, Alexander Stoutenberg, Teunis Burggraaf, Barend Ten Broek, and Cornelis Lakeman. These sixteen household heads averaged thirty-six years old. Their wives and children numbered fifty-nine. The average age of the women was thirty-one and of the children six. Of the latter, fifteen were three or younger. Two mothers were nursing babies three months old or younger, and Cornelia Van der Meer, wife of Dirk, gave birth to a child two weeks into the trip. Ellen Jongewaard, wife of Cornelis, had five children, ages eight to infancy, and since the Jongewaards outfitted two wagons for the journey, Ellen drove one of them to Oregon. Pieter and Merte Noteboom had nine children; of these one was three, another one, and a baby two months old. Alida Van der Meer, eighteen and unmarried, accompanied her siblings; some of her married sisters among the Van der Meer clan could certainly use her help.[23]

In addition, the caravan included at least four single men. Gerrit Roorda was twenty-three and worked as a wagon-driver for Luitje Mars. Gerrit, a member of the Roorda family discussed below, kept a daily logbook of the overland trip. Cornelis Van Blokland, also twenty-three, joined his older brother Jan Van Blokland, who was part of the Rijsdam family group. Unidentifiable were A. and J. Van der Meulen, who may have immigrated in 1849 or 1855 as members of Van der Meulen families, each of whom had children with names starting with A. and J. The Van der Meulen brothers were also associated with the Rijsdam family.[24]

The Overland Trail to Oregon
Every journey on that two-thousand-mile trip to Oregon was fraught with infinite hazards and dangers, even if two men (Jongewaard and Van der Meer) in the party were retracing a path of twelve years earlier and even if nearly 300,000 people over the last two decades had made the trail a virtual highway. By the mid-1860s the Great Road West was shared by numerous freighters, stagecoaches, Mormon Church trains, a telegraph wire, and serious preparations well underway for a transcontinental railroad, although no track extended out of Omaha yet. The route also claimed federal road improvements, bridges and ferries, military forts and patrols offering symbolic security, and numerous commercial establishments along the way selling or trading supplies, equipment and livestock as well as providing blacksmith services and wagon repairs.[25]

The Dutch-Americans surely planned carefully, studied guidebooks and maps, and gathered necessary staples and supplies for the journey. Generally, the cost to travel the overland route varied greatly according to exact point of origin, individual traveling style, ability to use draft animals, wagons and other trail equipment already on hand, and one's willingness to sacrifice and be frugal during the transit process. Data is not available itemizing the expenditures of the Pella Dutch, but for comparison, historian John Unruh cited the case of a party of eleven going to Oregon in 1853 from Indiana with three wagons, a carriage and assorted livestock at a cost of $846.32.[26] Although not all of the Dutch overlanders had substantial resources, most of them, according to their economic standing discussed earlier and based on the census of 1860, did have adequate means to draw upon once they liquidated their property to finance their relocation.

Despite all these considerations, they faced challenges untold from an ever-changing topography – prairie, plains, mountains and high desert. Unpredictable weather that was mostly hot, dry and windy could turn violently stormy with rain, hail and lightning. A thunderbolt or untended campfire could ignite grassland fires. Choking dust and buffalo gnats were common annoyances. A lack of sufficient forage along the trail caused livestock to weaken or fail. Equipment, if worn or accidentally broken, required repair. People still took sick or suffered injury. Daily food preparation was necessary and clothes needed laundering and mending. And in the Dutch case here, a small group of people of finite means and abilities had to make and break camp day after day, live out of wagons, and constantly move on for six months. This was the reality of the overland migration that had acquired the illusion of a routine by the 1860s.

To a large extent, it was anything but routine because of intensive red-white conflict all along the Oregon Trail by mid-1864. Civil War manpower needs to the east left comparatively small numbers of soldiers – essentially the eleventh Ohio Volunteer Cavalry Regiment – to patrol the central overland route, and regional warriors exploited this opportunity to prey on westering migrants. In April Colorado volunteers began scattered attacks on the Northern Cheyenne and Arapaho that spawned retaliatory raids along postal, freight and emigrant routes. This general uprising ultimately culminated in the massacre of Black Kettle's village at Sand Creek in November by Colonel John M. Chivington and his militia from Denver. In the early summer Brigadier General Robert B. Mitchell, commander of the District of Nebraska, antagonized the Sioux and Pawnee in the Platte River valley with condescending threats that provoked young warriors. They then attacked stagecoaches and stations, freighters and supply depots, road ranches and small wagon trains on the overland route from Fort Kearny to South Pass, a distance of 800 miles or more. By mid-August the native Americans had "laid waste the country" and halted all movement on the Oregon Trail along much of the upper branches of the Platte River. The overland mail, which had been running regularly on a daily schedule for more than three years, stopped, and the flow of emigrants across the plains ceased entirely. Hundreds of wagons loaded with all kinds of freight were forced to corral at the most convenient point and remain in place for weeks. Farther west, aggressive military action in 1863 out of Utah Territory by Brigadier General Patrick E. Connor and

California volunteers against the Shoshonis fed vengeful retaliations the next year. The Snake River route from Fort Hall to as far as Fort Walla Walla was subjected to frequent hit-and-run attacks to make it a "continual battle ground."[27] Into this ventured the Dutch-Americans.

The First Group Accross the Plains
In the first week of May 1864 the hegira of eighty Pella Dutch to Oregon began with a seasonally timely start.[28] They headed west following Iowa roads through Pleasantville, Indianola, Winterset, and Greenfield. Springtime rains that turned the Iowa roads into mud made even the first leg of the trip troublesome. The Dutch-Americans, however, had plenty of oxen among them, and if one of the wagons got mired in the mud, sinking down to the axles, the teamsters merely hooked as many yoke of oxen as necessary to concentrate the brute power of the beasts on the problem and dislodge the vehicle from the earth's grip. At Lewis, in Cass County, they came to the deeply rutted trace of the Mormons, which took them to Council Bluffs. There on May 28 they crossed the Missouri and joined the Platte River road in Nebraska Territory. A few days later near Columbus, the overlanders in the train that now consisted of twenty-four wagons examined their equipment to make sure all was in good order for the plains crossing. An inspection of Luitje Mars' wagon, pulled by five yoke of oxen, judged it structurally unreliable for the long haul, and he had to buy a new one for $150, a price that was $50 above a more usual charge in the Mississippi valley.[29]

On June 12 near Fort Kearny, Mars' stepson John Ellerbroek, ten years old, was seriously hurt. While seated in the wagon and attempting to crack the whip over the oxen, he lost his balance, fell to the ground, and both front and back wheel of the big vehicle carrying two and a half tons of freight rolled over his body. Alive but unconscious, his mother tended to him unceasingly until he regained consciousness. As John later wrote:

> My mother [Jannetje Van der Meer] was a true Christian woman and I heard her pray that I might get well and her prayers were answered. I said, "I will get well," and I did. And the strange thing was that when I lay in the wagon, the same thing happened on a wagon train that was ahead of us. A boy also fell out of a wagon and under the wheels and he was instantly killed. We passed them when they were burying him. His intestines were crushed and he lived but a few minutes. It is a wonder that I pulled through. I therefore positively believe that there is a God, and that He answers prayer if we have faith in Him, but without faith there is no answer.[30]

As the Dutch-Americans followed the North Fork of the Platte River, they began to see "a lot of Indians" – some friendly, some not. As a precaution, Captain

Jongewaard told the boys of the train not to tamper with any belongings of native Americans, particularly at burial sites where personal artifacts were encased, providing a temptation for souvenir-gathering youngsters. By so doing Jongewaard was recognizing common human behavior: ancestral graves of native Americans deserved respect and veneration just as did those of his Dutch forebears in the Old Country. He warned that desecration of those sites would surely incur the wrath of Indians. Perhaps Jongewaard had heard from others that tensions were particularly high between reds and whites on the road ahead.[31]

Just beyond Fort Laramie, the Dutch-Americans caught up with a group who had lost some of their livestock to native American raiders. This party joined the Jongewaard train, forming a caravan of 80 wagons. Over the next few days they passed several fresh graves by the roadside with crude headboards stuck in the ground and inscribed with the date of death and the words "Killed by Indians." Although the re-enforced overlanders posted a double guard from this point, warriors made an early morning strike on July 13 about sixteen miles east of Deer Creek Station on the North Platte River, scattered horses, mules and oxen, and managed to steal seven mounts.[32] Several riders pursued the Indians and others followed on foot. Shots were exchanged. One horse on which Arie Jongewaard was riding was wounded in the leg and another killed. One native American sustained a bullet injury in the crossfire and fell from his pony, but his comrades rescued him. With that the raiders departed, abandoning the livestock. Except for a few horses, including the best team belonging to Captain Jongewaard, the emigrants recovered most of their animals.

Three of the Dutch-Americans, Teunis Burggraaf, Barend Ten Broek, and Izaak De Vries, the son of Jannetje Van der Meer and stepson of Luitje Mars, headed for Deer Creek Station where 40 soldiers were encamped, to report on their run-in with the Indians. But while on the way they ran afoul to a patrol of soldiers, who mistook them for horse thieves. It was common at the time for whites to engage in horse stealing on the trail and sell the stolen property to agents of the southern states for the Confederate army. Reportedly, a reward of $500 was offered for the capture of a white horse thief. Thus, the Dutchmen now became the pursued and drew fire from the troops. Izaak's horse was shot, but Izaak managed to escape and hide. The other two, when captured at a river crossing, successfully explained their innocence to the soldiers and were freed to return to their wagon train on foot. Isaak, alone and horseless, wandered for two more days before fortuitously finding his way back to camp, where the rest of the party, having waited suitably long, was about to "give him up for lost" and depart. Izaak, dazed and sore, got a hero's welcome.[33] Jannetje surely prayed as thankfully that her firstborn had been spared as she had prayed over her child John Ellerbroek.

On several more occasions before reaching Oregon the Dutch group met native Americans, but no more serious clashes occurred. At one meeting the different cultures engaged in friendly trade, primarily handwork by Indians for food from the whites. Intercultural commerce could, however, pose its own complications and misunderstandings. Seeing Ellen Jongewaard admire a skillfully decorated native American blanket wrapped around an infant, one Indian woman shocked Ellen by offering to trade, not the blanket, but the papoose, in exchange for Ellen's baby daughter. The native American baby actually belonged to another woman and was perhaps an adopted child from another tribe. At another meeting when hunger-driven Indians came at breakfast time to trade for food, they happened on Luitje Mars, an especially religious man, engaged in his morning devotions. They watched in wonder at this man, slender and tall at six and a half feet, with sloping shoulders, a small head, long hair tufted over his ears, a ring beard on his jaw and a medium long beard under his chin, as he prayed "earnestly and long in a sonorous tone of voice with his face uplifted and his eyes closed…"[34] Surely the native Americans recognized a "shaman" when they saw him.

After passing Deer Creek station the large caravan diminished in size as smaller trains of twenty wagons or less separated from the big convoy during the latter half of July. Over the next weeks groups reassembled and parted again, a process common on the trail. At one point the Rijsdam family network, which had started out a week earlier from Iowa than the bulk of the Dutch-Americans but had become delayed after losing some livestock, joined the Pella column. Later, Cornelis Jongewaard and Gerrit Jot left the caravan after they disagreed about making a certain encampment, only to reunite a few days later. Trail diarist George Roorda wrote on July 23 that his train consisted of only 10 wagons, "all from Pella, Iowa," but soon they were part of larger company again.

The caravan crossed the continental divide at South Pass on July 29 and ferried across the Green River five days later. During August and September the overlanders traveled through Bear Lake Valley, came within five miles of Fort Hall, followed the course of the Snake River, and passed through the mining community of Boise City. Here Mars sold three yoke of oxen to local residents for $123 in gold dust, and Arie Jongewaard sold four cows for $63 in dust. Such transactions, not unusual along the trail, allowed these men to replenish their financial reserves. On September 17 the emigrants crossed the Snake River leaving Idaho Territory and entering Oregon. Ten days later the caravan suffered its first and only fatality when a baby in the Gerrit Jot family died; they buried the child in the town of La Grande. On October 1, with autumn upon them and winter fast approaching, the Rijsdam family group separated from the main convoy. They stopped in northeastern Oregon to settle permanently in the Grande Ronde Valley in Union County, but the other Pella Dutch continued on.[35]

The last stretch of the Oregon Trail was notoriously rough and rocky despite road improvements, and it took a final toll on the oxen. On certain days water was scarce; on others grass was hard to find. On October 6 Roorda reported the "one of our cattle gave out." Some oxen became so foot sore that the teamsters, not insensitive to the misery of the poor beasts, fashioned shoes of rawhide for them. On October 18, the overlanders arrived at The Dalles and the next day boarded the river steamer *Orenota* with wagons and livestock for a one-day passage down the Columbia River to Portland. On October 25, after six long months on the trek, some of the party stopped at Oregon City, and others stayed near Butterville. Roorda wrote in his trail logbook that they camped by the house of John Zumwalt and began working for him by digging potatoes, a job most familiar to the Dutch.[36]

Failure at the West Coast

The hegira was over, but Oregon was not Canaan. It was also nothing like the fertile, arable land of Marion County, Iowa, where a nineteenth-century midwestern farmer did not have to contend with trees of gigantic proportions and sometimes rocky soil or cope with an overabundance of rain. Environmental adjustment was most demanding, perhaps overwhelming. But far more devastatingly, during the course of the next year and a half, several members of the group died. Some may have become mortally sick with a fever or suffered accidental death. The exact causes or number of deaths are unknown, but among those to die were Pieter and Merte Noteboom and a three-year-old child, leaving behind a family of eight orphans. A child of Dirk and Cornelia Van der Meer died, as did Arie Jongewaard and two of his children and the second Mrs. Lakeman as well. Amid this crisis, character and resourcefulness were tested. Leendert Van der Meer, in particular, faced his responsibilities as a family man and assumed legal guardianship of the Noteboom minors – Arie, fourteen, Isaac, twelve, Gerrit, ten, Alida, nine, twins Pieter and Johannes, seven, Neeltje, five, and Maria, two.[37]

In Oregon, the Dutch-Americans had to face their limitations and isolation and confront options. The catastrophe particularly strained the support capability of the Van der Meer family network, a small group possessing limited resources and few communal allies. One source notes that Pella relatives responded to distant family members in need and "at a great expense, sent one to Oregon" to render assistance.[38] The ultimate strategy, however, was to get the Dutch-Americans safely back in Iowa after a wartime interlude in Oregon that had brought unforeseen and extreme hardships for some of the families. Significantly, repatriation to the Pella area would be during peacetime when no draft or call to arms threatened to disrupt their lives or challenge their way of life. In all probability the Van der Meer network pooled their available finances to allow about half of their number to make the journey eastward. Accordingly, Leendert Van der Meer's family, now enlarged with two additional offspring and five of the Noteboom children, the Cornelis Jongewaard family that included another child, Arie Jongewaard's widow and a surviving child, the Kleins with two more children, and the Mars returned in 1866 to Marion County and the security of that larger and more settled ethnic enclave where other kinfolk continued to live.

The return route was by ship over the most efficient and quickest passage, not by wagon over that long trail of two years earlier. The Dutch Oregonians sailed nearly 5000 miles down the west coast of the continent with a usual coaling stop at Acapulco or Manzanillo, traveled by train over the 47-mile crossing of the Isthmus of Panama, and went by steamer 1500 miles to New Orleans and another 1400 miles on up the Mississippi to Iowa.[39] Scheduled time for such a journey was about twenty-five to thirty days. Although rates varied greatly by month and steamship line, prices in 1866 to go from San Francisco to New York on the Central American Transit Company were $150 for first class, $100 for second, and $50 for steerage. The charge for cabin passage on a river steamboat from New Orleans to St. Louis was $15 to $20. The cost on the Panama Railroad was $25 for first class and $10 for second. By ship or train, children under 12 commonly traveled at half-fare; children under five rode at quarter price or sometimes free.[40]

Others of the Oregon group, including the three remaining Noteboom orphans, stayed a few more years in the Pacific Northwest, perhaps to acquire the resources for their return to Iowa or to give Pella relatives time to accumulate additional funds for assistance. In 1869 midwestern kinfolk informed the Dutch Oregonians that new settlement opportunities loomed in northwest Iowa, convincing those now in readiness to move once again. In October the Dirk Van der Meer family with two additional children, the Christiaan Nieuwendorp family with two more children, and Cornelis Lakeman, now a widower a second time with a child from each marriage, returned to Pella. In their company was Gerrit Roorda, who documented the briefest log of this "go-back." Departing from Portland on September 24, they took a coastal ship 850 miles to San Francisco arriving there in three days. They then boarded an eastbound train on the transcontinental railroad, newly completed on May 10, 1869, that carried them 2000 miles to Omaha by October 6. Coach fare (second class) on the train from Sacramento to Omaha was $33.20. From Oregon to Pella, this return journey lasted two weeks. If the Jots, Stoutenbergs, Burggraafs, and Alida Van der Meer remained in the Pacific Northwest, they became lost to history, although family folklore says Alida married and stayed in Oregon.[41]

Prepared by the Gold Rush
The overland Dutch migrants to Oregon were not the only Pella emigrants during the Civil War. Another group shared the same angst and response, and they similarly involved a tight-knit kinship group who formed the core of their band of exiles. At the center was the Roorda family. The history of their transoceanic and transcontinental relocations began in 1853 when Isaac, single and 21, left Friesland and sailed for America on the ill-fated ship *Willem and Mary*, as part of Oepke Bonnema's colonization effort to Wisconsin. Bonnema was a wealthy Frisian farmer who organized a group of 192 emigrants and financed their transport through the sale of his estate. The vessel shipwrecked on May 5 during a storm near the coast

of the Great Bahama Island, and the captain and crew abandoned the passengers. The latter suffered for several days aboard the damaged ship from thirst, starvation, and an outbreak of yellow fever that killed many of them. Nearby islanders sighted the southward drifting ship and dispatched a schooner to rescue the survivors. Ninety-two persons of the group ultimately reached Wisconsin, and in mid-July, they founded the settlement of New Amsterdam fourteen miles to the north of the confluence of the Black River and the Mississippi. Isaac Roorda was not, however, among these pioneers, for he escaped from the foundered *Willem and Mary* on a long boat and later boarded a ship bound for England. There he spent the winter of 1853-54, during which time he wrote an account of his experiences of the shipwreck to finance his second attempt to reach America. In 1854 he successfully reached its shores and settled, not in Wisconsin, but in the Pella colony in Marion County, Iowa.[42]

Isaac's relocation triggered a familial chain migration, for in 1855 his two brothers Wieger and Anne arrived in Pella, and two years later the parents, Epke and Foukje, and four younger siblings, Hendrik, Gerrit, Hinke, and Jan, joined the forerunners. Epke followed his trade as painter in the Pella area, assisted by his son Wieger. Isaac, Anne, and Gerrit all took up farming in the Dutch enclave. Three of the Roorda sons soon married three of the five daughters of Abraham and Aaltje Buwalda, a Frisian family that immigrated as part of the colony pioneers of 1847. In 1857 Boutje Buwalda married Isaac Roorda, two years later Tryntje married Wieger, and in 1863 Doetje married Anne. Three Roorda men and three Buwalda women in paired unions inextricably connected the two family histories. It must also be noted that a fourth Buwalda daughter, Paulina, married Engel Verploegh in 1859.[43]

Engel came to Pella in 1847 as a twenty-four-year old single farmer from Gelderland, sailing on the same ship as the Buwaldas, and, like Cornelis Jongewaard and Leendert Van der Meer, he participated in the California Gold Rush. In 1853 he hired on with a thirty-wagon caravan passing through Pella bound for the gold fields and assumed duties as an ox-driver for the six-month journey westward on the Mormon-Oregon-California Trail. In time, however, he learned that his widowed mother and six surviving siblings had arrived in Pella from Gelderland. Accordingly, Engel returned to Iowa by a ship along the West Coast to Panama, on foot across the Isthmus, by ship again to New Orleans and then mostly by walking overland to Pella. Once back in Marion County Engel traded his fortune in gold for Iowa's complement – land. In August 1858 he bought forty-seven acres of farmland in section 35 of Lake Prairie Township, and within seven months married Paulina.[44] In sum, Engel knew something about travel to the West Coast and back whether by land or by sea. His experience would provide reference information for developments that unfolded in the 1860s affecting the kinship group of the Roordas and Buwaldas into which he had married.

The Departure of a Second Group

The Roordas, like the Van der Meers and Rijsdams, soon experienced in an equally intense way the agony of the Civil War, for the war effort required of them the ultimate sacrifice. With the outbreak of the conflict, Hendrik Roorda enlisted in the Union Army, one of the seventy-five Pella Dutch to serve as a wartime soldier. In 1862 the Roorda family learned that Hendrik died of sickness at the age of twenty-three in the vicinity of Shiloh and was buried at Corinth, Mississippi, thus becoming one of the eleven Dutch-American fatalities to the war.[45] His name joined the list that also included Izaak Van der Meer and Teunis Van Blokland.

By 1864 the on-going Civil War, the military draft, and the demand of Iowa's governor that aliens become naturalized citizens or leave the state compelled another group of Pella Dutch to out-migrate to Oregon – this one centered on the Roorda-Buwalda-Verploegh family connection. As with the Pella overlanders to the Pacific Northwest, the precise motivation for each and every person cannot be definitively delineated, but a descendent of Engel Verploegh noted that he "probably took the trip to Oregon to escape the draft" having, as an immigrant, "no close ties for the North or South."[46] Others were vulnerable to wartime pressures as well.

This second band of Dutch-Americans to exit Pella totaled at least fifty-eight persons, comprising eighteen family units that included two adult single men and twenty-one children. In 1864 the average age of ten household male heads whose age is known was thirty-three; their wives averaged twenty-nine. An average age of the children could not be determined from available data.[47]

On the brink of departure to Oregon, the family and financial standing of most of the out-migrants precluded hiring military substitutes or paying the $300 commutation fee, but disposal of assets could permit relocation financing. Isaac, thirty-two, and Boutje Roorda had four children five years old or younger. They farmed in Summit Township in Marion County on land worth $250 in 1860 and held $50 of personal property. Wieger, thirty-seven, and Tryntje Roorda reported $300 in real estate in Lake Prairie Township and $50 in personal property, but had no children. Anne, twenty-seven, and Doetje Roorda were recently married, had no children, claimed no real estate, and had only $50 of personal property. Engel, now forty, and Paulina Verploegh, with three children six years old or younger, farmed 47 acres in Lake Prairie Township valued at $1,000 and had $400 in personal property.[48]

Two brothers of Engel, Koenraad and Govert Verploegh, were part of this extended family network of out-migrants. Both of them had arrived in Pella in 1853 accompanying their widowed mother. Koenraad was thirty in 1864 and married to Pietertje De Kock, a member of the Jan De Kock family that immigrated in 1856. They had two children three years old or younger and owned $150 of real estate in Lake Prairie Township with $50 of personal property. Govert, twenty-five, and Nellie Van Steenbergen were married in early 1864. Associated with this couple was Nellie's younger brother Leendert, who in 1864 was single and twenty-one. These siblings were children of the Cornelis Van Steenbergen family that emigrated from Gelderland in 1854.[49]

Other persons affiliated with the Roorda–Buwalda-Verploegh core enlarged this group migrating to Oregon in 1864, and some displayed familial connections of their own. Jan De Bruin, who emigrated singly from Gelderland in 1853, married Marie Van Genderen in 1856, the year she relocated from Zuid Holland with her widowed mother and two brothers. By 1864 when Jan was thirty-four, they had two children under the age of four and farmed in Marion County's Clay Township. There they owned real estate valued at $100 with other personal property worth $75. Marie's brother, Jan Van Genderen, was forty-five and single in 1864 and was associated with the De Bruin household. The family of Leendert and Neeltje De Penning moved from Zuid-Holland to Pella in 1854. Ten years later the couple had six children, the eldest a son of 18 who could be drafted in two years. Leendert, a forty-four-year-old tenant farmer in Lake Prairie Township, was of limited means, declaring only $100 of personal property. John Versteeg, a member of the Aart Versteeg family that emigrated from Gelderland in 1847, and Elizabeth De Visser, whose parents Alexander and Pieternella and four siblings were also among the 1847 Pella pioneers, were married in 1857. They reported $200 worth of real estate and $25 of personal property. By 1864 John, twenty-nine, and Elizabeth had two children under the age of four. John confirmed in a reminiscence written years later that following the outbreak of the Civil War "It was an awful time" and that in 1864 he and his family left with "15 [sic] families for Oregon." Hendrik Van Well immigrated singly to Pella in 1854 from Gelderland. Two years later his two older brothers chain migrated in his wake, and the three farmed together in Lake Prairie Township on land worth $1000. By 1864 Hendrik was thirty-nine and married to a widow named Jaantje, who had an eleven-year old daughter. These latter three joined the households chosing to leave Pella.[50]

Finally, acording to one source, still other Pella Dutch among these out-migrants were Mrs. Muilenburg and a son, Mr. and Mrs. Pete Steenbergen, Mr. and Mrs. Alexander Strentenberg and family, Mr. and Mrs. Stautenberg with three married daughters and their families, and Mr. and Mrs. Barendrich.[51] I have found no information to identify or describe further these persons.

The Journey by Rail and Boat ... and Back
The Roorda-Buwalda-Verploegh group and their associates decided to reach Oregon in 1864 not by wagon road west but by train to New York and then by steamship from East Coast to West via the Panama crossing.[52] This route was partially familiar to Engel Verploegh from his return journey after participating in the California Gold Rush. By the most efficient transportation of the day this trip was possible in twenty-five to thirty days at a cost of about $150 per adult using

least expensive travel rates. Although the information from the census of 1860 is not complete on the resources of all of the members of this party, most did have adequate means to afford the journey, and all obviously found the funds necessary to cover costs.

In 1864 no train served Pella; the nearest depot was twenty-five miles southeast at Eddyville. Here on the Des Moines Valley Railroad their journey began before springtime thaw, for they crossed the Mississippi River when it was still frozen by sled at Keokuk. No passage southward down the river to New Orleans was feasible since Union forces used the river almost exclusively for military purposes. Civilians had no assurance of the availability of steamboat service. Consequently, from Illinois to New York the party traveled for two to three days about 1,100 miles over rail at a cost of about $20 per adult. A steamship then carried them 2,500 miles for nine to eleven days on an Atlantic route past the Bahamas, through the Windward Passage between Cuba and Hispaniola, with a coaling stop at Kingston, Jamaica, to the Isthmus of Panama. Here they crossed on the Panama Railroad that had been in service since completion in 1855. This train ride across fever-infested terrain usually took four to six hours, but travelers had to allot a day for the ship to ship transit. On the Pacific coast they resumed ocean travel by "a small sail-ship" to San Francisco, a distance of nearly 4000 miles that usually took fourteen days by steamer but could be slower by sail. The party stayed a few days at San Francisco and then boarded another ship for the last 850 miles to Portland. Most of the group settled in the area of Oregon City and later some moved to Corvalis. The Roorda brothers worked as farmers and painted houses during their off-season.[53]

These seafaring Dutch Oregonians, like the Pella overland emigrants, were also temporary residents in the Pacific Northwest, and almost all returned to the Pella area in the aftermath of the Civil War when the threat of the draft, the divisiveness of wartime politics, and combat itself were no more. According to one source, only Mr. and Mrs. Alexander Strentenberg and family remained in Oregon City. Some of the returnees came back in 1866 and included the families of Jan De Bruin, Leendert De Penning, Hendrik Van Well, Mrs. Muilenburg and son, Mr. and Mrs. Pete Steenbergen, and the single men Jan Van Genderen and Leendert Van Steenbergen. The De Bruins added a child to their family while in Oregon. Leendert De Penning was a widower with six children on the return journey; his wife Neeltje had died in Oregon.[54] It is not known whether this band traveled in company with the returning group of 1864 overlanders that included the Leendert Van der Meers, the Jongewaards, the Kleins, and the Mars who took the sea and land route via Panama to get back to Pella, but it is highly probable that this occurred.

The remaining Dutch Oregonians left for Pella in the fall of 1869. The Roorda-Buwalda-Verploegh family connection was among them. A descendent of Engel Verploegh observed, "they stayed there [in Oregon] until the war was over." Nine children born between 1864 and 1869 to this kinship group increased their number.

Gerrit Roorda, who formerly traveled with the Mars family on the 1864 overland crossing, now joined his brothers on this return trip. Moreover, the family of John Versteeg, with two additional children, accompanied this party. One source affirms that Mr. and Mrs. Barendrich, Mr. and Mrs. Stautenberg and their three married daughters and families, and the families of Dirk Van der Meer, Christiaan Nieuwendorp, and Cornelis Lakeman were also part of this band. As noted earlier, according to the account of George Roorda, this group left Portland on September 24, and a sea voyage took them to San Francisco. Going inland to Sacramento, they boarded the transcontinental railroad for passage to Omaha, arriving on October 6. Another day by train brought them back to Pella.[55]

Conclusion

During the 1860s a collection of Pella Dutch families totaling 138 persons responded to demanding circumstances in rapid succession that carried them from the Midwest to the Pacific Rim and back again – in effect, migration under duress. Oregon was another "place of refuge" for some seeking a peaceful venue during the Civil War. It was also an interlude, not a permanent relocation resulting in colonization. Although the experience left them well traveled, if not well-worn, and caused severe hardships for some, including the loss of lives of several family members, it did not make them rootless or adrift from kinship and cultural connections. Once the Civil War was over almost all of the exiles returned to the ethnic hearth in Marion County among family and community. Except for the Rijsdam network that stayed in Union County, Oregon, a few others already noted who remained in the Oregon City area, those for whom information is not available, and the nine persons who died – except for these, a total of 132 Dutch Oregonians, including children born in the Pacific Northwest, repatriated to the Pella area where they re-established residency.

For the families of Cornelis Jongewaard, Cornelis Lakeman, and the Van der Meer network, however, the sojourn in Oregon was a prelude to another relocation. In the spring of 1870 they were among 253 settlers from Pella that homesteaded "free land" on twenty-nine sections in Sioux County, Iowa. Indeed, Leendert Van der Meer was a member of the leadership committee that selected and surveyed the settlement site in northwest Iowa.[56] The Oregon passage seasoned these folk for another out-migration from Pella of more enduring consequences that established it as the "mother colony" of another Dutch enclave in the Midwest.

The Civil War volunteers and the Dutch Oregonians were both exceptional outmigrants among the majority of the Pella Dutch who retained residency in Marion County during the 1860s. Whether soldier or civilian, the war years were disruptive, bringing dislocation, injury and death among both groups in the course of their very different responses to military conflict and producing geographic mobility in the extreme for most. Their various intra-decade relocations reveal what turmoil could stir in their lives beneath the guise of apparent steadiness suggested by decennial population persistence. The degree to which so many of them returned, however, to the Pella area before the decade ran its course suggests even more to what extent that community had become a lasting ethnocultural home for Dutch transplants to the United States.

Notes

1. Richard Doyle, "The Socio-Economic Mobility of the Dutch Immigrants to Pella, Iowa, 1847-1925," (Ph.D. Dissertation, Kent State University, 1982), 64, 107-108, 394, 397; Doyle, "Pella," *History of Pella, Iowa, 1847-1987*, 2 vols. (Pella, IA: Pella Historical Society, 1988/1989), 2:52.
2. Maris A. Vinovskis, "Have Social Historians Lost the Civil War? Some Preliminary Demographic Speculations," *The Journal of American History* 76 (June 1989): 34-58.
3. Robert P. Swierenga, "The Ethnic Vote and the First Lincoln Election," *Civil War History* 11 (March 1965): 27-43; K[ommer] Van Stigt, *History of Pella, Iowa and Vicinity*, trans. Elisabeth Kempkes (Pella, IA: Weekblad Print Shop, 1897); Cyrenus Cole, *Souvenir History of Pella, Iowa* (Pella, IA: The Booster Press, 1922); Jacob Van der Zee, *The Hollanders in Iowa* (Iowa City: The State Historical Society of Iowa, 1912); Jacob Van Hinte, *Netherlanders in America: A Study of Emigration and Settlement in the Nineteenth and Twentieth Centuries in the United States of America*, general editor Robert P. Swierenga, trans. Adriaan De Wit (Grand Rapids, MI: Baker Book House, 1985); Henry S. Lucas, *Netherlanders in America: Dutch Immigration to the United States and Canada, 1789-1950* (Ann Arbor: University of Michigan Press, 1955).
4. Robert P. Swierenga, *Dutch Households in U.S. Population Censuses 1850, 1860, 1870*, 3 vols. (Wilmington, DE: Scholarly Resources, 1987). Supplementary information was also found in idem, *Dutch Immigrants in U.S. Ship Passenger Manifests, 1820-1880* (Wilmington, DE: Scholarly Resources, 1982); idem, *Dutch Emigrants to the United States, South Africa, South America, and Southeast Asia, 1835-1880* (Wilmington, DE: Scholarly Resources, 1983).
5. Van der Zee, *Hollanders*, 230, incorrectly states that sixty-three Pella Dutch volunteered, a number repeated by Lucas, *Netherlanders*, 563, and Van Hinte, *Netherlanders in America*, 432. Van Stigt, *History*, 115-120 and Cole, *Souvenir*, 131-135 provide a list combining both Dutch and non-Dutch Pella area participants in the Civil War.
6. Swierenga, "The Ethnic Vote"; Lucas, *Netherlanders*, 542-563; Van Hinte, *Netherlanders in America*, 418-430; Van der Zee, *Hollanders*, 221-229.
7. Van der Zee, *Hollanders*, 230; Van Hinte, *Netherlanders in America*, 432; Lucas, *Netherlanders*, 563.
8. Van Stigt, *History*, 115-120; Cole, *Souvenir*, 131-135. I cross-checked the names for Dutch ethnicity against Swierenga, *Dutch Households*.
9. Swierenga, *Dutch Households*.
10. James M. McPherson, *Battle Cry of Freedom: The Civil War Era* (New York: Oxford University Press, 1988), 600-603. After the first draft in July 1863, three more followed the next year.
11. Van der Zee, *Hollanders*, 230; Van Hinte, *Netherlanders in America*, 432.
12. For the Law of 1795 and amendments, see William J. Bromwell, *History of Immigration to the United States* (1856, New York: Arno Press, 1969), appendices.
13. Doyle, "Socio-Economic Mobility," 121, table 16 at 122.
14. Brian W. Beltman, *Dutch Farmer in the Missouri Valley: The Life and Letters of Ulbe Eringa, 1866-1950*, (Urbana: University of Illinois Press, 1996), 289; H.J. Brinks, "Pella in 1855," *Origins* 15.1 (1997): 21-23 for a letter of Teunis Van Veenschooten dated 12 December 1855; Van

der Zee, *Hollanders*, 230, 402, n. 208; Van Hinte, *Netherlanders in America*, 433, 435; Charles L. Dyke, *The Story of Sioux County*, (Orange City, IA: n.p., 1942), 402. The only draft in Iowa occurred in the fall of 1864 and involved 1,862 men. See Hubert H. Wubben, *Civil War Iowa and the Copperhead Movement* (Ames: Iowa State University Press, 1980), 63; Eugene C. Murdock, *One Million Men: The Civil War Draft in the North* (Madison: University of Wisconsin Press, 1971), 352. The exemption provisions stirred controversy generally and helped to provoke draft riots in New York City, Milwaukee, and elsewhere.

15. Brian W. Beltman, "The California Gold Rush and a Few Dutch Argonauts from Pella," paper presented at the Twelfth Biennial Conference of the Association for the Advancement of Dutch-American Studies in Pella, Iowa, 1999 and publication forthcoming in *Origins* (2000); Swierenga, *Dutch Households*; Van Stigt, *History*, 37, 78-79; Cole, *Souvenir*, 35, 61-62. The quote from the Jongewaard correspondence of 3 August 1863, is found in H.J. Brinks, "Dutch American Reactions," and Christine Jacobs, "Avoiding the War," *Origins* 6.1 (1988): 6, 23. Frederik Lakeman returned to Pella by 1870 and farmed property valued at $2,800.

16. Swierenga, *Dutch Households*; Van Stigt, *History*, 37; Cole, *Souvenir*, 35.

17. Toni Rysdam-Shorre, *Gerrit…A Dutchman in Oregon* (Bend, OR: South Forty Publications, 1985), 44, 47, 51-56, 64, 71-73, 138; Swierenga, *Dutch Households*; Van Stigt, *History*, 41, 43, 68, 91, 120; Cole, *Souvenir*, 39, 43, 49, 88, 134. In October 1864 Confederate troops captured Egidius Rijsdam near Tifton, Georgia, and he remained a prisoner of war at Andersonville until 1865. Upon release he received his military discharge and returned to Iowa.

18. Family biographical information for the next few paragraphs derives from Swierenga, *Dutch Emigrants*; idem, *Dutch Immigrants*; idem, *Dutch Households*; Van Stigt, *History*, 74-75; Cole, *Souvenir*, 55-57; Hester Vande Garde, *History and Genealogy of the Arie Noteboom Family, 1750-1986* (Orange City, IA: n.p., 1986).

19. Vande Garde, *Genealogy*, 12, 181; Van Stigt, *History*, 119-120; Cole, *Souvenir*, 134.

20. Swierenga, *Dutch Households*; Van Stigt, *History*, 39, 41, 44, 74; Cole, *Souvenir*, 37, 40, 45, 56.

21. Van Hinte, *Netherlanders in America*, 436, quoting Van Stigt; Wubben, *Civil War Iowa*, passim; Olynthus B. Clark, *The Politics of Iowa during the Civil War and Reconstruction* (Iowa City: The State Historical Society of Iowa, 1911), 138-142 on charges of "treason" against some Iowans for opposition generally to the war policy and Republican leadership. See also Robert E. Sterling, "Civil War Draft Resistance in the Middle West," (Ph.D. Dissertation, Northern Illinois University, 1974).

22. Dyke, *Story*, 402, 429; Alvin M. Josephy, Jr., *The Civil War in the American West* (New York: Knopf, 1992), 239.

23. Vande Garde, *Genealogy*, 181-182; Dyke, *Story*, 402-403, 429-430; Rysdam-Shorre, *Gerrit*, 56, 67-82. Note that Gerrit Rijsdam, 57, and his son Arie, 15, accompanied his two daughters and their husbands to Oregon. Mrs. Rijsdam and three minor daughters remained in Pella, perhaps intending to relocate later. In 1866, however, Mrs. Rijsdam died, causing Gerrit and Arie to return to Pella in 1869 to attend to family matters. Gerrit then went back to Oregon in 1870 with two minor daughters still single. Arie stayed in Pella and married, but relocated to Oregon in the late 1870s. Two older married sisters and their families from Pella ultimately resettled in Oregon also.

24. "Roorda Day Book," 40; Swierenga, *Dutch Households*; Cole, *Souvenir*, 106, 39, 44, 94, 57, 88.

25. See generally, John Unruh, *The Plains Across: The Overland Emigrants and the Trans-Mississippi West, 1840-60* (Urbana: University of Illinois Press, 1979), *passim* and esp. tables 1 and 2 at 119-120, 123-131, Table 4 at 185, and chapter 6; Merrill J. Mattes, *The Great Platte River Road* (Lincoln: University of Nebraska Press, 1969); Wallace Stegner, *The Gathering of Zion: The Story of the Mormon Trail* (Lincoln: University of Nebraska Press, 1964); John Mack Faragher, *Women and Men on the Oregon Trail* (New Haven, CT: Yale University Press, 1979), esp. chapters 1 and 3.

26. Unruh, *The Plains Across*, 407-408. Other cost estimates for overland travel range from $500

to $1500 for one family. See Lillian Schlissel, *Women's Diaries of the Westward Journey* (New York: Schocken Books, 1982), 23; Julie Joy Jeffrey, *Frontier Women: The Trans-Mississippi West, 1840-1880* (New York: Hill and Wang, 1979), 28; Bernard DeVoto, *The Year of Decision: 1846* (Cambridge, MA: The Riverside Press, 1943), 147.

27. Josephy, *The Civil War*, 246-251, 257-259, 263-267, 299-313; Mattes, *Great Platte River Road*, 158-159, 230-231, 473-475; Eugene F. Ware, *The Indian War of 1864*, ed. Clyde C. Walton (New York: St. Martin's Press, 1960), 139-229; David P. Robroack, "The Eleventh Ohio Volunteer Cavalry on the Central Plains, 1862-1866," *Arizona and the West* 25 (Spring 1983): 23-48; Agnes Wright Spring, *Caspar Collins: The Life and Exploits of an Indian Fighter of the Sixties* (1927, Lincoln: University of Nebraska Press, 1969), 57-60; Myra E. Hull, ed., "Soldiering on the High Plains: The Diary of Lewis Byram Hull, 1864-1866," *Kansas Historical Quarterly* 7 (February 1938): 13-17; Fred B. Rogers, *Soldiers of the Overland* (San Francisco: Grabhorn Press, 1938), 146; Stan Hoig, *The Sand Creek Massacre* (Norman: University of Oklahoma Press, 1961), 36-53, 91-97. See also the numerous references in Corporal Hervy Johnson's correspondence during the summer of 1864 to depredations by Indians. See William E. Unrau, ed. *Tending the Talking Wire: A Buck Soldier's View of Indian Country, 1863-1866* (Salt Lake City: University of Utah Press, 1979), 135-173. For another 1864 caravan, see T. A. Larson, ed., "Across the Plains in 1864 with George Foremen," *Annals of Wyoming* 40 (April 1968): 18-19.

28. The *Roorda Family History*, held in the Central College Archives at Pella, Iowa, contains the "1861 [sic] Day Book of Gerrit E. Roorda," 38-43, which is a daily logbook of the 1864 overland journey. Dyke, *Story*, 402-412, provides the reminiscences of three children of the Dutch Oregonians: Cornelis Jongewaard's daughter Janna and Jannetje Mars' children John and Mary Ellerbroek, all who related their stories to Dyke. I have supplemented their recollections with notes from Vande Garde, *Genealogy*, 181-184 and Rysdam-Shorre, *Gerrit*, 71-73. See also a reference in Lucas, *Netherlanders*, 399, which contains several factual errors.

29. "Roorda Day Book," 38-39; Dyke *Story*, 403-404. On the wagon price, see Helen McCann White, ed., *Ho! For the Gold Fields* (St. Paul: Minnesota Historical Society Press, 1966), 11.

30. Quote of John Ellerbroek is from Dyke, *Story*, 409.

31. "Roorda Day Book," 39; Dyke, *Story*, 404.

32. "Roorda Day Book," 40; Dyke, *Story*, 405-408. Deer Creek Station is the site of modern Glenrock, Wyoming. In July 1864 Sioux warriors attacked a train west of Fort Laramie and captured Fanny Kelly and her niece and Sarah Larimer and her son. See Fanny Kelly, *Narrative of My Captivity Among the Sioux Indians* (1872; reprint, New York: Corinth Books, 1962).

33. "Roorda Day Book," 40; Dyke, *Story*, 405-408. The quote is John Ellerbroek's.

34. Dyke, *Story*, 409-411, 413-414. The quote is Janna Jongewaard's.

35. "Roorda Day Book," 40-43; Rysdam-Shorre, *Gerrit*, 73. See also endnote 25.

36. Dyke, *Story*, 411; "Roorda Day Book," 43.

37. Vande Garde, *Genealogy*, 183, 224, 257; Rysdam-Shorre, *Gerrit*, 73; Swierenga, *Dutch Households*. If some died in Oregon, it should be noted that my count reveals 10 births among the Dutch Oregonians between May 1864 and October 1869.

38. *The Sioux County Herald*, 30 May 1873, 4. I am indebted to Earl William Kennedy for sharing this source with me.

39. Sketchy folk history contends that the five Noteboom children journeyed by themselves via clipper ship from the West Coast around the Horn to the East Coast, a distance of 17,000 to 18,000 nautical miles, and then overland to Iowa, another 1,200 miles by rail. This does not seem credible. The cost of transportation around the Horn alone exceeded $300 per person and would surely have been prohibitive, and since several families consisting of adults and children took the shorter, cheaper middle route, it is not likely that five children were sent a separate way without adult care. To be sure, children did help take care of children on such journeys. One participant recalled that Isaac, 12, was given a mature responsibility: he was put in charge of his five-year-old sister Neeltje on the return. Once in Marion County again, several

relatives of Leendert took the Noteboom children into their respective families. Leendert kept the twins, his brother-in-law Dirk Van den Bos eventually cared for Gerrit and Alida, and grandfather Izaak welcomed little Neeltje. Vande Garde, *Genealogy*, 183, 224; Dyke, *Story*, 411.

40. John Haskell Kemble, *Panama Route, 1848-1869* (1943; reprint, Columbia: University of South Carolina Press, 1990), 106-108, 147-148, 195; Louis C. Hunter, *Steamboats on the Western Rivers* (1949; reprint, New York: Octagon Books, 1969), 381.

41. Vande Garde, *Genealogy*, 183-184; Dyke, *Story*, 411; "Roorda Day Book," 44. On train fare, see Oscar Osburn Winther, *The Transportation Frontier: Trans-Mississippi West, 1865-1890* (Albuquerque: University of New Mexico Press, 1964), 122.

42. *History of Pella*, 1:467; Loren Lemmen, "The Wreck of the *Wiliam and Mary*," *Origins* 13.2 (1995): 2-9; Van Hinte, *Netherlanders in America* 105, 165-167; Lucas, *Netherlanders*, 210, 485-486. See also Lucas, *Dutch Immigrant Memoirs and Related Writings*, 2 vols. (1955; reprint, Grand Rapids: Eerdmans, 1997), 2:138-139, "John Karsten's A Half Century of Dutch Settlement in Wisconsin, 1847-97," and 2: 188-189, "Anna Brown's Life Story of John Tuininga."

43. *History of Pella*, 1:466, 471, 493, 290; Swierenga, *Dutch Households*.

44. *History of Pella*, 1:633, 645-647; Beltman, "The California Gold Rush"; Swierenga, *Dutch Households*.

45. *History of Pella*, 1:466; Van Stigt, *History*, 119-120; Cole, *Souvenir*, 134.

46. *History of Pella*, 1:646.

47. Swierenga, *Dutch Households*; *History of Pella*, 2:55.

48. Swierenga, *Dutch Households*.

49. Swierenga, *Dutch Households*; *History of Pella*, 1:632-633, 2:55.

50. Swierenga, *Dutch Households*; *History of Pella*, 1:310, 595, 2:55; J[ohn] Versteeg. "Een oude heschiedenis nog eens over verteld," *Pella's Weekblad*, 6 October 1922. I am indebted to Janet S. Sheeres for translating this document.

51. *History of Pella*, 2: 55; Swierenga, *Dutch Households*. These names suggest obvious questions: was Pete [Van?] Steenbergen related to Nellie Van Steenbergen Verploegh, was Alexander Strentenberg really Alexander Stoutenberg (see text at 16), was Stautenberg also perhaps Stoutenberg, and was Barendrich maybe Barendregt? Of the Hendrik Barendregt family that immigrated in 1846, son Jacob married Johanna De Visser, a sister to Elizabeth De Visser Versteeg. By 1864 Jacob, a carpenter, was twenty-seven, and he and Johanna had three children, owned no real estate and had only $50 of personal property. Perhaps they emigrated with the John Versteeg family.

52. Allie Brunia, a daughter of Isaac Roorda, penned a brief reminiscence of the journey to Oregon. See her "A Trip to Oregon in 1864," in *History of Pella*, 2: 55.

53. Kemble, *Panama Route*, 107-108, 147-148, 189, 195; Hunter, *Steamboats*, 551; *History of Pella*, 2: 55.

54. *History of Pella*, 2: 55, 1: 310; Swierenga, *Dutch Households*.

55. *History of Pella*, 1: 646, 2: 55; Swierenga, *Dutch Households*; "Roorda Day Book."

56. Beltman, "Ethnic Territoriality and the Persistence of Identity: Dutch Settlers in Northwest Iowa, 1869-1880," *The Annals of Iowa* 55 (Spring 1996): 101-137.

Appendix A

Dutch Civil War Volunteers from the Pella Community

Total: 75; Wounded: 18; Died: 11

Bauman, Hendrik (wounded)
Bouman, Jacob L.
Bousquet, Herman F.
Bousquet, Henry L.
Bousquet, John J. (wounded)
Brink, Gerrit
DeBruin, Kryn
DeKock, Stephanus (wounded)
DeLeeuw, Cornelis
DeZeeuw, Cornelis (died)
Dingemans, Daniel
Dingemans, Jan W.
Duinink, Cornelis
Engelsma, Martin
Groen, Jan
Hesseling, Henry J.
Hol, Gerrit
Hol, Martinus
Kegel, Jacob
Klyn, Cornelis (died)
Klyn, John C.
Kolenbrander, Herman (died)
Koolbeek, Jacob A. (died)
Koolbeek, Johan
Langerak, William
Meyer, Jacob
Nieremeyer, John Sr. (died)
Nieremeyer, John Jr.
Nieremeyer, Simon
Paardekooper, Gerrit (wounded)
Paardekooper, Willem
Rhynsburger, Adrianus J.
Rhynsburger, Dirk (wounded)
Rhysnburger, Marinus (wounded)
Rijsdam, Egidius (wounded)
Roelofsz, Peter
Roorda, Henry (died)
Rubertus, Herman D.
Scheffers, Govert
Schippers, Nicholas (died)
Simons, Lybert (wounded)
Sipma, Sjoerd
Sleyster, Wernerus

Soeten, John
Steenhoek, Gysbert (wounded)
Stegeman, D.
Ten Hagen, Pieter
Tilma, Myndert
Tol, Dirk (wounded)
Van Blokland, Teunis (died)
Van Marel, Arie (wounded)
Van Rips, Daniel (wounded)
Van Rooijen, Pieter (wounded)
Van Steenwijk, Gerard
Van Steenwijk, Jan
Van Steenwijk, Willem
Van Veenschoten, Evert
Van der Kamp, Gerrit
Van der Kolk, Wiggert (died)
Van der Ley, John (wounded)
Van der Linden, Lukas
Van der Meer, Izaak (died)
Van der Waa, Hendrik J.
Verhoef, Leendert (wounded)
Vermeulen, James Adz.
Vermeulen, John (wounded)
Versteeg, Gysbert
Verwers, Jan
Vogelaar, Jacob (died)
Vogelaar, Leendert
Vos, John Adz.
Vos, Joseph
Walraven, Maarten (wounded)
Wijkhoff, John W.
Wolvers, Cornelis (wounded)

Urbanization and Assimilation Among the Dutch Catholic Immigrants in the Fox River Valley, Wisconsin, 1850-1905[1]

Yda Schreuder

If America was born on the frontier, it was in the city that she matured. In 1860, less than a quarter of the population lived in a city or town; by 1910 nearly half the population was urban.[2] Nineteenth-century historiography, based largely on Turner's Frontier Thesis, has concentrated immigration research primarily on rural settlements in the West. However, from the Civil War onwards most migration was not from old land to new land but from country to city and from one city to another.[3] Each upswing in the economy tended to draw workers from lower wage rural areas to higher wage industrial areas. In the Fox River Valley, Wisconsin, this pattern was well established by 1870. Consequently, the frontier phase of settlement was very brief and industrialization and urbanization occurred soon after the Civil War. For Dutch immigrants, the urban environment rather than the frontier was the social environment in which assimilation took place.

In my contribution to this volume I will elaborate on some aspects of this experience as it affected the Dutch Catholic immigrants. I will pursue this by using examples from my own research on the Dutch Catholic immigrant community in the Fox River Valley of Wisconsin and I hope that in this way I will make a contribution to a better understanding of and appreciation for the differences in experiences and behavior between the Dutch Protestant and Dutch Catholic immigrant groups in the United States.[4]

The Fox River Valley was opened up for settlement in the 1840s. The first Dutch Catholic immigrants settled there in 1848 as a result of Father Van den Broek's efforts to repopulate the area with Catholic immigrants after he had lost his mission among the Menominee Indians due to government removal policies. Van den Broek had been a missionary in the area since the mid-1830s and was quite familiar with local conditions. During a return visit to the Netherlands in 1847, he wrote and distributed pamphlets and promoted emigration in Catholic newspapers. A large majority of the immigrants he recruited came from the eastern part of the province of Noord-Brabant. As a result of his efforts three vessels with a total of approximately three hundred people left the Netherlands in the spring of 1848. This group settled in the area of Little Chute of the Fox River Valley in northeastern Wisconsin, the area of Van den Broek's Indian mission. Settlement dispersed quickly throughout the area but focused on the Fox River. Immigration from the same area in the Netherlands continued until World War I and even thereafter.[5]

The socio-economic environment in which the first immigrants arrived in the middle decades of the nineteenth century changed rapidly from a frontier society to a more specialized industrial society during the second half of the century. In this chapter I will analyze the dynamic economic geographic forces that affected the social order of the Dutch Catholic immigrant settlement. I will trace the development of industrial and urban employment and relate the immigrant experiences to these changes. Dutch Catholic immigrants were more inclined toward urban residence and assimilation than their Dutch Protestant frontier brethren were.[6] Part of the explanation lies with the urban-oriented nature of the Catholic Church in the nineteenth century which gave a definite direction to settlement concentration and established conditions favorable to interaction and assimilation within the Catholic faith. The other part of the explanation lies with the rapid socio-economic changes that occurred in the area of settlement in the second half of the nineteenth century. These changes had an impact on the second generation immigrants in particular and were reflected in high intermarriage rates among urban immigrants, many of whom had moved from rural communities in the Fox River Valley to urban centers like Green Bay and Appleton. In order to understand the process of assimilation among the Dutch Catholic immigrants in the Fox River Valley, we will first concentrate on the economic geographic changes in the area in the second half of the nineteenth century.

The Fox River Valley: The Pioneer Periphery
The Fox River Valley was in the first phase of European settlement in the 1840s. Land availability and employment opportunities were significant factors in the decision to settle the area. As western lands were opening up and being made accessible to East Coast and foreign markets, towns abounded with activities in road construction, canal building, and other sorts of commercial and local industrial activities. During the first phase of frontier development, relative isolation and low population densities limited commercial agriculture and industrialization, but mercantile enterprises and land speculation created a boomtown atmosphere that was conducive to attracting settlers. The initial Dutch Catholic settlement of the Green Bay-Fox River Valley area exemplified these conditions as recently surveyed lands and employment with the canalization project of the Fox River offered ample opportunities for the Dutch immigrants who settled here. This first phase in frontier development has been referred to as the "pioneer periphery." Characterized by an sudden rapid influx of pioneer settlers (immigrants included),

Father Theodore Van den Broek (1783-1851).
Holland Museum Collection at the
Joint Archives of Holland.

Historical Marker.
Holland Museum Collection at the
Joint Archives of Holland.

the frontier offered opportunities for land speculation and mercantile trade and Green Bay was in the vanguard of this development in the early 1840s when most trade took place by waterway. Located at the mouth of the Fox River with access to the Great Lakes, Green Bay was geographically well situated to take advantage of the sudden surge in economic activities. It had been part of the fur trade since the seventeenth century and business interests made Green Bay one of the major participants in the development of the state.[7]

An enthusiastic participant in the development of the Green Bay-Fox River Valley area was Morgan L. Martin, who throughout the 1840s and 1850s remained active in attempts to canalize the Fox River and make it suitable for water transportation. In addition, a system of locks and dams served to create water power for milling grain and sawing wood for planks. Martin held extensive landed property in the Fox River Valley and in his mind development of the area, immigration, and agricultural settlement were part of one and the same scheme; namely, to conduct profitable business.[8] There is strong evidence to suggest that Dutch immigration and settlement in the area were related to his efforts to canalize the Fox River and construct the dams and locks and to dispose of lands from the land grant associated with the project.[9] Land disposal and employment among the first group of Dutch Catholic immigrants suggest that early Dutch settlement in the area was to a large extent influenced by the Fox River canalization project. While land purchase was the obvious objective of most first generation immigrants during the first phase of frontier development, many immigrants were unable to gain access to land and found their way to towns and cities in the region to work in industry and other non-agricultural occupations. Little Chute, located at the southern end of the Fox River near a water power site, was the main settlement during the early phase of development of the area but employment conditions and land availability associated with the Fox River canalization project guided the subsequent orientation towards settlement along the Fox River and towards Green Bay.

The Fox River Valley: the Specialized Periphery
The next phase in the development of the area can be characterized as the "specialized periphery." Improved transportation had diminished isolation and cash crop production and processing industry developed. Town centers grew in size, especially those most centrally located and best connected with the port of entry (Green Bay) and outside markets. Expanding regional markets resulted in an increased demand for consumer goods, machinery, and building materials. Some of these goods were now manufactured locally.[10] Immigrant employment and settlement were accordingly affected and following the mainstream of development, changed from an agricultural-rural to an industrial-urban orientation. For a short time, the Fox River became the main transport route and concentrated traffic on Green Bay. At the time of the Civil War, the city was the primary port of entry and

trans-shipment center for the Fox River Valley and inland counties along Lake Winnebago.[11] After the Civil War, traffic diverted to Chicago and Milwaukee as a result of the railroad. The Chicago-Northwestern reached Green Bay in 1862, and soon thereafter the waterway became obsolete. Improved transportation had a significant impact on economic specialization of the area. Better access to Eastern markets resulted in export of farm produce and Wisconsin ranked second after Illinois as a wheat producing state by 1860. During the period 1860-1865, the state produced approximately 100 million bushels of wheat, of which two-thirds were exported. Wheat remained the main crop until 1870. Thereafter, competition from western producers caused a rapid decline in wheat production.[12]

Although the Fox River waterway lost its function as a transportation route, the river remained an important source of waterpower for industrial production. Flour milling, saw milling, wood working, and paper making industry all powered by waterwheels, developed quickly as markets for these products expanded and industrial and consumer needs throughout the state and nation increased.[13] After the Civil War, with the introduction of steam power, certain industries expanded and concentrated production in locations along the Fox River. Paper making eventually became the major industry in the area. Appleton, De Pere, and Green Bay all were important industrial centers by the end of the century.[14]

With the shift in industrial location came population redistribution from smaller towns and rural areas to larger cities along the Fox River. During the Civil War and thereafter (1860-1870), the population increased rapidly in size and in ten years, the number of settlers almost doubled. The increase of the Dutch Catholic immigrant population was approximately 70 percent. Most of the increase in the number of Dutch immigrants occurred in De Pere township along the middle course of the Fox River and in Kaukauna township, adjacent to the village of Little Chute. Initially, most of the increase in the Dutch immigrant population of the middle section of the Fox River Valley was the result of direct immigration from the Netherlands. Only a third of the increase was due to internal migration.[15] While clearly oriented towards settlement along the Fox River, the Dutch immigrant settlement remained primarily rural-agricultural until 1870. Appleton and Green Bay, the largest urban centers in the area, represented relatively small Dutch immigrant populations. Appleton, in fact, counts fewer Dutch immigrant households in 1870 than in 1860. Both Green Bay and Appleton have fewer than fifty Dutch-born heads of household in 1870, while the concentration in the rural area around De Pere adds up to over on hundred households in 1870. Kaukauna township remained the largest concentration of Dutch immigrants with 129 households or 709 Dutch-born immigrants in 1870.

As was the case during the initial settlement phase of the pioneer periphery, settlement choice reflects occupational choice. During the first few years of settlement, land sales and employment associated with the canalization project of the

Fox River dictated where Dutch immigrants settled in the region. Because most Dutch immigrants had limited financial means, employment on the canalization project was a necessity in order to earn enough money to purchase land. Since farmland prices increased rapidly and most of the lands with access to the waterway were occupied by the mid-1850s, many Dutch immigrant families were forced to find suitable property elsewhere in nearby townships. However, most immigrants were still able to buy land as their occupational designation and property values in the 1860 census manuscripts indicate. Immigrants who did not purchase land before 1860 were likely to disappear from the area's census records or become urban residents in later years. Occupations listed in the 1870 census included construction and wood working, suggesting the beginning of industrial employment in sawmills, planing factories and on construction sites.

Like was the case in the previous period, the occupational and settlement structure of Dutch immigrants during the settlement phase of the specialized periphery reflect choice of employment and residence in accordance with the stage in frontier development. The 1860 census demonstrated that an overwhelming majority of Dutch immigrants became farmers. By 1870, the emphasis was shifting towards non-agricultural and urban employment.

The Fox River Valley: The Transitional Periphery
The socio-economic and demographic changes in the Green Bay-Fox River Valley area, observed for the period after the Civil War, continued during the last quarter of the nineteenth century. Industrialization and urbanization took place at an increasingly rapid rate as the nineteenth century progressed. Dutch Catholic immigrants and their offspring took part in the general cityward movement. The beginnings of this process were documented in the previous section. Here we will focus on the third phase in the development of the frontier, referred to as the "transitional periphery."[16] During this final phase of development of the frontier, integration within the continental transportation system and full connection within the region allowed interior district centers to be freed from commercial dependence upon the regional center (Green Bay). Increased flexibility of choice in interregional shipment and changing competitive positions within the national economy led to a shift in agricultural and industrial specialization and different functions of urban centers. In fact, this phase is characterized by substitution in agriculture from wheat production to dairy farming, and specialization in manufacturing in the form of the paper industry. The partial loss in the mercantile function of the regional center – Green Bay – was compensated for by expansion of industrial activities. Interior centers experienced the most dramatic shifts during this phase. While some centers lost their function to national producers, others specialized in some particular product and found markets nation wide. Many of the smaller flour and saw milling operations disappeared from the area while paper

production developed into a prominent industry. This latter phase in frontier development was reached one or two generations (three or four decades) after initial settlement and coincided with a stage in development at which land scarcity and declining agricultural profits occurred. As a result, westward migration among rural settlers was common during this phase, while employment opportunities in industry created another migration stream.[17] Adaptation to dairy farming was one aspect of the transitional phase. Farming the northern pine lands following the lumber industry was another possibility for settlers in the area to adjust to the changing economic geographic circumstances. Dairy farming required more capital investment and was more labor intensive than wheat cultivation which relieved some of the land-scarcity problems. However, towards the end of the nineteenth century, rural settlement decline set in as higher wages in industry made industrial employment more attractive.

In the Green Bay-Fox River Valley area, the paper industry was the main urban industrial employer during the last quarter of the nineteenth century. Wood pulp, a by-product of the lumber industry in the northern pine woods, was the main raw material for the paper industry. Most of the early paper mills in the valley had taken over deserted flour mills. Flour milling had been declining in the area during the late 1860s and early 1870s after railroads diverted wheat transport to Milwaukee and Chicago and expansion of wheat production in the western states made Minneapolis the milling center for the Upper Midwest. Until 1880, the industry concentrated in the area around Appleton-Kaukauna. During the next few decades, the paper industry located throughout the Fox River Valley. By 1890, the area dominated paper making in the state of Wisconsin and by 1900 paper and pulp industry had risen to eighth place among Wisconsin's industries.[18] The growth of paper manufacturing more or less shaped the pattern of urban development in the Fox River Valley while the combined effect of decline in agriculture and expansion of industry resulted in a redistribution of population in the area. Cities and villages along the Fox river increased in size while some rural townships lost population.

Intermarriage and the Process of Assimilation

Most of the Dutch Catholic immigrant population in Brown County (in which Green Bay and De Pere are located) followed in the pattern of population redistribution just described. By 1905, approximately 50 percent of the immigrants of Dutch descent (first and second generation) are classified as urban. In Outagamie County (in which Little Chute and VandenBroek township are located), only about 20 percent of the immigrants of Dutch descent are urban residents. In fact, compared to the other immigrant groups and U.S. native born settlers, Dutch Catholic immigrants in Brown County maintain their rural orientation.

The different orientation between the Dutch Catholic immigrants from the original, mostly agricultural settlements (in the area around Little Chute), and the

Dutch Catholic immigrants in more urbanized areas, is also evident from the inter-marriage rates measured for different settlements. Intermarriage rates among first- and second-generation Dutch immigrants for 1905 show lower percentages for rural townships than for urban centers in the study area. The initial settlement of Little Chute and VandenBroek township had the lowest intermarriage rates among both first- and second-generation Dutch immigrants. In other, later settled, rural township like Buchanan and Freedom, second-generation Dutch immigrants had married outside their original group in fairly large numbers. However, intermar-riage rates were highest in urban centers in the area. Analysis of the intermarriage data illustrated that mixed marriages occurred more frequently among skilled workers, small proprietors, professionals, and businessmen, than among farmers, farm laborers, and general laborers. The intermarriage distribution suggests that social upward mobility was a factor in intermarriage. Upper and middle class urban immigrant residents were more likely to marry members of other groups. While this is primarily the result of group size, intermarriage rates among second generation immigrants do suggest that a disproportionate number of Dutch immi-grants married German immigrant members. Relative to the population composi-tion in the area of study, intermarriage rates among Dutch immigrants and mem-bers of the German immigrant group prevail.

In *Assimilation in American Life* (1964), Milton Gordon describes intermarriage or marital assimilation as the final stage in the assimilation process. In this socio-logical study, assimilation is described as process in which members of a minority or immigrant group lose their ethnic identity in a host or core society.[19] Gordon introduces the concepts of primary and secondary group relationships. Primary group relationships are personal relationships between relatives and friends. Sec-ondary group relationships involve contacts in the workplace or other institutions in society. When personal and marriage relationships develop across ethnic bounda-ries, assimilation takes place, according to Gordon. Implied in Gordon's model is the urban environment as the socio-economic environment in which assimilation occurs. As the city offers greater and more diverse employment opportunities and easier contact with members of other groups, intermarriage is more likely to hap-pen. In rural areas, on the other hand, where opportunities and contacts are fewer, lower intermarriage rates are found. Here church and community formed the nucleus around which a variety of social relationships evolved, and marriage took place most likely with members of the same group. Geographical and social mobil-ity are thus considered key factors in the intermarriage and assimilation process.[20]

Conclusion
What does this tell us about the differences in experiences between the Dutch Catholic immigrants and the Dutch Protestant immigrants? Robert P. Swierenga argues in his edited volume *Belief and Behavior* that "economics explain the 'why'

of immigration, but religion largely determines the 'how' of immigration and its effects."[21] Whereas Dutch Protestant immigrants tended to isolate themselves within their exclusive religious-ethnic communities, the Dutch Catholic immigrant experience in the United States showed evidence of the international character of Catholicism which weakened their group identity and facilitated assimilation. This widely shared interpretation of the experience of the Dutch Protestant and Dutch Catholic immigrants – derived from research conducted by numerous Dutch immigration historians, including Swierenga, H. Van Stekelenburg, and myself – has been at the core of some of the debates about religion and immigration behavior in the last decade.[22] For the most part, our views and observations overlap but differences in emphasis given to the factors that explain variation between Dutch Protestant and Dutch Catholic immigrant experiences remain.

Swierenga points out that in the United States, only three of twenty-five primarily Dutch Catholic churches were urban-based in 1920.[23] He found that there were no mutual connections between them and that all three of them were short-lived. In contrast there were over five hundred Dutch Calvinist congregations in 1920. However, whereas Swierenga emphasizes religious aspects of faith and belief in his explanation of the differences, I am inclined to emphasize the geographical location and the institutional structure of the Catholic Church. From Swierenga's perspective or point of view, church communities with an orthodox theology stressed cultural tradition and separation from mainstream America and religious faith was the key to the establishment and preservation of ethnic enclaves.

I have argued that whereas the Catholic Church did not encourage frontier colonization in the same way that Protestant churches did, the historical geographical development of the Dutch Catholic immigrant community followed a very different course. The established Catholic Church hierarchy was urban-based and internal urban-oriented migration brought Dutch Catholic immigrants and their children in contact with members of other Catholic groups. Schools and charitable organizations were integrated at the diocese level, and Irish, German, Belgian, and Dutch Catholic immigrants, in most instances, shared the same parish church, making intermarriage a likely occurrence, especially for the second-generation immigrants who grew up speaking English and were associated with the American way of life. Whereas, in 1860 less than a quarter of the population lived in a city or town; by 1910 nearly half of the u.s. population was urban. From the Civil War onwards most migration was not from old land to new land but from country to city and from one city to another. Each upswing in the economy tended to draw workers from lower wage rural areas to higher wage industrial areas. In the Fox River Valley of Wisconsin this pattern was well established by 1870. Consequently, the frontier phase of settlement was very brief and industrialization and urbanization occurred soon thereafter. For the Dutch Catholic immigrants, the urban environment rather than the frontier was the social environment in which assimilation took place and in this they were no different from most other immigrant groups in the United States in the nineteenth century. The Dutch Calvinist immigrant experience was an exception rather than the rule.

At the end of the nineteenth century, during the last stage in frontier development, rural depopulation and industrialization and urban growth created the conditions under which different immigrant groups intermixed and intermarried. Thus, geographical and social mobility explain the assimilation process among Dutch Catholic immigrants and their descendants in the Fox River Valley-Wisconsin. Evidence shows that intermarriage was lowest in primary or initial settlements and were highest in the secondary and urban settlements. Also, intermarriage was highest among skilled workers, small proprietors and professionals, while laborers and farmers had much lower intermarriage rates. Intermarriage with German immigrants suggests that the host society in Wisconsin towards the end of the nineteenth century was German-oriented. Unlike the Protestant Church, the Catholic Church was in a sense an assimilationist force. Urban rather than frontier-oriented, the Catholic Church gave definite direction to settlement concentration and established conditions favorable to assimilation within the framework of the Catholic Church. This particular pattern of assimilation suggests religious plurality in late nineteenth century America, confirming Herberg's thesis of the Triple Melting Pot, at least with respect to Catholic immigrant groups in medium-sized cities in the Midwest.[24] Thus the role of the church can be considered crucial in the process of assimilation. The Catholic Church, in general, was against frontier settlement. In fact, the leadership feared that dispersal would lead to loss of faith and confrontation with nativist groups, and that remoteness would deprive Catholics of proper care and support. Catholic services were concentrated in urban centers reinforcing the urban character of the Catholic Church and encouraging incorporation of different immigrant groups into the larger Catholic community.

Notes

1. This article is an adaptation from the author's book: *Dutch Catholic Immigrant Settlement in Wisconsin, 1850-1905* (New York: Garland, 1990). The materials for this paper were derived from chapters 5 and 7 in particular.
2. Stephen Thernstrom, "Urbanization, Migration, and Social Mobility in Late Nineteenth-Century America," in B.J. Bernstein, ed., *Towards a New Past: Dissenting Essays in American History* (New York: Pantheon, 1968), 158-176.
3. Richard A. Easterlin, *Population, Labor, Force, and Long Swings in Economic Growth: The American Experience* (New York: Columbia University Press, 1968), 21-41.
4. Yda Schreuder, *Dutch Catholic Immigrant Settlement in Wisconsin, 1850-1905* (New York: Garland, 1990).
5. For a brief description of the Dutch Catholic immigrant settlement in the area, see Henry S. Lucas, *Netherlanders in America: Dutch Immigration to the United States and Canada, 1789-*

1950 (Ann Arbor: University of Michigan Press, 1955), 213-225 and 522-528.

6. Yda Schreuder, "Dutch Catholic Immigrant Settlement in Wisconsin," in Robert P. Swierenga, ed., *The Dutch in America: Immigration, Settlement, and Cultural Change* (New Brunswick, NJ: Rutgers University Press, 1985), 105-124; Yda Schreuder, "Americans by Choice and Circumstance: Dutch Protestant and Dutch Catholic Immigrants in Wisconsin, 1850-1905," in Robert C. Ostergren and Thomas R. Vale, eds., *Wisconsin Land and Life* (Madison: University of Wisconsin Press, 1997), 320-330.

7. E.R. Muller, "Selective Urban Growth in the Middle Ohio Valley, 1800-1860," *Geographical Review* 66 (1976): 178-199; and by the same author, "Regional Urbanization and the Selective Growth of Towns in American Regions," *Journal of Historical Geography* 3.1 (January 1977): 21-39.

8. Vilas A. Bender, "Morgan Martin and the Improvement of the Fox River," (Masters Thesis, University of Wisconsin, Madison, 1951).

9. Yda Schreuder, "Immigration and Frontier Development: Dutch Catholic Settlement in the Fox River Valley of Wisconsin in the Nineteenth Century," *Upper Midwest History* 5 (1985): 45-59.

10. Margaret Walsh, *The Manufacturing Frontier: Pioneer Industry in Ante Bellum Wisconsin, 1830-1860* (Madison: State Historical Society of Wisconsin, 1972).

11. Alice E. Smith, *Millstone and Saw: The Origins of Neenah and Menasha* (Madison: State Historical Society of Wisconsin, 1966).

12. F. Merck, *Economic History of Wisconsin during the Civil War* (Madison, 1916), 19.

13. Walsh, *Manufacturing Frontier*, 98-125; Smith, *Millstone and Saw*.

14. Charles N. Glaab and Lawrence H. Larsen, *Factories in the Valley: Neeneah-Menasha, 1870-1915* (Madison: State Historical Society of Wisconsin, 1969).

15. The background of the Dutch immigrant population was determined on the basis of a linked data set derived from the U.S. Federal Manuscript Census of 1850, 1860, and 1870, and Dutch municipal records of emigrant households (see, Yda Schreuder, "Municipal Records in Nineteenth Century Dutch Emigration Research," *International Migration Review* 11.1 (1987): 114-122. The linked record file lists approximately 650 family households or single individual entries for the three census years, totaling over 3,000 individuals of Dutch descent. Of the 56 percent or 34 identified and linked Dutch born family households of De Pere township and village, 25 families derived directly from the Netherlands while 9 families came from townships in the study area.

16. Muller, "Regional Urbanization"; R. Higgs, "The growth of cities in a Midwestern region, 1870-1900," *Journal of Regional Sciences* 9 (1969): 369-375.

17. Allan G. Bogue, *Money at Interest: The Farm Mortgage on the Middle Border* (Ithaca, NY: Cornell University Press, 1955); Douglas North, *Growth and Welfare in the American Past: A New Economic History* (Englewood Cliffs, NJ: Prentice, 1966); John C. Hudson, "Migration to an American Frontier," *Annals, Association of American Geographers* 66 (1976): 242-265; Michael P. Conzen, "Local Migration Systems in Nineteenth Century Iowa," *Geographical Review* 64 (1974): 339-362.

18. Glaab and Larsen, *Factories in the Valley*; Dorothy M. Heesakker, "The Paper mill Industry in the Lower Fox River Valley, Wisconsin, 1872-1890," (Masters Thesis, Loyola University, Chicago, 1965).

19. Milton M. Gordon, *Assimilation in American Life: The Role of Race, Religion, and National Origins* (New York: Oxford University Press, 1964).

20. See also, Josef J. Barton, *Peasants and Strangers: Italians, Rumanians, and Slovaks in an American City, 1890-1950* (Cambridge, MA: Harvard University Press, 1975).

21. Robert P. Swierenga, "Religion and Immigration Behavior: The Dutch Experience," in Philip R. Vandermeer and Robert P. Swierenga, eds., *Belief and Behavior: Essays in the New Religious History* (New Brunswick, NJ, Rutgers University Press, 1991) 164-188.

22. Robert P. Swierenga, "Religion and Immigration Patterns: A Comparative Analysis of Dutch

Protestants and Catholics, 1835-1880," *Journal of American Ethnic History* 5 (Spring 1986): 23-45; Swierenga, "Religion and Immigrant Behavior,"; Henry A.V.M. van Stekelenburg, "Dutch Roman Catholics in the United States," in Swierenga, ed., *The Dutch in America*, 64-77; Yda Schreuder, "Ethnic Solidarity and Assimilation among Dutch Protestant and Dutch Catholic Immigrant Groups in the State of Wisconsin, 1850-1905," in Rob Kroes and Henk-Otto Neuschäfer, eds., *The Dutch in North-America: Their Immigration and Cultural Continuity* (Amsterdam: VU University Press, 1991), 195-218; and Schreuder, "Americans by Choice."

23. In "Religion and Immigrant Behavior," 174.
24. Will Herberg, *Protestant, Catholic, Jew: An Essay in American Religious Sociology* (Garden City: Doubleday, 1956).

The North Brabant Case: Emigration to the United States, 1947-1963

Henk van Stekelenburg

A London Committee

In November 1944 the allied forces had liberated large parts of the southern provinces of the Netherlands, and a small part of the Province of Gelderland. Up till the final removal of the German occupation forces from Dutch soil in May 1945 the Dutch government resided in London. In November of 1944 the Dutch government had commissioned a study group for reconstruction problems to explore the issue of emigration.[1]

This committee approached the question thoroughly: was the government to stimulate emigration, discourage it, or leave it free? Which measures had to be taken? Was it desirable to redistribute the population within the Dutch colonial empire? Was it wise to allow the unrestricted settlement of people and corporations all over the free world? The committee left aside the problems of relocation within the European boundaries created by the inundations in the Netherlands during the war and the annexation of German territory after the liberation.

The committee expected many Dutchmen to be interested in emigration due to the impact of the economic crisis of the 1930s, the war, and the occupation. In addition, the fear of continuous unemployment, the uprooting during the war, and a desire to bury the past and start anew could fan the emigration fever.

The committee advised the government not to encourage emigration in the first few years after the war, since everyone was needed to rebuild the country. Their report noted, however, that it was important to secure the fundamental right of freedom of movement and to maintain the pre-war institutions that had provided assistance to emigrants in the past. The committee could not make a definitive judgment about whether the Netherlands were overpopulated and recommended the establishment of a new institute to determine whether redistribution of the population was desirable. The committee further explored the opportunities offered by the traditional immigration countries overseas.

The chances for new immigrants in the United States were rather limited. The

155

Dutch had a small share of the national origins quota.[2] Those who wanted to emigrate had to face a long waiting period and needed an "assurance" or "affidavit of support." This certificate stated officially that an American citizen or organization would have to stand surety for a period of five years for the immigrant and his or her family. Group migration was no alternative, since the United States wanted to encourage assimilation. Despite these obstacles, the committee expected that the United States would continue to attract Dutch immigrants.

Up to this point the committee report was hardly remarkable. However, the final part revealed a need for a fundamental reorganization of the care for the emigrants. The committee concluded that it was in the Dutch interest to maintain contacts with the immigrants. In the past the cooperation with Dutch diplomatic and consular services in the countries of destination had been rather poor. The homeland had expressed little interest in the emigrants in the new country, but the war had underscored the importance of maintaining the ties with the Dutch abroad.

The committee proposed one central bureau under able supervision and with representatives in each country of immigration. While the state should subsidize the office, the status of this bureau had to be independent, because independent organizations had easy access to foreign authorities. The office had to be advised by a group of specialists from social institutions and business organizations and chaired by a government appointee.

The new office was to be commissioned to research the question of emigration, inform the Dutch population, advise the Dutch government, consult with Dutch diplomats in immigration countries and with the settlement bureaus in the Netherlands and abroad, and also to examine potential emigrants, organize group settlements, and provide facilities to emigrants.

The most remarkable feature of this proposal was the private character of the organization in combination with state funding and cooperation with government officials. Another striking component is the emphasis on group migrations and actual government support to make the settlements a success. As a final recommendation the committee advised the government not to wait until the entire country had been liberated, but to begin consultations immediately with immigrant countries and localities where Dutch tended to emigrate.[3]

It was clear that the committee sought to continue pre-war structures, which had to be improved by increased efficiency, cooperation between private and public sectors, more finances, and closer ties with former fellow countrymen. A large part of the proposals would be realized in the following decade.

The Post War Active Emigration Polity of the Dutch Government (1947-1962)
Despite the activities of this committee, it was not the Dutch government, but Dutch private agricultural organizations that took the initiative to advance emigration in 1946. They had for some time experienced the need of small farmers from

the sand areas, who possessed too little land to make a living for their predominantly large families. The mentality in many rural areas was reluctant to accept fundamental structural adaptation. Many children remained at their mixed farming homesteads, depressing the profits of these farms. New opportunities for reclamation of acreage in newly claimed land, such as the Noordoostpolder, were too few to provide a solution for this "small farmers" question. Children of small farmers could not start as independent farmers, causing a pressing young farmers problem, especially in the sand soil areas in the eastern and southern parts of the Netherlands. Emigration offered a solution. The first option was to start agricultural colonies in France and South America (Brazil and Argentina), because other destinations did not appreciate colonies which prevented rapid integration.

Most likely the agricultural sector had the highest level of organization in the Netherlands, in which almost twenty per cent of the working population found employment in 1947. In the following decade the countryside changed dramatically, as the following table shows. These changes were especially strong in Noord-Brabant.

Table 1: Percentages of three sectors of employment in the Netherlands and Noord-Brabant between 1947 and 1960.[4]

	Agriculture		Industry		Services	
	1947	1960	1947	1960	1947	1960
Netherlands	19	11	35	42	42	45
Noord-Brabant	24	11	42	53	33	36

The so called pillarization had reached its climax in the 1950s. This metaphor describes the separate organization among liberal-conservatives, Roman Catholics, Protestants, and Social-Democrats, each with its own political parties, labor unions, media, schools, social and medical care, sport associations etc. At the top of these pillars, the elites cooperated pragmatically. The Protestants and Roman Catholics joined hands in rejecting a neutral society, which was the ideal of the other two groups. In contrast with the Social Democrats, the confessionalists wanted to limit the influence of the central government to those areas to which is was entitled (Protestants) or in which the private sector failed (Roman Catholics). They also wanted the central government to subsidize their own educational and social institutions and to increase the welfare system.

This attitude explains the prevailing tension between the government and confessional emigration organizations while they were forced to cooperate. The Dutch government's primary fear was overpopulation, and it intended to use emigration to relieve the labor market from its pressure. The private religious organizations were primarily interested in the material, religious, and moral well-being of the emigrants.

Within a year after its founding on July 15, 1946 the Centrale Stichting Landbouw-Emigratie (CSLE, the Central Foundation Agricultural Emigration), an initiative of three national farmers' and greengrocers' unions and the three daylaborers' unions (neutral, Roman Catholic and Protestant), announced its intention to start the agricultural emigration. This event confronted the Dutch government with a *fait accompli*. The secretary of social affairs had to recognize the CSLE and its member organizations as mediators of emigration. When in 1949 non-agricultural workers were also allowed to emigrate, their organizations, such as the labor unions and shopkeepers organizations, received the same status. One can imagine that the government bureaus, which used to exclusively handle mediation of emigration as a matter of the international labor market, regretted this trend. They continued to cater to a large number of potential emigrants, which created a mishmash of institutions dealing with offering information, registration, and assistance to aspiring emigrants. For instance, in 1951 Noord-Brabant counted 29 offices for application. The final stage of the transaction, the provision for foreign currency, possible subsidies, transport, contacts with emigration authorities and emigration-attachés, was centralized in The Hague: until 1952 the *Stichting Landverhuizing Nederland* (Emigration Foundation of the Netherlands, SLN) was the central office, while, later a new complex structure was formed as part of the Ministry of Social Affairs and Employment, in which the *Nederlandse Emigratiedienst* (the Dutch Emigration Service NED) coordinated the activities.

In 1951, the emerging cooperation between government and private sector was formalized by an Act on the Organizations for Emigration (*Wet op de organen voor de emigratie*). A description of this climax of private and public understanding should be treated elsewhere; here it suffices to conclude that the beginning in 1951 a coherent and forceful emigration policy could start, while in the following years the need to emigrate decreased as a result of the increasing standard of living and modernization, despite the influx of about 300,000 repatriates and people from the East Indies and a growing labor force. The conclusion of sociologist B.P. Hofstede is fully justified: "The Government's emigration policy, a purposeful line of conduct based on economic and demographic principles, landed in a vacuum very soon after it became institutionalized; by the time it was put into effect it had almost become an anachronism. As the Government finally acknowledged, the accent had gradually come to lie mainly on the social aspects, but the intrinsic social function of emigration has never really constituted a convincing political argument."[5]

The Dutch government's active emigration policy ended in 1962. The social character of the 1951 law secured its validity, due to the power of the private organizations who maintained their networks in the Netherlands and in the recipient countries. In 1992 the government discontinued its emigration policy and subsidies, thus terminating the carefully constructed organization for emigration.

The Post-War Emigration Policy of the United States
Due to the relatively small number of Dutch-Americans who had entered the United States in the nineteenth century, the quota system, which set a maximum on emigration to the United States between 1924 and 1965 meant that only an annual 3,153 visa were available for Dutch citizens. This number was further decreased to 3,136 when the *Immigration and Nationality Act* of 1952 (*Public Law 414*) was passed. In the midst of the Cold War, this act tightened the requirements for political reliability, while old obstacles banning people with physical, mental, or moral deficiencies (including homosexuals) remained. Immigrants with a solid education, technical skills, special expertise or extraordinary abilities received preferential treatment because the American economy needed these people. The quota could be raised for specially designated groups, such as relatives and refugees. The stipulation of the need to find someone to provide surety to avoid the immigrant becoming a public charge and the low quota caused a waiting list for emigration to the United States of 40,000 people in 1952.[6]

In the following years some substantial, but temporary, changes provided extra places for emigrants.[7] The Refugee Relief Act (Public Law 203, 1953) made provisions for an extra 214,000 immigrants, among whom were 17,000 "refugees" from the Netherlands. The flood of February 1953 had made a large impression overseas and its victims were eligible for entrance to the United States. When few flood victims expressed a desire to leave the country, a strong lobby, and support of some American members of Congress with sympathy for the Netherlands, accomplished the extension of the term "refugee" to include also indirect victims of the Flood, existing "war victims" and repatriates from Indonesia. Between 1945 and 1953 169,000 people had left Dutch East India to settle in the Netherlands, followed by an additional 67,000 people between 1953 and 1957 and another 50,000 after 1957, a grand total of 386,000. Only those of Dutch ethnic origin were welcome in the United States, not those of pure Indonesian descent.

The biggest obstacle for people in those new categories was to find sponsors. While farmers, farm laborers, and able craftsmen had no difficulty finding Americans among farmers and employers' organizations willing to sponsor them, clerks and unskilled laborers often faced a problem. Because many repatriates and Indonesians lacked contacts in the United States, voluntary agencies helped out. Religious organizations, such as the World Council of Churches, the Church World Service, the National Catholic Welfare Conference, the Calvinist Resettlement Service and the Hebrew Immigrant Service maintained close contacts with the American Consul-General in Rotterdam and the NED in Den Haag and made arrangements to accommodate and place emigrants. The CWS represented 23 denominations and acted as sponsor for 64 per cent of the newcomers, while the Roman Catholic organization sponsored 19 per cent and the remainder of 17 per cent used other organizations, relatives, or friends.[8] These provisions enabled 15,182 people to settle under the RRA between August 1953 and December 1956.

When Sukarno's policy of confrontation caused an exodus of Europeans from Indonesia, Congressmen F.E. Walter and J.O. Pastore introduced additional acts to increase the entrance of Dutch *repatrianten*. The Pastore-Walter Acts I and II (1958 and 1960, Public Law 85-862 and Public Law 86-648) allowed an extra 9,000 to 10,000 Dutch citizens to enter the United States.

Among all categories of those leaving Indonesia, especially the Indo-Europeans were most successful in establishing themselves in the United States. Most of them settled in California, which offered better prospects, more homes, and a milder climate, while discrimination was absent. Rijkschroeff estimated that about 23,000 to 24,000 Indo-Europeans settled there, but most likely they counted for more than 30,000. Once settled, they could welcome their relatives when the quota system was abandoned, and an estimated 30.000 people joined them in the period 1965-1973.[9] According to B.R. Rijkschroeff's very cautious calculations more then 40 per cent of the Dutch immigrants in the United States between 1953 and 1963 came from Indonesia.[10] The most well-known voluntary agencies were the Church World Service (CWS) of the World Council of Churches and the National Catholic Welfare Conference (NCWC) of the American Roman Catholic bishops.

The overrepresentation of the Dutch from Indonesia increased the national average of married couples and families. It also increased the number of people working in services. Members of this group were used to higher salaries, had received more education, originated directly from the large Dutch cities and more people in this group indicated that they did not belong to a church.[11]

Up till 1954, the Dutch central emigration authorities were not involved in the process, except in supplying foreign currency or subsidies. The data for research are only complete after 1954, when the NED made lists of departures. Since the great majority of emigrants leaving Noord-Brabant for the United States in the period 1947-1963 were not from Indonesia, we can get a more detailed view of their features.

Noord-Brabant Emigration to the United States
About ten percent of all Dutchmen emigrating overseas originated from the province of Noord-Brabant. In the period between 1946-1963, when 409,716 and 41,150 left the Netherlands and Noord-Brabant respectively, twelve and thirteen per cent of the Dutch population lived in this province, according to the censuses of 1947

and 1960 respectively. The emigration rate for Noord-Brabant was about eighteen per cent lower than the national level.

| Netherlands | 9,625,499 inhabitants | emigration rate: 4.26 % |
| Noord-Brabant | 1,180,133 inhabitants | emigration rate: 3.48 % |

An overview of the flow of emigrants between 1948 and 1963 shows the impact of political decisions, such as the Pastorale-Walter Acts, which greatly expanded emigration to the United States in the years after 1954 while the numbers to other destinations dropped.

Table 2: Noord-Brabant Emigrants Assisted by the SLN and NED and the country of destination (not included is migration to the [former] overseas parts of the empire.

YEAR	CAN.	U.S.	AUSTR.	NW.Z.	S.AFR.	BRAZ.	REST
1948	787	108	78	28	124	22	19
1949	595	90	180	35	115	169	34
1950	827	76	1,027	82	65	88	23
1951	1,762	72	1,211	369	111	20	32
1952	2,264	173	1,930	589	124	20	24
1953	2,507	*	1,286	374	191	49	133
1954	1,877	114	1,844	126	168	41	70
1955	725	193	1,951	170	121	53	67
1956	842	475	1,246	202	75	22	85
1957	1,163	636	693	137	64	30	57
1958	684	316	838	250	119	37	77
1959	517	405	910	232	90	17	22
1960	601	716	887	140	22	21	24
1961	236	512	429	96	24	14	25
1962	195	455	185	116	27	20	29
1963	182	137	177	76	47	26	26
Total	15,764	4,478	14,872	3,022	1,487	649	747

* In Rest Category

Source: CBS, Statistiek van de buitenlandse migratie.

The slight lag in the rate of emigration from Noord-Brabant does not immediately justify conclusions about its climate for emigration. The relatively large proportion of emigration from the big cities of the province of Holland, the late start of emigration to Canada, and a small share of returning Dutchmen from Indonesia can offer partial explanations. More clues are provided by the differences between regions and sectors. In the period 1950-1954 the percentage of agrarian emigrants among the entire Brabantse emigrant stream was higher than the national figures. This result is not surprising considering the larger share of agricultural workers in the Noord-Brabant economy in 1947. The young farmers' problem was urgent in the sand soil regions of the province.[12] The scope of this article precludes a complete overview of the emigrant flow from Noord-Brabant. A rich source of data allows us to examine the emigration in the years of the extra quota, 1955-1963.

Conclusions Drawn from Departure Lists in the Period 1955-1963
It is almost certain that the card index of all emigrants serviced by the SLN and her successor the NED has been destroyed. Fortunately, the Archives Department of the Ministry of Social Affairs and Employment kept the so-called departure lists.[13]

The lists for the United States extend from 1954 to 1982. Before 1954 the SLN and NED were only involved in matters of currency and subsidy, while the processing of emigrants happened at the American Consulate-General in Rotterdam. The increase in emigrants and the subsequent need to find transport facilities and sponsors after 1954 necessitated the involvement of the NED. Table 3 shows the spread of emigrants per municipality in Brabant, starting from 1955, since 1954 counted only two units from this province.

Table 3: Municipalities in Noord-Brabant supplying ten or more emigrants to the United States, 1955-1963.[14]

MUNICIPALITIES IN NOORD-BRABANT 1947-1963	NUMBER OF INHABITANTS AT 1 JAN. 1961	HOUSEHOLDS EMIGRATING TO THE US 1955-1963	PERSONS EMIGRATING TO THE US 1955-1963	RATE OF EMIGRATION PER 1,000 INHABITANTS
Baarle-Nassau	4,507	2	11	4.09
Bergen op Zoom	35,452	27	73	2.05
Boekel	5,711	4	10	1.75
Boxmeer	9,184	7	30	3.26
Boxtel	16,936	11	33	1.94
Breda	108,658	129	409	3.76
Budel	8,237	5	16	1.92
Cuyk	7,658	6	18	2.35

Deurne	19,641	6	19	0.96
Dinteloord	4,503	2	10	2.22
Dongen	14,271	6	12	0.84
Drunen	7,582	10	29	3.82
Eindhoven	168,858	296	676	4.00
Etten en Leur	14,422	3	11	0.76
Fijnaart en Heiningen	4,992	3	16	3.20
Geertruidenberg	4,665	2	13	2.78
Geffen	2,975	3	13	4.36
Geldrop	19,420	12	40	2.05
Gemert	12,512	11	45	3.59
Gilze en Rijen	15,016	14	45	2.99
Grave	6,201	6	20	3.22
Helmond	43,400	22	73	1.68
'S-Hertogenbosch	72,684	63	68	0.93
Loon op Zand	15,407	6	15	0.97
Made en Drimmelen	7,389	2	14	1.89
Mierlo	9,171	5	23	2.50
Mill en St.Hubert	8,176	3	18	2.20
Oisterwijk	11,404	14	41	3.59
Oosterhout	25,324	10	24	0.94
Oss	30,672	42	134	4.36
Raamsdonk	8,781	3	10	1.13
Roosendaal enNispen	38,836	12	37	0.95
Schijndel	13,876	3	13	0.93
St. Oedenrode	10,841	9	31	2.85
Sprang-Capelle	6,277	5	16	2.54
Steenbergen en Kruisland	11,835	5	12	1.01
Tilburg	138,546	158	469	3.38
Uden	16,039	29	103	6.42
Valkenswaard	19,303	11	45	2.33
Veghel	13,541	12	40	2.95
Veldhoven	19,218	21	80	4.16
Vlijmen	9,783	4	11	1.12
Vught	22,843	15	39	1.70
Waalre	9,495	11	34	3.58
Waalwijk	18,154	17	55	3.02

Source: *vertreklijsten van de Directie Emigratie in het archief van het Ministerie van Sociale Zaken en Werkgelegenheid in Den Haag.*

In contrast to the previous table, this overview is exclusively derived from the emigration to the United States arranged by the NED in these nine years. A massive exodus to the United States did not happen in the Netherlands, nor in Brabant. Yet, in the decade between 1954-1963 an extra group of 35,000 Dutchmen were allowed to enter the United States. The RRA-program, which enabled 15,182 Dutchmen to emigrate between August 1953 and December 1956 had a success rate of 90 percent. The Pastore-Walter Acts (1958 and 1960) each added 9,000 extra emigrants, and the increasing number of repatriates used this opportunity gratefully. In this decade about 25,000 repatriates and 10,000 others emigrated to the United States.

Noord-Brabant provided 3,416 emigrants according to the lists of departures (3,845 according to the CBS data) to the United States between 1955 and 1963. It is impossible to indicate precisely the proportion of repatriates in Noord-Brabant. Since most people in this category left large cities, the relatively high level of emigrants from Eindhoven suggests a large part of Dutchmen from Indonesia. The local census shows that Eindhoven's population increased with 1,894 people from Indonesia and New-Guinea between 1950 and 1963.[15] Several hundreds of them are likely to have belonged to the group of 676 emigrants from this city settling in the United States. Also Breda and Tilburg supplied hundreds of repatriates, though the contract-pensions hosting the repatriates were also present in smaller towns. A remarkable feature is the departure of military employees from towns surrounding the air force bases in Volkel, Eindhoven, and Gilze-Rijen: from Uden eleven and from Gemert four heads of families or single men left; from Eindhoven thirteen and from Veldhoven four left; and from Gilze-Rijen five emigrated. Military personnel show up regularly in the lists. Clearly agricultural emigration was marginal in this period and few unskilled laborers left.

Table 4: Total number of employees from Noord-Brabant to the United States 1955-1963.

Agriculture	Industry	Building Industry	Services
46	459	58	464

Comments: Agriculture includes greengrocers, dairy farmers, and forestry workers; industry includes craftsmen such as blacksmiths, shoemakers, mechanics, and white collar workers such as analysts and engineers.

Source Vertreklijsten NED in Arch. Ministerie van Sociale Zaken en Werkgelegenheid in Den Haag.

Conclusion

The extension of possibilities for emigration from the Netherlands to the United States was not a result of demographic policies. The United States was not interested in it and the Dutch government was no longer concerned about massive unemployment. The young farmer problem had been solved. Humanitarian considerations caused the temporary relaxation of the restrictive American immigration policy. Especially the Indonesian Dutch profited especially from this measure. As time progressed, the nature of the selection meant a loss for the Netherlands, which experienced a period of economic growth. While opposition to the emigration policy of the Dutch government increased, confessional associations, responsible for the placing of emigrants in the United States continued their influence, until the emigration wave had slowed down.

Noord-Brabant showed no regional pattern of emigration to the United States as had been the case before 1940, nor was it a predominantly agrarian phenomenon. City dwellers, and among them many repatriates, replaced them.

* Translation by Hans Krabbendam

Notes

1. Nota Emigratiebeleid Reconstructie Commissie in Algemeen Rijksarchief (ARA/te 's-Gravenhage, Archief van het Kabinet der Koningin 1898-1945, toegangsnr. 2.04.14, inventarisnr. 9104.
2. Since 1924 the quota was based on the number of Dutch immigrants in the 1890 U.S. census. Two (later three) per cent of that number were issued as visa (in fact permits to stay) to which certain special cases were added.
3. Group migrations were mainly agrarian colonies, for instance in Brazil, which the Dutch government actively supported.
4. Source: *CBS-volkstellingen*. Comment: an "other" category remains, with a maximum of 4 per cent. The data are taken from A.H. Crijns, *Van overgang naar omwenteling in de Brabantse land- en tuinbouw 1950-1985. Schaalvergroting en specialisatie* (Tilburg: Zuidelijk Historisch Contact, 1998), table 5, 48.
5. B.P. Hofstede, *Thwarted Exodus: Postwar Overseas Migration From the Netherlands* (Den Haag: Staatsuitgeverij, 1964), 180-181.
6. Gerald F. de Jong, *The Dutch in America, 1609-1974* (Boston: Twayne, 1975), 179.
7. The following paragraphs are based on Eline Attema's M.A. thesis (Leiden 1994): "Een enkele reis overzee: Het emigratiebeleid van de Nederlandse regering (1945-1993) en haar bemoeienis met de emigratie naar de Verenigde Staten." Attema consulted the records of the Dutch Foreign Office.
8. B.R. Rijkschroeff, *Een ervaring rijker. De Indische immigranten in de Verenigde Staten van Amerika* (Dordrecht: Eburon, 1989), 35. He lists the Catholic Relief Service instead of the National Catholic Welfare Conference.
9. Ibid., 20-22 and C. Annink in W. Willems and L. Lucassen, eds., *Het onbekende vaderland. De repatriëring van Indische Nederlanders, 1946-1964* (Den Haag: Sdu Uitgeverij, 1994), 153.
10. Rijkschroeff, *Een ervaring rijker*, 22.

11. Ibid., 4.

12. T.P.W. Dielissen, "Brabantse boeren, aspirant-emigranten," (M.A. thesis, Catholic University Nijmegen 1993), 41.

13. Archief Ministerie van Sociale Zaken en Werkgelegenheid, 's-Gravenhage, Directie Emigratie, cartotheek (vertreklijsten).

14. The 1947 census counted 143 municipalities in Noord-Brabant. In 1958 Alem, Maren and Kessel were reorganized; a part merged with Lith and Empel-Meerwijk, another part with the Gelderland towns of Maasdriel and Rossum. In 1960 De Werken was absorbed by Werkendam. In 1961 Noord-Brabant counted 141 municipalities, of which 97 had less than ten emigrants to the u.s.

15. *Statistische Jaarboeken Eindhoven*, 1957, 1960 and 1970.

SECTION 4

DUTCH-AMERICAN RELIGION

Main Reformed Denominations in the Netherlands 19th Century. Adapted from R.P. Zijp, *Anderhalve eeuw gereformeerden 1834-1984*, (Utrecht: Stichting Het Catharijneconvent, 1984), 123.

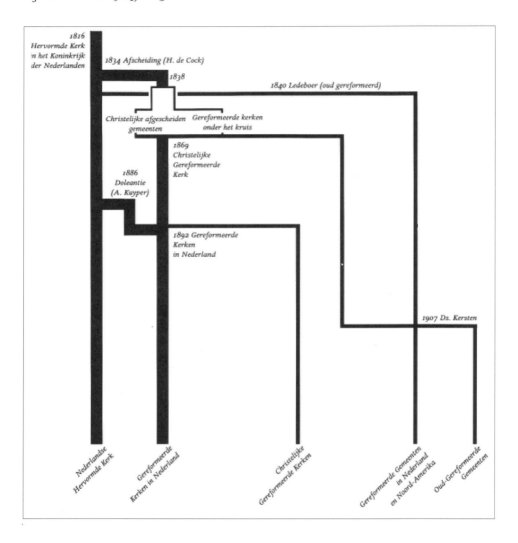

Dutch Immigration and Membership Growth in the Reformed Church in America: 1830–1920

Donald A. Luidens and Roger J. Nemeth

Introduction

The history of Dutch immigration to America is long and distinguished. For more than 350 years, the Dutch have played a significant role in shaping American culture. American politics, literature, education, science, sports, military, and fine arts have all felt the contributions made by Dutch immigrants and their descendents. Indeed, one would be hard pressed to identify any area of American life that has not been influenced in some significant way by the Dutch, albeit some areas more than others. Arguably, the American institution most affected by Dutch immigrants has been religion. Since the founding of New Amsterdam in 1624, Dutch members of the Reformed Church in America, Roman Catholicism, and the Christian Reformed Church, have left their mark on the religious landscape by creating and sustaining thousands of congregations and missions throughout America and the rest of the world.

This paper explores the growth of the Reformed Church in America (RCA) between 1830 and 1920, the heyday of Dutch immigration.[1] The focus of our study is how and where RCA membership grew during the 90-year period beginning in 1830, and how it was associated with Dutch immigration. Data for this study come from decennial U.S. Census reports on population and yearly official membership statistics from the RCA.

Dutch Immigration

The first wave of Dutch immigrates to the United States began in 1623 with the founding of New Netherlands. Concentrated along the Hudson River valley from New Amsterdam (New York) to Fort Orange (Albany), and what is today northern New Jersey, the Dutch colony grew to a population of roughly 10,000 by the time it fell into English hands in 1664. Immigration from the Netherlands had begun to fall long before the English takeover, and it would not rebound until the middle of the nineteenth century. As late as the 1820s Dutch immigration to the United

States averaged fewer than 40 persons a year.[2] Although the 1830s witnessed a substantial increase in Dutch immigrants, it was not until the latter half of the 1840s that Dutch emigration to America began in earnest once again. It continued (with several notable ups and downs) until the U.S. Immigration Acts of the 1920 severely curtailed Dutch (and other European) immigration numbers.

When compared to most Western European countries, Dutch immigration to the United States was relatively meager. During the one hundred and twenty-five years leading up to the end of World War II, only about 265,000 Dutch relocated to the United States. This figure pales in comparison to the 6.1 million Germans, 4.7 million Italians, 4.6 million Irish, and 2.7 million English emigrants who braved the trans-Atlantic crossing during the same time period. It is how and where the Dutch settled, and not the overall size of their numbers, that largely explains their disproportionate influence on the American religious landscape.

Table 1: Number of Dutch Immigrants Admitted to the United States by Decade: 1820-1920

Decade	Number of Immigrants	Percent of Total
1820s	1,105	.5%
1830s	1,377	.6%
1840s	7,624	3.4%
1850s	11,122	5.1%
1860s	8,387	3.8%
1870s	14,267	6.5%
1880s	52,715	24.0%
1890s	29,349	13.4%
1900s	42,463	19.3%
1910s	51,252	23.3%
Total	219,661	99.9%

Data from the U.S. Census and reported in Lucas (1955: 641).

Table 1 presents data on the number of Dutch immigrants admitted to the United States in each decade for the 100-year period beginning in 1820. These data clearly reveal that the Dutch immigrating prior to 1840 comprise a rather insignificant proportion of the total immigration for this period. Of the total of nearly 220,000

Dutch emigrating to the United States, only 1.1 percent did so in the 1820s and 1830s. The 1840s represent the first large wave of Dutch immigration of the nineteenth century. In addition to their comparatively large numbers, the immigrants of the 1840s also differed from their earlier counterparts in their primary motives for emigrating. Economic considerations are nearly always a motive for emigration, and they were certainly important for the Dutch emigrating during the nineteenth century. While few Dutch emigrated because of pure economic desperation, most did so out of "… a conscious calculation that their future in America promised more prosperity for them and their children than if they remained in their homeland."[3] While economic factors were important for the Dutch emigrating in the 1840s, religious motives were also paramount. The late 1840s witnessed the beginning of the emigration of several thousand Seceders (*Afscheiding*) from the Netherlands Reformed (*Hervormde*) Church, and most did so as part of entire congregational units. The emigration of Seceders was particularly heavy in the later half of the 1840s and 1850s.[4] This group immigration continued for about a decade when economic depression in the United States and later the onset of the Civil War severely discouraged immigration.

One of the most significant characteristics of this congregational group immigration was the creation of several *kolonies*. Dutch *kolonies* were small Midwestern settlements founded and almost entirely populated by pietist Dutch Calvinists during the mid-nineteenth century. The primary motivation among the Dutch for creating these communities was to maintain a strict Calvinist way of life and to limit cultural assimilation. Rev. Albertus Van Raalte's congregation of 100 settlers, emigrating from the Netherlands in November 1846, founded the first of the Dutch *kolonies* in Holland, Michigan in 1847.[5] Several other groups locating in Iowa, Wisconsin, and Illinois soon followed Van Raalte's congregation. These groups also emigrated, en masse, in family units and as members of congregations.

The clustering of Dutch emigrants in the United States was quite remarkable. Few immigrant groups to the United States have demonstrated a stronger propensity to cluster than the Dutch. Commenting on this particularly strong desire to cluster, Swierenga points out that the geographical origins of Dutch emigrants were as clustered as the areas they settled in the United States. He notes that for the period from 1820-1880, nearly 75 percent of all Dutch emigrants to the United States came from only 12 percent of all township units in the Netherlands. Moreover, 5 percent of all Dutch municipalities sent out one-half of all emigrants, and only 2 percent of them supplied one-third of all emigrants. Swierenga likens this immigrant stream to:

> … a clump of drinking straws, each carrying peoples from specific Dutch villages to specific American communities…. The fact that, over a period of six decades, three-fourths of the emigrants came from only 134 municipalities in the Netherlands, and in America three-fourths settled in only 55 townships and city

wards by 1870, indicates the localized processes at work. It was clearly a migration of transplanted communities and family chains: parents and children, siblings, grandparents, in-laws, and friends moving in an ever-widening circle from particular localities in the fatherland to particular communities in the States.[6]

U.S. Census data on foreign-born residents indicate that this clustering continued throughout the nineteenth and early twentieth centuries. Presented in Table 2 is the percentage of Dutch born residents living in three Eastern states or seven Midwestern states. These data indicate that as late as 1900, eighty-nine percent of all foreign-born Dutch lived in only ten states; a substantially larger percentage of them lived in the Midwest than the East.

Table 2: Foreign-born Dutch Residents in the U.S. Census: 1850-1920

Region	1850	1860	1870	1880
East	(3,531) 36%	(7,448) 26%	(10,189) 22%	(13,748) 24%
Midwest	(5,434) 55%	(17,869) 63%	(31,988) 68%	(38,034) 65%
Total in U.S.	9,848	28,281	46,811	58,100

Region	1890	1900	1910	1920
East	(16,942) 21%	(20,312) 21%	(26,577) 22%	(27,847) 21%
Midwest	(56,832) 69%	(64,320) 68%	(74,540) 62%	(77,714) 59%
Total in U.S.	81,851	94,992	120,053	131,766

Data from Total in U.S. Census reported in Lucas (1955). East comprised of New Jersey, New York, and Pennsylvania. Midwest comprised of Illinois, Indiana, Iowa, Minnesota, Michigan, Ohio, and Wisconsin.

The relative growth in the foreign-born Dutch population differs greatly in the East than in the Midwest. Although the *number* of Dutch born residents in the East increased every decade between 1850 and 1920, their *percentage* of the national total declined fourteen percent in twenty years - from a high of thirty-six percent in 1850 to twenty-two percent in 1870. Thereafter, it stabilized at just over twenty percent. The Midwest, on the other hand, exhibits a pattern of both increasing number and increasing percentage of Dutch born up to 1890. The number of foreign-born Dutch residing in the Midwest grew so rapidly that its share of the national total reached nearly seventy percent by the end of the nineteenth century.

Although the number of foreign-born Dutch residing in the East and the Midwest continued to increase after 1900, their proportion of the total number of foreign-born Dutch living in the United States declined. The reason for their declining percentages lies in the increasing number of Dutch born residents settling further West after 1900 (especially in South Dakota, Utah, Washington, and California).

RCA *Membership Growth*

Presented in Table 3 are data on RCA membership for the total denomination, for eastern counties from 1818-1920, and for midwestern counties beginning after 1860. Prior to 1830, RCA membership grew slowly. Increasing fewer than 2,000 members between 1818 and 1830, this period pales in comparison to the growth (both in terms of numbers and percentages) following 1830. During the next fifty years membership in the RCA grew nearly six-fold, from fewer than 14,000 members in 1830 to nearly 79,000 communicants in 1920. The dramatic increase in membership following 1830 mirrors the growth of Netherlanders admitted to the United States up to 1880. The decade of the 1880s, however, proved to be pivotal for the future relationship between immigration and RCA membership growth.

Because of their long history in United States, RCA churches in the East had become fairly Americanized by the time Dutch immigrants began arriving in the 1840s. Although most of the immigrants who were members of the Seceder church in Netherlands (*Afgescheidenen*) followed Van Raalte's move and joined the RCA, many soon had reservations about the piety of their Eastern brethren. One issue in particular, membership in the Freemasons, became very divisive. While Calvinist churches in the Netherlands were opposed to Freemasonry in general, the RCA in the East had by the nineteenth century accepted it as part of American society. Many new Dutch immigrants in the Midwest thought that membership in the Freemasons was anti-Christian and that membership in a lodge or in any secret society should be forbidden.

The controversy came to a head in 1882 when several congregations in the Midwest began leaving the RCA and joining the Christian Reformed Church (CRC). The immediate impact of what came to be known as the Secession of 1882 was the loss of nearly 1,000 members, almost entirely from the Midwest. While its full effect on the RCA may never be fully known, the Secession of 1882 had a detrimental impact on immigrant recruitment as well. Because of the Masonic issue, the RCA lost recognition of its mother church in Netherlands, and in 1882 began counseling its members immigrating to the United States to not join the RCA. Instead, they were directed to the fledging CRC.

Table 3: Growth in RCA Membership 1830 – 1920

Year	Entire Membership	Eastern Counties	Midwestern Counties	Rest of the U.S. Counties
1818[1]	(11,919)	(11,919) 100.0%	(0)	(0)
1830	(13,701)	(13,701) 100.0%	(0)	(0)
1840	(24,253)	(24,217) 99.9%	(36) 0.1%	(0)
1850	(34,598)	(34,047) 98.4%	(551) 1.6%	(0)
1860	(47,420)	(43,759) 92.3%	(3,661) 7.7%	(0)
1870	(63,032)	(56,404) 89.5%	(6,603) 10.5%	(25) 0%
1880	(78,546)	(68,160) 86.8%	(10,386) 13.2%	(0)
1890	(90,348)	(75,463) 83.5%	(14,748) 16.3%	(137) 0.2%
1900	(108,568)	(86,466) 79.6%	(21,724) 20.0%	(378) 0.4%
1910	(115,403)	(87,322) 75.7%	(26,754) 23.2%	(1,327) 1.1%
1920	(136,350)	(96,089) 70.5%	(38,748) 28.4%	(1,513) 1.1%

1. The earliest available data on yearly RCA membership is 1818.

One can begin to glean a sense of the impact that the Secession of 1882 had on RCA recruitment of immigrants by looking at the growth of the CRC and the relationship between the RCA's growth and immigration rates. Between 1880 and 1900, the CRC grew from slightly more than 12,000 members to over 47,000 members, and while the RCA also grew, it did not grow as fast as would have been expected given immigration rates. From Table 1 one is able to calculate the average number of immigrants per decade, the average number of new RCA members per decade, and compare these figures before and after 1880. For each decade between 1830 and 1880, there was an average of 8,555 Dutch immigrants to America and an average gain of 12,969 RCA members. This calculates into a ratio of 1.5 RCA members per immigrant. Obvious, the RCA augmented immigrant growth by adding new members through natural increase (i.e. offspring of existing members). After 1880, there was an average of 43,945 Dutch immigrants per decade compared to an average of 14,451 new RCA members. These figures produce a ratio of 0.3 RCA members per immigrant. Although these figures do not take into account changing fertility patterns and internal migration, (and should not be taken as a precise measurement), they do give a general indication of how severely the RCA was affected by the 1882 Secession. Had the RCA continued to experience the same ratio of members to immigrants after 1880 that it enjoyed in earlier decades, its growth rate could have been as much as five times greater.

Data in Table 3 also show where in the United States RCA membership was growing. Prior to 1850 nearly the entire denomination was located east of the Allegheny Mountains. Indeed, with the exception of a couple of churches in central Illinois and another in Maine, all RCA congregations before 1850 were located in New Jersey, New York, or Pennsylvania.[7] Between 1830 and 1850, RCA membership in the East grew rapidly, increasing by nearly 20,000 communicants (or nearly 150 percent). After 1850 the East continued to grow in every decade up to 1920, and even at this late date its membership represented over 70 percent of the entire denomination. Although it was still growing and continued to enjoy numerical dominance in the denomination, the percentage of RCA members residing in the East was waning. Indeed, the shrinking percentage of members living in the East, a trend begun in 1850, would continue until the present.

Conversely, membership numbers for the Midwest reveal a pattern of continual growth. Beginning with a modest thirty-six communicants in 1840, the number and percentage of RCA members living in the Midwest increased with every decade. By 1920 more than one-forth of the entire denomination resided in one of seven Midwestern states. The seventy-year period, starting in 1850, witnessed the shift of the denomination's demographic center westward from its historical beginnings in New York City and the Hudson River Valley to faster growing regions of the Midwest. It is important to note that a decline in membership (or even a slow drop in growth) in the East did not initiate this transition. Rather, it resulted from RCA membership growing at a faster pace in the Midwest than in the East. The extraordinary growth in RCA membership in the Midwest during this period was, at least initially, the result of Dutch immigration patterns.

As for the rest of the United States, RCA membership never reaches a significant mass before 1920. RCA presence in areas outside the East and the Midwest begins in earnest only after 1890. Although membership growth gains momentum during the next twenty years, the proportion of RCA members residing in counties in the rest of the United States was still only one percent in 1920.

Immigration and Membership Growth

One indication of the influence of immigration on RCA membership growth can be gleaned from examining county-level data on foreign-born Dutch residents in the United States. Presented in Table 4 are correlation coefficients measuring the relationship between the size of a county's RCA membership and the number of foreign-born Dutch residing in the county. This figure indicates the relative Dutchness of a county as compared with the size of its RCA composition. The higher the coefficient, the more Dutch the RCA is in a county.

Table 4: Correlation Between RCA Membership and Number of Born in the Netherlands

| | County-Level Data | |
| | Eastern | Midwestern |
Year	Counties	Counties
1870	.34* (47)	.95 ** (25)
1871	.25* (48)	.90 ** (32)
1890	.21 ns (52)	.92 ** (50)
1900	.38 ** (54)	.87 ** (75)
1901	.45 ** (55)	.87 ** (78)
1920	.45 ** (56)	.87 ** (81)

ns = not statistically significant
*   = significant at .05 level
** = significant at .01 level

Eastern counties include counties with at least one RCA congregation. All but two of these congregations were in New Jersey, New York, or Pennsylvania. Midwestern counties are counties with at least one RCA congregation in Illinois, Indiana, Iowa, Minnesota, Michigan, Ohio, or Wisconsin.

The coefficients for Eastern counties throughout this period indicate that the size of the county's RCA membership is only weakly to moderately associated with the size of the Dutch born population in a county. Interestingly, the strength of the relationship decreases up to 1890, but increases thereafter. Since the number of Eastern counties with RCA members remains relatively stable throughout the fifty-year period, this would seem to confirm that by the time Dutch immigration had reached sizable numbers in the mid-nineteenth century, RCA membership in the East had come a long way in the process of Americanization. By 1890, the RCA in the East had expanded beyond its ethnic roots to include many non-Dutch. The increasing correlations after 1890 indicate that RCA membership was increasingly concentrated in counties with relatively high foreign-born Dutch.

Comparing the correlation coefficients for the two regions reveals a much stronger association between RCA membership and the size of the Dutch born population in the Midwest. Indeed, the relationship is two to three times stronger in the Midwest than in the East for any given year. In 1870, the entire RCA membership in the Midwest was concentrated in only 25 counties, and the size of a county's RCA membership was directly related to the size of its Dutch born population. In fact, the .95 correlation coefficient indicates that the relationship between the two variables could hardly have been any stronger! In the Midwest, almost every Dutch born immigrant was in the RCA, and virtually every RCA member was Dutch born. The figures in Table 4 indicate that over the next fifty years the number of Midwestern counties with RCA congregations more than tripled, expanding into areas that were not as heavily populated with Dutch. Even after this rapid expansion, however, the relationship between RCA membership and the Dutch born population continued to be quite strong. The slight drop after 1890 can be attributed, in part, to diffusion of RCA members into neighboring counties and to the birth of new members in the United States. It is clear from these data that the RCA began in the Midwest as an immigrant church, heavily influenced by Dutch settlement patterns, and continued to be so even as late as 1920.

Further indication of the influence of Dutch immigration is found in the localized concentrated pattern of RCA membership. Earlier in this paper we reported that the Dutch were notable among immigrant groups because of the extent to which they settled in clusters. This propensity among Dutch emigrants has a long history and was evident even among emigrants in the seventeenth and eighteenth centuries. Swierenga makes the point that even as late as 1790:

> ... more than 125 years after the English seized New Netherlands, 80 percent of the Dutch Americans yet resided within a fifty-mile radius of New York City, where they comprised one-sixth of the population. Eighty years later, in 1870, after sixty to seventy thousand of the "new emigrants" had arrived, over 90 percent could be found in only eighteen counties or city wards in seven Midwestern and mid-Atlantic seaboard states.[8]

In addition to New York City, other well established Eastern centers of Dutch settlement were the corridor from northeastern New Jersey to New Brunswick, and the farming region of the upper Hudson River valley around present-day Albany and Schenectady.

By examining the geographical distribution of its membership one can begin to see the influence Dutch settlement patterns had on the RCA. Presented in Figure 1 is the percentage of the total RCA membership located in each county for 1830. This graph reveals that not only was RCA membership limited to three states, but the entire membership was confined to a total of only forty counties. More impressive is the proximity of RCA membership to the New York City-Hudson River-Erie Canal waterway. With over 80 percent of its members residing in counties along this water route, the distribution of RCA membership forms what can be described as an "inverted L" pattern, beginning at New York harbor, traveling north up the Hudson River, and moving westward along the Erie Canal. Figure 2 indicates that the inverted L pattern of RCA membership persisted well into the twentieth century.

Table 5: Percentage of RCA Membership Located in Established Core Centers in the East

Year	New York City Core[1]	Northeastern New Jersey Core[2]	Albany Core[3]	Combined Core
1830	25.0	12.9	11.0	48.9
1840	18.4	12.5	16.7	47.6
1850	18.5	14.4	13.3	46.2
1860	19.7	13.7	10.6	44.0
1870	18.8	14.4	10.7	43.9
1880	17.9	14.1	9.2	41.2
1890	15.8	17.2	7.8	40.8
1900	18.4	16.5	7.2	42.1
1910	17.5	18.3	6.4	42.2
1920	15.0	18.0	6.3	39.3

1. New York City Core consists of the following counties: Bronx, Kings, Queens, and New York.
2. Northeastern New Jersey Core consists of the following counties: Bergen, Essex, Hudson, and Sommerset.
3. Albany Core consists of the following counties: Albany, Rensselaer, and Schenectady.

The concentration of RCA members along this inverted L can be explained by the immigration and dispersion pattern of Dutch folk coming to the New World. For

Figure 1: Percentage of RCA *members in Eastern Counties: 1830*

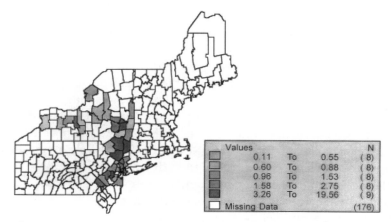

PRORCA 1830 -- (MEM 1830) PER 100 (RCA 1830) UNITS CREATED BY THE EQUATION: RATE =
100 * ("MEM 1830"/"RCA1830")

Figure 2: Percent of RCA *Members in Eastern Counties: 1920*

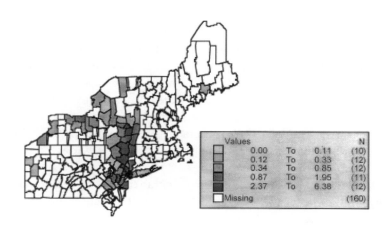

nearly 9 out of 10 Dutch immigrants between 1820 and 1880, New York City was the port of entry into the United States.[9] Like most immigrants in New York, the route most traveled westward by the Dutch was the Hudson River-Erie Canal waterway.[10] The significance of this waterway for the development of western New York and the Midwest is reflected in the population explosion in those areas soon after the canal opened in 1825. In Michigan alone there was an 84-fold increase in population between 1820 and 1860, from just fewer than 8,900 to nearly 750,000.

Looking at the percentage of members residing in three long-established core centers further reveals the extent of the denomination's concentration. Listed in Table 5 is the percentage of members living in the eleven counties that comprise centers of RCA membership in the East: New York City, the New Jersey corridor (from Bergen to Middlesex counties), and the Albany/Schenectady area. New York City, with one-fourth of the denomination's entire membership, was clearly the most dominant magnet at the beginning of the Dutch immigration era. Its percentage of RCA members exceeded the total for the other two core centers combined. Collectively, these three core centers comprised nearly one-half of the entire RCA membership in 1830. While the next 90 years witnessed a steady decline in the proportion of RCA membership in New York City and Albany/Schenectady, Northeast New Jersey's proportion increased. The net effect of these changing fortunes is that these three core areas continued to comprise nearly 40 percent of the denomination's total membership as late as 1920. It is important to note that while their *proportion* of the RCA's membership slipped from 50 to 40 percent during this period, their *number* of RCA members actually increased. Their share of members declined only because membership in the Midwest was growing at even a faster pace.

The large numbers of Dutch folks emigrating after 1840 settled in the newly formed states that once comprised the Northwest Territory. Relatively cheap land that could be developed into farms and established transportation routes encouraged these Dutch immigrants to initially settle an area encircling the southern portion of Lake Michigan and parts of central and western Iowa. As mentioned earlier, many of these emigrants in the 1850s and 1860s were Seceders from the Reformed Church in the Netherlands and were influenced by religious motives to create *kolonies* in an effort to resist cultural assimilation in America. By 1870, four centers or magnet areas of Dutch settlement had emerged in the Midwest. The largest of these magnet centers, and their rapid growth, is evident in Figures 3 and 4.

The largest of the Midwest magnet areas included the original Holland, Michigan *kolonie* on the western shore of Lake Michigan. This center for Dutch immigration eventually comprised a four-county area and the city of Grand Rapids. Two other magnet centers located along Lake Michigan were Cook County (including Chicago) in Illinois, and Milwaukee and Sheboygan counties in Wisconsin. Lo-

Figure 3: Percentage of RCA Members in Midwestern Counties: 1870

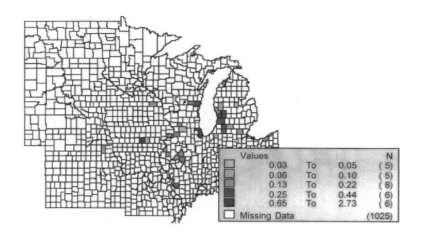

PRORCA 1870 -- (MEM 1870) PER 100 (RCA 1870) UNITS CREATED BY THE EQUATION: RATE = 100 * ("MEM 1870"/"RCA 1830")

Figure 4: Percent of RCA Members in Midwestern Counties: 1920.

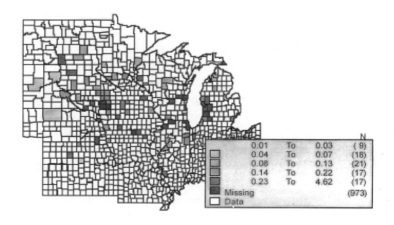

cated in Iowa were two more magnets for Dutch immigration, centered on the *kolonies* of Pella and Orange City.

Table 6: Percentage of RCA Membership Located in Emerging Core Centers in the Midwest.

Year	Holland Core[1]	Iowa Core[2]	Chicago Core[3]	Sheboygan Core[4]	Combined Core
1880	6.2	1.4	1.1	1.0	9.7
1890	5.9	2.5	1.8	1.1	11.3
1900	6.8	2.8	2.6	1.4	13.5
1910	8.4	3.5	2.2	1.7	15.7
1920	10.1	4.2	2.8	1.8	18.9

1. Holland Core consists of the following counties: Allegan, Holland, Kent, and Muskegon.
2. Iowa Core consists of Mahaska and Marion Counties, and Sioux County (which is not contiguous with the other to counties..
3. Chicago Core consists of only Cook County in this analysis. DuPage and Will Counties later become part of this expanding core center.
4. Sheboygan Core consists of Fond du Lac and Sheboygan Counties.

Listed in Table 6 is the percentage of the denomination living in each of the emerging core areas of the Midwest. During the forty-year period beginning in 1880, all four core areas experienced rapid growth in numbers and in their share of RCA members. The Holland core began as the largest of these Midwest RCA magnets and continued to be so with over 10 percent of the denomination's membership in 1920. Like New York City in the East, it was clearly the denominate magnet for RCA members in the Midwest. The other three core centers experienced exceptional growth, doubling or tripling in their share of RCA members. Collectively, these four Midwest centers doubled their proportion of RCA members by 1920. While their collective figure represents only one-half the percentage of RCA members residing in the established core areas of the East (18.9 percent compared to 39.3 percent), it represents the beginning of a westward trend that would continue for the next 70 years.

The rapid growth in membership in the Midwest would soon have significant impact also on the direction and leadership of the denomination. The establishment of Hope College and Western Theological Seminary (both in 1866) in Michigan and Central College in Iowa (acquired from the Baptists in 1916) meant that

Midwestern congregations no longer had to look to the East to education their children and to fill their pulpits. Indeed, by 1920 Western Seminary had more ministerial candidates enrolled than the 150 year old New Brunswick Seminary in New Jersey (twenty-one and nineteen seminarians respectively), and Hope and Central Colleges were accounting for nearly two-thirds of the total number of future seminarians.

The growing influence of Midwestern churches in the RCA is also evident in financial matters. Although many Midwestern RCA congregations were heavily indebted to churches in the East for support during their initial years of ministry, by 1920 this situation had all but ceased. Although Eastern congregations were still contributing about two-thirds of the total giving in the denomination, Midwestern congregations were continually increasing their support. For example, the proportion of total giving in the RCA coming from Eastern churches declined from a high of 83 percent immediately after the Civil War to about 63 percent in 1920. Moreover, when the per capita giving for the two regions is compared, figures for the Midwest show continued improvement. So dramatic was the increase in per capita giving that by 1920 the newly arrived Midwestern immigrants were giving proportionally the same amount as the much more established Eastern members of the RCA.

The growing influence of Midwestern members can be illustrated in several decisions made by the denomination during the early decades of the twentieth century. One action, in particular, points to the shifting power relations within the RCA; the ability of Midwest congregations to block the union of the RCA with the Reformed Church in the United States (RCUS).[11] The RCUS was considered by many in the Dutch-born Midwest to be too liberal and, perhaps more importantly, too German. Although RCA ministers in the East had advocated union for a long time, it was widely believed that a merger would result in many Midwestern congregations leaving the RCA. In describing the outcome of this regional conflict, Van Hinte argues that the issue was finally dropped and "...to strengthen the bond and to recognize the strength of the West, the highest church gatherings of the Reformed Church, the General Synods, were held several times in the Young-Dutch colonies at Grand Rapids, at Holland in Michigan, at Englewood, which was the 'Dutch' part of Chicago, and even at Pella, Iowa."[12] The union of the RCA and the RCUS is just one of many regional conflicts within the RCA illustrating the enormous social, political, and religious differences between Dutch-born RCA members in the Midwest and their more "Americanized" counterparts in the East.

Discussion
The influence of Dutch settlement patterns in the United States has been truly remarkable. By clustering their communities around core magnet areas, first in the East and later in the Midwest, the Dutch were able to exercise a level of influence

in America that far exceeded their numbers, and it had the affect of sustaining Dutch ethnicity in the United States for many generations. One institution emblematic of Dutch presence in America has been the RCA. While helping to sustain Dutch ethnicity in the United States, it has at the same time been heavily influenced by it. Beginning with the very first Dutch immigrants in the seventeenth century, and continuing through the early decades of the twentieth century, how and where Dutch settled profoundly influenced where RCA members were to be found.

The highly concentrated distribution of its members served the RCA well in many ways. First, it allowed the RCA to create a presence in areas of the East and the Midwest that far exceeded the size of its membership. When viewed within mainline Protestantism, the RCA was then, and still is, only a small player. For example, other old-line denominations such as the Presbyterians, Lutherans, and the old Congregationalists (the United Church of Christ) all had national memberships that towered over the 136,000 RCA communicants in 1920. By clustering their congregations in a few magnet centers the RCA became a "known commodity" in particular areas within the East and Midwest. As such, it was considered a "mainline denomination" early in the twentieth century, as evidenced by its pivotal role in the founding of the Federal Council of churches and other ecumenical endeavors (e.g. the Christian Missionary Society).

Clustering also helped in planting new churches starts in these magnet areas. By "mothering" new churches, older and larger churches in these regions assisted hundreds of newer churches establish themselves. Moreover, because the RCA had established name recognition in these core areas; it helped Reformed churches compete with churches from other denominations for new members.

It was also helpful in exercising RCA polity to have churches relatively close to one another. The organizational units of the RCA, beginning at the local congregational and classis levels and proceeding up to the regional and national judicatories, all benefited by having representatives living within relatively close proximity. In an age when transportation was primarily by wagon, boats, and later trains, having its membership clustered certainly made it easier to have frequent congregational and denominational meetings.

Having its membership so heavily concentrated among pockets of Dutch immigrants, however, was not entirely beneficial. Because the RCA has been so closely associated historically with Dutch immigration, the denomination found it difficult to move beyond being thought of as an immigrant church. Indeed, many even today refer to the RCA as the "Dutch Reformed Church." The Secession of 1882 and the passing of the Immigration Acts of the 1920s meant that the RCA could no longer hope to replenish its numbers with Dutch immigrants. Thus, the denomination became heavily dependent on the children of existing members for its source of new members. The relatively high fertility of families during the late decades of the nineteenth century and the high retention of members' children allowed the denomination to continue to grow. But even during this period of numerical growth, the RCA was not keeping pace with the growth in America's population. The declining fortunes of the RCA are illustrated in Figure 5.

Presented in Figure 5 is a comparison of the birthrate for white women in the United States and the percentage of the population that were members of the RCA.[13] The trend line for birthrates and the trend line for RCA membership were moving in opposite directions prior to 1880. As birthrates tumbled, the percentage of the population belonging to the RCA increased. This can be accounted for by the large waves of Dutch immigrants in the 1840s and 1850s that immigrated in congregational units and eventually joined the RCA. The RCA reached its apex in terms of U.S. market share in 1880 and it declined thereafter. The outcome of the 1882 Secession and the declining significance of immigration for the RCA are clearly evident in the high correlation between the trend lines after 1880. As early as 1880, the future growth of the denomination was closely tied to the falling birthrates of its members.

The long-term influence of what happened after 1880 can be seen in recent membership data. Currently, the Midwest as a region enjoys numerical dominance in the denomination. With nearly twice the number of members, the Midwest has now replaced the East as the demographic center of the RCA (fity-nine percent and thirty percent respectively). Only about eleven percent of the denomination's total membership is found outside this two regions. Moreover, the reliance of the RCA

Figure 5: Comparison of U.S. Birthrate and Proportion of U.S. Population that is RCA.

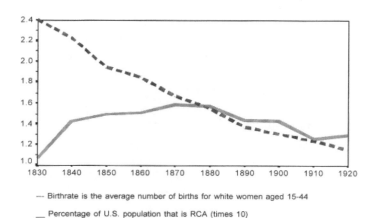

--- Birthrate is the average number of births for white women aged 15-44

__ Percentage of U.S. population that is RCA (times 10)

on replenishing its numbers with the offspring of members can be seen in the persistence of Dutch ethnicity. In a denominational survey conducted in 1991, slightly more than one-half of all members, and nearly 70 percent of all clergy, reported having Dutch ancestry.[14] Interestingly, proportion of members and clergy claiming Dutch ancestry has not declined, at least since 1976. Sharp regional differences in ethnicity are also evident in these data. Nearly three times as many members reported Dutch ancestry in the Midwest, as did members in the East (seventy percent to twenty-five percent respectively).

Birthrates in the United States continued to drop during most of the twentieth century. Currently, birthrates for white women have fallen below replacement levels (i.e. the rate needed to replace parents), and are about one-half of what they were at the beginning of the century. Because of the post-World War II baby boom, the RCA did not feel the consequences of this profound decline in its future source of membership until the 1950s when churches in the East began losing members at an alarming rate.[15] The East was particular vulnerable to membership loss because it had lower birthrates than any other region, and because RCA congregations in the East have been located in inner-city neighborhoods. The massive out-migration of millions of Americans beginning after World War II from urban centers to the burgeoning suburbs meant that many long-standing, urban congregations found themselves in declining neighborhoods. Moreover, despite moderate success at starting churches in suburbs, their number did not keep pace with the decentralization of urban centers.

For most of the twentieth century, the Midwest experienced continual growth. After birthrates resumed declining following the boom of the 1950s, RCA membership in this region continued to growth until the early 1980s. At this time, membership growth in Midwest began to slow, and this region is currently experiencing a slight decline. The primary reason why the Midwest did not begin to lose members earlier is because churches in this region have been able to augment internal growth with recruitment of church members from other denominations. Survey data on denominational switching indicate that more RCA members have transferred from the CRC than any other denomination.[16] Since CRC membership is highly concentrated in the Midwest, RCA congregations in this region have long benefited from this pattern of denominational switching more than RCA congregations in other regions. Moreover, the switching of CRC members has helped to maintain the level of Dutchness in Midwestern RCA congregations. The recent downturn in RCA membership in the Midwest may indicate that this source of new members is dwindling.

Another reason for the decline in RCA membership in the East and Midwest is also demographic in nature. The heavy concentration of RCA congregations in the Northeast and the upper Midwest left the denomination ill suited to respond to the tremendous regional shift in population during the twentieth century. The Sunbelt to Frostbelt population migration trend already evident by 1920, and accelerating after World War II, meant that the denomination's membership was concentrated in regions that were either losing population or growing only slowly. In spite of several church growth programs in fast growing areas in the South and West, the denomination's share of the nation's population has continued to decline throughout the century. The RCA has found it difficult to plant successful new churches in areas where other mainline Protestant denominations have long histories and established name recognition (e.g. Presbyterians, Methodists, and Baptists).

Conclusion

For better or worst, the present geographic concentration and composition of the RCA membership was largely set during the period between 1830 and 1920. By the latter date, the concentration of members in magnet centers in the East and Midwest was clearly evident. Moreover, Dutch immigration's declining influence on RCA membership, and the denomination's growing dependence on natural increase as its source for future members, were trends that have their origins during this period of extraordinary growth.

While the impact of Dutch immigration on RCA membership has been enormous, it has also been very uneven. Its influence has differed greatly over time and between regions. In the East, Dutch immigration had only a minimal effect on RCA membership growth throughout the entire period between 1830 and 1920. Its impact on the Midwest, however, was immense and vital in expanding the denomination up to the 1880s. Thereafter, the impact of Dutch immigration on RCA membership growth waned quickly.

Much about the present makeup and distribution of RCA members can be learned by examining trends evident in the nineteenth and early twentieth centuries. Additionally, many of the challenges facing the denomination today can be traced to developments during this time period. If the RCA is to be successful in meeting these challenges it will need a clear understanding of the forces that have been instrumental in shaping its current configuration and the pressures that will continue to shape it in the future.

Notes

1. What is now known as the Reformed Church in America (RCA) was founded in 1628 in New Amsterdam by the first wave of Dutch immigrants to the United States. Since its founding it has undergone several name changes including the "Reformed Dutch Church in North America," the "Dutch Reformed Church in North America," and the "Reformed Dutch Church in the United States of America." Because the Reformed Church in America was used as its name for most of the years under consideration, we will use RCA to refer to the denomination throughout the paper.

2. For Dutch immigration figures for the nineteenth and early twentieth centuries see Robert Swierenga, "Dutch Immigration Demography, 1820-1880," *Journal of Family History* 5 (Winter 1980): 390-405 and Robert Swierenga, "Exodus Netherlands, Promised Land America: Dutch Immigration and Settlement in the United States," in J.W. Schulte Nordholt and Robert Swierenga, eds., *A Bilateral Bicentennial: A History of Dutch-American Relations, 1782-1892* (Amsterdam: Octagon Books, 1982).

3. Ibid., 128.

4. For data on the emigration of Hervormde and Afscheiding members between 1837 and 1857 see Elton Bruins and Robert Swierenga, *Family Quarrels in the Dutch Reformed Churches of the 19th Century* (Grand Rapids, MI: Eerdmans, 1999), 7.

5. For fuller accounts of the settling of the Holland *kolonie* see Jeanne Jacobson, Elton Bruins, and Larry Wagenaar, *Albertus C. Van Raalte: Dutch Leader and American Patriot* (Holland, MI: Hope College, 1996), 28-57, Henry Lucas, *Netherlanders in America* (Ann Arbor, MI: University of Michigan Press, 1955), 68-150 and Jacob van Hinte, *Netherlanders in America: A Study of Emigration and Settlement in the 19th and 20th Centuries in the United States of America*, Robert P. Swierenga, general editor, Adriaan De Wit, chief translator (Grand Rapids: Baker Book House, 1985), 132-137.

6. Swierenga, "Exodus," 134-135.

7. During the 1830s and 1840s the RCA launched several "mission" churches in Ohio, Indiana, and Michigan. These were lackluster efforts, with little lasting effect.

8. Swierenga, "Exodus," 133.

9. For a listing of ports of arrivals used by Dutch immigrants between 1820 and 1880 see Robert Swierenga, ed., *The Dutch in America: Immigration, Settlement, and Cultural Change* (New Brunswick NJ: Rutgers University Press, 1985), 4.

10. Many Dutch immigrants traveling the Hudson River-Erie Canal water route received assistance from RCA congregations along the way. An example of this is the help given to Rev. Van Raalte and his congregation by Rev. Wyckoff and Second Reformed Church Albany, details of which can be found in Jacobson et al, *Van Raalte*, 29-30.

11. For a fuller description of this account, see Van Hinte, *Netherlanders*, 848-849.

12. Ibid., 849.

13. The figures for the percentage of the U.S. population that were RCA members had to be multiplied by 10 so that it could be compared to the birthrate in Figure 3.

14. For a complete description of this study and its findings see Roger Nemeth and Donald Luidens, "The RCA in the Larger Picture: Facing Structural Realities," *The Reformed Review* 47 (Winter 1993): 85-112 and Roger Nemeth and Donald Luidens, "The Persistence of Dutch Ethnicity: Dutch Clergy in the Reformed Church in America," *Journal for the Scientific Study of Religion* 34 (June 1995): 200-213.

15. For a fuller account of RCA membership trends during the twentieth Century see Roger Nemeth and Donald Luidens, "The RCA: A Virtual Denomination?" *The Church Herald* 55 (November 1998): 8-11.

16. For a demographic profile of RCA members see Donald Luidens and Roger Nemeth, "In Search of the RCA," *The Church Herald* 49 (September 1992): 8-11.

Forging a Religious Identity: The Christian Reformed Church in the Nineteenth-Century Dutch Immigrant Community

Richard H. Harms

During the 1850s in West Michigan, Classis Holland of the Reformed Church in America (RCA) experienced a series of secessions that set about ten percent of that Dutch immigrant community religiously apart.[1] These various groups of seceders were united in their core complaint of not being able to accept to the 1850 union of Classis Holland to RCA.[2] But consensus on the complaint did not lead to a common path these groups chose to follow. The largest seceding group, that of 1857, began in the same direction as that blazed by the small South Holland, Michigan group in 1852 and the larger Drenthe, Michigan group in 1853, but ultimately took a divergent path and formed a new denomination, now known as the Christian Reformed Church (CRC).

Uncertain Beginning
Much has been written about why the secession of 1857 occurred. Writers from the CRC and the RCA carried forward, well into the twentieth century an extensive, at times vitriolic, debate about the legality of the secession.[3] Yet no one has focussed on how the four congregations of the 1857 departure, initially comprising of two ministers and an estimated 750 souls, formed a unique denomination. How did a relatively few Dutch immigrants form a separatr denominational identity when on the surface, there was little to distinguish them from their ethnic and religious kin? Both those who remained in the RCA and the seceders subscribed to a common Reformed faith and doctrine. In fact, after the secessions both groups accepted each other's members and ministers with a relative facility.[4] Yet fifty years later the CRC celebrated its semi-centennial, installed its two-hundredth minister, was operating a seminary and beginning to developed a four-year liberal arts college, administering mission efforts, and had grown to 66,000 members in 167 congregations.[5] As James Bratt notes, focussing on the RCA west of the Alleghenies during the first decade of the twentieth century, the CRC and the RCA West were approximately equal in size.[6]

What is particularly remarkable about this, is that at the point of their leaving the

RCA in 1857 and for the next several decades, the four congregations give no clear evidence that they intended or intend to become a separate denomination. There is no doubt that they were determined to be rooted in what they saw as the fundamentals of the 1834 secession from the *Hervormde Kerk*, the established church of the Netherlands.[7] Central to these fundamentals was Calvinism suffused with Hendrik De Cock's view of church polity that required a strict adherence to the church order formulated at the Synod of Dordt in 1618-1619, as Herbert Brinks convincingly demonstrated.[8] But what is not clear is how this determination led to creating a unique denomination. Instead a series of challenges and questions over the next twentythree years forged a unique denomination. Once forged, this denomination was different from what was the majority in 1857. As Brinks demonstrates, thanks to the ministerial corps that developed, the CRC was deeply rooted in the conservative Dutch Calvinism of the northern Netherlands. But the question remains, how did the CRC reach this point?

This process involved the, at times simultaneous, and intertwined efforts of considering affiliation with the Presbyterian Church as other Dutch immigrants were doing,[9] ensuring viability, which included selecting a name, among the numerically much larger of their ilk in the RCA, attempting to link to the church in the Netherlands they had left,[10] when linkage efforts with the church in the Netherlands came to naught, and lastly, providing for the growing demand for ministers. This culminated in 1876 with the opening of a Theological School (now Calvin Theological Seminary and Calvin College) and the realization among the membership over the next few years that the 1857 secession movement had become a separate denomination.

Having presented their documents of secession to Classis Holland of the RCA in early April 1857, the four congregations, Graafschap, Grand Rapids, Noordeloos, and Polkton, met as a classis later that month to discuss their future course. Unfortunately the minutes of that meeting are lost so actions taken and even the very date are not known, but it is clear from the second classical meeting in October that the overarching requirement for viability was the need for competent clergy, since by that second meeting Hendrik G. Klijn had returned to the RCA leaving the future CRC with one minister, Koenraad Vanden Bosch, to itinerate through the West Michigan forests from his congregation at Noordeloos.[11]

The lack of ministers exacerbated a host of other problems. When resolution was particularly difficult, classis often turned to Presbyterian ministers Roelof Smit (Drenthe) and Jacob R. Schepers (South Holland), seated as fraternal delegates, to provide advice and counsel. This contact led to one of the first questions for the CRC to answer: how would they relate to Presbyterians?

Contacts with Presbyterians
Initially, the CRC invited the Dutch Presbyterians to join. This began at the October 1857 classical meeting when a visitor from a small Presbyterian congregation in

Grand Haven that had been organized in 1855 by Smit and Schepers expressed interest in joining the CRC.[12] Ultimately the Grand Haven congregation decided against joining the CRC.[13] In 1860 Drenthe rejected a similar invitation because the Presbyterians permitted them to follow the Church Order of Dordt.[14]

Invitations from the Presbyterians for the CRC to join them were also declined. Objections began with the use of hymns during Presbyterian worship, which had been one of the complaints against the RCA.[15] More importantly, the Presbyterians did not subscribe to the Church Order of Dordt, which the Dutch immigrants held as absolute, as Brinks notes.[16] The Presbyterian willingness to permit Dutch-speaking congregations to subscribe to Dordtian church order was not enough to assuage this concern by the CRC, because of the Presbyterian insistence that all church business be conducted in English, a language with which the Dutch immigrants, as a whole, were not fluent.[17] The discussions of union culminated at the July 1863 classis held at Zeeland, where Milwaukee, a congregation that has joined the CRC few months earlier, had Vanden Bosch formally propose joining the Old School Presbyterians whose doctrine as late as 1869 the CRC recognized as pure and acceptable.[18]

Shortly before that classis, Wilhelmus H. Van Leeuwen had come from the Netherlands to lead the Grand Rapids congregation, as the second CRC minister. He preached the opening sermon at the classis to a large crowd.[19] Enthused by this reception and the fact that a second minister had been obtained, the CRC decided against union. As a result Milwaukee, which saw little chance for obtaining a minister in the near future, left the CRC for the Presbyterian Church, which was organizing a number of Dutch congregations in Wisconsin.[20] But contact continued with the CRC ultimately absorbing a number of the West Michigan Presbyterian congregations. South Holland joined Graafschap CRC in 1867, Zeeland joined the First Zeeland CRC in 1874, and Drenthe organized as a CRC congregation in 1886.

As this contact with the Presbyterians began, the CRC also had to deal with challenges to the group's viability. The October 1857 classis received reports that Klijn had returned to the RCA and that Polkton, having sent no delegates, had opened its pulpit to any Dutch minister, regardless of denominational affiliation.[21] Within months, Polkton also returned to the RCA. These disappointments were balanced a bit by news that Vanden Bosch had organized a congregation at Vriesland, Michigan (a few miles east of Zeeland) on 17 April 1857.[22] Less than a year later a small group in Zeeland wanted to organize as a congregation, but was not permitted to do so until 1864.[23]

Choosing a Name

The organization of Vriesland and interest from Zeeland buoyed the CRC sufficiently so that in 1858 classis could began considering the matter of a name for the group. This proved to be particularly nettlesome, perhaps reflecting the CRC's uncertainty of its own identity, and the discussion had to be tabled when a consensus could not be reached. Three classical meetings later, the name Holland Reformed Church was approved.[24] This caused confusion for governmental officials since the RCA at the time was known as the Dutch Protestant Reformed Church.[25] Therefore in 1863 the name was changed to True Holland Reformed Church.[26]

The debate over the name continued. In 1864 Jacob R. Schepers, seated at classis as a fraternal delegate, unsuccessfully suggested changing the name to Christian Seceding, to reflect the name of the denomination in the Netherlands. Later in 1864 and twice in 1867, the Paterson, New Jersey, congregation asked that word True be removed so that immigrants could more easily distinguish between the Dutch speaking CRC and the English speaking True Protestant Dutch Reformed Church.[27] Repeated suggestions in 1868 by Vriesland, in 1872 and 1877 by Classis Illinois to remove True from the name were rejected. Not until 1880, when the members of the CRC realized (as well be demonstrated below) that they were a unique denomination was a consensus on a name achieved – Holland Christian Reformed Church.[28]

Relationships With the Seceders in the Netherlands

During these same years, the CRC repeatedly and unsuccessful sought direct linkage to the *Christelijke Afgescheidene Gemeenten* and its successor in the Netherlands. This linkage was sought because the CRC considered members of the Dutch church their theological kinsmen. Further, such a tie would have greatly facilitated the transfer of memberships and ministerial credentials for those emigrating to the United States. This immigration was crucial to growth of the nascent CRC which insisted on maintaining Dutch as its ecclesiastical language.

The effort at linkage caused a bit of a problem within the CRC since its members were from both this larger Dutch branch in the *Afscheiding* and the smaller *Gereformeerde Kerken onder het Kruis (Kruisgezinden)*.[29] In 1844 the *Kruisgezinden* had formed their own denomination.[30] This division was very much in evidence in the early CRC even though those from the *Kruisgezinden* were the minority in the CRC, because they filled prominent roles such as Jan Gelock, a lay leader in both the Grand Rapids congregation and in the denomination until death in 1889. Apparently a number of people in Grand Rapids were from the *Kruisgezinde* tradition, for already in 1858 the congregation asked classis for permission to call a *Kruisgezinde* minister. Since the majority in the CRC was from the larger *Christelijke Afgescheidene Gemeenten*, classis decided that such ministers were outside the pool of those that guaranteed ecclesiastic purity and therefore required that they be examined for orthodoxy. Grand Rapids then flirted with joining the Presbyterian Church by opening its pulpit to ministers from that denomination without classical approval. In 1863 Grand Rapids made its unhappiness again know to classis and received permission to call W.H. Van Leeuwen, a former minister in the *Kruisgezinden*. The next year, in October, Douwe J. Vander Werp, who had also begun his ministry in the *Kruisgezinden*, arrived to lead the Graafschap congregation. Presumably, both underwent some sort of examination, although there is no record of this.

The desire for a direct relationship with the church in the Netherlands was so strong that in 1860, without classical approval, Graafschap declared that it was affiliated with the Dutch church. Classis reprimanded Graafschap for exceeding its authority but also quickly noted that such affiliation was not necessarily wrong. Yet approval of such linkage did not come from the *Christelijke Afgescheidene Gereformeerde Kerken*, instead such status was accorded the RCA.[31] The CRC complaint that it was being treated as stepsister received the non-committal reply in 1860 that the Dutch church recognized all churches who followed Reformed doctrine and church polity.[32]

This perceived rebuff from the Dutch church quieted the CRC efforts at linkage until Van Leeuwen took up the issue shortly after his arrival in 1863. In addition to offering to teach any students for the ministry in his parsonage and prodding the denomination to inaugurate a mission program,[33] Van Leeuwen seems to have been confident that he could obtain the recognition from the *Christelijke Afgescheidene Gereformeerde Kerken*. His efforts had the same result as those of 1860 since the Dutch church still could not understand the reasons for CRC separation from the RCA.[34]

The failure to receive *Christelijke Afgescheidene Gereformeerde Kerken* recognition in 1863 was much better received than it had been in 1860 and for a few years the efforts at linkage seem to have been put in abeyance. One reason may have been that the United States Civil War had stanched the flow of immigrants, making the need for easier transferring of memberships and credentials less immediate. Further, the pressing need for ministers from the Netherlands was ameliorated somewhat with the arrival of Van Leeuwen and Vander Werp and success in recruiting ministerial candidates from the CRC's own numbers. In 1864 Jan Schepers, a member of the Vriesland congregation, presented himself to be trained for the ministry. After being approved for this by classis, he began introductory instruction with Van Leeuwen, who had been a teacher prior to entering the ministry, a year later classis assigned him to study theology with Vander Werp.[35]

Growth Through New Wave of Immigrants
With the end of the U.S. Civil War, the wave of Dutch immigrants began to build, particularly from the northern Netherlands. In spite of the lack of recognition from *Christelijke Afgescheidene Gereformeerde Kerken*, a sizable number of these immigrants joined the CRC. Between 1864 and 1870, fourteen congregations joined the denomination. Interestingly, more than half of these came to the CRC following dissatisfaction with other affiliations. The first of these was Paterson which successively had been in the RCA and the *Kruisgezinden*.[36] Pella (1866) and Chicago (1867) both had been in contact with the RCA. Cincinnati (1866), Wellsburg (1868)[37]

Figure 1: - Growth of the Christian Reformed Church, 1857-1907

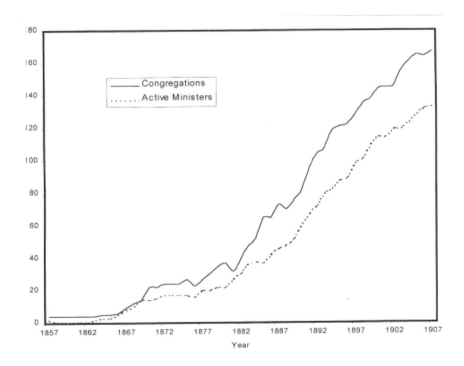

Source: Database of CRC statistics from Classical, General Assembly, and Synodical Minutes, 1857-1907; *Yearbooks* of the CRC, 1880-1907; and biographical data on CRC pastors compile by the author and available at the Archives in Heritage Hall, Calvin College, Grand Rapids, MI. Since consecutive membership data is not available until 1880, with publication of the yearbooks, the numbers of congregations and ministers are used as a proxy for growth since reports on total membership do not begin until 1880 and these report have significant missing data.

and Lafayette (1869) had had contact with, or part of, the Presbyterian Church, while Grand Haven (1866) and East Saugatuck (1869) had among their founding members those who had belonged to the Presbyterian Church. The growth of the CRC following the Civil War in indicated by the solid line on Chart I.

As this growth began, there was also an influx of six ministers in rapid succession beginning in 1866 with Willem Frieling and Arend H. Bechtold. Roelof Duiker, Johan B. DeBeer, Hendrik R. Koopmans, and Ede L. Meinders joined the next year. This growth caused the denomination to be divided into two classes.[38] Unfortunately, five of the six ministers left for the RCA, four within the next five years. Bechtold left within a matter of months, De Beer in 1868, Koopmans in 1869, Duiker in 1872,[39] and Meinders in 1886. The CRC dealt with this depletion was offset somewhat by calling ministers from the Netherlands and by graduating parsonage trained ministers, Jan Schepers in 1868, Jacob Noordewier, Jan Stadt, Jr., and Willem Greve in 1869. The demand for ministers, however, continued to outpace the supply (see Chart II).

Publication and Publicity

This growth somewhat eased the financial impecunity that the CRC had experienced since 1857. As a result a church periodical was begun, which also proved to be a further step in establishing CRC legitimacy in the eyes of others. A half-hearted effort in 1867 led to one issue of *Stem Uit Het Westen* (Voice from the West). This was followed six months later with *De Wachter* (The Watchman) published by Cornelius Vorst in Holland, Michigan and edited by Vander Werp, who continued pastoring the Graafschap congregation and tutoring theological students. According to Vorst, the purpose of *De Wachter* was to counter the attacks on the CRC by *De Hope*, whose editor was a RCA member.[40] *De Wachter* provided the CRC with an official voice emanating from Holland, the center of nineteenth-century Dutch immigration to West Michigan.

Shortly after the copies of *De Wachter* were sent to the Reformed Church of South, the CRC received formal recognition from that church. Begun be missionaries from the *Hervormde Kerk*, the South African church, organized in 1859, held the Church Order of Dordt, the Heidleberg Catechism, and the Belgic Confessions as their forms of unity. Theologically and ethnically both were from the same branch of the Reformed faith.[41] Because CRC wanted to participate in missions, but did not yet have the means to establish its own mission program, it sent money to the South African church for its mission work.[42]

Free copies of *De Wachter* to the Netherlands also produced interest and rekindled efforts at linkage by the CRC.[43] In 1869, as the *Christelijke Afgescheidene Gereformeerde Kerken* and most of the *Kruisgezinden* were in the process of merging into the *Christelijke Gereformeerde Kerk* (CGK), Rev. J. Nentjes of the Noord Holland provincial assembly wrote the CRC asking for an explanation of separation from the

RCA in 1857.[44] The CRC immediately set about collecting the necessary information, including statements from the True Protestant Dutch Reformed Church[45] delineating why it had left the RCA in 1822. Vander Werp and Rev. Frederik Hulst, who had come from the Netherlands a few months earlier, were assigned the task of collecting and compiling the data.

To insure that this information would reach the Netherlands in time for their synodical meeting, the CRC's general assembly met in April 1869, two months earlier than scheduled. The response was published and distributed as *Brochure op Kerkelijk Gebied*.[46] One copy was specifically sent to Van Velzen, head of the Dutch church's theological school in Kampen.[47] The brochure does little to explain the events of 1857, instead focussing on what had happened in the RCA between 1857 and 1869 to support the validity of the 1857 secession. For the CGK, the desired explanation was not provided and no official ties resulted.

But the brochure did have an impact. On July 6, 1869, Van Velzen wrote Classis Michigan a letter acknowledging receipt of the brochure and accompanying letter. He went on to state that it seemed to him that the RCA was following the same course as that of the *Hervormde Kerk* since the secession of 1834. He also explained the Dutch synod's decision by noting it had not been able to choose one side or the other, instead deciding to open ecclesiastical fellowship to both the RCA and the CRC, allowing its ministers and members to transfer to either denomination.[48] For the CRC, this equality in recognition, although short of the desired linkage, was a significant accomplishment.

Education

Another development during the late 1860s that caused the CRC to further and more concretely define itself as a Dutch and a Reformed denomination, distinct from other forms of Protestantism in the United States was support for Christian day schools.[49] Although members from both the RCA and the CRC supported and opposed such schools, ultimately most in the CRC supported separate Christian day schools, while most in the RCA saw little need for such separation. Many, including Van Raalte, saw schooling as a means to Americanization and the unique American system of local control of the public schools provided sufficient assurance that Christian education, even in Dutch in some locations, could be provided in the public schools. But others, particularly those in the CRC, based on their experiences in the Netherlands with government controlled public education, were unsure that such arrangements are benefit everyone. They further felt that schooling both provided education and served as a means for preserving the faith which imbued education with a greater urgency.[50] Initially, because of limited financial means, such instruction was limited to sessions during the summer or on Sundays supplementary to the education provided through the public school structures.[51]

During the 1860s, it became clear to the parents that their children could do little with a Dutch language education in an English speaking world. Limited measures were attempted to provide some education in English, within the Dutch curriculum. In 1864, for instance, Van Leeuwen was asked to contact the English speaking True Protestant Dutch Reformed church for suitable English language books. And in 1869, Jacob R. Schepers, on the verge of transferring to the CRC, was asked by the CRC general assembly to investigate suitable books in English that could be used for instruction in Christian day schools.[52] By the end of the decade, in spite of the importance a Dutch in ecclesiastical situations, day school education was delivered in English, rather than Dutch.[53]

The concession on language of instruction did not diminish support for separate Christian day schools. By the 1870s, as a bit more money became available to CRC members, the drumbeat to support Christian day schools grew. At that 1871 general assembly, the delegates were charged to look for specific people within the denomination who had an aptitude for teaching.[54] Two years latter that matter was made more imperative with each congregation instructed to establish both Christian day schools and Sunday schools.[55] The next year each congregation was asked to publicly report on progress that had been made toward this goal.[56] As a result support for Christian day schools fell more and more within the purview of the CRC ultimately becoming a point of demarcation with the RCA.

As support for Christian day schools began to grow within the CRC, Vander Werp began to advocate opening a theological school. The CRC could look to the South African Church as a model. That church established a theological school to train its own ministers with two instructors and five students in November 1869.[57] At the CRC general assembly of 1870 Vander Werp proposed such a school. The proposal was well received, but lack of funding prevented its adoption.[58] The next year's assembly also deferred due to lack of finances, but did provide funds for William Hellenthal to study at the Kampen theological school of the CGK.[59] A graduate of Hope College, in Holland, Michigan, Hellenthal wished to study for the ministry in the CRC and his formal training at Hope had prepared him for more than tutoring in a parsonage. Any hopes for more direct linkage to the CGK through Hellenthal ended when he died of small pox, shortly after arriving in the Netherlands.

Seminary
The need for ministers in the CRC continued. Vander Werp's 1873 request again was declined due to lack of finances, did lead to an inquiry about the qualifications of a Kampen student for teaching in place of Vander Werp. During the 1874 discussion of the need for a school, the Grand Rapids delegates proposed calling a minister to their congregation, who could also teach in a theological school, rather than in the parsonage. In this manner, the congregation and the denomination could share the expense. The assembly acceded to this and a trio of ministers from the

197

Netherlands was formed.[60] All three ultimately declined to come and Vander Werp continued teaching, with a denominational stipend for the first time in addition to his ministerial salary.

At the 1875 general assembly another trio was formed with J. Bavinck as the first choice. Bavinck declined, and because of the national economic depression in the United States during the mid 1870s, neither of the others was called.[61] A few months later Vander Werp was diagnosed with oral cancer and could no longer teach. Classis Michigan arranged to have Gerrit E. Boer, an 1865 graduate of Kampen who had come to serve the Grand Rapids congregation in 1873, teach the students provisionally until the next general assembly. Because of the urgent need for an instructor, the assembly met in February, four months ahead of schedule. The two efforts to call a professor from the Netherlands having failed, the assembly realized that serious action was need. All agreed that $1,800, for salary, housing and moving expenses, would be needed to call an instructor. An additional $300 to $1,000 would be needed for moving expenses if this person came from the Netherlands.[62] Such an amount seemed beyond reach, so it was decided to call a CRC minister rather than one from the Netherlands.

This decision marks the beginning of a redefinition of how the CRC saw itself. Granted, when Gerrit E. Boer accepted the call to be the docent, he was required to agree that the CRC was "a historical continuation of the church in the Netherlands,"[63] and the model for the theological school, in terms of curriculum, governance, and student regulations, was Kampen.[64] But from this point forward the need to support a theological school forced the CRC to come together as a denomination. After 1876 there is indication of any CRC efforts at becoming part of the CGK as had been the case until that point.

Economic necessity further forced the CRC to select a geographic focal point, other than Holland, Michigan, then generally viewed as the center of West Michigan Dutch immigration. In addition to providing $1,300 for Boer's salary and housing, there was the matter of finding a facility to house the theological school. The solutions came from Grand Rapids whose congregation offered free housing plus $400 toward the salary, if Boer were allowed to remain in Grand Rapids.[65] Seeing no other possibility raising the needed funds, the general assembly accepted. Grand Rapids further offered the upper floor of its primary school as a location for the theological instruction at a modest rent of $52 annually. The two-story brick building had been completed just the year before and had a large room upstairs that could be used for a lecture hall and a smaller room for tutorial instruction. This offer also was accepted.[66]

The location of the theological school at Grand Rapids came a time when the city was on the verge of dramatic economic growth resulting from the sudden expansion of the furniture industry. This expansion created many jobs which drew a large numbers of Dutch immigrants to Grand Rapids, giving the city an ever

Figure 2: Minsterial Corps of the CRC *Percentage of Denominationally Trained Ministers*

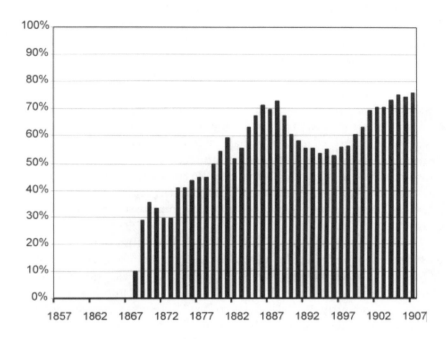

Source: database of CRC statistics from Classical, General Assembly and Synodical minutes, 1857-1907; *Yearbooks* of the CRC, 1875, 1881-1907; and biographical data on CRC pastors compiled by the author and available in heritage Hall, Calvin College, Grand Rapids, Michigan.

increasing numeric, and resultant economic, edge over other cities with CRC congregations. Between 1879 and 1889 six new congregations organized in Grand Rapids: Eastern Avenue in 1879, two years later Alpine Avenue, in 1884 Coldbrook Avenue joined, having left the RCA three years earlier, in 1887 both Franklin (Fifth Avenue) Street and Lagrave Avenue, and in 1889 West Leonard Street. Other communities, particularly Holland and Zeeland, did not acquiesce to the school's location in Grand Rapids. But the requests to move the school and offers of facilities for the school various subsequent general assemblies and synods failed.[67] Grand Rapids became the focal point of the CRC.

The school began to supply a steady flow of ministerial candidates into the denomination. But the growth of CRC during the 1880s, due also in some measure to the Masonic controversy in the RCA that resulted in the CGK recommending their departing members joint he CRC rather than the RCA,[68] and the growth of immigration, was such that the school's graduates could not closed the gap with the ever growing number of congregations (see Chart I). But the school did provide, for the first time, a relatively stable percentage of the total minister corps to be CRC trained (see Chart II).

Another indication that the CRC finally saw itself as a unique denomination came at the 1879 general assembly. The delegates agreed to the proposal, this time from Classis Iowa to assume the title of synod in place, whereas a general assembly would have been between synod and classis. In Reformed churches a synod is the highest court. Moreover, the delegates approved extending correspondence beyond the GKN and the Reformed Church of South Africa to include the *Alt Reformierte Kirche* in Germany and the Free Evangelical Church in Silesia.[69] Feelings toward the RCA were not ameliorated. Classis Illinois considered one of Boer's statements that the RCA was a sister church to be "a slap in the face" and he was forced to explain that he meant the RCA was a sister church in confession, but not so in practice and teaching.[70]

A sense of the identity forging process can be drawn from Table I. Note that the first United Statets trained presiding officer was elected in 1879.[71] During the 1890s those trained at the CRC's Theological School consistently begin to be elected to the post. The process had taken more than two decades, and did not have as its goal, the goal that was achieved. The CRC, wanting to be different from the RCA by returning to what its members saw as the theological fundamentals, were forced to form a new denomination, rather than returning to a former structure. The question now becomes: have former and later divisions within the Reformed community had similar experiences? Is the CRC case typical or atypical? Careful analysis of recent divisions in the CRC, for instance, may shed some light on this.

Table 1: General Assemblies/Synods and Presiding Officers

Year	Location	President Officer	Training of Presiding Officer
1865	Graafschap	Douwe J. Vander Werp	H. De Cock/T.F. DeHaan
1866	Grand Rapids	Douwe J. Vander Werp	H. De Cock/T.F. DeHaan
1867	Grand Rapids	Douwe J. Vander Werp	H. De Cock/T.F. DeHaan
1868	Graafschap	Roelof Duiker	W.A. Kok
1869	Chicago	Koenraad Vanden Bosch	W.A. Kok/F.A. Kok
1870	Chicago	Willem H. Frieling	W.A. Kok
1871	Chicago	Roelof Duiker	W.A. Kok
1872	Chicago	Douwe J. Vander Werp	H. De Cock/T.F. DeHaan
1873	Chicago	Koenraad Vanden Bosch	W.A. Kok/F.A. Kok
1874	Chicago	Douwe J. Vander Werp	H. De Cock/T.F. DeHaan
1875	Chicago	Willem H. Frieling	W.A. Kok
1876	Chicago	Gerrit E. Boer	Kampen
1877	Chicago	Willem H. Frieling	W.A. Kok
1878	Chicago	John Kremer	Kampen
1879	Chicago	Leendert Rietdijk	D.J. Vander Werp
1880	Chicago	Roelof T. Kuiper	W.A. Kok
1881	Grand Rapids	Leenert Rietdijk	D.J. Vander Werp
1882	Grand Rapids	Willem H. Frieling	W.A. Kok
1883	Grand Rapids	Jan H. Vos	W.A. Kok, Kampen
1884	Grand Rapids	Lammert J. Hulst	W.A. Kok/T.F. DeHaan
1886	Grand Rapids	Leenert Rietdijk	D.J. Vander Werp
1888	Grand Rapids	Evert Bos	Kampen
1890	Grand Rapids	Lammert J. Hulst	W.A. Kok/T.F. DeHaan
1892	Grand Rapids	Andrew Keizer	CRC
1994	Grand Rapids	Klaas Kuiper	Kampen
1896	Grand Rapids	Andrew Keizer	CRC
1898	Grand Rapids	Jacob Manni	CRC
1900	Grand Rapids	Andrew Keizer	CRC
1902	Holland	Gabriel D. De Jong	CRC
1904	Holland	Evert Breen	CRC
1906	Holland	Hendrik Van Hoogen	Kampen
1908	Muskegon	Jacob Manni	CRC

Source: Minutes of CRC General Assemblies and Synods, 1865-1907; Biographical data on CRC Ministers, Archives in Heritage Hall, Calvin College, Grand Rapids, MI.

Notes

1. These reasons are succinctly presented in footnote 1 of: Herbert J. Brinks, "Religious Continuities in Europe and the New World," in Robert P. Swierenga, ed., *The Dutch in America: Immigration, Settlement, and Cultural Change* (New Brunswick: Rutgers University Press, 1985), 219-220.

2. A thorough presentation of this dissatisfaction is presented in chapter 3 of Elton J. Bruins and Robert P. Swierenga, *Family Quarrels in the Dutch Reformed Churches of the 19th Century* (Grand Rapids: Eerdmans, 1999). Bruins and Swierenga have woven together the events in South Holland (Michigan) in 1852, with those in Drenthe in 1853, with those culminating in 1857 in Graafschap, Grand Rapids, Noordeloos and Polkton.

3. Bruins and Swierenga, *Family Quarrels*; for a summary of the, at times vitriolic, polemics from both side on the legitimacy of what happened in 1857 see the fine bibliographic essay on pages 139-140.

4. The net flow of ministers between the two denominations favored the RCA, with six leaving the RCA for the CRC and twentytwo leaving the CRC for the RCA. Source, author's database of biographical information about CRC ministers.

5. Statistics are drawn from CRC Yearbooks, 1875, 1881-1907; CRC Classical Minutes, 1857-1870; and CRC General Assembly Minutes, 1865-1880.

6. James D. Bratt, *Dutch Calvinism in Modern America: A History of a Conservative Subculture* (Grand Rapids: Eerdmans, 1984), see particularly his table on 222-223.

7. Although *Hervormde Kerk* can be accurately translated as Reformed Church, due to the several Dutch words that were used in naming denominations that can be translated by the English word Reformed, the original Dutch names will be used in this article.

8. Brinks, "Religious Continuities," 209-223.

9. See for instance: Menno Borduin, "Het Hollandsche Element in de Presbyteriaansche Kerk," *De Gereformeerde Amerikaan* 8 (March 1904): 119-125 and Gerrit Bieze, "The Holland Presbyterian Churches in America, c.1850-1925," unpublished manuscript, Archives in Heritage Hall, Calvin College, Grand Rapids, Michigan. The whole matter of Dutch Presbyterianism requires extensive and detailed research, which is beyond the scope of this paper.

10. Geert Egberts Boer summarizes this view when discussing the importance of Christian day school, *De Wachter* 8 (16 September 1875): 1.

11. Vanden Bosch traveled by ox cart, initially blazing his own paths to Grand Rapids, about thirty miles eastward, Vriesland fifteen miles eastward and southward, or Graafschap, ten miles southward.

12. CRC Classical Minutes, 7 October 1857 reports that Rev. Vanden Bosch was to go to the Grand Haven congregation to administer baptism. For convenience, the movement that begins with the 1857 secession will be called the CRC, even though denominational identity does not come until the late 1870s.

13. Art. 15, CRC Classical Minutes, 5 April 1861, Peter. D. Van Vliet, "Christian Reformed Grand Haven," *The Banner* (6 May 1909): 292-293, and Bieze, "The Holland Presbyterian Churches," 8. The economic depression of the late 1850s caused the congregation to dwindle, with the remnant joining the CRC as a branch of the Noordeloos congregation in 1861. Vanden Bosch at one point claimed the Grand Haven branch was independent due to its former status as a Presbyterian congregation (Art. 7, CRC Classical minutes, 1 June 1864) but classis viewed the group as a branch of first Noordeloos and later Grand Rapids, until they organized in 1866. See: CRC Classical Minutes: Art. 13, 3 February 1863; Art. 10, 1 June 1864; Art. 9, 5 April 1865; and Art. 8, 21 February 1866.

14. Art. 3, Minutes of the Drenthe Scots Presbyterian Church, 17 August 1860, Heritage Hall, Calvin College, Grand Rapids, Michigan.

15. CRC Classical Minutes, Art, 7, 4 February 1863 and Art. 4, 3 February 1864.

16. Brinks, "Religious Continuities."

17. CRC Classical Minutes, Art. 7, 4 February 1863; Art. 9, 22 July 1863.

18. In 1859 Smit tried to mediate conflict between members in Zeeland and Noordleoos, CRC Classical Minutes, Art. 3 and Art. 6, 5 October 1859 and Art. 9, 1 October 1862. In 1861 Smit unsuccessfully proposed a joint publication program between the West Michigan Dutch Presbyterian congregations and the CRC, CRC Classical Minutes Art. 2, 5 June 1861.

19. W.H. Van Leeuwen, "Leerrede Gehouden Ter Opening Onzer Klassicale Vergadering" (Grand Rapids: J. Quintus, 1863) available in the Archives in Heritage Hall, Calvin College, Grand Rapids, MI. In the introduction Quintus quotes the newspaper coverage of the event from *De Grondwet*, 29 July 1863 which indicates that Dutch members of the CRC, the RCA, and the Old School Presbyterians, packed the church and stood outside to hear the sermon).

20. In 1862 Vanden Bosch went to Milwaukee and established a congregation (CRC Classical Minutes, Art. 11, 1 October 1862), but there is no specific mention that this congregation joined the CRC. Presumably this is the Wisconsin congregation mentioned in the next classical meeting (Art. 7, 4 February 1863). According to Borduin the lack of ministers in the CRC, caused this congregation to join the Presbyterian church, Menno Borduin, "Het Hollandsche Element in de Presbyteriaansche Kerk," *De Gereformeerde Amerikaan* 8 (March 1904): 121. For a discussion of the Presbyterian Church in Wisconsin, see: Gerrit Bieze, "The Holland Presbyterian Churches in America, c. 1850-1925," unpublished manuscript, Archives in Heritage Hall, Calvin College, Grand Rapids, MI.

21. CRC Classical Minutes, 7 October 1857. The clerk of that session made many spelling errors and did not divide the minutes into separate articles.

22. Notulen (Minutes), T.R.D.C., 1857-1894, Vriesland, MI, Archives in Heritage Hall, Calvin College, Grand Rapids, Michigan.

23. At the same time forty families in the Zeeland RCA congregation, being denied permission by Classis Holland of the RCA to organize a second congregation, joined the United Presbyterian Church. In 1874, this congregation sold its church building to and most of the members joined the Zeeland CRC. CRC Classical Minutes, Art. 4, 20 October 1858; Minutes of the First Old School Presbyterian Church of Zeeland, 1863-1874, Archives in Heritage Hall, Calvin College, Grand Rapids, MI. Zeeland had begun as a branch of Noordeloos and its organization occurred in 1862, again in 1864 and again in 1866, resulted from repeated protests from Vanden Bosch who insisted he was the lawful minister of Zeeland and Zeeland's equally insistent position that he was not. Numerous efforts to mediate having failed at both the classical and general assembly levels, Classis Michigan in 1869 dictated that he had been, but was no longer the minister of Zeeland and that the organization of 1864 was valid, to which Vanden Bosch protested to no avail. CRC General Assembly Minutes, Art. 38, 1872; Classis Michigan Minutes, Art. 22, 28 April 1969. See the note on p. 196 of: Gerrit J. Haan, "Geschiedenis der Eerste Chr, Geref. Kerk van Zeeland, Michigan," *De Gereformeerde Amerikaan* 6 (May 1902) for a summary of the First Presbyterians Old School congregation. More detail can also be found in *First Zeeland crc Centennial, 1862-1962* (Zeeland: 1962), 11, 15.

24. CRC Classical Minutes, Art. 4, 2 February 1859.

25. Minutes of the General Assembly, Art. 47-48, 1879.

26. CRC Classical Minutes, Art. 9, 22 July 1863.

27. This church seceded from the RCA in 1822 and was located primarily in eastern New York and New Jersey. Although English speaking, this denomination and the CRC perceived a commonality since both had left the RCA. For an example of this commonality see: Herbert J. Brinks, "Church History via Kalamazoo, 1850-1860," *Origins* 16.1 (1998): 36-42.

28. Minutes of the General Assembly: Art. 22, 1867; Art. 22, 1869; Art. 18, 1872; Art. 37, 1877; Art. 47-48, 1880.

29. That is, the Christian Seceded Congregations and the Reformed Churches under the Cross.

30. Bruins and Swierenga, *Family Quarrels*, 30; in 1844.

31. The *Christelijke Afgescheidene Gereformeerde Kerken* themselves were a small minority on the Dutch Reformed scene and having received recognition from the RCA were perhaps reluctant to recognize secessionists from the RCA. According to 1856 data, 2.7 percent of Dutch reformed congregants belonged to the *afgescheidene* churches, while 96.8 percent belonged to the state church. *The Christian Intelligencer* (25 September 1856): 50.
32. CRC Classical Minutes, Art. 9, 3 October 1860.
33. Ibid., Art. 3, 22 July 1863.
34. Van Raalte's visit in 1866 the Dutch church's synod in the Netherlands, in which his brothers-in-law Simon Van Velzen and Anthony Brummelkamp both were ministers, understandably did little to help the Dutch church understand why the immigrant church community had divided.
35. Schepers was a cousin of Jacob R. Schepers. For an a brief biography of Jan Schepers see: Richard H. Harms, "Jan Schepers, 1832-1902: Pioneer Pastor," *Origins* 16.2 (1998): 50-52.
36. Under the leadership of its minister, J. De Rooij, the congregations had affiliated with the RCA 1856-61 and with the Kruisgezinden, 1861-62. *Mededeelingen uit de Historie der Eerste Chr. Ger. Gemeente te Paterson, NJ* (Paterson: De Telegraaf Drukkerij, 1906), 5-8.
37. For a summary of the Wellsburg (Steamboat Rock) experience see: Ede. L. Meinders, "Rise of this Church," unpublished manuscript in the Archives in Heritage Hall, Calvin College, Grand Rapids, Michigan.
38. Art. 11, Minutes of CRC General Assembly, 1868.
39. Duiker returned to the CRC in 1881 but then went back to RCA a second time in 1887. He was much respected in the CRC serving a the president of the General Assembly in 1868, one year after his arrival, and again in 1871.
40. *De Wachter* 7 (18 March 1876): 2.
41. John Dolfin, "The Reformed Church of South Africa," *The Banner* (4 February 1909): 72-76.
42. CRC Classical Minutes, Art. 47, 2 October 1867; Classis Michigan Minutes, Art. 20, 2 September 1868; and the goodwill is notes in CRC General Assembly Minutes, Art. 27, 1871.
43. Classis Michigan minutes, Art. 14, 8 January 1868 and Art. 20, 2 September 1868.
44. CRC Classical Minutes, Art. 30, 6 January 1869.
45. The True Reformed Protestant Dutch (TRPD) church in New York and New Jersey had separated from the RCA in 1822. TRPD minister John Berdan was known among the West Michigan Dutch through his letters to Paulus Den Blyker during the mid 1850s that were critical of the RCA and had circulated through the Dutch immigrant community. Herbert J. Brinks, "Church History via Kalamazoo, 1850-1860," *Origins* 16.1 (1998): 41. The CRC classis corresponded with Berdan about possible union for several years during the late 1850s and early 1860s. Talk of union between the two ended because the TRPD used hymns and denied infant baptism. Van Leeuwen, reinvigorated the discussion shortly after his arrival in 1863. The subsequent discussions were amicable leading to closer ties and full union in 1890.
46. [Douwe J. Vander Werp], *Brochures op Kerkelijk Gebied* (Holland, MI: C. Vorst, 1869). An English translation available in the Archives in Heritage Hall, Calvin College, Grand Rapids, Michigan For a brief discussion of these efforts see, Kromminga, *The Christian Reformed Tradition*, 120-121.
47. Classis Michigan minutes, Art. 17, 20 April 1869.
48. Classis Michigan minutes, Art. 29, 29 September 1869.
49. James D. Bratt, "The Reformed Churches and Acculturation," in Swierenga, ed., *The Dutch in America*, 194-195.
50. Bruins and Swierenga, *Family Quarrels*, 73
51. For a detail discussion of CRC schools see: George Stob, "The Christian Reformed Church and Her Schools," (Th.D. dissertation, Princeton Theological Seminary, 1955). Stob notes in chapter 5 that the premise of such schools was to provide a sound Reformed and Dutch instructional foundation for public education.

52. CRC Classical Minutes, Art. 7, 3 February 1864; CRC General Assembly Minutes, Art. 25, 1869. Another language factor had developed in 1866 when Ridott, Illinois joined the CRC. Ridott was made up of German immigrants from the *Alte Reformierde Kirche*. These immigrants spoke primarily German, unlike the German immigrants in Graafschap, Michigan who used Dutch in their liturgy, and were as familiar with Dutch as with German. For a more detailed discussion of the German speaking immigrants in the CRC, see: Herbert J. Brinks, "Ostfrisians in Two Worlds," in Peter De Klerk and Richard R. De Ridder, eds., *Perspectives on the Christian Reformed Church: Studies in Its History, Theology, and Ecumenicity* (Grand Rapids: Baker Book House, 1983).

53. In 1875 the CRC general assembly formally decided to remove Dutch as a requirement in Christian day schools. CRC General Assembly Minutes, Art. 4, 1875.

54. Ibid., Art. 21, 1871.

55. Ibid., Art. 8, 1873.

56. Of the nineteen congregations represented, six reported operating schools, with Grand Rapids having the best program with a building, a teacher, and an assistant teacher. One of the six, Muskegon, reported operating a school in cooperation with the RCA congregation in that city. Nine congregations reported that they had no school nor did it appear that this would occur in the foreseeable future. Of the remaining four, Niekerk reported that it had had a school, but not at present; Paterson, NJ was providing some language instruction on Sundays; Graafschap had a building but no teacher; and Holland indicated that it was working on establishing a school. Grand Rapids, Muskegon, Grand Haven, Kalamazoo, Vriesland, (all in Michigan) and South Holland, IL had a functioning program, interestingly Vriesland complained that its schools, which were publicly supported did not teach enough in English. Cleveland and Cincinnati, OH, Lafayette, IN, Chicago, Collendoorn (East Saugatuck), MI, Ridott, Noordeloos and Zeeland reported no schools. CRC General Assembly Minutes, Art. 4, 1875.

57. John Dolfin, "The Reformed Church of South Africa," 73-74.

58. CRC General Assembly Minutes, Art. 32, 1870.

59. Ibid., Arts. 39 and 40, 1871.

60. Ibid., Art. 15, 1873 and Art. 15, 1874.

61. Ibid., Art. 10, 1876.

62. Ibid., Art. 18, 1876.

63. Ibid., Arts. 21-22, 1876.

64. Ibid., Arts. 26, 30, and 34, 1876. For a fuller description of the school see Stob, "The Christian Reformed Church and her Schools," chapter 8.

65. The students also petitioned to stay in Grand Rapids. Assembly Minutes, Art. 29, 1876. Apparently from their few months with Boer, they preferred Grand Rapids to Muskegon, where they had studied with Vander Werp. CRC General Assembly Minutes, Art. 29, 1876.

66. CRC General Assembly Minutes, Arts. 26-28, 1876. It could also be argued that holding the general assembly meetings in Chicago was part of this shift in focus away from Holland, but it seems Chicago was the more centrally located rail connection for the various congregations and thus this could have been more of a practical consideration.

67. CRC General Assembly Minutes, Art. 37, 1877 and Art. 28, 1878.

68. Much has been written on the Masonic controversy, see for instance Kromminga, *The Christian Reformed Tradition*, 116-118 and Bruins and Swierenga, *Family Quarrels*, chapter 4.

69. CRC General Assembly Minutes, Art. 18a, 1879. Rev. Matse of the Silesian church had been a fraternal delegate at the 1878 general assembly.

70. Ibid., Art. 31.

71. Since the presiding officers are elected by the delegates, the choice can be seen as a measure of ability and respect accorded by peers.

Earliest known image of the Williams Street School, where
the Theological School held classes on the second floor.
Archives: Calvin College, Grand Rapids, MI

Section 5

Portrait Gallery

Lammert J. Hulst

Lammert J. Hulst: The Pastor as Leader in an Immigrant Community

James D. Bratt

Robert Swierenga's work on Dutch-American immigration offers a twofold testimony to the themes of continuity and persistence. It testifies in the first place to the remarkable perseverance in pursuing his task that has made Bob a model among students and scholars alike, and that has produced a series of data and publications unparalleled in American immigration historiography for comprehensive scrutiny of their subject population. In the second place his analysis discloses how fully his subjects shared these qualities with the author. The chains of Dutch migration were closely linked indeed, and the climate, soils, occupations, and social networks that the emigrants left behind they managed to find or replicate, time and again, at the end of their journey. We come away from reading Bob's studies convinced that the Dutch of the nineteenth century did not so much seek a new life in America as opportunities to reclaim an old life, and that they achieved this end.[1] This story of determination and success might seem to offer up yet a third testimony, to the "American dream," except that the persistence of the past and the disinclination for the new contradicts some dearly held convictions of American self-congratulation. For that irony, as for the data and model he has bequeathed to us and scholars still to come, we owe Bob our hearty thanks.

Criticisms of the type of work Bob has pursued are often twofold as well. Quantitative social history is impersonal, it is said, substituting post-facto statistical abstractions for the range of individual cases that composed the real action on the ground. A second and related objection notes that reconstructing channels of movement does not tell us who dug them in the first place and why, or who directed the flow of immigrants through them and how. The first objection might be designated a call for the particular, the second the question of leadership. If the proper response to these objections is not to reject the quantitative model for the humanist alternative but rather to try mesh the two, then one long-term test of Bob's project will be to determine how well its generalizations comport with a range of individual cases, particularly with the careers of those figures acknowledged at the time to be leaders in the Dutch-American community. This essay offers one such test in the case of the Rev. Lammert Jan Hulst.

The Life

It is hard to imagine a better test case than that of L.J. Hulst, so representative was he of the immigrant population, so influential in its long-term positioning in the United States, yet so opinionated and colorful in his individuality.[2] In origins, religious disposition, time of arrival, and place of settlement, Hulst played par for the course. He was born (in 1825) to a modest farming family of pietist-conventicle inclinations and went over with them as a boy in the 1834 Secession from the *Nederlandse Hervormde Kerk*. He witnessed the Seceders' harassment at the hands of the authorities; in fact, being from Gemeente Dalfsen, in Overijssel, he could remember seven decades later a confrontation between no less than A.C. Van Raalte and the local constable during a service the Seceders were holding in a barn.[3] In his early teens Hulst earnestly sought and found salvation, then seemingly lost it only to find it again in a pious family for whom he worked as a farm hand. Almost immediately he felt a call to the ministry and tested by a process of prayer and sign-reading intense enough to satisfy Gideon himself. Passing through the parsonage school of Wolter A. Kok in Hoogeveen, he was ordained in 1849 to the ministry of the Seceders' *Christelijke Gereformeerde Kerk* and successfully served three northern Netherlands congregations (Birdaard and Ferwerd in Friesland, and Stadskanaal in Groningen) over a span of twenty five years. Then, in 1874, at 49 years of age, he emigrated with his wife and seven children to the United States, first taking a parish of the Reformed Church in America (RCA) in Danforth, Illinois, then switching in just two years to "a wider field of service" in Grand Rapids, Michigan.[4] There in a city poised for national leadership in the furniture industry, poised as well to become the first harbor of the imminent high tide of Dutch-American immigration, Hulst was installed as the founding pastor of Fourth RCA on the near Northeast side. Five years later, he led his congregation out of the RCA in protest of the denomination's toleration of Freemasons in its membership; shortly thereafter he led them into affiliation with the denomination that would soon be renamed the Christian Reformed Church (CRC).

Hulst's action, said the CRC's first historian, Henry Beets, was significant in its own right and symbolic of important broader trends. In bringing some well established congregations, including Van Raalte's own, into the CRC; in signifying a new cadre of leadership for a fellowship that had often lacked the same; and most of all in winning the Netherlands mother church's endorsement for the CRC on the verge of peak Dutch immigration, West Michigan's anti-Masonic crusade and Hulst's leadership therein helped ensure a prosperous future for his new denomination.[5] Hulst lived up to the part too. He served as chief editor of the CRC's official paper, *De Wachter*, from 1884 to 1888, and associate editor long after that. He was twice president of the CRC's Synod. For a time he filled in for the departed Professor Geerhardus Vos (who left for Princeton in 1893) teaching dogmatics at the church's Theological School in Grand Rapids. These duties came on top of his pastoring the Coldbrook CRC (as it had been renamed) for thirty years, which entailed a weekly round of eighteen catechism classes, a Saturday evening Bible study for young people, a dozen pastoral visits, and three sermons a Sunday.

But Hulst brought along his polemical side into the CRC too. He resolutely opposed the formation of English-language congregations in Grand Rapids, alleging that two of these – LaGrave Ave. and Broadway, the latter drawing heavily off Coldbrook's membership – had not received due blessing from their mother congregations, and arguing besides that the Anglo-American ecclesiastical style which the English language brought with it spelled grave danger for authentic Reformed life and doctrine.[6] He also opposed the theology and cultural attitudes associated with Abraham Kuyper. As Kuyper's Neo-Calvinist movement caught fire in the Netherlands in the 1880s, the new Dutch immigration brought with it Kuyperian zealots, especially to urban centers and educational facilities such as Grand Rapids and its Theological School. Hulst never threatened to bolt over these issues as he had with lodge membership, but he never stopped pushing the Secessionist over against the Neo-Calvinist cause in the CRC,[7] never ceased warning the denomination about the flood of worldliness he saw lapping at its doors, and sometimes blamed the first of these for aiding and abetting the second.

In short, Hulst remained a Seceder confessionalist from the start to the bitter end – and the end for him at Coldbrook in 1906, at age 82, was a touch sour. He resisted the new language, the new hymnody, the new theology, the advent of Sunday School at the side of catechism, the young upstarts in his congregation who did not know their place, and especially their suggestions that he retire. If his was a representative Dutch American life, the question remains how he as an under-educated, denomination-jumping, resistance-oriented pastor became a leader in that community, and why that leadership eventually faded. The answer lay first in Hulst's very typicality but second in the adaptability he brought to his role. These rested in turn on the community's explicitly and implicitly recognized grounds of authority. Hulst succeeded by fixing early onto that bedrock. Late in his career he found its plates shifting.

Spiritual Resources
Hulst's own claim to authority is evident in the biblical text which he used for his ordination sermon, for the semi-centennial celebration of that event, and for the opening line of his memoirs, Amos 7: 14-15: "I am not a prophet nor a prophet's son" but have been called by God from pasture and field to be a preacher to Israel.[8] The plain people to whom Hulst spoke these words – whether in the farm districts of Friesland or in the factory streets of Grand Rapids – knew whereof he spoke and

heard in him a kindred voice. They remembered the context in which the Amos spoke and its close fit with their own times: God's plain man was to prophesy truth to power. Hulst's power lay first of all then in his declaration of modesty and in his recitation of just the narrative a Seceder audience took as the proper elevation.

The story began with Hulst, fifteen years old, on his knees nightly in agonized prayer over the assurance of his salvation. The hopeful answer he received did not prevent a falling away when he, ironically, took up the shepherd's trade in the employ of his own father and at the expense of any regular Christian fellowship. Four years later his faith was renewed by a spiritual conversation with the daughter of his boss, a Seceder farmer.[9] The story might have led on to an appropriately carnal conversation with the young lady, except that Hulst now turned his introspections to the prospect of becoming a minister; young Jenny married another and went to an early grave. Marriage for Lammert would wait until his ordination when he quickly sought a suitable partner to make his position more seemly. The happy bride was Elbertje Hellenga, eighteen years old in 1850, thus seven years Hulst's junior, and the eventual recipient of just two pages in his 164-page memoir. Hulst's true passion lay with the ministry. To this call his memoir gave the close recounting a later age would devote to youthful romance: first hopes, daunting obstacles, the crucial word of encouragement, the hard tests of the first theology lesson, the first sermon, the final candidate's exam.[10] His call *had* to be authentic, Hulst concluded, because he had brought to it no money, no adequate preparatory education, no learning in the biblical languages, yet out of it had drawn a lifetime of effective service.

Hulst did not remain an unlettered populist, however. In his first pastorate he studied Latin, Greek, and Hebrew a year at a time; devoted himself to learning logic, modern literature, and the history of theology; and soon qualified to set up a parsonage school of the sort he himself had attended.[11] Most of all he devoted himself to the study of Reformed theology, hammering away at its sixteenth- and seventeenth-century founders. This self-tutored mastery of the core of orthodoxy would ever remain Hulst's chief claim to authority, for it was a broadly if not easily accessible record packed in the few texts that often adorned the farmer's and fisher's bookshelf, and if such as one as he could master it, so in theory could they. But formal authority does not become practical leadership without adaptability. Hulst demonstrated that most of all in a process of self-criticism that led him to change his own theological convictions. Accustomed to near-mystical reflections on the secret counsels of divine predestination, Hulst determined that brand of Calvinism to be unpreachable. Instead he brought divine election down to earth. God's covenant with Abraham, not the eternal covenant within the Trinity, was the starting point of Christian faith and life, he taught. He suppressed his native mysticism much as he opposed the kindred supralapsarian teachings of the Kuyperians, and for the same reason: they made the church too narrow (only the demonstrably elect) or too broad (all reality reflecting God's will), and left the believer uncertain.[12]

His conversion and his unassailable orthodoxy gave Hulst a bully pulpit in church controversies. But to him these were not just a lever *on* the church but close to *being* the church itself. In both his American battles over Freemasonry in the RCA and Neo-Calvinism in the CRC, Hulst first and last invoked Reformed confessional piety as being the mark of the church and scorned his opponents' moves as "playing church." To move from "God's honor" to "the salvation of man" was to be more "Methodist" than Reformed, with grave consequences: "... then the expansion of the church and the honor of its members becomes the focal point, until the church is no longer the church of Christ but a human institution bearing the name of a Christian church."[13] The drive for human glory and social show accounted for the RCA's blindness regarding the lodge, Hulst declared; it came in more intellectual and cultural dress among the Kuyperians; it animated no little of the move to English in the CRC; and it always betrayed the design of an elite to wrest God's treasure from the hands of the lowly. A eulogist at his death in 1922 made this his epitaph: "We must bear in mind that generally the spirit of error begins to develop in the circles of the learned ... [while] Reformation generally originates with the common folk."[14]

Comparatively little of Hulst's time was given to church polemics, however. Rather, he was a pastor in season and out, and it was as a pastor that he had to sustain his leadership. By his own account he grew in the role, but then he had plenty of opportunities to learn. His memoirs give more space to vignettes of his counseling practice than to any other subject, and through his fine ear for dialogue and quick repartee we get a lively sense of the spiritual crises of everyday life, from marital discord to wandering sons, bad loans, gambling addiction, a Scrooge of a elder, and a gift of (ratty) rattan chairs in his Illinois parsonage. Significantly, most of the American incidents involved materialism and its various seductions, but that did not move Hulst to social theorizing or systemic analysis. Rather he was attuned to individual character and sympathetic with human frailty, aiming not to adjudicate an ethical principle or condemn a sinner but to improve the situation at hand. Hulst often used these tales to illustrate one or another of his theological points, but the reader gets the impression that it was in the case of the village doubter converted on his deathbed, of a young woman debating the signs and seals of the sacraments, or of a promising seminarian lost to adultery that Hulst confirmed for himself the effectiveness of his covenant preaching and the true measure of conversion.[15]

Thus, however adamant Hulst sounded on orthodoxy, he was long-suffering in pastoral practice. While the state had to accent punishment to uphold the right, he explained, the church had to emphasize "the *love* which seeks to save." He grew increasingly skeptical of formal church discipline as the years passed, precisely because he thought it was so seldom done from that motive. When he left Coldbrook in 1906, the congregation had to erase from the rolls a long lists of delinquents – many of them young men – with whom Hulst had tried to maintain a pastoral relationship.[16] Perhaps Hulst was so reluctant to give up hope because his own children were not all in the fold. His brightest star, son Henry, had undertaken seminary studies at Princeton, only to lose faith in Scripture as divine revelation. Hulst did not hide his sorrow at this outcome, but he did not scoff either at the national reputation Henry went on to achieve in medical practice.[17] From such a record – candid but not overwrought – he would seem to have increased his authority by showing he had grounds for empathizing with other people's suffering. This was a crucial feature in Hulst's character. As subsequent heresy hunters in the CRC would discover, he who would be a watcher on the walls of Zion can quickly become a trumpet of self-righteousness and wind up ridiculed or in exile; Hulst's self-criticism and patent humility spared him that fate.

When he did take up polemics it was to defend the prerogatives of his office or the church's public standards as he understood them; when it came to the personal, he could be remarkably generous. His leading opponent in the Masonic controversy at Fourth Reformed, for instance, was Frans Van Driele, an eminent local businessman and a pioneer of the Grand Rapids' Dutch community – a candidate for the elitism that Hulst liked to skewer. Yet Hulst remembered the person and gave Van Driele high marks for his insight and integrity: "He was truly a valuable person. He feared God, was friendly toward the lowly, and dared to refute the powerful." As a newcomer to a strange city, "I learned a great deal from him … [and] found in Frans a trusted person to answer my questions."[18] Likewise, in his account of the Masonic conflict, Hulst decided to pass over "some unpleasant details … that perhaps might awaken some undesirable bitterness," and he leavened the harshest episodes with a touch of humor. At the classis meeting called to consider deposing him from the ministry, he asked permission to read a "little piece" that he had prepared to explain his position. The chair forbade it and ordered him to simply plead guilty or not guilty. That's not so easy, Hulst replied. Nonsense, answered the chair.

"Well now, let me read the little piece and the nonsense will be explained." But no, that could not be…. [The chair decided:] "We will have to declare that Rev. Hulst was summoned but did not appear." "But," someone shouted, "there he sits big as life." "Well," says a third, "he is there in the flesh but not in the spirit." Rev. Hulst felt the urge to ask in turn whether his spirit was seen walking away. But he bethought himself in time that at that moment such a well-deserved remark would not improve the situation.[19]

In sum, Hulst's personal character was crucial not only to his religious authority but also to his immigrant audience, many of whom were lean in resources, insecure in status, sensitive to slights and arrogance, yet needing an unambiguous assertion of standards. Hulst met the challenge by being firm on abstractions and tender to persons, by submitting himself to the standards he would impose on others, and finally by taking due account of his standing in the eyes of the transcendent authority to whom leader and community alike felt beholden. "If I could look back on my work with satisfaction," he wrote in his 59th year in the pulpit,

> then I would imagine myself to have received due compensation – but that's not how things stand. My work, in the light of God's holiness, has been so tainted that I can look back at it only with shame. And I will be glad if God, for Christ's sake, will provide for me a little place with the least of believers in the Father's eternal home.... Even though I consider myself totally undeserving, my hope remains in this. May this witness serve to make the proud humble and to encourage the poor sinner to hold on to God's promise in Christ.[20]

Social Deployment

The challenge of a religious *leader* is to deploy spiritual resources effectively in concrete situations. Thus Hulst's success depended considerably upon his place and appeal within Dutch-American *social* networks. We need not recount here the central importance of (Christian) Reformed churches in the immigrant network but can take it as accepted that, to put it mildly, Hulst had inherent prestige as a minister. But not all ministers were equally prestigious, so a closer look is needed at how Hulst presented himself and what network assets he depended on. The traits of his ministerial training – humble origins, diligent labors, and upward mobility via community service – need not be rehearsed here either, although they are much to the point. They were supplemented, however, by two additional features.

The first was so notable that a long-time observer of the Grand Rapids CRC scene, writing a generation after Hulst's death, remembered first of all "something *patriarchal* in his appearance as well as ministerial."[21] The same impression was conveyed in Hulst's own lifetime, as the denominational and local daily press marked the various anniversaries of his birth or ordination to the ministry with tributes to an ancient veteran of the pulpit: "our Nestor," a "veteran of the Secession," the last of the old fathers. "Patriarch" suited Hulst's own self-image too. He reflexively spoke of "my consistory," "my catechumens," the "youth" who gathered at "my house" for Bible lessons. He could not be lured by calls from Van Raalte's church to leave "my dearly beloved Coldbrook congregation," so soon the calls stopped coming.[22] The old age which some at Coldbrook argued as reason for retirement he took as redoubling his authority. Perhaps the most revealing statement on this score came as he recollected his call to the United States:

> ... my wife had never interfered in any call I received, nor had she voiced her opinion on what she thought I should do. She now let me feel that she was

strongly against my accepting this call. Under these circumstances my conscience was somewhat bound not to accept it.... [Later that week she asked] "what are you going to do?" "Well, *vrouw*, if you were for it as much as I presume you are against it, we would go to America. And I say this not as a reproach but I acknowledge thankfully that you have always let me be free to make the choice. Though, this is not an ordinary call, and therefore I hope in this to receive a signal from God whether or not to stay." She answered, "Yes, I hesitate to make such a long trip to a strange land, and that with seven children but I want you to make a decision freely without my opinion. I am beginning to think also it might be better to go than to stay here." With these words the stumbling block was rolled away from my feet and the way was opened to move to America.[23]

Hulst also ruled as a patriarch. He never liked formalized rules and bureaucratic procedures; these were part of the "playing-church" game that signaled ill health in the body. He took dissent in the congregation as a personal challenge, and he nurtured spiritual sons on "his" consistory to check rivals and thwart enemies. In Grand Rapids Frans Van Driele, "father" of the whole community, hardly fit that role, but after the schism Sipke S. Postma, an old catechumen of Hulst's in Friesland, rose to the part and filled it for 25 years. Hulst's final battle at Coldbrook started with the arrival of a "young man" who wished to have the young people run their own society, to hold some services in English, to blow out the musty air with fresh breezes of "progress." Hulst could hardly hide his injured pride when the English-language issue came to a congregational vote, nor did the 3-1 margin in his favor satisfy him. Fathers should not have to be sustained by the formal vote of their children; "from that time on," Hulst lamented, "our mutual relationship left something to be desired."[24]

Patriarchy had a general sanction in Hulst's Victorian generation, but the circumstances of immigration probably increased its appeal. The migration process was often hard on older sons, whose paternal role-models more easily lost status in moving from old country to new. The wisdom and authority displayed in the pulpit – alternatively, behind the bar in the ward heelers' saloon, at the dock by the *padrone*, or on the factory floor by the foreman – could provide young men with a welcome replacement. Just as Hulst's patient work with wandering sons of the church bespoke his own sense of this role, his passion against Freemasonry becomes clearer in this light. On the one hand Masons looked like a patriarchal dream, composing an all-male order hierarchically arrayed to inculcate ancestral wisdom in their young recruits. On the other hand the lodge in Hulst's America represented a threatening alternative to the church, since in the northern cities of the late nineteenth century they had more male members than did churches. Besides their extra-Christian ritual and teachings, then, lodges could strike Hulst as a false patriarchy, elitist in airs, sequestered from the public accountability, and abandoning true male responsibility to family and society.[25]

Something of that abandonment seems to have troubled Hulst's own youth, at least as he recalled it in his memoirs. His father barely appears in its pages, and then only as part-owner of the flock of sheep whose tending led young Lammert astray. It is Hulst's older brother Jan who emerges as his spiritual guide and, at the critical moment, promises the funds to pay for his ministerial training. The training itself came from the Rev. Kok, who was not only a teacher but "truly a Father to his students." Such Hulst ever tried to be in his own work. In fact, nothing so closely fits Hulst's self-image as his early memories of Gerrit Hoekman, a kindly elder in his boyhood village who did so much that a father was supposed to do. Childless himself, Hoekman regularly gathered children around him for instruction in the Lord, supplying the vacuum left by the officious, superficial clergyman of the town.[26] Hulst's favorite time as a minister would always be the evening Bible studies with young people, preferably in his own parlor. No wonder he found answers to his theological difficulties in God's covenant with Abraham, first of the patriarchs.

Hulst's second social asset was chain migration and its attendant localism. Hulst first caught "immigrant fever" when his younger brother Frederik left for the United States, but his subsequent invitation to join him did not suffice to draw Lammert over. Only when a former deacon of his emigrated to Danforth, Illinois, whence a pastoral call soon arrived, did Hulst follow. When Danforth proved to be too narrow a field for his labors, Hulst moved to Fourth Reformed which was attractive not only because of its strategic location in Grand Rapids but because a good share of the congregation were old neighbors. By this time Frisians and Groningers were starting to dominate the Dutch domiciles of the Coldbrook area, and Hulst's presence drew even more. Eventually 35 percent of the Frisian-born residents in the district hailed from Ferwerdadeel, around Hulst's old parish.[27] Hulst thus followed but also dug deeper the channel of specific locale migration that afforded immigrant and leader alike a familiar body of people and customary set of rules.

Localism was also marked in the process whereby Hulst's congregation moved from the RCA to the CRC. Their official letter of departure cited the familiar litany against Freemasonry, but it began by recalling the unease with which they had watched the RCA remove theological education from Holland to New Brunswick, New Jersey.[28] This might have been an economy measure on the part of the denomination, but in the eyes of many "in the West" it looked like a piece of imperialism by which the most important ingredient of their future well-being, the reliable training of the ministry, passed from local to distant, elite, east-coast control. The passage in local leadership symbolized by the death of A.C. Van Raalte in 1876 did not help the RCA cause either, but perhaps more important was Van Raalte's relative marginalization in west Michigan years before and the inability of his successors to claim the full sway of his mantle.[29] That Hulst arrived in west Michigan the same year that Van Raalte died had more than symbolic import, not least because the younger man had his own claim to the mantle from having been in Van Raalte's orbit during the holy days of Seceder suffering. More practically, the Dutch immigrants pouring into the area preferred Hulst's city to Van Raalte's rural county, and were more likely to hail from Hulst's northern than from Van Raalte's central provinces in the Netherlands. As a known commodity, Hulst for all his modest education and recent emigration was a more desirable leader than was an old legend.

But Hulst would learn that familiarity comes and goes as networks change. By the end of the nineteenth century the Dutch had arrived in such numbers, from such an array of localities, and across such a span of destinations that new networks were required to harness them and a new brand of leader to guide them. Local leadership, so effective in the process of transplantation, was inadequate to the task of nationwide coordination, and men like Hulst began to sense the strain. He was elected president of the CRC Synod one more time in 1890, at age 65, but thereafter found himself in an increasing number of losing battles. He leveled his Secessionist guns against Neo-Calvinist theology in an 1891 book arguing infra- vs. supralapsarianism, but if that helped to drive Geerhardus Vos away, twenty years later he was at the same job with less success. His *Oud- en Nieuw Calvinisme* came out with the help of G.K. Hemkes in 1913, but the American-born, Neo-Calvinist friendly, university-trained Ph.D. Ralph Janssen came on the Calvin Theological Seminary faculty anyway and soon was attracting the better students.[30] The Broadway CRC had long since been organized as an English-language congregation with many of Hulst's former catechumens filling its pews. When Hulst finally left Coldbrook for the small country parish of Eastmanville, Michigan, he scared most potential successors away; with its building in disrepair and its membership down to 185 families (from a peak at 300 in 1894), the Coldbrook congregation had to issue ten calls before it received an acceptance, from J.J. Hiemenga.[31]

Hiemenga would go down in the congregation's annals as "the builder." He succeeded in replacing the old sanctuary and recovered most of the lost membership by showing the busy, energetic spirit that the era deemed "progressive" but that Hulst always suspected of being more show than substance. Hiemenga would add to his triumphs by becoming the first president of Calvin College, which in the first twenty years of the new century grew from a pre-seminary academy into a four-year liberal arts institution. The college occupied a new campus on the southeast edge of town, adjacent to the leafy, brick Ottawa Hills neighborhood that developers were building on an old golf course. There the Grand Rapids elite could remove from the central city with its noise and smoky factories. Districts like Coldbrook, which featured such annoyances in abundance, were plagued by high transience. Dutch residents there showed lower rates of home ownership and a higher incidence of unskilled manual laborers than did any other Dutch enclave in the city.[32] The immigrant chain had tied Hulst to common people and mean streets; the future belonged to the more fortunate on shady avenues.

Hulst's waning comports exactly with the model of leadership succession that Josef Barton found among communities of central and southern European immigrants. The first generation looked to "local leaders" who, for all their common origins, managed to rebuild the sort of voluntary associations they knew in the old country as a means of preserving the newcomers' dignity. But "group leaders" had to emerge in the next generation to knit the widely dispersed ethnic enclaves into a national network and to handle its increasing complexity with more sophisticated organizations and communications. "In an early stage the modern leader is a centralizer, building the big organizations that take over some of the functions of the small community" and bequeathing to their people "an increasingly differentiated, professional, and bureaucratic type of leadership."[33] Such was J.J. Hiemenga; such, with even more success, was Henry Beets who, more than anyone else in the twenty years after Hulst's retirement, was Mr. CRC: editor of its new English-language periodical, *The Banner*, protagonist of world missions, promoter of all its institutions, and all-purpose emissary to outsiders. As Barton further predicates of such leaders, Beets came not from the center but from the margins of the community's life[34] – not being native to the Secession but having converted in America, and in Kansas at that – and had appeal precisely because he was not identified with either side in the Seceder-Kuyperian quarrel, yet merited some association with both.

Beets was too affectionate and too genuine to earn Hulst's reproof as a "church player." But, then, the winds did not long blow the "progressives'" way. Hiemenga's capital campaign at Calvin College failed, and he went back to the pastorate. Beets tired of the denomination's bitter theological wars in the 1920s and devoted himself to missions. In 1922, the year that Hulst died, Ralph Janssen was demoted from the seminary faculty by a coalition of Confessionalists and stern Kuyperians; two years later the former purged the latter and reigned alone for the next thirty years.[35] Their victory was signified in 1928 when Henry J. Kuiper replaced Beets as *Banner* editor and became the denomination's foremost voice. Kuiper's language might have been English and his preferred music revivalist hymns, but his voice was that of strict piety, straight orthodoxy, and fervent anti-worldliness. He lacked only Hulst's humor and self-deprecation to be his perfect successor.

Notes

1. The Dutch were hardly the only group showing this pattern. T.H. Breen finds it among 17th-century immigrants to Massachusetts Bay in *Puritans and Adventurers: Change and Persistence in Early America* (New York: Oxford University Press, 1980), 3-105; Jon Gjerde finds it among 19th-century immigrants from northern Europe to the upper Midwest in *The Minds of the West: Ethnocultural Evolution in the Rural Middle West, 1830-1917* (Chapel Hill: University of North Carolina Press, 1997); and Victor Greene finds it among eastern European immigrants to urban America in *For God and Country: The Rise of Polish and Lithuanian Ethnic Consciousness in America, 1860-1910* (Madison, WI: State Historical Association of Wisconsin, 1975).
2. The chief sources on Hulst are his autobiography, *Drie en Zestig Jaren Prediker* (Kampen: Kok, 1913); Jacob G. Vanden Bosch, "Lammert Jan Hulst," *Reformed Journal* 7 (December 1957): 17-21; and Jacob Noordewier, "Memoriam," in *Yearbook of the Christian Reformed Church, 1923* (Grand Rapids: Christian Reformed Publishing House, 1923), 127-136. A good analysis by one of his students and successors is Henry Beets, "Rev. L.J. Hulst, a Man of Note," *Banner* (31 August 1922): 532-534. The biographical file on Hulst in the Heritage Hall archives, Calvin College and Seminary, has numerous clippings from denominational magazines and local newspapers giving much the same information.
3. Hulst, *Drie en Zestig Jaren*, 12-13.
4. Quotation ibid., 111.
5. Beets itemizes these points in his "Voorwoord" to Hulst, *Drie en Zestig Jaren*, vii-ix, and repeats them in his account of the Freemasonry controversy in *De Christelijke Gereformeerde Kerk in Noord Amerika* (Grand Rapids: Grand Rapids Printing Co., 1918), 174-189.
6. Hulst, *Drie en Zestig Jaren*, 152-154.
7. Hulst's principal critiques of Neo-Calvinist theology were *Supra en Infra* (Grand Rapids: Doornik, [1891]); and, with G. K. Hemkes, *Oud- en Nieuw-Calvinisme* (Grand Rapids: Eerdmans-Sevensma, 1913).
8. Hulst's sermon on the 50th anniversary of his ordination, *Herdenking van zijne Vijftig-jarige Evangeliebediening* (Grand Rapids: J.B. Hulst, 1899) is reprinted in English translation in *A Century of Faithfulness, 1882-1982: Beckwith Hills Christian Reformed Church*, in Heritage Halls archives, Calvin College and Seminary. In that sermon Hulst notes that he preached the same text at his ordination. See also his *Drie en Zestig Jaren*, 1.
9. Hulst, *Drie en Zestig Jaren*, 26-31.
10. Regarding the two women, ibid., 40-41; on his educational hurdles, 32-40.
11. Ibid., 51-55.
12. Ibid., 57-65; Hulst and Hemkes, *Oud- en Nieuw Calvinisme*, 29-41.
13. Hulst, *Drie en Zestig Jaren*, 126.
14. Noordewier, "Memoriam," 127-128.
15. Theses incidents and more are recounted in Hulst, *Drie en Zestig Jaren*, 72-79, 86-104, 112-117, 142-151.
16. Hulst, *Drie en Zestig Jaren*, 83, 136 (quotation); Vanden Bosch, "L.J. Hulst," 21.
17. Hulst, *Drie en Zestig Jaren*, 134-135; Vanden Bosch, "L.J. Hulst," 21.
18. Hulst, *Drie en Zestig Jaren*, 121.
19. L.J. Hulst, "History of the Separation of the Congregation of Coldbrook in Grand Rapids from the Reformed Dutch Church in America" (English translation typescript in Hulst papers, Heritage Hall archives, Calvin College and Seminary), quotations 28 and 20, respectively.
20. L.J. Hulst, "Felicitatie," *De Wachter*, 22 September 1909.
21. Vanden Bosch, "L.J. Hulst," 17.
22. Hulst, *Drie en Zestig Jaren*, 133.
23. Ibid., 107-108.

24. Ibid., 156-158, quotation 158.

25. For gender-role analysis and statistics on lodge membership, I have relied on Mark C. Carnes, *Secret Ritual and Manhood in Victorian America* (New Haven: Yale University Press, 1989). See also Lynn Dumenil, *Freemasonry and American Culture, 1880-1930* (Princeton: Princeton University Press, 1984).

26. Hulst, *Drie en Zestig Jaren*, 23 (on Kok), 3 (on Hoekman).

27. David Vander Stel, "The Dutch of Grand Rapids, Michigan, 1848-1900: Immigrant Neighborhood and Community Development in a Nineteenth-Century City" (Ph.D. dissertation, Kent State University, 1983), 205-210.

28. Hulst, "History of Separation," 18.

29. Elton J. Bruins," The Masonic Controversy in Holland, Michigan, 1879-1882," in Peter de Klerk and Richard R. De Ridder, eds., *Perspectives on the Christian Reformed Church: Studies in Its History, Theology, and Ecumenicity* (Grand Rapids: Baker Book House, 1983), 60-61, argues the importance of van Raalte's death in this process.

30. James D. Bratt, *Dutch Calvinism in Modern America: A History of a Conservative Subculture* (Grand Rapids: Eerdmans, 1984), 46-49, 105, 244-245 (note 51).

31. *Souvenir: Fiftieth Anniversary, 1882-1932: Coldbrook Christian Reformed Church*, 19ff. Copy available in Heritage Hall archives, Calvin College and Seminary. For a look at Hulst in the context of his congregation's longer history, see James D. Bratt and Christopher H. Meehan, *Gathered at the River: Grand Rapids, Michigan, and Its People of Faith* (Grand Rapids: Eerdmans, 1993), 67-73.

32. Vander Stel, "The Dutch of Grand Rapids, Michigan," 205-210.

33. Josef J. Barton, "Eastern and Southern Europeans," in John Higham, ed., *Ethnic Leadership in America* (Baltimore: Johns Hopkins University Press, 1978), 150-175; quotations from Higham's summary of Barton's argument, 11.

34. Barton, "Eastern and Southern Europeans," 170.

35. Bratt, *Dutch Calvinism*, 93-119.

The Summer of Dominie Winter's Discontent[1]:
The Americanization of a Dutch Reformed Seceder

Earl Wm. Kennedy

I became acquainted with Robert Swierenga's work almost two decades ago through his article analyzing the 1857 Dutch Reformed schism, which marked the parting of the ways of the denominations now known as the Reformed Church in America (RCA) and the Christian Reformed Church (CRC).[2] This statistical study showed that the 1835-1880 immigrants who joined the RCA tended to come from the more populous, "cosmopolitan" areas of the Netherlands, while most of those who went into the CRC originated in the more outlying, rural, "localistic," traditional regions, largely in the north, such as Groningen; this geographical correlation became more pronounced after 1857.[3]

The Calvinist seceders who left the "liberal" Reformed state, or public, church (*Hervormde Kerk*) in the Netherlands beginning with the *Afscheiding* (Secession) of 1834, were themselves soon embroiled in internal disputes between the "northern" party of the Revs. Hendrik De Cock and Simon Van Velzen, the "Gelderland" (or "southern") party of the Revs. Anthony Brummelkamp and Albertus C. Van Raalte, and the maverick "Scholtians," named for the Rev. Hendrik Pieter Scholte. The northerners were generally the strictest in their adherence to the doctrine, discipline, and worship prescribed by the Synod of Dordt (1618-1619); the Gelderlanders added a dash of pragmatism and mission to their Calvinism, stressing the free offer of the gospel to all; and Scholte's followers, least bound to the Reformed heritage, were the most individualistic, biblicistic, and evangelical. Roughly speaking, the northern party was the forerunner of the CRC, while the Gelderland party – with some help from the Scholtians – became the backbone of the midwestern RCA, as exemplified in the colonies of Holland, Michigan, and Pella, Iowa, set up in 1847 by Van Raalte and Scholte, respectively.[4] Members of both the *Hervormde Kerk* and the various *Gereformeerde kerken* (Reformed [seceders'] churches), also known pejoratively as *Afgescheidenen* (Seceders), emigrated to the United States in increasing numbers beginning in the mid-1840s, but, for a number of reasons, the *Afgescheidenen* became the dominant force among the Dutch Reformed immigrants.[5]

Orange City

In recent years I have been doing research for a book on the first half century (1871-1921) of the RCA and the CRC in Orange City, Sioux County, in the northwest corner of Iowa. This colony, begun in 1870, was settled almost exclusively by people from Pella and vicinity, encouraged by that city's enterprising mayor, Henry Hospers, a member of its First Reformed Church. Many from that congregation helped organize the First Reformed Church of Orange City on 6 May 1871, with the blessing (from afar) of their Pella pastor, the Rev. Egbert Winter (1836-1906).[6] He reported the news of its formation, by the Classis of Illinois, in a letter in the weekly newspaper of the Western RCA, *De Hope*, published in Holland, Michigan. He observed that there was a great need for a lively and zealous minister there, it being a field with great potential.[7]

But Dominie Winter's hopeful tone was dampened after his pastoral visit to Orange City over two Sundays, 18 and 25 June 1871. He discovered that a serpent had entered the Edenic Orange City garden. In his eyewitness report to *De Hope*, Winter first describes the land, the climate, the railroad plans, and the steady influx of settlers (over 200 families already). More important, however, is the religious situation. Although interest in the preaching of the gospel is widespread there, "it pains us that the *Afgescheidene* brothers still continue their withdrawn standpoint and life also there in that new region, where earlier no worshipers of the living Covenant-Jehovah resided. The banner of schism and discord should not have desecrated this new soil.... Alas, they seem to busy themselves with certain *ideas* which are more *ecclesiastical* than *spiritual* – and, again, alas! – to be little concerned about the more *important* and more *spiritual realities* of inner and mutual amalgamation, with which the actual life of faith stands so closely bound...." Why should old divisions be imported into this new area, when a fresh start ought to be made "with a truly cordial church union? ... *Afscheiding*! – we must say that that word is a soul-racking dissonance among the children of God. *Afscheiding*– from friends of truth and fellow heirs of the same Fatherly House. – Oh, it must be a grating dissonance for Heaven!" After this *cri de coeur,* Winter sets forth the urgent need for a pastor in Sioux County who would also set up a school. In spite of these problems, the religious prospects for the new colony are, with human effort and God's blessing, very favorable, and many Dutch immigrants will doubtless settle there. "EENDRAGT MAAKT MAGT."[8]

Less than three weeks after Winter left Orange City, and only four days after he penned the letter, and nearly two weeks before it actually appeared in print, the First Christian Reformed Church of Orange City was organized on 14 July 1871, thus fulfilling Winter's worst fears.[9] Barely surviving the 1870s, it began rapid growth in the next decade, attracting many Seceder immigrants from the Netherlands, and becoming the mother church of the CRC in the west. Its slightly older sibling rival, the First Reformed Church, also prospered and gave birth to many daughter churches.[10]

My present purpose is to examine the factors which may have led Dominie Winter to his passionate outburst. Such strong language was common then in the heat of the ecclesiastical warfare between the western branch of the RCA and *De Ware Hollandsche Gereformeerde Kerk* ("The True Holland Reformed Church"), as the CRC then (1864-1880) somewhat immodestly dubbed itself.[11] Winter's tale, although not entirely unique, will help to illumine the not always edifying RCA-CRC *broedertwisten* ("brothers' quarrels") as well as other aspects of the immigrant Calvinist experience. His is the story of an immigrant who moved both literally and figuratively from the original home of the northern party, Dominie De Cock's Ulrum, to become a sturdy advocate of Reformed, even Protestant, ecumenicity in the midwestern RCA.

Groningen

Egbert Winter was born in the hamlet of Zoutkamp, parish of Vierhuizen, province of Groningen, 5 January 1836, just over a year after the Afscheiding began in the adjacent town of Ulrum[12] He was the son of Jurrien Pietersz. Winter, a blacksmith, and his wife Reinje Aries Van Weerden,[13] who had become members of De Cock's far-flung Secession parish after leaving their local church, whose pastor, by complaining about De Cock's baptizing children from other parishes, was the first to get him into the ecclesiastical trouble which eventually led to his secession.[14] In fact, Egbert's mother was one of the first converts in the revival connected with the schism and remained a De Cock admirer until her death in Holland, Michigan, a half century later.[15] The Winter family's early association with De Cock is also shown by the fact that in 1833 he baptized, as one of seventeen non-Ulrum infants, Egbert's older sister, Eike.[16] The next year, their paternal grandfather was one of many in the Ulrum congregation to sign the famous "Act of Secession and Return" (to the Reformed faith).[17] Presumably Egbert was baptized by De Cock in the Seceder church in 1836.[18] Later that year, Egbert's father was one of three nominated as elder for the Zoutkamp area of the parish.[19] When Egbert was quite young, the family moved to Ulrum.[20]

Michigan

The Winters emigrated to the United States, apparently in stages, in 1848 and 1850, with Egbert arriving in the latter year at age fourteen.[21] They settled near Holland, Michigan, where Jurrien Winter rose from laborer to farmer by the time of his death in 1861.[22] Egbert's parents' Michigan church affiliation is as yet unknown, but he made his own public confession of faith at the First Reformed Church of Holland, under Van Raalte's ministry, on 5 August 1855, when he was still a teenager.[23] It is uncertain to what extent, if any, this was a declaration of religious independence on his part. But, from then on, Winter, like about a dozen other future ministers (several with "northern" backgrounds) who came under Van

Egbert Winter, Seminary Graduation Photo, 1863
(RCA Archives. New Brunswick, NJ)

Raalte's influence in this decade, was firmly on the path to Americanization as he studied under American-born instructors from the older, eastern RCA, first at the Holland Academy, and later at Rutgers College and what is now known as New Brunswick Theological Seminary.[24] Put in terms of the Netherlands situation, then losing some of its immediacy for the immigrants, Winter had shifted from De Cock's northern party to Brummelkamp's Gelderland group. He could not look back in quite the same way as his mother always did to the good old days of De Cock,[25] who died when Winter was only six, although he would retain an appreciation for the stand taken by De Cock and Scholte in 1834.[26] Winter's Michigan pastor and religious mentor, the "Gelderlander" Van Raalte, advocated the natural, gradual Americanization of the Dutch immigrants and their integration into the eastern RCA.[27] Yet in 1857, just as Winter was nearing the end of his studies at the Holland Academy, a small but significant separation from the RCA by northerners hostile to Van Raalte's orientation and program occurred among the Michigan immigrants. This second "separation and return" would become the nucleus of the CRC and would deeply affect Egbert Winter and his ministry a decade later in Pella.[28]

Winter had begun attending what became the Holland Academy, presumably in preparation for the gospel ministry, several years before he made his confession of faith (1855).[29] He was probably among those boys who received beginning Latin instruction from the academy's first teacher about 1852; in those early days, Van Raalte would visit after school once a week to give the pupils their catechism lessons; Winter was well catechized by Van Raalte.[30] Late in life, Winter, in a laudatory sketch of Van Raalte, recalled how popular with the congregation had been the latter's Sunday afternoon teaching and preaching the catechism in the old log church (which preceded the "Pillar Church" of 1856). Van Raalte was "at once orthodox and evangelical, ... a mild Calvinist, modelled after ... the Heidelberg Catechism." Moreover, "those who suspected him of a want of orthodoxy, betrayed a sad lack of the evangelical spirit. Of this, hyper-calvinistic narrowmindedness [meaning the CRC] alone was capable."[31]

But of course it was not Van Raalte alone who impacted Winter during his time at the academy, from which he graduated in 1858.[32] The instructors imported by Van Raalte from the East to teach the young men Latin, Greek, English, mathematics, etc., certainly played their part as well. Two in particular deserve mention here: the Rev. John Van Vleck (1828-1865), principal 1855-1859, and Abraham Thompson (1833-1886), instructor 1857-1858. Van Vleck and Thompson were both Rutgers College graduates, with the former also a graduate (1855) of the seminary in New Brunswick. Thompson and Winter went (with several other Dutch-born Holland Academy graduates) to New Brunswick, New Jersey, for the fall semester 1858, to study at the seminary and college, respectively. Van Vleck left Holland a year later to teach at an academy in Kingston, New York.[33]

Egbert Winter moved to New Brunswick when he was twenty-two years old and would leave there five years later, with a B.A. from Rutgers College (1860; he had entered in the junior class) and a M.A. from its graduate school, the seminary (1863). Already knowing from Holland a number of his fellow New Brunswick students, he would soon become acquainted there with American-born young men from the RCA and other Protestant denominations. His seminary teachers were committed to the doctrinal standards of the RCA in general and to the Canons of Dordt in particular. In response to CRC allegations about the unorthodoxy of the eastern RCA, *De Hope* published testimonies in the late 1860s from two midwestern, Dutch-born, former students at the seminary as to the purity of the Calvinism taught by, among others, its professors of didactic and polemic theology, Samuel A. Van Franken (died 1861) and his successor Joseph F. Berg, both of whom had doubtless also taught Winter.[34] Berg, earlier a pastor in the German Reformed Church, was already renowned before he came to the seminary for his writings attacking Roman Catholicism, the German Reformed Mercersburg theology (which he saw as tending toward "Romanism"), and premillennialism.[35]

Berg's concerns coincide with a couple of the major issues of the time when Winter was studying in New Jersey. Although it was the era of the Civil War, the national crisis seems not to have been particularly disruptive of academic, theological, and ecclesiastical activities in the RCA in general or in the New Brunswick area in particular.[36] Life went on. Several topics were regularly featured during the 1860s in the RCA periodicals, *The Christian Intelligencer* in the East and *De Hope* in the Midwest.[37] First, there was the fear of "Romanism." The hordes of immigrants – many of them Roman Catholics – entering the United States from Ireland, Germany, and (soon) southern Europe, frightened not only the "native Americans" but all Protestants, including RCA members born in the Netherlands; the specter of the western frontier falling into the clutches of Rome was dwarfed only by that of the "papists" subjugating the big eastern cities and ultimately the United States government.[38] Memories of the Reformation and the Counter-Reformation had been revived by the post-Napoleonic resurgence of the Catholic Church in Europe, especially under Pope Pius IX, with his Dogma of the Immaculate Conception of the Blessed Virgin Mary (1854), Syllabus of Errors (among them the separation of church and state, nonsectarian schools, religious toleration, Bible societies, and various manifestations of "modernism"; 1864), and Dogma of Papal Infallibility (1870).[39] The Evangelical Alliance, begun in Europe in 1846 and the United States in 1867, was partly an effort at a cooperative Protestant response to the Catholic threat. Among other things, it promoted missions and an annual week of prayer in congregations of its constituent denominations during the first full week in January; the Evangelical Alliance was a forerunner of the modern ecumenical movement.[40] The RCA weeklies gave the Alliance good publicity.

In addition to the negative task of warning about Roman Catholicism, *The Christian Intelligencer* and *De Hope*, like other evangelical periodicals, gave extensive coverage to the missionary enterprise and mandate. The nineteenth century was "the great century" for Protestant (especially American and British) foreign missions. For its size, the RCA played a disproportionately large role in this enterprise, with its pioneering work in India, China, Japan, and Arabia; and not a few of its missionaries were New Brunswick Seminary products, at least three of them graduating while Winter was at Rutgers.[41]

Moreover, there was a growing concern for domestic missions to reach the unchurched and godless, including the immigrants, in the burgeoning cities as well as on the rapidly moving western frontier.[42] Evangelistic efforts among urban Jews became popular and were increasingly linked with resurgent premillennialism, as negative "signs of the times" (e.g., wars, immorality, unbelief) undermined some people's faith in earthly progress.[43] Where or when Egbert Winter "caught" his particular premillennial "bug" is unclear, except that it was not from his anti-chiliastic theology teacher at New Brunswick, Joseph F. Berg; in any case, it was "in the air."[44] While most Protestants were not yet willing to let social and cultural pessimism stop them from making at least some effort to fight the ills of the day (e.g., slavery, drunkenness, Sabbath desecration, and the like), the emphasis gradually shifted to a more private religion and evangelism. Thus such vehicles of outreach as the American Bible Society, the American Sunday School Union, the American Tract Society, and the Young Men's Christian Association increasingly gained favor with the churches. In the face of the enormous challenges of the era, most American-born and Americanized immigrant Protestants saw the need to cooperate in these and other evangelical parachurch organizations, each set up with a specific goal.[45] The above-named four societies, like the Evangelical Alliance, were regularly endorsed by the RCA weeklies.

Then, in 1857, just when it seemed that evangelical Americans, more than ever before, badly needed to band together to fight Rome, secularism, and immorality, to reform society, and especially to preach the gospel to the nation and the world, the CRC schism erupted in Michigan and soon spread to nearby states. Although *The Christian Intelligencer* did not give much coverage to this secession, *De Hope*, in Holland, Michigan, at the geographic center of the dispute, was begun in part to refute CRC charges against the RCA, particularly its older, eastern wing. *De Hope*'s first editor was Van Raalte's son-in-law, the Rev. Pieter J. Oggel, Winter's predecessor in the Pella church. *De Hope*, as representative of the immigrant RCA churches, and Winter shared a common dismay that the CRC could fuss about petty matters while "the fields were white unto harvest" and "Rome was burning." The CRC's very existence showed to its RCA critics how out of touch these new seceders were with the urgent spiritual needs of the day - not to mention out of touch with American life. In spite of Oggel's best intentions, *De Hope* got embroiled in a seemingly endless, unprofitable controversy with the CRC, especially as championed by its weekly newspaper, *De Wachter* (1868). And Winter would, willy-nilly, become enmeshed in the quarrel, too.

One last ingredient was needed to energize the mainstream American churches and voluntary societies to enable them to fulfill effectively their multifaceted mission: revival. Earlier years had seen the Great Awakening and the Second Great Awakening, as well as the socially informed urban evangelism of a Charles G. Finney. The 1860s witnessed the beginning of the work of Dwight L. Moody, a pragmatic, Arminian, premillennial layman, and his songleader Ira D. Sankey, whose gospel songs, widely used in evangelistic meetings and the Sunday school, would help to transform American hymnody. These men, their message, and their methods eventually gained widespread RCA support, in spite of occasional Calvinist demurrers. The middle years of the nineteenth century witnessed what some have called "the triumph of Methodism" and the continued waning of Calvinism.[46] "Perhaps the closest thing to a truly national revival"[47] began in a congregation of the Reformed Protestant Dutch Church (RCA) on Fulton Street in New York City at a noon businessmen's prayer meeting in the fall of 1857, the same year, by an odd coincidence, that the CRC seceded in Michigan. This "prayer meeting" or "businessmen's" revival of 1857-1858, featuring interdenominational participation and speakers in "union" prayer meetings, was promoted by the YMCA and was quickly headlined by the religious and secular press; it stressed individual conversion and piety (as soon embodied in Moody), not social reform (as seen in Finney).[48] *The Christian Intelligencer* carried a regular front-page column on it for many years, even after its zenith.[49]

The prayer meeting revival spread rapidly to many cities across the United States, including New Brunswick, where Egbert Winter had arrived in 1858, just when the awakening was peaking. The degree to which he was influenced by the revival is unknown, but one of his classmates reports that "in the college and in the Seminary he was foremost in the religious activities of student life...."[50] Moreover, the seminary faculty minutes of May 1858 speak of "a great awakening of religion," while in May 1860 they tell of a union prayer meeting with Rutgers College.[51] Engelbert Christian Oggel, the brother and successor of P.J. Oggel as editor of *De Hope*, attended New Brunswick Seminary 1863-1866, just after Winter graduated. The younger Oggel tells of a "catholic" (ecumenical) experience he had as a seminary student, when there were monthly Sunday evening prayer meetings in one of the churches to pray for the conversion of the heathen. These union prayer services were attended by Reformed, Presbyterians, and Baptists. "We sang and prayed together...," heard messages, and gave offerings "for this great cause. Through such meetings we learned to know, value, and love each other."[52] Moreover, already in Winter's day the seminary student body was quite diverse, including Methodists, Episcopalians, Presbyterians, and others, in addition to the eastern and midwestern Dutch Reformed core.[53]

Egbert Winter was apparently no exception to the platitude that students commonly learn more outside of class than in it. Whatever he may have been imbibing about the truths of Dordtian Calvinism from his seminary teachers should be viewed in the context of the larger life of the church and nation. His subsequent career can be better understood in light of the situation circa 1860 sketched in the preceding paragraphs. Winter would be more akin in mentality to the evangelical Reformed churches in the east (and also to that of the Gelderland party of Van Raalte) than to that of De Cock, the northern party, and the CRC. It is not that the CRC had no exposure at all to Winter's world; it is rather that the CRC seemed, for whatever reasons, to be impervious to it. That he was more open to the American environment may be due to many factors, which, to explore, would probably involve largely fruitless speculation, given the paucity of the evidence.

A safe guess, however, is that one factor opening him up to (further) Americanization was his union with the daughter of an American-born RCA minister. On 26 May 1863, less than a month before he received his seminary degree, he married Mary Emma, the daughter of the Rev. John Cannon Van Liew of New Brunswick.[54] Whether Winter knew his father-in-law, who died early in 1861, is uncertain. What is interesting about the relationship is not merely that Van Liew had been a preacher and teacher in New York and New Jersey but that he was a nephew of the Rev. Isaac N. Wyckoff, the Albany pastor who had befriended the 1846-1847 Michigan immigrants on their way west and had arranged the 1850 "marriage" of Classis Holland to the Dutch Reformed church in the east; this merger was, of course, anathema to the seceders of 1857. It is unknown whether Winter was acquainted with Wyckoff (who died in 1869), but the genealogical connection suggests that Winter's marriage further cemented his eastern RCA ties.[55]

The bond was strengthened further by his call to be the minister of the Reformed Church in Cuddebackville, New York (near the New Jersey border), where he was examined, ordained, and installed on 11 August 1863. The sermon was preached by Winter's former Holland Academy teacher and friend, the Rev. John Van Vleck, a man greatly admired by his pupils in both Michigan and Kingston, New York.[56] He was pastoring a church only a little over twenty miles up the road from the Cuddebackville congregation. Winter, who was only the second pastor of this English language church organized in 1854, seems to have been the first midwestern Dutch immigrant to serve an RCA congregation in the east.[57] He may have taken this charge partly so that his bride, who was possibly in fragile health, could live near her family in New Brunswick. In any event, she died at Cuddebackville on 23 March 1864, after less than ten months of marriage, and was buried in her home town. A year later, Winter's mentor Van Vleck also died (of tuberculosis).[58] Thus, two of Winter's ties to the east were severed with the deaths of his wife and his former teacher. Then, toward the end of 1865, Winter married Minerva, daughter of William Cuddeback of Cuddebackville.[59] This, too, may have prompted Winter to think of leaving Cuddebackville, because it can be awkward to have one's wife's kinfolk in the congregation, especially when the town bears their name. However this may be, early in 1866 Winter accepted the call to be the pastor of the First Reformed Church of Pella, and the Cuddebackville church publicly expressed its high regard for him and its regrets at his departure.[60]

Pella

Although this was in a sense a return "home" to his own Dutch-speaking immigrant people, Winter must have been gripped by a strong sense of a "missionary" call to Pella, because several factors militated against an easy time there: he had been in the east, longer away (eight years) from the Dutch environment than most Michigan seminarians; he did not know Iowa; his wife was not Dutch; and above all, he had a very difficult ministerial assignment, namely, to succeed the gifted and largely beloved Pieter J. Oggel, and to tame an unruly congregation on the verge of splitting after more than three pastorless years. This was, however, no leap in the dark.

A very brief excursus on the previous history of the First Reformed Church of Pella is necessary at this point. The only church in the colony during the first few years after its founding in 1847 was Hendrik Pieter Scholte's non-denominational "Christian Church." During the early 1850s opposition to Scholte's theology, churchmanship, and business practices gained momentum, so that, finally, Van Raalte was called in from Michigan in 1856 to organize the First Reformed Church as a part of his Classis Holland. This congregation had relatively little natural cohesion, its "inclusive" conglomeration of Scholtians, Gelderlanders, and northerners being held together mainly by its dislike of Scholte's ideas or ways, or both. It took four years and seven calls (including two to Van Raalte) to procure a resident pastor, P. J. Oggel, who served fairly effectively, given the circumstances, for three strenuous years (1860-1863), resigning for health reasons. The main problem (among many) over the first decade of the church's existence was the recurring unhappiness of the northerners with the Scholtians, especially with regard to the latter's influence in the Sunday school (e.g., the Scholtians' permission of "non-Reformed" teaching in the Sunday school, or their suggestion that there be a "union" Sunday school with the Pella Baptists).[61]

On 1 August 1864, about half way through the congregation's second pastorless period, Egbert Winter's name first appeared in the consistory minutes as one of three ministers (the other two were in Michigan) to be invited to Pella to preach, presumably as both pulpit supply and potential pastor.[62] This was only about four months after his first wife's death in Cuddebackville. Someone in Pella must have known that this young widower in the faraway east might now be available for a call to the frontier. That someone was almost surely the Rev. Abraham Thompson, who knew Winter well from their Holland and New Brunswick days, and who, as founding pastor of Pella's English-language Second Reformed Church (1863), was working closely with the consistory of First Church during its pastoral vacancy (1863-1866).[63] Although Winter did not accept the 1864 invitation to visit Pella, he was again (March 1865) asked to come, which he did in July and early August 1865, just when the situation in the congregation was taking a critical turn.[64]

The chief "troublemaker" seems to have been Adriaan Nultenbok, an 1855 immigrant who within a year had become an elder in the strictest Calvinist conventicle in Pella; he and his group had been incorporated in 1856 into the "united" Reformed congregation, which he had then served regularly as an elder.[65] By December 1864, however, he had evidently begun to give up on the RCA and declined to be nominated for re-election.[66] He had been presumably among those who wrote the Rev. Douwe J. Vander Werp of the infant CRC in Michigan early in 1865 requesting "that someone come there [to Pella] to preach, and that their desire is that a congregation be established there."[67] When Winter was in Pella that same summer, Nultenbok was one of those who had to be visited by him and the elders for plotting a Seceder congregation there and collecting funds for its minister.[68] Just after Winter left Pella, Nultenbok and another member asked the consistory to let Dominie Vander Werp preach at First Reformed Church; this request to have the fox in the chicken coop was, predictably, denied, whereupon Nultenbok and his cohort declared themselves to have seceded from the congregation.[69]

At a congregational meeting 27 September 1865, in a close vote which was immediately made virtually unanimous, Egbert Winter was called to be the pastor of the discord-riven First Reformed Church of Pella.[70] Not surprisingly, given the tenseness of the situation, he did not make his decision quickly. Correspondence was exchanged; he had questions needing answering.[71] It was in this period, too, that he remarried, presumably making him readier (with a life-partner) to say "I do" to Pella, which he did in early January 1866[72] Arriving there in late February, he was soon installed as pastor by his friend Abraham Thompson, who on this occasion preached for the first time in the Dutch language.[73] The Winter-Pella honeymoon, however, was short-lived.

At the end of March a congregational member had to be visited by a consistory committee for holding a fund-raising meeting at his home to bring Vander Werp to preach[74] The CRC Classis, meeting on 6 June 1866, in response to a second request from Pella people who desired to secede from the RCA congregation there, authorized him to travel to Pella to investigate the situation and, if need be, organize a church.[75] On 2 July, a First Church member asked, on behalf of himself and some others in the congregation, that the consistory permit Vander Werp to preach in the unused, small Stone Church in town for about three Sunday mornings. Understandably, the request was turned down, because consistory recognized that Vander Werp intended to set up a seceder congregation[76] – which he in fact did on 12 August 1866. The official letter of Afscheiding, dated 2 August 1866, was signed by forty-two persons (although Vander Werp reported to the CRC synod that the Pella church began with sixty-two members).[77] The seemingly inevitable had come to pass.[78]

Winter's coming did not precipitate the split but certainly reinforced its inevitability, and he could not have failed to have taken personally the departure of so many from the congregation upon his arrival. But how could those imbued with a northern mentality – focused backward on Dordt – realistically be expected to embrace a pastor tinged with premillennialism,[79] the American zeitgeist, and the missionary spirit, a man trained first by the "Gelderlander" Van Raalte and then in the evangelical, inclusive, ecumenical east – even if he *had* been baptized by Dominie De Cock himself and raised in a family committed to the Groningen version of the 1834 Secessionist faith? How could Winter possibly have competed for the hearts of the northern party in Pella against the likes of a Douwe J. Vander Werp, who had been De Cock's right hand man (undoubtedly known to Winter's parents in the Netherlands) in the Afscheiding and later had been prepared by him for the pastorate? Vander Werp was the genuine article, uncontaminated by the American experience, since he had emigrated only recently and as an older man. He quickly became the backbone of the CRC, trained five of its future ministers, and was the first editor of *De Wachter*.[80]

The Nultenbokite exodus (which took several years) did not, unfortunately for Winter and the congregation, bring peace to the First Reformed Church of Pella. The disputed election of an elder in January 1868 led to a prolonged controversy which badly divided the consistory, put Winter through much anguish, and ultimately seems to have played a role in the forming of a third Reformed congregation in Pella, late that same year.[81] As if this were not enough trouble for one year, a bitter quarrel between an elder and a layman erupted, and a member had to be disciplined for denying the deity of Christ.[82] Evidently worn out by all the tumult of his first three years in Pella, Dominie Winter requested and got an extended out-of-town vacation from April to September 1869.[83] The following year he lost still more members of his congregation when they left for the new colony in Sioux County. His later ministry in Pella and elsewhere seems to have been happier but need not concern us here.[84]

Several of Winter's contributions to *De Hope* during his early Iowa years reveal something of the outlook which so repelled the Pella seceders and which made him, in turn, so hostile to them. In a letter dated 28 February 1868, he praises a "Christian convention in Iowa" which he was privileged to attend in which participants from various evangelical denominations spent a couple of days listening to speakers, praying, and talking about matters such as evangelism (even street preaching) and spiritual renewal. "Instead of arguing so much about points of difference, would it not be healthier to talk about the true unity of the heart. Although total unity of ideas is not to be expected here, one still needs to preserve, cultivate, and reveal basic heart unity." The opening address was delivered by Dwight L. Moody, whose spirit and words Winter receives with great appreciation – and no hint of criticism.[85] The great evangelist, it should be recalled, was anything but a card-carrying Calvinist.

A few months after the convention, Winter penned a sarcastic response (entitled *Wat Nog?* – "What Next?") to a report in *De Wachter* that the Baptist minister in Pella had preached one Sunday in Second Reformed Church when Dominie Thompson had to be absent. The CRC piece had asked "What next?" after relating this distressing bit of ecumenicity. Winter replies that Vander Werp, *De Wachter*'s editor, had preached various times in Van Raalte's church in Holland, Michigan: *wat nog?* – that John Bunyan was a Baptist: *wat nog?* – that the missionary Adoniram Judson was a Baptist: *wat nog?* – and that the preacher Charles H. Spurgeon is a [Calvinistic] Baptist: *wat nog?*[86] Thus, Winter, although committed to the Reformed faith, continued to value fellowship with people of other evangelical denominations. For example, he took a leading role, along with a Baptist, at the fifth annual Marion County Sunday school convention at the end of May 1870, held in Pella's Second Reformed Church.[87]

A different sort of contribution to *De Hope* came in January 1869, when Winter told of a recent trip he had made to the Rocky Mountains. He saw the pathetic spiritual conditions there and the urgent need for home missionaries in Wyoming and Nebraska. Undoubtedly his vision for the west would help him to view a colony in Sioux County, to be settled the next year, as a kind of missionary outpost from which (Reformed) Christians could unitedly bring the gospel to those farther west.[88] Then, in February, he added an article both urging the end of the ecclesiastical battles between the RCA and the CRC and confessing that this is probably a vain hope, since the Afgescheidene "brothers" *will* not be convinced of the error of their ways.[89] The next notable contributions by Winter to *De Hope* – already mentioned at the beginning of this article – would be those describing the Orange City colony in the summer of 1871.

Conclusion

The "brothers' quarrels" of the Netherlands and Pella continued in Orange City. Not surprisingly, the Rev. Seine Bolks (1811-1894) and the Rev. Jan Stadt (1828-1900), the first pastors of the RCA and CRC congregations there, were disciples of Van Raalte and Vander Werp, respectively. The composition of these churches and their consistories in the nineteenth century fairly well fits the pattern discerned by Robert Swierenga in his statistical studies (with "northeners" predominating in the CRC). The First Reformed Church began numerically stronger, with its earliest consistory and members coming largely from Pella's First and Third churches. The Christian Reformed in Orange City started feebly, with a few Pella people, some of whom soon defected to the Reformed, perhaps because they thought a slightly tainted live preacher – Bolks – was better, especially for their children, than "canned" sermons read by an orthodox elder. Before long, however, the Christian Reformed had a pastor and a substantial influx of immigrants from the northern provinces of the Netherlands; the 1880-1882 Masonic controversy in Michigan helped divert many Seceder immigrants away from the RCA and into the CRC (because the RCA's toleration of Freemasonry cost it the endorsement of the Seceder church in the Netherlands), although it had little direct impact on the Orange City situation, because there were virtually no Masons there in 1880. By 1900, both the Reformed and Christian Reformed congregations, which were unable to live either with or without each other, were thriving in Orange City. Their stories continue to this day and remain to be told.[90]

This is not the place to deal with the questions of Americanization and the "ultimate" rightness or wrongness of the RCA and CRC in Michigan, Pella, Orange City, or anywhere else. Suffice it to say that such debates between heritage and outreach, identity and communication, are not unique to the Dutch Reformed, and will doubtless go on for as long as the church exists – or at least, as Dominie Winter might say, until the millennium.

Notes

1. Thanks and apologies to William Shakespeare and John Steinbeck. For help with this article in general, I am indebted to the staff and facilities of the Albertus C. Van Raalte Institute and the Joint Archives of Holland, both located at Hope College, Holland, Michigan. Additional assistance came from Western Theological Seminary (Holland, Michigan) and Northwestern College (Orange City, Iowa) libraries and from Heritage Hall of Calvin College (Grand Rapids) and the churches whose minutes were used.

2. Robert P. Swierenga, "A Denominational Schism from a Behavorial [sic] Perspective: The Dutch Reformed Separation," *Reformed Review* 34 (Spring 1981): 172-185. Although it is anachronistic to name these denominations "RCA" and "CRC" before 1867 and 1890, respectively, I shall do so for the sake of simplicity.

3. Ibid., 181-185. Swierenga himself has Groningen forebears.

4. Robert P. Swierenga and Elton J. Bruins, *Family Quarrels in the Dutch Reformed Churches in the Nineteenth Century: The Pillar Church Sesquicentennial Lectures* (Grand Rapids: Eerdmans, 1999), 27-34; Earl Wm. Kennedy, "Eden in the Heartland," *The Church Herald* 54 (March 1997): 9, 15; Henry Beets, *De Chr. Geref. Kerk in N. A. Zestig jaren van strijd en zegen* (Grand Rapids: Grand Rapids Printing Company, 1918), 27-48, 79-84; D. H. Kromminga, *The Christian Reformed Tradition: From the Reformation Till the Present* (Grand Rapids: Eerdmans, 1943), 79-98; Herbert J. Brinks, "Religious Continuities in Europe and the New World," in Robert P. Swierenga, ed., *The Dutch in America: Immigration, Settlement, and Cultural Change* (New Brunswick: Rutgers University Press, 1985), 209-223. Brinks' thesis is convincing, namely, that the American Dutch Reformed schism of 1857 was rooted primarily in internal differences among the 1834 seceders.

5. Swierenga, "A Denominational Schism," 175, 180; Swierenga and Bruins, *Family Quarrels*, 5-8, 99-103.

6. Jacob Van Hinte, *Netherlanders in America: A Study of Emigration and Settlement in the Nine-*

teenth and Twentieth Centuries in the United States of America (1928), Robert P. Swierenga general editor, Adriaan De Wit, chief translator (Grand Rapids: Baker, 1985), 463-482; Henry S. Lucas, *Netherlanders in America: Dutch Immigration to the United States and Canada, 1789-1950* (Ann Arbor: The University of Michigan Press, 1955), 334-345.

7. E. [Egbert] W. [Winter], *De Hope*, 1 [actually 8] June 1871, 3 (letter, Pella, 24 May 1871, reporting on the latest Classis Illinois meeting [no date]). All translations of untranslated materials are mine.

8. "Unity makes strength" (the RCA motto). E. Winter, "Een Nieuw Veld," *De Hope,* 27 July 1871, 1-2 (letter, Pella, 10 July 1871); the CRC periodical *De Wachter,* 11 August 1871, quickly responded to his attack.

9. Consistory Minutes, 12 June, 7 August 1871, First Christian Reformed Church, Pella; *De Wachter,* 14, 28 July, 11 August 1871; I. Van Dellen, "De Chr. Ger. Gem. te Orange City, Iowa," *Voor het Jaar 1907. Jaarboekje ten dienst der Christ. Gereformeerde Kerk in Noord Amerika* (Grand Rapids: J.B. Hulst, [1907]), 107-108; Van Hinte, *Netherlanders in America*, 482.

10. Van Dellen, "De Chr. Ger. Gem. te Orange City," 108-114; Bill and Nella [Earl Wm. and Cornelia B.] Kennedy, "First Reformed Church, Orange City, Iowa, 1871-1996" ([Orange City, Iowa: Pluim Publishing Company, 1996]; copy at the Joint Archives of Holland), 4-8; Van Hinte, *Netherlanders in America*, 512-517.

11. Beets, *De Chr. Geref. Kerk in N. A.*, 122-123. The Belgic Confession, Article 29, distinguishes the true (i.e., Reformed) from the false (i.e., Roman Catholic) church; the implied designation of the RCA as the "false church" was not lost on the RCA, especially in an era of renewed anti-Romanism.

12. Russell L. Gasero, *Historical Directory of the Reformed Church in America 1628-1992* (Grand Rapids: Eerdmans, 1992).

13. Helena Visscher Winter and Sara Fredrickson Simmons, "The Families of Jan Harm [sic] Woltman (c. 1789-1819)[,] Jurrien Peter [sic] Winter (1796-1861) and Reena [sic] Aires [sic] Van Weerden (1791-1884). 150 Years in America" (Holland, MI, 1998, photocopy), 4, Herrick Public Library, Holland, Michigan. Robert P. Swierenga, ed., *Dutch Emigrants to the United States, South Africa, South America, and Southeast Asia, 1835-1880: An Alphabetical Listing by Households and Independent Persons* (Wilmington, DE: Scholarly Resources, 1983), 339; Robert P. Swierenga, ed., *Dutch Immigrants in United States Passenger Manifests, 1820-1880: An Alphabetical Listing by Household Heads and Independent Persons* (Wilmington, DE: Scholarly Resources, 1983), 1169.

14. Lucas, *Netherlanders in America*, 46-48; Van Hinte, *Netherlanders in America*, 90; H. Algra, *Het Wonder van de 19e Eeuw: Van vrije kerken en kleine luyden* (Franeker: T. Wever, 1966), 109-110; J. Wesseling, *De Afscheiding van 1834 in Groningerland, deel 1: De Classis Middelstum* (Groningen: De Vuurbaak, [1972]), 41; Swierenga and Bruins, *Family Quarrels*, 16-20; *Biografisch lexicon voor de geschiedenis van het Nederlandse protestantisme*, eds. D. Nauta et al. (Kampen: Kok, 1983), 2:129-132; Gerrit J. ten Zythoff, *Sources of Secession: The Netherlands Hervormde Kerk on the Eve of the Dutch Immigration to the Midwest* (Grand Rapids: Eerdmans, 1987), 110-127.

15. Egbert Winter, "De Grafstede," *De Hope*, 20 May 1884, 4 (a tribute, at his mother's death, to her piety). Reinje Aries Van Weerden (1791-1884) bore at least ten children to two husbands, made shoes to augment the family income, lived a very long time, and evidently exerted a strong Christian influence on her descendants. By her first husband, a Woltman, she became the grandmother of the Rev. Harm Woltman, a midwestern RCA pastor, who died young (1870), as well as of the wife of the Rev. Peter Lepeltak, another midwestern RCA pastor, who had a long and effective career. By her second husband, Reinje was not only the mother of the Rev. Egbert Winter but the grandmother (through two other sons) of two more RCA ministers (named for Jurrien Winter) and of a Congregational minister named for his childless uncle Egbert. Winter, "Families," 4, 7, 12-13, 17; Elton J. Bruins, *The Americanization of a Congregation*, 2nd ed. (Grand Rapids: Eerdmans, 1995), 150, 196; Gasero, *Historical Directory of the RCA*.

16. Wesseling, *De Afscheiding in Groningerland*, 1:38-39.
17. G. Keizer, *De Afscheiding van 1834. Haar aanleiding, naar authentieke brieven en bescheiden beschreven* (Kampen: Kok, 1934), between 576 and 577.
18. De Cock was not much in Ulrum after 1835, but a pastor was needed to perform baptisms, and he was the only Seceder minister in the area; Wesseling, *De Afscheiding in Groningerland*, 1:75.
19. Ibid., 1:78.
20. *The History of Marion County, Iowa* (Des Moines, 1881), 686, says that he was six years old; evidently this information was from Egbert himself.
21. Mrs. Winter's children by her first marriage (to a Woltman) emigrated with the Winters; see note 15 above. Winter, "Families," 4, 31; Swierenga, *Dutch Emigrants to the U.S.*, 339, 341; Swierenga, *Dutch Immigrants in U.S. Passenger Manifests*, 1066, 1169, 1177-1178; Robert P. Swierenga, ed., *Dutch Households in United States Population Censuses, 1850, 1860, 1870: An Alphabetical Listing by Family Heads* (Wilmington, DE: Scholarly Resources, 1987), 1266, 1277, 1387-1388; J.W. Beardslee, "The Passing of Dr. Winter," and J.H. Karsten, "Michigan Letter," *The Christian Intelligencer*, 19 December 1906, 834.
22. Egbert's parents are buried in Holland's Pilgrim Home Cemetery. Swierenga, *Dutch Households in U.S. Censuses*, 1266; Winter, "Families," 6; "Pilgrim Home Cemetery," Herrick Public Library, Holland.
23. Winter's older brother's first child, a daughter, was baptized in this church the next month, but it was nearly two years more before her parents made their confession of faith. MS, First Reformed Church membership book [beginning 1854], 26, Joint Archives of Holland; Winter, "Families," 17.
24. "Americanization" can be a slippery concept, into which we will not go; Bruins, *Americanization*, 144-145.
25. Winter, "De Grafstede, " 4. His mother, remaining in Holland, never lived with him during his ministry. He came to a Michigan pastorate in 1884, only a month before she died.
26. Egbert J. Winter, "Separatist Church of Holland," MS, Society of Inquiry of New Brunswick Theological Seminary, 10 February 1862 (thanks to Russell L. Gasero, the archivist of the RCA, New Brunswick, NJ, for locating this document); Winter, in excellent English, takes a moderate view of the Hervormde Kerk, believing it to have suffered from rationalism in 1834 but to have recovered somewhat since then, partly because of the Secession.
27. Van Raalte's merger of Classis Holland with the RCA in 1850 reflects this outlook. His vision for Christian education could not have been achieved without eastern money and teachers. On Van Raalte and Americanization, see Jeanne M. Jacobson, Elton J. Bruins, and Larry J. Wagenaar, *Albertus C. Van Raalte: Dutch Leader and American Patriot* (Holland, MI: Hope College, 1996), 59-68.
28. Kromminga, *The Christian Reformed Tradition,* 107-111, 116; Beets, *De Chr. Geref. Kerk in N.A.*, 77-120; Van Hinte, *Netherlanders in America*, 366-381; Lucas, *Netherlanders in America*, 511-513.
29. Karsten, "Michigan Letter," 834. Karsten was Winter's college and seminary roommate. Confession of faith was commonly done at about the age Winter did it. It did not necessarily mean that he had not been a believer before 1855.
30. D. Broek, "Interesting School-Remembrances, *De Grondwet*, 3 January 1911, 11; Beardslee, "Passing of Dr. Winter," 834.
31. E. Winter, "Albertus Christiaan van Raalte," De Grondwet, 22 August 1911, 11.
32. "Third Annual Catalogue and Circular of Hope College 1866-1867," 37 ("Graduates of the Germinal School"), Joint Archives of Holland.
33. An account of the course of instruction at the Holland Academy may be found in the catalog, ibid.; also see "The Holland Academy," *The Christian Intelligencer*, 24 June 1858. For the academy's teachers at this time, see Wynand Wichers, *A Century of Hope 1866-1966* (Grand Rapids: Eerdmans, 1968), 47-52. Van Vleck, a very able scholar and teacher, had a difficult

relationship with Van Raalte; Jacobson, Bruins, and Wagenaar, *Albertus C. Van Raalte*, 77-82.

34. R. Pieters, "De Ger. Kerk," *De Hope*, 18 November 1868, 1; D. Broek, "De Leer der Gereformeerde Kerk," *De Hope*, 13 January 1869, 1. Pieters (class of 1861) and Broek (class of 1864) quote from their class notes to prove that Van Vranken (not named) and Berg fully held to the Canons of Dort. Howard G. Hageman, *Two Centuries Plus: The Story of New Brunswick Seminary* (Grand Rapids: Eerdmans, 1984), 54, 67-68, 80-81.

35. Ibid., 80; John W. Beardslee III, ed., *Vision from the Hill: Selections from Works of Faculty & Alumni, Published on the Bicentennial of the New Brunswick Theological Seminary* (Grand Rapids: Eerdmans, 1984), x-xi, 49-55.

36. Hageman, *Two Centuries Plus*, 83-84; Wichers, *Century of Hope*, 57-59.

37. The *Christian Intelligencer* was spot-checked, and *De Hope* was carefully surveyed.

38. Winthrop S. Hudson and John Corrigan, *Religion in America: An Historical Account of the Development of American Religious Life*, 5th ed. (New York: Macmillan, 1992), 233-240.

39. Clyde L. Manschreck, ed., *A History of Christianity: Readings in the History of the Church from the Reformation to the Present* (Englewood Cliffs, NJ: Prentice-Hall, 1964), 366-369, 371-375.

40. Ibid., 465, 477.

41. Jacob Chamberlain (1859) and John Scudder (1860) to India, and James H. Ballagh (1860) to Japan; Gasero, *Historical Directory of the RCA.*; Eugene Heideman, *A People in Mission: The Surprising Harvest* (Reformed Church Press, 1980), 1-11.

42. Hudson and Corrigan, *Religion in America*, 222-227.

43. George M. Marsden, *Fundamentalism and American Culture: The Shaping of Twentieth-Century Evangelicalism: 1870-1925* (New York: Oxford University Press, 1980), 32-39, 48-62; Timothy P. Weber, *Living in the Shadow of the Second Coming: American Premillennialism 1875-1982*, enlarged ed. (Grand Rapids: Zondervan, 1983), 41-42, 141-154.

44. Egbert Winter, "Dogmatic Theology," vol. 7, chap. 4, sect. 3, pp. 62-91, "The Second Advent of Christ," bound typescript in Western Theological Seminary Library; after explaining the postmillennial (and implicitly the amillennial) and premillennial views, he opts for the latter, which he says he has held "for years" (90); but he rejects the secret rapture of the church (78); his is a moderate, cautious but firm premillennialism, not dispensationalism. Karsten, "Michigan Letter," 834; Nicholas M. Steffens, "Rev. Dr. Egbert Winter," *De Hope*, 18 December 1906, 4. If Winter had not met premillennialism in Michigan or in the east, he certainly found it when he went to Pella in 1866; Earl Wm. Kennedy, "Prairie Premillennialism; Dutch Calvinist Chiliasm in Iowa 1847-1900, or the Long Shadow of Hendrik Pieter Scholte," *Reformed Review*, 46 (winter 1992): 154-158. Abraham Thompson, Winter's teacher in Holland and colleague in Pella, at least later mildly favored premillennialism; *De Hope*, 20 November 1878, 3.

45. Hudson and Corrigan, *Religion in America*, 147-150, 174, 224-227.

46. Ibid., 224-230, 172-174.

47. Kathryn Teresa Long, *The Revival of 1857-58: Interpreting an American Religious Awakening* (New York: Oxford University Press, 1998), 7; Timothy L. Smith, *Revivalism and Social Reform in Mid-Nineteenth-Century America* (New York: Abingdon Press, 1957), 63-79.

48. Hudson and Corrigan, *Religion in America*, 174. Long, *Revival*, 93-126, argues that the 1857-1858 awakening, unlike the New England revival tradition of Finney and others, did not have much of a vision for social reform.

49. William Anderson, "First Anniversary of the Fulton-st. Daily Prayer-Meeting," *The Christian Intelligencer*, 30 September 1858, 54. Anniversary speakers included Dutch Reformed, Presbyterian, Baptist, and Congregational ministers.

50. Beardslee, "Passing of Dr. Winter," 834.

51. May 1858 and May 1860 New Brunswick Theological Seminary faculty minutes, in the seminary archives (thanks to President Norman J. Kansfield of the seminary for this information).

52. E. Chr. Oggel, "Ik geloof een heilige, algemeene christelijke kerk," *De Hope*, 25 November 1868, 1; these prayer meetings were still continuing.

53. Norman J. Kansfield, telephone conversation with the author, 28 May 1999, citing the school's 150th anniversary book (1934).

54 . It was actually a Rutgers College M. A. degree. *The Christian Intelligencer*, 4 June 1863 and 25 June 1863.

55. *The Christian Intelligencer*, 7 and 21 February 1861; Edward Tanjore Corwin, *A Manual of the Reformed Church in America (Formerly Reformed Protestant Dutch Church) 1628-1878*, 3rd ed. (New York: Board of Publication of the Reformed Church in America, 1879), 514, 561-562. On Wyckoff, see Swierenga and Bruins, *Family Quarrels*, 49-54.

56. *The Christian Intelligencer*, 25 June 1863, 3; "The Rev. John VanVleck," *The Christian Intelligencer*, 6 April 1865, 2.

57. Gasero, *Historical Directory of the rca*.

58. *The Christian Intelligencer*, 31 March 1864, 3; "Van Vleck," *The Christian Intelligencer*, 6 April 1865, 2; Gasero, *Historical Directory of the* RCA.

59. *The Christian Intelligencer*, 7 December 1865, 3; the exact date of the marriage is not mentioned.

60. *The Christian Intelligencer*, 8 February 1866, 3.

61. Kennedy, "Eden in the Heartland," 8-10, 15; K. Van Stigt, *Geschiedenis van Pella, Iowa en Omgeving* (Pella: Weekblad Drukkerij, 1897), 3:108-110; Consistory Minutes, 14 March, 13, 27 June, 11, 18, 25 July, 1 August, 26 December 1859; 9 January, 27 February, 26 November, 3 December 1860; 14 January, 13 May 1861; 11 July 1864, First Reformed Church, Pella.

62. Ibid., 1 August 1864.

63. Thompson and Winter had overlapped three years in New Brunswick. Gasero, *Historical Directory of the rca*. Possibly Winter's other Holland Academy mentor, Van Vleck, had played a similar role by introducing him to the Cuddebackville church.

64. Consistory Minutes, 14 March, 17 April, 29 May, 24, 31 July 1865, First Reformed Church, Pella.

65. Van Stigt, *Geschiedenis van Pella*, 2:127-128; 3:131. Nultenbok, aged forty-two or forty-three, had emigrated as a "Roman Catholic" (surely a misprint!) from Dussen, Noord Brabant, with a wife but no children; a carpenter, he evidently prospered moderately in Pella; Swierenga, *Dutch Emigrants*, 187; Swierenga, *Dutch Immigrants*, 682; Swierenga, *Dutch Households*, 735. Nultenbok and his group had withdrawn in 1857 from the Pella Reformed church because it had "sinned" in joining the RCA, but they soon returned; Consistory Minutes, 22 June, 5 October 1857, First Reformed Church, Pella.

66. Consistory Minutes, 19 December 1864, First Reformed Church, Pella.

67. "CRC Classis Minutes," 5 April 1865, Article 16, quoted in Henry Beets, "The First Christian Reformed Church at Pella, Iowa," 2 (MS, Heritage Hall, Calvin College), translated from the original article in Dutch in *De Gereformeerde Amerikaan* 10 (1906): 366-374. Beets comments that, for some unknown reason, the synod did not act on this for a year.

68. Consistory Minutes, 24, 31 July, 7 August 1865, First Reformed Church, Pella.

69. Ibid., 21, 28 August 1865.

70. Ibid., 27 September 1865. The vote was sixty-seven for Winter and sixty for the Rev. Peter De Pree, a young RCA home missionary in the Pella area, and, like Winter, a product of Holland Academy, Rutgers College, and New Brunswick Seminary; Gasero, *Historical Directory of the RCA*.

71. Consistory Minutes, 23 October, 13 November, 4 December 1865, First Reformed Church, Pella.

72. Ibid., 15 January 1866.

73. Ibid., 26 February 1866; *The Christian Intelligencer*, 15 March 1866, 2. Was Thompson the first easterner to preach in Dutch in a midwestern congregation? Just after Winter came, the consistory, by majority vote, requested to transfer the congregation from the Dutch-speaking Classis of Holland to the English-speaking Classis of Illinois (to which Second Church, Pella, belonged), which was nearby; this decision probably did nothing to encourage the Pella northerners to stay in the RCA, although Winter preached exclusively in Dutch in Pella;

Consistory Minutes, 19 March 1866, First Reformed Church, Pella.

74. Ibid., 26 March 1866.

75. Beets, "The First Christian Reformed Church at Pella," 2.

76. Consistory Minutes, 2 July 1866, First Reformed Church, Pella.

77. The extra twenty presumably included both the few who had seceded previously and those who separated after 2 August but before Vander Werp left town. Ibid., 6, 20 August 1866; Consistory Minutes, 13 August 1866, First Christian Reformed Church, Pella; Beets, "The First Christian Reformed Church at Pella, 2; Van Stigt, *Geschiedenis van Pella*, 3:118-119, 131-133.

78. Incidentally, five years later Adriaan Nultenbok, as a Pella Christian Reformed Church elder, helped organize the Christian Reformed congregation in Orange City; Van Dellen, "De Chr. Ger. Gem. te Orange City, Iowa," 107.

79. Consistory Minutes, 7 October 1872, First Christian Reformed Church, Pella; the first point of this "public declaration," soon to appear in *De Wachter*, is "to oppose the teaching and introduction of Chiliasm, an opinion so commonly permeating the ministry and membership of the Dutch Reformed Church in America"; Beets, "The First Christian Reformed Church at Pella," 3.

80. H. J. Brinks, "Germans in the Christian Reformed Church 1857-1872," *Origins* 9.2 (1991): 39-41; Beets, *Chr. Geref. Kerk*, 39, 43-44, 147, 149, 158-160, 163-164; Wesseling, *Afscheiding van 1834 in Groningerland*, 1:101, 106-110; D. Nauta et al., eds., *Biografisch lexicon voor de geschiedenis van het Nederlandse protestantisme*, (Kampen: Kok, 1988), 3:392-393; Swierenga and Bruins, *Family Quarrels*, 95-96, call Vander Werp "the Van Raalte of the Christian Reformed Church."

81. Consistory Minutes, 1, 6, 13, 20, 27 January, 3, 17 February, 23 March, 6, 20, 17 April, 4 May, 8, 24, 29 June, 6 July, 5, 26 October 1868, First Reformed Church, Pella; Consistory Minutes, 16 November 1868, Third Reformed Church, Pella. Other factors in the division were the large size of First Reformed Church and possibly its dubious Calvinism (especially with the Scholtians still present); Henry T. Rozendaal, *Heralds of Truth: A Brief History of the Churches of Pella* ([Pella], 1969), 21-23. During the course of the controversy, Winter complained that he had never before had such a difficulty of conscience, and eventually he had to ask consistory's forgiveness for his erroneous interpretation of church law (he had been overruled by classis); Consistory Minutes, 20 January and 6 July 1868, First Reformed Church, Pella.

82. Ibid., on the quarrel: 22 June, 6 July, 31 August, 7 September, 5, 26 October 1868; 15, 22 March 1869; on the heresy: 23 March, 28 September 1868.

83. Ibid., 5 April, 6 September 1869.

84. After leaving Pella in 1884, Winter served as pastor of the Second Reformed Church, Grand Rapids, and professor of theology at Western Theological Seminary, Holland.

85. E. Winter, "Christelijke Conventie in Iowa," *De Hope*, 11 March 1868, 1.

86. E. W., "Wat Nog?" *De Hope*, 5 August 1868, 1 (letter, Pella, 23 July 1868), in response to an article in *De Wachter*, 26 June 1868; *De Wachter*, 23 October 1868, 4, replies that Winter errs in putting the revered Bunyan in the same category as the suspect Spurgeon.

87. A.T. [Abraham Thompson], *De Hope*, 15 June 1870, 1 (letter, Pella, 1 June 1870).

88. E. Winter, "Roepstem uit het Westen," *De Hope*, 20 January 1869, 1; 27 January 1869, 1 (letter, Pella, 30 December 1868).

89. E. Winter, "Nog niet genoeg?" *De Hope*, 24 February 1869, 1.

90. Earl Wm. Kennedy, "A Tale of Two Churches: Orange City's First Reformed and Christian Reformed Congregations during Their First Thirty-Five Years," Proceedings of the Association for the Advancement of Dutch-American Studies Conference, September 1985, Northwestern College, Orange City, Iowa (Joint Archives of Holland, photocopy), 99-121.

Geerhardus Vos (1862-1949)
(Photo: Heritage Hall, Calvin College).

Geerhardus Vos as Introducer of Kuyper in America

George Harinck

Paradox

Most Reformed Dutchmen know at least two facts about the Dutch Reformed presence in the United States: the existence of Dutch immigrant communities in the midwest since about 1850 and the presentation of the Stone lectures on Calvinism by Abraham Kuyper at Princeton Theological Seminary in 1898. Looking closer, these two facts seem difficult to connect. Why did not Kuyper deliver his lectures to his brethren in the midwest, and why were sophisticated Presbyterians at Princeton interested in this beggar-like Dutch Neo-Calvinist?

A key to solve this paradox offers the experiences of Geerhardus Vos (1862-1949). Vos was of Dutch descent, but he spent the major part of his career as a professor of biblical theology at Princeton Theological Seminary (1893-1932). This was the community where he worked and lived, with his American wife Catherine Frances Smith and their four children, publishing in English, and hardly ever speaking Dutch anymore.

Today Vos is largely a forgotten man, only known to a small circle for his biblical theology.[1] In Dutch literature on the history of Neo-Calvinism Vos' name is hardly ever mentioned. In American historical literature, he plays a more or less isolated role in the history of Reformed theology and its seminaries.[2] Peter S. Heslam in *Creating a Christian Worldview: Abraham Kuyper's Lectures on Calvinism* of course mentions Vos, but because Kuyper and his lectures are the subject of the book, Heslam does not pay attention to the specific role of Vos in the event.

This absence of Vos is partly understandable, because he did not like to be in the spotlight. He preferred to live his life as a scholar and a mystic between walls of books.[3] But his monastic lifestyle cannot conceal his crucial role in introducing Kuyper and his Neo-Calvinism in the Christian Reformed and Presbyterian circles of America. He is not just one of the many Dutch immigrants, listed and classified by Robert Swierenga to figure in his statistics. For one thing, Vos has had a hand in shaping Swierenga's Christian Reformed world, scholarly as well as religiously, and played an important role in Swierenga's major field of Dutch-American studies, and, if I may add a personal note, Robert and Joan Swierenga resemble Geerhardus and Catherine Vos in their hospitality to Dutch friends – I cherish recollections of happy hours in their house at the lake.

In this essay I will tell the story of Geerhardus Vos as an introducer of Kuyper and Neo-Calvinism in the Reformed and the Presbyterian communities in the United States, relating the successes and the failures of this introduction to ambivalences in Vos' personal life and the theological agenda of the Dutch and American communities he belonged to.

A Dutch Youth

In order to understand Vos' role, we have to start at the beginning. Geerhardus Vos was born on March 14, 1862 in the Frisian city of Heerenveen in the Netherlands. His parents, Jan Hendrik Vos (1826-1913) and Aaltje Beuker (1829-1910), were both from the county of Bentheim, a part of Germany close to the Dutch border province of Overijssel. They belonged to the Seceders, a group of Reformed people in the Netherlands and parts of the German border region who had left the old Hervormde Kerk in 1834 and next years in protest against non-Reformed theology and church polity. These German Seceders were akin to the Dutch Seceders and played a considerable role in the history of the Reformed churches, in the Netherlands as well as in the United States.[4]

One of the most prominent was Jan Hendrik Vos. He decided to become a pastor, left Bentheim and was educated in the Netherlands, first by the Rev. W.A. Kok and the Rev. J. Bavinck at their theological school in Hoogeveen and after 1856 at the *Theologische School* of the *Christelijke Afgescheiden Kerk* at Kampen, founded in 1854. After his studies Vos returned to Bentheim and was ordained on September 19, 1858 as minister of the Seceded *Altreformierte Kirche* in Uelsen, Bentheim.

In Heerenveen, the Netherlands, a *Christelijke Afgescheiden Gemeente* was founded in 1851, and in November 1860 Vos became its pastor. There Geerhardus was born, the first of four children. He received a life-long social influence of the Seceder milieu in which he grew up, as he wrote at the time of his retirement: "I have always been more averse than sympathetic to 'coming forward.' Maybe this is the remnant of the somewhat world-averse spirit of the old-Seceder pietism my parents lived in."[5] He may have turned into other roads theologically in later years, but in his religious life he stayed near the truths his parents embraced.

His father went from place to place and Geerhardus lived in the rectories of the *Christelijke Gereformeerde Kerk* at Katwijk aan Zee (1865), Lutten (1870), Pernis (1874), and Ommen (1878). The growing *Christelijke Gereformeerde Kerk* lost its sectarian image during these years and the Seceders gradually grew into Dutch society. Geerhardus was a clever boy and it is a sign of the cultural emancipation of his parents that they destined him for higher education. Since there were hardly any Christian gymnasia in the Netherlands at that time, in the summer of 1877 he was sent to the municipal gymnasium of Amsterdam.[6] Since 1873 his mother's younger brother, Henricus Beuker (1834-1900), had been the minister of the *Christelijke Gereformeerde Kerk* in this town. The choice of the Amsterdam Gymnasium was undoubtedly influenced by the fact that the Beuker family could take care of young Geerhardus. He lived in Beuker's Amsterdam parsonage for several years.

Geerhardus had a gift for study, was industrious and had the energy to work. When he started in the third form in 1879, he was allowed to be examined privately for the fourth form at Christmas time. In June 1880 he was promoted to the fifth and last form.[7]

At this stage Kuyper enters his life. As a Reformed pupil interested in spiritual affairs at a public gymnasium, Vos had a fascinating time in Amsterdam in the late 1870s. The *Hervormde Kerk* of the capital was in commotion, moved by orthodox preachers such as A. Kuyper (1837-1920) and F.L. Rutgers (1836-1917). Both actively promoted the Reformed cause in this church over against moderates and modernists. Together they were deeply engaged in the initiative to found a Calvinistic university and prepared the opening of the *Vrije Universiteit* in October 1880. They also planned the founding of a Reformed gymnasium. These developments did not leave the municipal gymnasium untouched. In 1878 parents requested that Vos' school be closed for one afternoon a week in order to enable the Jewish, Roman Catholic, *Hervormde* or *Christelijke Gereformeerde* boys to attend their religious education. (There were no girls in gymnasia at that time.)[8] The curatorium objected, but a reaction was bound to come: ten years later a Reformed gymnasium in Amsterdam was founded. In the end, this Reformed revival did not stop in Amsterdam, but spread over the whole country. In Vos' Amsterdam years the capital became the center of new life in the *Hervormde Kerk*.

Because he had completed his secondary education in 1881, enrollment at the new *Vrije Universiteit* in town would have been a serious option for Geerhardus. But the Seceder community was ambivalent toward this Calvinistic university. One of the main reasons was that the theology department was free from any church. Uncle Beuker gave a typical Seceder comment on this 'free' department in November 1878: "Such a stream or brook needs a Reformed church as a source to take its rise; and it needs a Reformed church as well as an ocean to empty itself into."[9]

But, to be honest, other ambivalences prevented a possible enrollment at the *Vrije Universiteit*. In the spring of 1881 his father decided to depart from Ommen, join the many Reformed emigrants and leave for the New World. The early 1880s were the heyday of the growth of these Dutch-American churches: "Every week big crowds of people from the Netherlands arrive", wrote Rev. G.E. Boer of Grand Rapids to a Seceder pastor in the Netherlands, "and for weeks at a row we announce their attestations in the Sunday services".[10] As a result of this ongoing stream of newcomers, a third Christian Reformed church was being founded in Grand Rapids, for which a new pastor was needed. Vos accepted a call from this Spring Street Christian Reformed Church in Grand Rapids, Michigan. We do not know why Vos, having rejected an earlier call from America in 1877, at the age of fifty-five decided to leave to the new world. Was it a flight away from his recently united fatherland Germany as a rising power?[11] Anyhow, at that time it meant a serious break in the life of his family and in the long run he withdrew his gifted eldest son from the *Christelijke Gereformeerde* Kerk.

When Geerhardus left the gymnasium on 16 July 1881 with an honorable judicium, he concluded both his boyhood and his Dutch life. For ten days later, on Wednesday, July 27, Vos preached for the last time in the Netherlands, in the Amsterdam Bloemgrachtkerk of his brother-in-law Beuker. In the next days the Vos family traveled with a group of emigrants via Antwerp, and left for Philadelphia on the first of August aboard the Red Star Line-steamer *Belgenland*.[12] What of the old world would last in Geerhardus' soul, and what would the new world bring him?

Study in Grand Rapids and Princeton

At the time the Vos family arrived in Michigan, the Christian Reformed community was in full development. While the *Vrije Universiteit* was founded and strained the relations in the field of Reformed theological education in the Netherlands, Christian Reformed theological education in the United States took shape as well. The Christian Reformed Church, founded in 1857, was an immigrant church and relied heavily on its Dutch mother-church, the *Christelijke Gereformeerde Kerk*. Through the years, quite a number of Seceder pastors had emigrated to Dutch settlements in the United States, as ministers or teachers. In 1873 and 1875 J. Bavinck twice had declined a call of the Christian Reformed Church to educate the theological candidates of the young American church. In 1876 the Christian Reformed Church had founded its own Theological School in Grand Rapids, Michigan and appointed the Rev. G.E. Boer as its first teacher. It was theological education in its infancy, but this school in Grand Rapids was the first step towards a position independent of the Netherlands.

It was in this place and in these circumstances that the Vos family settled in 1881. Geerhardus enrolled at the small Theological School in Grand Rapids, intending to become a minister like his father. Seemingly he excelled as a student, for within a year, in April 1882, he was appointed as an assistant teacher. This remarkable arrangement made ends meet, because there was no money to appoint a second teacher, and Geerhardus apparently was too well educated to profit much from Boer's instruction. He kept this position until the summer of 1883, when he declined an appointment for the next course.[13]

In 1883 Geerhardus became a candidate-pastor in the Christian Reformed Church.[14] But he was not satisfied yet. To complete his theological education he first moved to the Presbyterian Princeton Theological Seminary that summer, never to enter the pastorate at all. Because of his preliminary (self-)studies in Grand Rapids he was admitted to the second class of the curriculum. He was a good student and in 1885 he received the Hebrew Fellowship for graduate study in Berlin, awarded by the Princeton faculty for his thesis' on *The Mosaic Origin of the Pentateuchal Codes*.[15] Vos left for the home country of his parents in the autumn of 1885 and studied in the booming capital of united Germany, with theological professors such as August Dillmann, Hermann Strack, and Bernhard Weiss.

Appointments in Amsterdam and Grand Rapids
So, after four years of absence Vos was back in Europe. The young theologian visited his family in the Netherlands several times and it became known to Dr. Abraham Kuyper, founder of the *Vrije Universiteit* and its professor of dogmatics, that the young Vos excelled in his studies.

Here was a big opportunity for Kuyper. Just at that time, in the summer of 1885, the Old Testament professor of the *Vrije Universiteit*, F.W.J. Dilloo, had resigned and returned to his former congregation in Prussia. With the future of his weak university at stake, Kuyper did not waste much time and in the spring 1886 he asked the twenty-four-years old Vos to consider an appointment in the Old Testament chair at the *Vrije Universiteit*.[16] It was an offer Vos was interested in, but in his answer he showed some hesitation as well:

> Naturally I considered the country where my parents live as the assigned circle where God wanted me to labor to the measure of my capacities and opportunities. Then you placed another prospect next to this one, that, if it were realized, would replant me into the old native soil and on the other hand pull me away from my newly won circle of friends and separate me from that which is dear to me.[17]

He intended to become Americanized, but as a young immigrant he still could easily be puzzled by different perspectives. The situation became complex when the *Christelijke Gereformeerde* weekly *De Bazuin* of 16 July 1886 announced that Vos had been appointed as a teacher at the Theological School in Grand Rapids by the synod of the Christian Reformed Church.[18] The letter of appointment, dated at the end of June, and received in Berlin in the first half of July, certainly came too early in Vos' life. He first wanted to write a dissertation.

The *Vrije Universiteit* expected much from Vos too, and gradually Vos came to share this enthusiasm. His opinions had changed since his stay in Europe. The personal contacts with faculty and board had been positive, and the welcoming of the Doleantie of 1886 – a Reformed secession from the Hervormde Kerk led by the *Vrije Universiteit* professors Kuyper and Rutgers – by Christelijke Gereformeerden like his uncle Beuker, contributed much to his positive mood. Now an ecclesiastical connection with the theological department of the university seemed at hand. Beuker, previously critical of the *Vrije Universiteit*, now endorsed it. Vos was touched by the excitement and expectation that beset the young *Vrije Universiteit* in the decisive year of 1886, and attracted by its maturing theological principles over against the dominant critical theology of the German schools he knew so well. Just as he was troubled by the low academic standards and poor prospects of the Theological School in Grand Rapids, he was attracted by the program and the potentialities of theological education at the *Vrije Universiteit*. In short, Kuyper and his drive to reform culture had put a spell on him.

However, his parents in the United States were not touched by the quickly changing situation within the Dutch Reformed community caused by the Doleantie. Perhaps they still considered Kuyper's attitude in the first place as a neglect of the *Christelijke Gereformeerde Kerk*, but above all they wanted their eldest son to leave Europe, to stay with his own kin and accept the call to the School in Grand Rapids.

The board of the *Vrije Universiteit* wanted a quick decision. It made provisions for him to continue his studies while he served as professor, and appointed him on September 15, 1886.[19] But solidarity with his parents forced the young Geerhardus to decline the call of the *Vrije Universiteit*. In a sad letter to Kuyper, written on October 7 in the parsonage of uncle Beuker in Leiden, he explained why:

> The correspondence with my parents made it necessary for me to make a choice which had become doubly difficult after acquaintance with the *Vrije Universiteit*. Had not such tender motives as the relation between parents and child mixed up in our consideration and made that choice totally inevitable, that would not have been done. The impulse of undivided sympathy with the glorious principle that your institution represents and seeks to propagate drove me, as it were, within her walls. It would have been an honor and a delight to me to be permitted to serve the *Vrije Universiteit* with my frail energies.
>
> The circumstances, as they have formed themselves under God's rule, apparently do not allow that. My parents cannot view the case in the same light in which I learned to look at it as of late. In case I, against their advice and wishes, dared to follow the inclination of my heart, I would bring grief to them, from which I have to save them at any cost. Taking this into consideration, I see no other way than to choose the field of activity assigned to me in America.[20]

Vos' "no" was a severe blow for the *Vrije Universiteit*, all the more because the same meeting of curators that had to accept Vos' refusal also had to deal with the departure of another theologian, Ph.J. Hoedemaker, who opposed the Doleantie.

In the same month, Vos finally was ready to accept the appointment at Grand Rapids, but his study was delayed for two years because of his bad health.[21] In the autumn of 1886 he did not return to busy Berlin, but left for Strassburg, to write his dissertation at the modern Kaiser-Wilhelm-Universität. After a year, he still was not at peace with his decision, as he wrote in an ambivalent mood to his friend Herman Bavinck from Strassburg:

> I am going to America with the feeling that my place is not there. And I leave the Netherlands with the knowledge that even if my work be insignificant, I could do it there with joy and sympathy. More than once I have regretted that last year when they made me a proposal in Amsterdam, I did not make a decision. And I still sometimes doubt if I may or even should return, especially if it is wise to go there without having accomplished my goals here.[22]

In the spring of 1888 he received his Ph.D at Strassburg University. His dissertation, supervised by the Arabian and Syriac expert Th. Nöldeke, was not on German critical theology, but on the collation, translation and introduction of an Arabian text.[23]

After having said goodbye to friends like the *Christelijke Gereformeerde* dogmatician Herman Bavinck (1854-1921), professor at the Theological School at Kampen since 1882, he sailed off to the United States on May 19, 1888. Bavinck considered his departure a loss for the *Christelijke Gereformeerde Kerk*.[24] Vos never returned to the Netherlands or Europe again. On September 4, 1888 he was installed as a teacher in dogmatics and exegesis at the Theological School at Grand Rapids.

He had passed by the *Vrije Universiteit*, but via his inaugural address "De uitzichten der theologie in Amerika"[25] he imported Kuyperian insights into the Christian Reformed community. According to Kuyper, the United States represented the world's happiest conjunction of church and state, of piety and liberty, brought about by Calvinism.[26] Calvinism would blossom there one day. Vos agreed, and introducing these Kuyperian notions, he rejected apologetics, and advocated a Christian idealistic life-embracing view opposing the dominant American spirit, embodied in Herbert Spencer's philosophy of evolution. The principles of this view had to be formulated by theology. In order to do this, the Reformed in America had to rely on Dutch theology: "God wants us to benefit and be blessed by the wonders He has worked there."

In the next years he taught at least twenty-five hours a week and wrote lengthy lectures on dogmatics, philosophy, New Testament Greek and idolatry.[27] One may doubt whether he was on the right place, but in Grand Rapids he proved to be the learned man Kuyper and Rutgers would have liked to attach to the *Vrije Universiteit*.[28]

Introduction of Kuyper and Bavinck in the United States
Vos' departure turned out to be a blessing in disguise for the *Vrije Universiteit*.

When Vos returned to the United States in the summer of 1888, there was a debate, "unrivalled in American Presbyterian history,"[29] on the revision of the Westminster Confession. Many Reformed churches throughout the world had revised their confessions, and now Charles Briggs (1841-1913), professor of Hebrew at Union Theological Seminary in New York, and other American Presbyterians favored a revision, in order to reject in the name of theological progress what Briggs in 1889 called "orthodoxism," the preference of tradition to truth.[30] Related to the revision issue was Briggs' opposition to the doctrine of biblical inerrancy. His most important opponent was the young B.B. Warfield (1851-1921), professor of dogmatics at Princeton Theological Seminary since 1887, who defended the Westminster Confession as "the best, safest and most acceptable statements of the truths ever formulated" and would only favor revision that reached "even clearer and more precise definition."[31] Warfield defended the concept of inerrancy, one of the pillars of Princeton orthodoxy.

Briggs and Warfield were co-editors of *The Presbyterian Review*. In October 1889 their disagreement led to the discontinuation of the journal. Warfield immediately started a new theological journal, the *Presbyterian and Reformed Review (PRR)*. It became a rallying point of Reformed orthodox theology, and Warfield tried to assemble all arguments and all help against higher criticism and revision of the confession, and against modernism in general. The first issue of *PRR* was released in January 1890.

The young Vos sided with Warfield. He had returned to the United States with the intention of working in accordance with Kuyper's theology. His class notes reveal a Kuyperian influence, including use of his phrases.[32] He knew that his intentions meant a change in the educational program of Grand Rapids, and that this would produce tensions in the Christian Reformed community. But a change was favored by the recognition of the poor academic standards of the School, as well as by the introduction of the coherent Kuyperian theology in the Christian Reformed Church via new immigrants and through Dutch and American Reformed journals. One of Vos' students, J. Van der Mey, described this change in 1896 in a letter to Kuyper:

Almost all the ministers of our church who were educated in America embrace your principles. This has two causes. First, the education under Prof. Boer and [G.K.] Hemkes was in every sense poor. After the graduates became ministers, they felt the lack of sound knowledge, and when they entered their congregations, they tried to improve themselves through continued study. And what did they use? They used the works of Abraham Kuyper! Secondly, those who were educated by Dr. Geerhardus Vos have come to your side as a consequence of the powerful training they enjoyed under Dr. Vos. Dr. Vos led us to Dr. Kuyper.[33]

Being a staunch Kuyperian, Vos introduced Kuyper to Warfield as a man who "has done more than anybody else for the revival of the old orthodoxism and the old orthodox theology in Holland, and unites in a wonderful manner the practical gifts of the leader of a religious movement with a well-trained systematic mind."[34]

This first stroke of Vos – Kuyper's only academic contact in the new world – was a hit. Warfield immediately sensed Kuyper could be a useful ally in his defence of Reformed orthodoxy. Warfield answered Vos: why not ask Kuyper for a contribution to the *Review*? Vos was eager to introduce the reviving Dutch Reformed theology, which had influenced him so strongly, to an American audience, and felt the need of strengththening the Reformed element in the Presbyterian Church. Now it was Vos' turn: he asked Kuyper to write an article for the *PRR* on recent theological thought or recent dogmatic works in Holland, and offered to translate it for him.[35] At the same time he asked Bavinck to send him recent Dutch theological publications that might be interesting for the *PRR*.

Kuyper was willing to write, but not on recent Dutch theology, because he either had to pass by in silence the orthodox movement, or speak largely about himself. Vos now advised Warfield to ask his friend Bavinck for the article on recent Dutch dogmatic developments, and to ask Kuyper to write on a topic of his own choice. Warfield agreed and Vos forwarded his requests in accompanying letters to the theologians in the Netherlands,[36] suggesting that Kuyper write on the revision issue, a subject Vos knew Kuyper had dealt with earlier.[37] Vos' letters to Kuyper suggest a feeling of indebtedness to the *Vrije Universiteit*. To Vos' relief, his interventions on behalf of Dutch Reformed theology and Reformed Presbyterianism were successful, for both Bavinck and Kuyper agreed to contribute to Warfield's journal. Kuyper's lengthy article on the subject proposed by Vos – Calvinism and confessional revision – was published in the July 1891 issue with sixteen extra pages.[38] Later on that year, Vos translated an article by Kuyper on the revision of the Westminster Confession.[39]

Vos' initiatives made it clear he was concerned about the situation of Reformed theology in America, and still felt closely connected with his Dutch friends and their work. Bavinck and Kuyper were right in assuming that the emigrant Vos had not left their circle. He was an outpost of their world, who might easily become a colleague in the Netherlands one day, or Kuyper might come over to the new world.[40] Vos had returned to Grand Rapids in 1888, but soon he knew he would not stay there the rest of his life. Several times he was approached to accept a call, from the Kampen Theological School or from one of the Presbyterian seminaries in America. It was difficult for Vos to make up his mind in these matters. The American way of life was attractive, he wrote Bavinck in 1891, but theologically he would prefer the *Christelijke Gereformeerde Kerk*.[41] Unable to get the best of both worlds, he had to live with this ambivalence.

The Road to Princeton

In the end, it turned out that Vos did not move to Amsterdam or Kampen, but to prestigious Princeton Seminary. In 1891 Briggs had delivered an inaugural address upon his induction into the chair of biblical studies at Union. Reiterating his established views on the Bible in a belligerent tone, this address was received as frontal attack on Presbyterian orthodoxy. It triggered his heresy trial in the church, as well as the establishment of a chair in biblical theology at Princeton, with Vos as the intended professor. As a briljant young theologian he was considered able to stand up to Briggs. Although Vos already wanted to leave Grand Rapids when the first call came from Princeton early in 1892,[42] he decided to stay. His theological reservations concerning the Presbyterian Church had vanished, but the postion of Calvinism in the Christian Reformed Church was still insecure and he was afraid of devastating his own work by leaving now. But in early 1893 he did not want to turn down a second call. Perhaps his relationship with the Congregationalist Catherine Smith, whom he would marry on September 7, 1894, helped him to leave Grand Rapids. By this time even his commitments to his parents could not held him there. The reasons for his acceptance were not just Princeton needs – "if Princeton goes down, the cause of orthodox theology and evangelical religion will receive a heavy blow"[43] – but conservatism within the Christian Reformed Church, the deplorable academic situation at the School in Grand Rapids and the severe critique on his supralapsarian (i.e. Kuyperian) teaching as well. In a way, Vos was saved by Princeton, for, as he explained to Bavinck in July:

> Still the long term work is barely attractive enough to remain. The young men that are studying are so underdeveloped with the results that these men pride themselves on their diligence with the reach so small that one must lose spirit. This year the exams were the worst. As I make that observation, I am pleased I am leaving…. I fear that the school here would have to undergo a radical reformation before there can be a change for the better. The two other docents do not do much daily work, and nevertheless make the church impossible; two or three better appointments need to be made.[44]

Princeton was a better place for Vos than Grand Rapids, strategically and intellectually (though it is unclear if he, speaking with a thick Dutch accent and in an intricate German style, reached the majority of his students any better in Princeton).[45] And a professorate in biblical theology – considered by him as an organic history of revelation – attracted him more than his demanding obligations in Grand Rapids had done. He was expected to give only two lectures a week, so there would be much time for study.[46] He became part of a renewal of the faculty of about a dozen members, as one out of six new professors appointed since 1887.

He was ordained by the Presbyterian Church of New Brunswick on April 24,

1894, marking his separation from the narrow-mindedness he had met within the Christian Reformed Church. Kuyper understood Vos' leaving Grand Rapids, "that would have killed him academically," but he did not agree wholeheartedly with his move to the Presbyterian world.[47] It is clear the Dutch Reformed Vos crossed a borderline by entering the Presbyterian world, but it certainly was not a farewell to his Dutch colleagues and their theology. Entering a Presbyterian world, he left the immigrant Dutch community and church, but as a friend and brother-in-arms he approached Kuyper and Bavinck. After Vos' departure Kuyper finally considered the Christian Reformed Church as a backwater, but it was not until Vos went to Princeton that Kuyper caught sight of Princeton Seminary.

Vos' personal relationship with Bavinck became especially close in these years. For the first time since Vos' leave for America in 1888 they had met each other again in the summer of 1892 in Grand Rapids. The ties of friendship were drawn tighter during Bavinck's three weeks stay at Vos' home.[48]

Starting anew in Princeton, Vos asked Bavinck how to lecture best at the Seminary and urged him to send information on any interesting theological news from the Netherlands. In 1893 he showed his disappointment when the merger of the Kampen School and the *Vrije Universiteit* was postponed. In Grand Rapids he had experienced the disadvantages of a theological department that was too tightly linked to the church – and this was the case in Kampen as well.[49] Calvinistic theology could bloom in a less church-controlled and more academic climate like that at the *Vrije Universiteit* or Princeton Seminary, Vos concluded from his first Princeton impressions in a letter to Bavinck, a month after his arrival: "Calvinistic sympathies are stronger now than when I was a student at this place. Warfield especially is very decided, and the others feel his influence."[50] He inaugurated at Princeton on May 8, 1894, with an adress on "The idea of biblical theology as a science and as a theological discipline."[51]

Kuyperian Agent among the Presbyterians

Over the years many of the Christan Reformed community's brightest sons followed Vos to Princeton for their graduate training.[52] But one of the first effects of his move happened in September 1894, when two of Bavinck's Kampen students from the Netherlands, B. Wielenga and W.W. Smitt, enrolled at Princeton Theological Seminary. It was Bavinck's initiative, but Vos was the agent, arranging housing and scholarships. Vos regarded their stay as a "welcome opportunity to tighten the relationship" between him and Bavinck, and between Princeton theology and Dutch Reformed theology. Vos' wish to furnish his bipolar orientation became a recurrent theme in his letters to the Netherlands.[53]

In his opinion such a relationship could be fueled by Bavinck's transfer from the Kampen Theological School to the *Vrije Universiteit*. When Bavinck considered a new call from the *Vrije Universiteit* in the early months of 1894, still in the vacancy of Dilloo, Vos wrote:

I do not doubt that you will do an excellent job in the field of Old Testament studies as well. You are still young enough to get thoroughly acquainted. But would it not be a pity if your position in Kampen were handed over to one of the extreme Secessionists? ... if the training at Kampen has to be directed totally in this spirit, then it is a sad situation for the scholarly prospects in the Reformed Churches of the Netherlands. It seems to me as if your work is the only counterweight to that direction. On the other side, it is true that the *Vrije Universiteit* is in urgent need of you. Certainly it needs to have a more solid foundation. If Kuyper would be taken from us, it would be doubtful if the *Vrije Universiteit* could maintain itself.[54]

In the end Bavinck declined the call again and worked on as a dogmatician in Kampen, until he finally left for the *Vrije Universiteit* in 1902.

But this change of position did not alter the balance of the relationship. It was a one way traffic from the Netherlands to the United States, an import of Dutch Reformed theology, but no export of Presbyterian theology. This was mainly because Dutch Reformed theology was in a creative and expanding phase in the first decade of Vos' Princeton professorate, while the Reformed Presbyterians were in a period of decline.

An illustration of this difference is the history of the American publication of Kuyper's three volume *Encyclopaedie van de heilige godgeleerdheid* (*Encyclopedia of Sacred Theology*) of 1893 and 1894. In this book Kuyper offered a general introduction to theology, its principles, and its relation to other disciplines, from a Calvinistic point of view.

Ever since the start of this project in 1889 Kuyper had had plans to publish this major work in English as well. He had not succeeded in attracting Vos to the *Vrije Universiteit*, but he could use him even more effectively in America to expand his reach into the new world. Vos' departure may well have put the idea into Kuyper's head. By October of 1889, Kuyper had already asked Vos to explore the possibilities for an American edition. It is interesting that he consulted Vos, who was out of his sight, and not a more experienced man in American affairs like N.M. Steffens of Western Theological Seminary of the Reformed Church in Holland, who cared for his son Frederik in Chicago, and with whom he corresponded on a regular basis in these years.[55] Vos was enthusiastic about the attempt to write a Calvinistic encyclopedia, but he doubted "the demand in this country for discussions of this sort, as people are apt to consider theology under an exclusively practical aspect."[56] He offered to do the translation for Kuyper himself.[57]

Kuyper finished the first part of his manuscript in 1893. By that time he wanted to publish the Dutch and American edition simultaneously. In the meantime Vos had transfered to Princeton, and was unable to translate the manuscript as quickly as Kuyper wanted. But he proposed other translators to Kuyper, who did part of the job, though problems with the translation delayed the publication. Another problem was to commit a publisher. Vos asked Warfield for assistance, and gave him the translation of the first hundred pages.[58] On February 26, 1894 Vos wrote to Kuyper:

> Dr. Warfield talked to me about it last week. The publishers seem to be afraid that the book is of too pure a scholarly tenor to be in much demand in this practical country. There is some truth in that.[59]

The market for translated Dutch academic publications was very small in America, and Vos had to plead for Kuyper intensively, until the renowned publishing house Scribner's of New York was disposed to publish the vehicle of Neo-Calvinism. The *Encyclopedia of Sacred Theology* appeared in 1897. This international platforming was a major achievement for Dutch Reformed theology, brought about by the agency of Geerhardus Vos.

Abraham Kuyper in Princeton

Vos did his best to promote other Dutch works of kindred spirits as well. He wrote an extensive review of Bavinck's *Gereformeerde dogmatiek* for *PRR*.[60] He succeeded in interesting Princeton colleagues in his Dutch involvement. This paved the way for what is considered the hallmark of the Reformed Dutch-American relationship around 1900: Kuyper's Stone Lectures at Princeton.

In October 1896 Princeton College celebrated its sesquicentenial. At this event the College would be renamed in Princeton University. Eminent scholars from American and European universities would be present to celebrate the event. Kuyper was invited too, and the trustees of the university offered him an honorary degree of doctor in divinity ("as a theologian") or in law ("as a public man") as well.[61] The degree would be bestowed at the University's inauguration ceremonies on October 22, in the presence of the president of the United States, Grover Cleveland. Kuyper was the only Calvinist of the five theologians, and the only one from the European continent, who would receive a honorary degree. Kuyper had already had plans for an American trip, but this was his big opportunity to speak to "one of the most distinguished audiences ever assembled in America."[62]

Vos and the faculty of the seminary did have a hand in this invitation and considered this possibility an eminent opportunity to meet Kuyper and introduce him to an American audience. For this reason, Vos was asked by the faculty to persuade Kuyper to acccept the invitation and make the long journey to New Jersey. Having corresponded personally with Kuyper for years, Vos now stressed that he wrote on behalf of all the faculty:

> Your work for the Lord and for Reformed theology and the Reformed churches

is cherished by us and with thanksgiving we enjoy the fruit which comes to us most recently in your beautiful *Encyclopaedie*. In my conviction, personal acquaintance between Dr. Warfield and others and you can be of significance for the future. Do not let that opportunity pass by.[63]

Initially Kuyper told Vos he would come, but in June he eventually had to decline the invitation. Serious conflicts at the *Vrije Universiteit* arose, parliamentary elections were scheduled in June, with unpredictable consequences, and Kuyper was under serious critique within the *Gereformeerde Kerken*. In August the synod of these churches would gather and decide whether objections made to Kuyper's Neo-Calvinistic theology would be assigned, and whether the theological education of the churches would be organized according to Kuyper's *Encyclopaedie* – free from the church and in a Neo-Calvinistic setting – or to the Christian Reformed seminary tradition of Kampen. The situation being tense in different fields, Kuyper could not be missed.

The Princetonians were disappointed, but not defeated. The university asked him to come next year, and on behalf of the seminary Vos invited him to deliver the Stone lectures – six to eight lectures on a theological subject – some time between September 1897 and April 1898.[64] This time Kuyper accepted both invitations. He proposed to speak on Calvinism, but postponed the lectures and the doctoral ceremony until October 1898. Kuyper wrote his manuscript in the autumn of 1897 and, learning from past experiences, Vos warned Kuyper either to send him the manuscript immediately for translation, or to postpone the lectures another year.[65] With Dutch-American help the final Dutch draft of the lectures was translated in the first week of October 1898 by J.H. DeVries, H.E. Dosker, A.H. Huizinga, Steffens, and Vos – just in time.[66]

When Kuyper arrived in New York his *Encyclopedia* had just appeared. Vos hoped the author's presence would help to promote the book.[67] Kuyper could now care for the business he had to delegate to Vos for so many years. Kuyper used this opportunity to offer Scribner's the manuscript of his Stone lectures. But, as Vos had already suspected, the publisher doubted the success of the *Encyclopedia* and rejected a second text by Kuyper.[68]

Kuyper's audience was impressed by his person and message, but the reception of Neo-Calvinism was as mixed as the success of his *Encyclopedia*: as Steffens had written to Kuyper so often, Calvinism was not fit for modern American culture, and it was a source of disunity among the Christian Reformed brethren of his time.[69]

Different Tensions
Even to his contemporaries it was largely unknown that Vos had a hand in introducing Dutch Reformed theology at Princeton Seminary, as Dosker wrote to Bavinck, some months after Kuyper's visit: "Because of his position in Princeton, a man like

Vos can have an immeasurable influence, if only he used his influence, and would not lock himself in his study cell."[70] Vos did use his influence, and he is the key to solve the paradox that Kuyper's heritage is best known in the Dutch communities of the midwest, but that he celebrated his finest American hour in the Presbyterian world of Princeton.

Vos' career and challenges are illustrative of the early history of Neo-Calvinism in the modern world. Attracted by the ideal of Reformed science at the *Vrije Universiteit*, Vos tried to contribute to it in the theology department, so crucial to this ideal, first at the Theological School in Grand Rapids, and, failing to succeed there, at Princeton Seminary. His successes and failures in doing so are related to two different tensions in the Dutch-American relationship. One is the ambivalence about Kuyper's theology within Dutch Reformed circles, welcomed by many Reformed people, but opposed by most of the Seceder theologians in the Netherlands as well as in the United States, and the other is the complex relationship between the American Presbyterian theology and Neo-Calvinism, the first welcoming the support of the latter, but not its substance. Combined with Vos' own ambivalence relating to Europe and the new world, Kuyper and the Seceder mentality, the church and academic research, the history of Kuyper's introduction is a true story of two continents. Seen from the Dutch side, it was a success that Vos introduced Kuyper in one of the centers of American religion of the turn of the century. The mood of this success is reflected in Kuyper's self-confident Stone lectures, presenting a radiant Neo-Calvinism, glorified in the United States. The Americans were charmed by it, but even the mild Vos doubted the possibilities for Neo-Calvinism in the new world.

All these tensions were manifested in Vos' life and career. That is why he is an interesting starting point for a balanced history of the attractions and diffenrences, the successes and failures, within this Dutch-American relationship. Like the life and career of Robert Swierenga, it is truly a story of the ambivalence felt by those living in two worlds. As the Dutch Jewish poet Jacob Israël de Haan wrote:

Who often said in Amsterdam: "Jerusalem"
And to Jerusalem was driven then,
Now whispers as a musing man:
"Amsterdam, Amsterdam."[71]

Notes

1. Richard B. Gaffin Jr., ed., *Redemptive History and Biblical Interpretation: The Shorter Writings of Geerhardus Vos* (Phillipsburg: Presbyterian and Reformed Publishing Company, 1980) containing a (not complete) bibliography of the writings of Vos, 547-559.

2. See: *Semi-Centennial Volume: Theological School and Calvin College 1876-1926* (Grand Rapids: Semi-Centennial Committee, 1926); David F. Wells, ed., *Reformed Theology in America: A History of its Modern Development* (Grand Rapids: Eerdmans, 1985). In William K. Selden, *Princeton Theological Seminary: A Narrative History, 1812-1892* (Princeton: Princeton University Press, 1992), 95, Vos is mentioned once, apart from the record of his death in 1932. Bradley J. Longfield mentions Vos only once in *The Presbyterian Controversy: Fundamentalists, Modernists, and Moderates* (New York: Oxford University Press, 1991). W. Robert Godfrey, "The Westminster school," in Wells, ed., *Reformed Theology*, 95. "It may be that Machen's knowledge of the Christian Reformed Church in America and the Gereformeerde Kerken in the Netherlands originated with Vos."

3. David B. Calhoun, *Princeton Seminary, Vol. 2: The Majestic Testimony, 1869-1929* (Edinburgh: The Banner of Truth Trust, 1996), 210: "Gentle and naturally retiring, Vos avoided active participation in public life and controversy." Henry E. Dosker to H. Bavinck, 25 February 1893: "Heard nothing from Vos. He is dryasdust and seems to become a bookworm more and more." H. Bavinck Collection. Historical Documentation Center for Dutch Protestantism, Vrije Universiteit, Amsterdam (HDC).

4. See: Gerrit Jan Beuker, "German Oldreformed Emigration: Catastrophe or Blessing?" in George Harinck and Hans Krabbendam, eds., *Breaches and Bridges: Reformed Subcultures in the Netherlands, Germany, and the United States* (Amsterdam: VU Uitgeverij, 2000), 101-114.

5. Vos to A. Eekhof, 28 October 1932, A. Eekhof Collection, HDC.

6. According to Ransom Lewis Webster, "Geerhardus Vos (1862-1949); a Biographical Sketch," *Westminster Theological Journal* 40 (1977-1978): 305, Vos visited a gymnasium in Schiedam as well. Vos was in the same class as J.W. Pont (1863-1939), professor at the Restored Evangelical-Lutheran Seminary at the University of Amsterdam, 1903-1933, and C.A. Verrijn Stuart (1865-1948), professor in economics at the Universities of Groningen and Utrecht, 1909-1934. In the class of 1879 was Abraham Kuyper's oldest son H.H. Kuyper (1864-1945), professor in church history at the Free University, 1900-1940. Naamlijst der leerlingen van het Amsterdamsche gymnasium, inv. nr. 219. Collection Curatoren van de openbare gymnasia en rector van het stedelijk of Barlaeus gymnasium, arch. nr. 260, Municipal Archives Amsterdam (MAA).

7. F.L. Rutgers to B. van Schelven, 27 August 1886. Collection Curators, Vrije Universiteit, Amsterdam (VU).

8. Copyboek van verzonden stukken, 1862-1881, inv. nr. 158, letter of 10 October 1878. Collection Curatoren, MAA.

9. Beuker in *De Vrije Kerk* 4 (1878): 548.

10. *De Bazuin*, 3 June 1881.

11. James T. Dennison, Jr., "Geerhardus Vos: Life Between Two Worlds," *Kerux: A Journal of Biblical-Theological Preaching* 14.2 (1999): 21, refers to a family tradition that German nationalism was a factor in the Jan Vos family's decision to emigrate to America.

12. In these days of very busy emigration—the *Christelijke Gereformeerde* weekly *De Bazuin* was full of advertisements for the ocean crossing—there was a rumor that the *Koninklijke Nederlandsche Stoomboot Maatschappij*, that had a frequent cheap and fast service from Amsterdam to New York with several steamers, such as the *Stella, Castor, Pollux*, and *Jason*, treated its passengers badly. There were reports of drunken sailors, bad food, and unhygienic conditions (*De Bazuin*, 26 August 1881). This may have been the reason Vos took the alternative route via Antwerp. See: R.P. Swierenga, "Going to America: Travel Routes of Zeeland Emigrants," *Nehallennia* 114 (1997): 19-22, special issue on emigration of Zeelanders to America, 1840-1920.

13. Summary of the theological instruction in the trustees' notebook, Collection Calvin Seminary, Heritage Hall, Calvin College, Grand Rapids (HH).

14. I do not know if he ever preached in the United States before 1888, but he did preach in the Netherlands, see: Gerrit Jan Beuker, *Abgeschiedenes Streben nach Einheit. Leben und Wirken Henricus Beukers 1834-1900* (Kampen: Mondiss, 1996), 246: "At the end of August 1887 Beuker preached to the *dolerende* congregation in Aarlanderveen, while his nephew, candidate G. Vos from the USA, conducted the service in Leiden."

15. London, 1886, with an introduction by William Henry Green, his Old Testament professor at Princeton.

16. Vos was not offered the *first* professorship in Old Testament at the Free University, as was stated incorrectly by Webster, *Vos*, 306.

17. Vos to A. Kuyper, 28 May 1886. A. Kuyper Collection, HDC. An annotated English edition of Gerhardus Vos' letters is being prepared for publication by James T. Dennison, Jr. and Kerux, Inc. of Escondido, California. The translations used here are from that forthcoming volume and are used by kind permission.

18. Vos was appointed by the synod on June 17, 1886. In the first round he had equal votes with J.Y. de Baun. After a serious discussion the synod decided to appoint the one who got two thirds of the votes. In the second round Vos got 42 out of 68, in the third round 46. *Acta van de generale synode van de Christelijke Gereformeerde Kerk,* Collection Christian Reformed Churches, HH. Webster incorrectly states that Vos was unable to consider the call of the Free University, because he already had accepted a call to teach at the Theological School at Grand Rapids. As a matter of fact, he did consider the call from the *Vrije Universiteit*, and only accepted Grand Rapids' call after rejecting the first. Webster, *Vos*, 305.

19. Minutes Directors, 25 September 1886, Collection Directors, VU.

20. Vos to Kuyper, 7 October 1886, Kuyper Collection, HDC.

21. Minutes of the Curatorium, 3 August 1887, Collection Calvin Seminary, HH.

22. Vos to Bavinck, 16 June 1887, Bavinck Collection, HDC.

23. The dissertation was titled *Die Kämpfe und Streitigkeiten zwischen den Banu Umajja und den Banu Hasim. Eine Abhandlung von Takijj ad-din al-makrizijj. Der Arabische Text nach der Leidener, Wiener und Strassburger Handschrift herausgegeben und zur Erlangung der Doctorwürde bei der philosophischen Facultät der Kaiser-Wilhelms-Universität zu Strassburg im Elsass eingerichtet* and was published in 1888 by E.J. Brill, Leiden. Dennison, "Geerhardus Vos," 24, confesses bewilderment about the choice of this topic. A possible explanation is, that Bavinck suggested Vos an Arabic subject as well as this university and this promotor. Bavinck's friend the Arabist C. Snouck Hurgronje had studied with Nöldeke in Strassburg in 1880-1881, and lectured at Leiden University. See: J. de Bruijn and G. Harinck, eds., *Een Leidse vriendschap. De briefwisseling tussen Herman Bavinck en Christiaan Snouck Hurgronje, 1875-1921* (Baarn: Ten Have, 1999), 76-91.

24. On 18 December 1888, Bavinck criticized Christians, who, instead of reforming society, seceded themselves from everything, "and, even worse, set sail for America, holding up the fatherland to unbelief, considering it as lost." H. Bavinck, *De katholiciteit van christendom en kerk*, ingeleid door G. Puchinger (Kampen: Kok, 1969), 35.

25. "Rede van Prof. G. Vos, Ph.D., bij het aanvaarden van zijn professoraat in de theologie aan de Theologische School te Grand Rapids, Mich., den 29en Aug. [sic!] 1888," manuscript, transcribed by J.B. Hoekstra, Pella, Iowa, 7 May 1889. *Collection Calvin Seminary.*

26. For Kuyper on America, see: James D. Bratt, "Abraham Kuyper, American History, and the Tensions of Neo-Calvinism," in George Harinck & Hans Krabbendam, eds., *Sharing the Reformed Tradition: The Dutch-North American Exchange, 1846-1996* (Amsterdam: VU uitgeverij, 1996), 97-114.

27. J. Noordewier, 'De oorsprong van onze Theologische School," in *Semi-Centennial Volume. Theological School and Calvin College 1876-1926* (Grand Rapids: Semi-Centennial Comittee, 1926), 18.

28. Beuker, *Beuker*, 327: "He is called the American Herman Bavinck — like him from German descent.

He was a real scholar like Bavinck – a man with wide horizons, who lifted the education at our School to a level that was unattainable before." Steffens to Kuyper, 1 December 1888: "I don't know if he [Vos] is in the right place. True science is not appreciated in in our Dutch American circles." Kuyper Collection, HDC.

29. Mark S. Massa, *Charles Augustus Briggs and the Crisis of Historical Criticism* (Minneapolis: Fortress Press, 1990), 77.

30. Calhoun, *Princeton Seminary*, 121.

31. J. DeWitt and B.B. Warfield, *Ought the Confession of Faith be Revised?* (New York: n.p., 1890), 39; B.B. Warfield, "The Final Report of the Committee on Revision of the Confession," *Presbyterian Reformed Review* 3 (1892): 329. (*PRR*)

32. J. Faber, *Amerikaanse afscheidings-theologen over verbond en doop* (Barneveld: De Vuurbaak, 1995), 17.

33. J. van der Mey to Kuyper, 18 February 1896, Kuyper Collection, HDC, translation in Herbert J. Brinks, *Write Back Soon: Letters from Immigrants in America* (Grand Rapids: CRC Publications, 1986), 122, 123.

34. Vos to B.B. Warfield, 22 October 1889, Collection B.B. Warfield, Princeton Theological Seminary, Princeton, NJ (PTS).

35. Vos to Kuyper, 1 February 1890, Kuyper Collection, HDC.

36. See: Warfield to Bavinck, 16 June 1890, Bavinck Collection, HDC; Vos to Kuyper, 12 July 1890, Kuyper Collection, HDC.

37. A. Kuyper, "Revisie formulieren van eenigheid," *De Heraut*, 30 March-6 April, 20 April-20 July 1879, republished as *Revisie der revisie-legende* (Amsterdam: Kruyt, 1880). Vos was a subscriber to *De Heraut*.

38. *PRR* 2 (1891): 369-399; also published in *The Presbyterian Quarterly* 18 (October 1891): 479-516, and in Dutch: *Calvinisme en revisie* (Amsterdam: Wormser, 1891).

39. A. Kuyper, "De revisie der Westminster confessie," *De Heraut* 6 and 13 September 1891; published in *The New York Observer*, October 1891.

40. Vos to Kuyper, 1 February 1890: "I was moved by what you wrote about your wish to see me yet one day labor beside you. I would consider it an honor, but it seems as if I will have to labor here. Fortunately there are people here who live in the Reformed truth and who have brought love for the Reformed truth from the old country. Your name, too, is held in great esteem here." Steffens to Kuyper, 25 April 1891: "I would like to send you Dr. Vos, if I had the power to do so. But as long as his parents live and he is unmarried, I don't think he will leave to the Netherlands." Kuyper Collection, HDC. Steffens to Kuyper, 7 May 1886: "I understand, how you have given thoughts to the plan, that it might be better to move with the Reformed people, either to Africa or to America." Kuyper Collection, HDC.

41. Vos to Bavinck, 30 June 1891, Bavinck Collection, HDC.

42. W. Henry Green to Warfield, 29 February 1892: "I enclose a letter just received from Vos, whose queries I will answer, and who suggests no obstruction in the way of his coming." Warfield Collection, PTS.

43. W. Henry Green to Vos, 19 March 1892, Courtesy Richard B. Gaffin. Jr.

44. Vos to Bavinck, 3 July 1893, Bavinck Collection, HDC. For the same negative opinion, see: Steffens to Kuyper, 25 January 1891: "It is a pity that the young man, Vos, wastes his power in such a place. Had he stayed in the Netherlands, he could have contributed much more." Kuyper Collection, HDC, translation in Brinks, *Write Back Soon*, 123. See: Henry Beets to Dirk Scholten, 6 February 1893, for an appreciation of Vos by one of his students in Grand Rapids: "We have a splendid professor in Dr. Vos. He is a Calvinist of the most pronounced type and a supra-lapsarian at that.... He is a young man of thirty and as kind and obliging and humble as I never saw a man before. And what a treasure of knowledge he may call his own! I suppose you know he is a close friend of your old professor Dr. Steffens and also to the Drs. Bavinck, Kuiper, Warfield, etc." Collection H. Beets, HH.

45. Calhoun, *Princeton Seminary,* 208: "Because of the weightiness of his lectures and his patient, methodical style of scholarship, the enrollment of Dr. Vos' elective classes was often sparse." But Cornelis van Til considered Vos "the greatest pedagogue I ever sat under." Dennison, "Geerhardus Vos," 19.

46. Vos to Bavinck, 3 July 1893, Bavinck Collection, HDC.

47. Kuyper to Bavinck, 24 January 1894, Bavinck Collection, HDC.

48. See: George Harinck, ed., *H. Bavinck, Mijne reis naar Amerika* (Barneveld: De Vuurbaak, 1998).

49. Vos to Bavinck, 3 July 1893: "Ik houd niet van een overdreven kerkisme hoewel ik er vroeger zelf aan geleden heb." Bavinck Collection, HDC.

50. Vos to Bavinck, 20 October 1893, Bavinck Collection, HDC. Cf. Vos to Kuyper, 26 February 1894: "I have begun my work here with pleasure. In the midst of the general defection, Princeton exerts a good influence. In the last years they have become more firm here as matters unfold." Kuyper Collection, HDC.

51. *Inauguration of the Rev. Geerhardus Vos as Professor of Biblical Theology* (New York: A.D.F. Randolph, 1894); republished in Gaffin, *Redemptive History*, 3-24.

52. James D. Bratt, *Dutch Calvinism in Modern America: A History of a Conservative Subculture* (Grand Rapids: Eerdmans, 1984), 107.

53. See: Vos to Bavinck, 21 November [1893], 1 February 1894, 22 December 1894, Bavinck Collection, HDC.

54. Vos to Bavinck, 28 March 1894. Bavinck Collection, HDC. It is interesting that Vos and Bavinck were both called with the same arguments. Greene urged Vos to come to Princeton: "Remember that the Master, under whose orders you serve, rules the whole field of battle, and not one corner of it merely. Is he not calling you to a point where you can do his work more effectively" (Calhoun, *Princeton Seminary*, 138). Some months later Kuyper urged Bavinck to come to the Free University with almost literally the same words: "We must not measure our positions and choices too narrow-mindedly and with small considerations, but have to ask: how and where can we serve best the great cause of our confession, in connection with the great struggle of this world?" Kuyper to Bavinck, 4 February 1894, Bavinck Collection, HDC.

55. There are fifteen letters of Steffens in the Kuyper Collection over the years 1882-1899, three of them are from 1888.

56. Vos to Warfield, 22 October 1889, Warfield Collection, PST.

57. Vos to Kuyper, 1 February 1890, Kuyper Collection, HDC.

58. See: A.H. Huizinga to Warfield, 13 February 1894, Warfield Collection, PST.

59. Kuyper Collection, HDC.

60. *PRR* 7 (1896): 356-363, translated in Dutch for *De Wachter*, 2-16 September 1896.

61. H.B. Tine to Kuyper, 11 April 1896, Kuyper Collection, HDC.

62. Calhoun, *Princeton Seminary*, 168.

63. Vos to Kuyper, 30 April 1896, Kuyper Collection, HDC.

64. Vos to Kuyper, 9 October 1896, Kuyper Collection, HDC.

65. Vos to Kuyper, 11 October 1897, Kuyper Collection, HDC.

66. P.S. Heslam, *Creating a Christian Worldview: Abraham Kuyper's Lectures on Calvinism* (Grand Rapids: Eerdmans), 62: unfortunately afterwards Kuyper altered the final manuscript for the publisher, "with a view to bettering the English," as Warfield noted, "but with the effect of waning it sadly...."

67. Vos to Kuyper, 11 October 1897, Kuyper Collection, HDC.

68. Ch. Scribner's & Sons to Kuyper, 17 October 1898, Kuyper Collection, HDC.

69. See: George Harinck, "A Triumphal Procession? The Reception of Kuyper in the USA (1900-1940)," in Cornelis van der Kooi and Jan de Bruijn, eds., *Kuyper Reconsidered: Aspects of His Life and Work* (Amsterdam: VU Uitgeverij, 1999), 273-282.

70. Dosker to Bavinck, 17 January 1899, Bavinck Collection, HDC.

71. Jacob Israël de Haan, "Onrust," in *Verzamelde gedichten* (Amsterdam: Van Oorschot, 1952), 2:358.

A Frisian in the American City:
The Letters of Pieter Ypes Groustra and His Family from Chicago, 1881-1946

Annemieke Galema

When the grain-ship *Castor and Pollux* set course for America from Amsterdam in the spring of 1881, the passengers realized that they would leave their native soil forever. A return trip was not feasible and this made it difficult to say goodbye. Most passengers had sold all their possessions to pay for the passage and keep sufficient money to make the transition. Moreover, it turned out that it was impossible to ship a complete household to America; the steamship company had fixed strict limits. Originally, the *Castor and Pollux* had not been put into service for the transportation of emigrants, but to export cheap American corn to Europe. Passengers were picked up on the way to New York for additional profits.

Among the many passengers on the ship were Pieter Ypes Groustra and his family, who had decided to emigrate to escape the severe poverty at home. Pieter was born on December 10, 1841 in Ee, a village in the municipality of Oostdongeradeel, in the northern Frisian clay region, where he grew up together with his two brothers Renze and Eelze.[1] He mastered carpentry and thus tried to earn a living, first with his wife Pietje Hiddes Van der Wal and after her death with his second wife Frederica Aukes.[2] In the early eighties, Friesland was struck by a serious agrarian crisis that had a negative effect on the entire economy. The farmers in the clay region, who depended heavily on agriculture, suffered severely because cheap American grain flooded the European market and depressed the prices. Small traders and artisans failed to get new orders and they feared the future.

Motivation and Preparation

Although we do not known exactly Groustra's motives for emigration, we can assume that this economic depression played an important part in the decision. Between 1880 and 1914 almost 10,000 emigrants left the northern clay region in Friesland for America.[3] In the year 1881, when Pieter set out, no fewer than 22 persons left his village. And many had preceded them: the Dongeradelen had a strong tradition of migration. By the middle of the nineteenth century, many

Pieter Groustra, his wife Jantje de Boer and his son Cornelis. The younger woman is probably daughter Geeske. (Chicago after 1901, private collection).

people from that region had moved overseas.[4] Their stories, letters and anecdotes were circulating in the village as a standard part of social life. During worship services ministers might read a letter from Iowa from the pulpit, sent by a former church member. Also local newspapers regularly published letters of those that had settled in America long ago. If this information kindled a positive imagination, a potential emigrant was born.

Dozens of the letters that Pieter Ypes Groustra and his family sent from America between 1881 and 1946 have been preserved.[5] These letters describe many experiences of the Frisians in the metropolis of Chicago. An impression of their writings gives us an interesting view on migration at the turn of the century.[6] The letters of the Groustra family can count as exemplary for the Frisian emigrants of this period, since they not only supply instantaneous snapshots but also offer insights in a full life story. They show how a Frisian family affiliated with the Dutch Reformed Church in Chicago and how this church was a platform for their well-being. The letters are representative of the migration movement and also touch two of Robert Swierenga's research interests: the history of the Dutch churches in America and the Dutch presence in Chicago.

Before Pieter and his wife Frederica departed, they had obtained information from J. Wijkstra in Ee, who was an agent of the *Prins & Zwanenburg* shipping agency, with branch offices in Harlingen, Amsterdam, Rotterdam, and Groningen. People could buy their tickets here and Wijkstra supplied laudatory brochures on the immense American country. In the promotion material made by the agency, advertisements could be found for the acquisition of land along the Northern Pacific Railroad, information on climate and distances, comparative figures concerning vegetation in different states and agricultural yields in certain areas that were recommended to emigrants. Wijkstra provided the Groustra family with a simple but useful dictionary of the English language. This was badly needed, since most emigrants only spoke Frisian and Dutch, the latter being their written language.

On May 21, 1881 Pieter and Frederica left for Harlingen with their sons Ype and Anton[7], who were nearly six and four years of age, and from there they went to Amsterdam by boat. They spent the night there before they embarked on the *Castor and Pollux,* which would take them to New York. They shared this experience with emigrants from all over Europe. The inns for emigrants in Amsterdam, Rotterdam, Hamburg, Antwerp, and Bremen had infamously poor hygiene and offered little room for the people and their luggage. On board, it was nearly impossible for the emigrants, who were of many nationalities, to develop mutual understanding, because they lacked a common language. Some of them had already been travelling for weeks from Eastern-European countries to reach the North Sea coasts to get transport to America.

The eighteen-day voyage that Pieter and his family undertook was full of storms and seasickness, bad food, lice and other vermin. In one of his letters he described the journey as very hard, though the time lost to stopovers was kept to a minimum. It is regrettable that Pieter's first letter with the record of travel, written after their arrival in New York, has not been preserved. His story really starts for us after he first encountered the skyscrapers in the metropolis and started his journey to Chicago overland.

To Chicago by Rail

In August 1881 Pieter described how the train journey to Chicago lasted two full days: "sitting night and day, in a heat that has never been felt by any of you." Moreover, they were not able to buy some refreshment, because they had had to pay 22.50 guilders for the excess baggage. This took the rest of their money and Pieter blamed his relatives in Friesland for lack of generosity: "Why, I often thought, did not my Brothers and Friends, who were still able to do so, give me some extra guilders for the journey, they knew [about] my penurious circumstances when I left." In the train the Groustra family had to live on the half-mouldy bread that they had taken from Ee, and cold water to quench their thirst. Pieter found it hard that he could not provide for the needs of his wife and children after such an exhausting journey.

Their arrival at Kensington Garden Station in Chicago was a shock from which they quickly recovered: "There we stood, not knowing what to do next. My wife was crying, 'Where to go without any money? Where could we stay the night?' I addressed my prayer to God in silence, but I did not at all feel depressed or lost. After a few moments of reflection I was taken to Boswinkel's address in Guslei Street, you know that his brother from Frederiksoord had given me a letter for him. It was an hour's run into town. When we got there, I handed the man the letter, also asking him to help a man in distress. He immediately invited us to his house, although his wife was sickly. We were exhausted, but we were entirely treated as friends."[8]

Pieter's connections were not exceptional. It is clear from the many immigrant letters that they often linked up with relatives, neighbors, or acquaintances who had already settled in America. The impression that the nineteenth century immigrants impulsively embarked on an adventure, is effectively made obsolete by the Groustra story. The "adventure" was very carefully prepared. Usually, the destination was known, and connections readily available. This was not only true for the emigrants from the north of the Netherlands, elsewhere in the Netherlands there also were networks that provided the emigrants support on their journey across the Atlantic.

After Pieter, Frederica, and their children had spent the night at Mr. Boswinkel's, they continued their journey to Roseland, a suburb to the south of Chicago. There they lodged with a Mr. Van Tuinen, probably an old acquaintance from Ee.[9] The accommodation was temporary: "After having stayed with the Van Tuinen's for a week, we could not get along anymore." The Groustras went to look for living accommodation and they found a room in a shed that had been built especially for the many newcomers. They bought all kinds of new furniture and Pieter remarked: "…of course everything on credit, that is what happens to most people that come here, they can be helped here, because the working man earns so much here, that he can pay on account." Immediately after their arrival, Pieter found a job as a carpenter in the Pullman factories, where railway coaches were made. Though he worked ten hours a day, Pieter did not complain at all, because it compared favorably with the work load in the Netherlands, while he boasted that his food was as good as the menu of "the best citizen in the Netherlands." His boss was also Dutch, as well as many of his colleagues on the work floor. He emphasized the familiarity among his neighbors, which counted a number of Frisians in the neighborhood. Pieter wrote somewhat proudly: "We speak Frisian daily, just as you do." But he felt compelled to write that the carpenters who were able to understand the English language earned a dollar more a day than he did.

Not Only the Nice Apples in Front of the Window
The first year after their passage the Groustras admitted to less positive experiences. The family was particularly troubled by the scorching heat of the Chicago summers. In the first few months they all started to suffer from "summer illness" and this meant doctor's bills. Pieter also had a financial misfortune, as he was taking legal action against a Frisian emigrant because of his misbehavior at work: "A brute from Friesland, with whom I worked, gave me a stroke with the saw, after which I had to stay home for five days and be treated by a doctor," he writes to the people in Ee in September 1881. We may assume that no work meant no income, and that the Groustras suffered from an event like this.

Religious life in America was a disappointment for him. Pieter did not approve of the fact that public life continued normally on Sundays. Trains were running, inns and pubs were open and spirits were drunk to excess. Since the Groustra family were members of the *Nederlandse Hervormde Kerk* in Friesland, they joined the Dutch Reformed Church (RCA) in Roseland. Pieter explains this as following: "the other *domini* (minister) does not meet the needs of my heart. He is exactly the same as domini de Jong in Engwierum." The Dutch Reformed Church in America had a Dutch identity. This made the Groustras initially feel at home among the other Dutch emigrants, though reservations soon emerged. Pieter Groustra believed he was able to judge the American religious climate, since he had mastered the English tongue sufficiently to attend a Baptist church service. He concluded several times that church life in America was too loose and he feared "fading borders" between church and society, and between churches of different denominations. Although he had become an elder in the Reformed Church in the meantime, he feared the dilution of the Reformed creed. Even the reputedly more strict Christian Reformed Church had started "following the stream as well."[10]

He admitted that he missed the Dutch way of believing: "my heart still belongs to our old tried and tested *Gereformeerde* faith..." Though he voiced his critical remarks about his RCA, the advice of his mother in Friesland made him decide to stay within this denomination, but not wholeheartedly.[11]

Pieter served as a part in the emigration chain, though he failed to talk his brother into emigrating. After a gap of seven years in the correspondence, Pieter began in 1888 to address his letters mainly to his brother Renze, who was also considering emigration. Pieter gave extensive and detailed advice to his brother. He warned him that in America manual labor offered a stable standard of living only if one spoke the language. The best argument was his own satisfaction: "And now we are doing so well. What a relief it is to me to be freed from the trouble and the sorrow that I struggled with in the old Fatherland, and of which I bore a good deal. I have to work here, but I have a delicious piece of bread."[12]

After a decade in the New World, Pieter openly admitted that he preferred America to the Netherlands. But we should exercise due caution with this information. On the basis of a large number of emigrant letters, however, it seems likely that many writers painted an overly-rosy picture of the situation overseas. For most people there was no way back and why then should one send complaints to the old fatherland? Moreover, they all longed to have their relatives and friends from the homeland around them. To send some positive impressions about America in a letter to the Netherlands could help their decision to join them. Still, Pieter seemed to have realistic expectations. He even wrote to Renze with some reservation: "Some people get disappointed here sometimes, because they had formed a completely wrong notion of America. If you have the courage to lose yourself for a few years and deny your favorite pursuit, then I see some light here for you ... I would not want to place the nicest apples in front of the window, but instead tell you the truth as much as possible."[13] Then he listed many necessities of life with their prices so that people in the Netherlands could draw a comparison between the cost of living in both countries. Thus the pros and cons were balanced. In the meantime the Groustra family had moved into a large house, with "a large kitchen, 2 nice living-rooms and 4 small bedrooms, and 4 cupboards for clothes etc., a good pump, a rainwater tank, and a fire cabin outside to make a fire in the summer." Compared to the place the family lived in during the first year after their arrival, their situation had improved considerably. Pieter even offered his brother an advance boat ticket, and reminded him to depart in the spring, which offered the best chances for work and the most favorable traveling conditions. Even this solid and generous advice failed to persuade brother Renze to venture upon the big passage.

The Secure Basis of Family and Work
By the time the Groustras had been in Chicago for a decade, the family had prospered: four children were born, namely Hylkje (later called Hilda) in 1884, Eelze

(later: Edward) in 1886 and the twins Cornelius (Neil) and Pieter (Peter) in 1889.[14] In 1889, Frederica wrote a passage in a letter for the first time, at least as far as we can conclude from the letters that are preserved. The most basic information from her side comes down to the fact that she thinks America is much better "for a person to provide for the necessities of his body." In 1891 her youngest daughter Geeske (Grace) came into the world. What happened to Frederica remains unclear, but by 1900 she had already passed away. In that year Pieter sent portraits of his family to his brother Renze, in which Frederica was missing. A housekeeper, Jantje de Boer from Hallum, took her place and he married her on December 10, 1901: "we have a very happy marriage, and the Lord gives us His blessing."[15] His sons Anton and Ype also got married in 1901.[16] His children followed the American custom to marry young: in 1906 he expected that in the next year his children Hylkje and Eelze – both in their early twenties – were going to take the same step.

After Jantje de Boer had been introduced in a letter to the relatives in Friesland as Pieter's new partner in life, she also started to write letters. Jantje was a frequent and informative writer, even though she had never met her husband's relatives. She often wrote about family affairs. It pleased the Groustras that their offspring had all settled down in the vicinity of Roseland with their partners. Around World War I Pieter still worked at the Pullman factories and Jantje proudly mentioned that no fewer than three of their sons were also employees there. Anton was the only one that earned his money elsewhere. As Pieter grew older, work started to become a burden to him. In recognition of his long employment, he was assigned lighter work around the age of seventy. But the number of working hours remained the same, which means that altogether he was still outdoors twelve hours every day. Cornelius, the youngest son who still lived at home, accompanied him to the factory every day. Around 1915 it was a privilege to be allowed to keep on working, since many people lost employment because of the war. Jantje wrote that "if you leave the house to do the shopping, on every corner of the street you see men, young men stand idle, which makes our hearts sad sometimes and one thinks this is a bad sign." In 1922 Pieter wrote about the big labor unrest in Chicago. The city seemed to be a center of agitation and Pieter thought: "sometimes I think we live on a volcano that can erupt any moment."

Despite these skeptical sounds, there were very positive developments: the Pullman Company offered a pension plan for the first time. It was available to anyone older than 70 who had been an employee for twenty or more years. Pieter used this provision from the time that he was 73 and Jantje hoped to enjoy a quiet old age.

'Maybe Something Got Lost in the Mail'
Very rarely the Groustras sent a letter to the Netherlands with one or two-dollar bills as small presents. When their relatives did not thank them quickly enough, Pieter or Jantje wrote a concerned letter, suggesting that the postal services might

have lost something. The general trend of the disappearance of European languages after World War I did not skip the Groustras. They started to mix the two languages. He chose the English variant for some words and wrote "photos" (for pictures sent overseas), "examination" (when he talks about examination for military service), "supporter" (when he talks about his son Cornelius, who was a great help at home) and "basement" (when he tells about the gas leakage that almost killed him). Already in a letter from 1920 there is a whole paragraph in English, which, as Pieter says, he wrote without being aware of it. But we do not get the impression that Pieter and Jantje completely abandoned the old world culture. They were still interested in the events in the Netherlands, particularly in the economic situation, but they identified with the American country, as his political comments revealed. Pieter opposed President Wilson and wrote in 1920: "We are in the middle of the storm of the forthcoming *Presidential election* and that means something here. What the future will bring is dark to me. We have had more than enough of Wilsonism. All spells anxious times.... Radicalism raises its head boldly and the foundations of the state are being moved, truly the future is dark. Fortunately we have escaped from the clutches of the "League of Nations" so far and the "Monroe Doctrine" lives on in the hearts of the noble people of the nation."[17] Politically, Pieter demonstrated obvious nationalist feelings for his new home country in his letters.

Pieter and Jantje sounded extremely confident in their letters. They got along well with one an other and the rest of the world. Pieter's son Ype married a German immigrant and his son Anton a woman from his native village of Ee. This demonstrated that different ways were possible. In fact, in their whole correspondence Pieter and Jantje Groustra did not show any regrets about their emigration. They were happily rooted in Chicago at the turn of the century. Pieter Groustra died on December 18, 1924 at the age of 83 and after a 23 years marriage with Jantje. During his entire life in America he had a desire to see relatives and best friends from the old fatherland. Jantje (a Frisian herself) maintained these contacts with Pieter's family. She explained her loyalty in writing as follows: "although we have never met, there is a bond. I loved my husband and thus his family was mine, just as my family was his." On December 13, 1938, she died too and the relatives in the Netherlands became aware of this, when son Cornelius answered a letter from his cousin who lived in The Hague. He writes in good Dutch, which means that the cultural heritage of Pieter and his two wives manifested in the second generation, to some extent. People probably do not want to be transformed in all respects from "genuine Frisian" to "real American" in one lifetime.

Robert Swierenga's present project is to document the history of the Dutch in Chicago. As to the Frisian community in the Windy City, I hope he can shed light on the Frisian strategies to distinguish themselves from the Dutch in general. Did they purposefully preserve something of their Frisian identity and how fast did they acculturate? A very challenging and interesting topic is the question of Frisians who did not affiliate with one of the Dutch churches in Chicago: with whom did they associate for their social and cultural life? And what were the economic implications for people who did not join one of the religious platforms? I hope that the Groustra letters are a useful part of his research concerning the Dutch in Chicago.

Notes

1. Pieter Ypes Groustra's father was Ype Pieters Groustra. Ype was born in 1811 in Epe (Gelderland) as the son of Pieter Jans Groustra and Reijnke Gerlofs, who were husband and wife in Nijkerk. In 1838 he married Hylkje Eelzes Kennema, who was the daughter of Eelze Hylkes Kennema and Geeske Hylkes Idsenga, husband and wife in Ee.

2. Frederica Maria Aukes was born on October 2, 1852, probably in Vledder. Her father became a schoolteacher in Ee.

3. We deal here with people from the following six municipalities: Oost- and Westdongeradeel, Het Bildt, Ferwerderadeel, Barradeel and Wonseradeel. The biographic data of this group of Frisian emigrants were taken from the Population Registers and were analysed for research. See Annemieke Galema, *Frisians to America, 1880-1914: With the Baggage of the Fatherland* (Groningen: RegioProject/Detroit: Wayne State University Press, 1996). Prof. Dr. R.P. Swierenga supervised my dissertation. I owe him a great debt of gratitude.

4. For instance Worp Van Peyma, a prominent Frisian farmer, who left Ternaard in 1849 with his family and some people from the region to go to Lancaster in the state of New York. Van Peyma, a member of the farmer's aristocracy, sprang from an old patrician family in Westdongeradeel. Before he left, he had occupied functions in the public sector with regard to the Frisian Water Authority [*Friese Waterstaat*].

5. Many thanks to the late G.R. Groustra, who generously placed his relatives' letters at our disposal, and also gave additional information. I also owe the Rijksarchief Leeuwarden a debt of gratitude for reproducing the originals.

6. These letters are part of a large collection of immigrant letters, collected in the Netherlands during a national campaign. The original letters (and sometimes the xerox copies) are held at the archives of Calvin College in Grand Rapids, Michigan. A representative sample was published in: H.J. Brinks, ed., *Dutch American Voices: Letters from the United States* (Ithaca and London: Cornell University Press, 1995).

7. Ype was born on October 18, 1875 and Anton Theodorus was born on June 18, 1877, both in Ee. In the United States people later called them by American names: Harry (Ype) and Anthony (Anton).

8. Letter from Pieter Groustra, August 15, 1881.

9. Most probably this Van Tuinen was Mr. Jacob Wessels Van Tuinen (born July 18, 1833 in Ee). According to my computer list on North-Frisian emigrants 1880-1914 (see note 3), he also left from Ee. According to the Population Registers, he left Friesland with his wife Wertje Ruurds Nicolai (born July 23, 1823 in Ee) and his daughter Aukje (born August 23, 1858 in Ee) on the same date as Pieter Groustra. Van Tuinen's son Johannes (though born November 25, 1863 in Ee) would have left a week earlier in May 1881. Groustra does not mention the Van Tuinen family as their traveling companions. Therefore it is likely that Van Tuinen had arrived in Chicago earlier. The removal from the Population Registers usually took place at the end of the financial year, that is if the emigrant in question did not sign out personally. Eventually, the

departure for America did not remain unnoticed in the relatively small rural communities, but after some months the registrar might have filled in the precise date of departure incorrectly.

10. Letter of Pieter Groustra from Chicago to his cousin Johannes Groustra in The Hague, April 16, 1920.

11. Letter of Pieter Groustra from Roseland to his mother in Ee, not dated.

12. Letter of Pieter Groustra from Roseland to his brother and sister in Friesland, October 22, 1888.

13. Brother Renze was an organ-builder by trade. He worked successively in Dantumadeel and Driesum. Later he went to the city of Groningen, where business turned out to be less flourishing. Then he got the idea of going to America.

14. Peter only lived for a short time: he died in the year of his birth.

15. It is not clear from the correspondence how Jantje joined the Groustra family as their housekeeper.

16. On July 24, 1901, Ype married Anna Albrecht, a woman of German origin. The letters make mention of two children from this marriage: Harold (born in 1903) and Estella Maria (born March 3, 1906). Anton married Gerry Postma (born in Ee) on April 25, 1901. They gave birth to a son (Pieter) in 1904.

17. In 1823, U.S. President James Monroe, in his annual message to Congress, warned European nations against interfering with internal affairs in the Western Hemisphere. This became known as the Monroe Doctrine.

America's Most Popular Dutchman: Hendrik Willem Van Loon

Cornelis A. van Minnen

When around noon on the 11th of March 1944 Franklin D. Roosevelt received a message that Hendrik Willem Van Loon had died, he immediately sent a cable from the White House to Van Loon's widow, offering his condolences and telling her, "Am shocked and saddened by the news that Hendrik's life came so suddenly to its close. He was my true and trusted friend." Just two months before Van Loon had turned sixty-two. He still had many plans for new books and he was deeply concerned about the war in Europe and with heart and soul actively involved with Nazi-occupied Holland. Van Loon's passing away not only shocked the Dutch community in the United States, but also many American celebrities. Hundreds of letters and cables expressing condolences were sent to Van Loon's widow, not only from the American president but also, among others, from First Lady Eleanor Roosevelt, former President Herbert Hoover, and authors like Pearl S. Buck, Carl Van Doren, Carl Sandburg, Van Wyck Brooks, and Librarian of Congress Archibald MacLeish. In addition, also Queen Wilhelmina of the Netherlands, Princess Juliana, and Dutch Prime-Minister Pieter Gerbrandy sent cables.[1]

On 14 March, with white-gloved policemen directing the traffic and private cars running a shuttle service between railroad station and church, almost 400 friends – many of whom were brought from New York City to the deceased author's hometown Old Greenwich, Connecticut, with extra railroad cars – gathered for the funeral services in the town's overcrowded First Congregational Church to pay Van Loon their last respects. The Netherlands government-in-exile in London, repre-sented at the funeral by its ambassador in Washington and Van Loon's close friend Dr. Alexander Loudon, sent a standing wreath of calla and madonna lilies with a simple white card reading "From a sad and grateful Holland."[2]

Bridge Between Two Countries
Who was this many-sided Dutch-American who had made his mark on America's cultural life as a historian, journalist, illustrator and especially popularizer of

Hendrik Willem Van Loon broadcasting to the Netherlands
during Word War II. New York 1943
(Photo: H.W. Van Loon Papers, Cornell University)

history and art and of whom the London *Times'* obituary stated that he "was one of the most engaging products of the marriage between Holland and the United States"?[3] Within the limited space of this short essay I hope to demonstrate that Van Loon, though almost completely forgotten now in both his adopted and native countries, deserves his rightful place in the historic gallery of those who made a remarkable contribution to Dutch-American relations. Especially during World War II, he served as a bridge between both countries and, indeed – as the expression goes – he was larger than life.

His physical appearance was impressive. Towering over six feet and three inches and weighing 290 pounds even when dieting – according to his own description his tailor was "Omar the tentmaker" – Van Loon, with his great moon of a face, timid, gray-green eyes glancing curiously over his horn-rimmed spectacles that coasted down his steep nose, his seventeen-and-a-half inch neck and size twelve-and-half shoes, looked like an amiable elephant, and in his cartoons he depicted himself as such. Indeed, as the *New Yorker* described him in a profile, he was "massively proportioned [and] Falstaffian in design." His production was equally gigantic: his more than forty, mostly self-illustrated books, sold over six million copies all over the world and were translated into more than twenty languages. In addition, he produced innumerable illustrations and articles for newspapers, magazines and periodicals, wrote prefaces, introductions and chapters in many books of others, had his own radio programs, delivered hundreds and hundreds of lectures and addresses before clubs and organizations both in and outside of the United States, and sent thousands upon thousands of often illustrated letters to many persons around the globe. His frequent travels took him to destinations in Europe, North and South America, New Zealand, Australia, Asia, and Africa. He estimated that he had spent three years of his life on the ocean. In short, this one-man factory brimmed over with energy.[4]

Upbringing and Education
Hendrik Willem Van Loon was born on 14 January 1882 in Rotterdam as the second child of a well-to-do family. Unfortunately, he held only bitter memories of an unhappy youth, dominated by his most unpleasant father who terrorized the family, and a beloved mother who died when he was only eighteen years old. He received his education at the gymnasium in Gouda – where the all-permeating smell of cheese caused his life-long distaste for this world-renowned Dutch dairy product – and at the private boarding school Noorthey in Voorschoten, a town near The Hague, which, as he recalled, provided him with "a beautiful base of snobbery." Following the death of his mother and the remarriage of his father to a much younger woman whom he sincerely disliked, Hendrik Willem at age twenty decided to leave the Netherlands and use the money he had inherited from his mother to cover the expenses of a few years study in the United States. Van Loon's uncle

Jan Hanken, a well-known doctor in The Hague, married to an American woman, was instrumental in getting him accepted as a student at Cornell University in 1902. After the first year there, he spent his second year at Harvard and then returned to Cornell where he took his A.B. in 1905. In 1906 he married the daughter of a prestigious Boston family, Eliza Bowditch, whom he had met aboard an oceanliner returning from a summer trip to Holland.[5]

After his graduation from Cornell, Van Loon served as an Associated Press correspondent in Washington, Moscow, St. Petersburg and Warsaw where he reported on the aftermath of the Revolution of 1905. His ambition was to become a professor of history at an American university and, as at that time Germany was considered to be the Mecca of scholarship, he decided to obtain his Ph.D. at a German university. From 1907-1911 he studied at the University of Munich and wrote his dissertation which he later reworked into his first book, *The Fall of the Dutch Republic*. During these years in Europe his two sons, Henry and Gerard Willem, were born. His affiliation with Cornell as a lecturer in European history was brief, for though he enjoyed an immense popularity among the student body, his Alma Mater did not want to extend his two-year contract as several of his colleagues considered his unconventional way of teaching with his characteristic drawings on the blackboard more a kind of vaudeville than solid scholarship.[6]

Van Loon returned to the Associated Press and served as a war correspondent in Europe during World War I. He reported, among other things, about the siege of Antwerp and in 1917 the ship on which he was sailing to Holland, one day out of port, off the coast of the Dutch island of Texel, struck a chain connecting two free-floating British mines. After two explosions, the passengers were ordered into lifeboats and each man was assigned an oar. The next morning all passengers, luckily there were no casualties, landed safely on shore at Den Helder. Van Loon's experience in the lifeboat – having to pull an oar and being packed with many people in a small boat – not only resulted in a hernia but also, as Van Loon later reported, was the source of a life-long trauma of claustrophobia. In this period, between 1915 and 1920, he published a small number of history books but they were not successful. Simultaneously, his marriage with Eliza Bowditch was also collapsing. While trying to make ends meet by publicity writing for some commercial businesses in New York, he met Helen Criswell, owner of a Greenwich Village tearoom. They were married in 1920 and a new period of his life was about to begin.[7]

Breakthrough
Van Loon's breakthrough came in 1921 with the publication of *The Story of Mankind*, his sixth book. It was an immediate bestseller which would earn him well over half a million dollars in royalties. In *The Story of Mankind* Van Loon gave his own interpretation of world history, from the caveman to the present, and the

volume included more than 150 illustrations. It was widely acclaimed in the American press and recommended to both children – the target group – and adults. Historian Charles A. Beard commended it as "a great book, one that will endure." Van Loon received endless invitations to speak about his book across the country and his breakthrough reached a zenith when in June 1922 the Children's Librarians' Section of the American Library Association at its annual congress in Detroit awarded him the first John Newbery Medal for "the most distinguished contribution to American literature for children." At age forty and exactly twenty years after his arrival in the United States the Dutch immigrant had become a celebrity. Indeed, he had realized his childhood dream: "From my tenth year on (or even earlier)" – so he wrote in his posthumously published and unfinished autobiography *Report to Saint Peter* – "I wanted more than anything else to be a very famous historian!"[8]

How different was the reaction to *The Story of Mankind* in Van Loon's native country. Whereas Charles Beard and other American historians praised it, the eminent Dutch historian Johan Huizinga who reviewed the Dutch translation of the book in *De Gids*, was horrified by Van Loon's bestseller in the United States. In his opinion *The Story of Mankind* was based on a series of errors and he loathed the illustrations. Furthermore, he thought that the author had repudiated himself by descending to the level of the child, which he considered "one of the curses of our century." That Van Loon's book was such a smashing hit in the United States was in Huizinga's view "a bad omen for our civilization." Van Loon's subsequent book, *The Story of the Bible*, was equally trashed in Holland – both text and illustrations – as was for instance expressed by a review in the daily newspaper *Algemeen Handelsblad*. It was clear that in the appreciation for Van Loon there was a big gap between the Netherlands and the United States.[9]

After teaching for an academic year at Antioch College, Ohio, and spending another year as columnist at the Baltimore *Sun*, Van Loon decided to make writing his full-time work and published one book after another. Historical personalities, art, folk songs, geography, navigation – he could write about any topic and had "an evangelist's zeal," as the *New York Herald Tribune* put it, to share his knowledge with everybody and anybody. In 1922 he contributed a chapter to the controversial book *Civilization in the United States* in which he criticized the lack of historical knowledge of most Americans and accused historians that "No one has ever been able to convince the man in the street that time employed upon historical reading is not merely time wasted." Here was the mission he saw for himself: bringing the man in the street into contact with the past as he was convinced that "History can never be detached from life."[10]

As a historian Van Loon did not put a high value on historical research. As the *New Yorker* wrote in an ironic portrait of the author in three installments in 1943, "… Van Loon is a self-contained universe. [His critics] cannot know that he has studied the universe by studying himself. He is his own source material and his own research.... The difference between Van Loon and other historians is that he goes to the vivid reality of his own personality for information, while his more anemic rivals are forced to derive their material second-hand from the dusty records of mere authorities." When his interviewer confronted him with the criticism of professional historians who accused him of factual errors in his works, Van Loon, who considered himself to be the victim of a professorial plot caused by jealousy of his successful booksales, rhetorically asked, "Who gives a damn about some little professor?" This dichotomy between popular and academic reactions to Van Loon's work was demonstrated time and again. Van Loon's massive 1937 bestseller *The Arts*, published simultaneously in the United States, Great Britain, Austria, France, and Italy, needed five persons to review it in the *Saturday Review of Literature*, each of whom discussed a single specific aspect of it: painting, sculpture, archeology, architecture, and music. Whereas the newspapers described *The Arts* as a tour de force, the professors in general considered the book a fiasco. "I get a little annoyed (I am sorry to say)," Van Loon once wrote in a letter to the *New York Herald Tribune*, "by repeated hints that since I refrain from footnotes I use no sources. A good history should be like a good dinner. One should be able to enjoy the fare without being reminded every two or three minutes where the cook got the capers or the butter."[11]

Protagonist Van Loon
In all of his books Van Loon himself plays a major role, even in biographies of historical persons, such as the Rembrandt biography he wrote in Veere, the Netherlands, or in the encounters with a series of historical figures in the same town he described in his bestseller *Van Loon's Lives*. In the *New Yorker* interview he disarmingly said that the common theme of all his books was "Van Loon on Life." Despite his enormous success, Van Loon was a hypochondriac. "I drug myself with work to dull the agony of melancholia," he often said. No one would be able to understand him, he thought, as his "five-track mind" went too fast for ordinary people to follow him. Therefore, behind the facade of success the real Van Loon went his solitary way. He expected that his work, like that of other geniuses, would probably be properly appreciated a hundred years after his death. His favorite New York spots were the Waldorf-Astoria and the Algonquin Hotel, popular in literary circles, were he often went for lunch, preferably surrounding himself with young ladies from book publishing circles. He then held his endless "five-track" monologues to an increasing number of people and gradually dominated the conversation in the whole restaurant while at the same time decorating the tablecloths with his characteristic drawings. The headwaiter at the Algonquin Hotel estimated that a regular Van Loon lunch took one tablecloth per hour. In his book *Van Loon's Lives*, the author wrote that he "wanted to sit and talk God out of his heaven and the Devil back into his hell." The Dutch literary critic and journalist Jan Greshoff,

who knew Van Loon rather well, wrote in his memoirs that Van Loon would have "exploded like a kettle filled with boiling water without a spout or lid if he had not expressed himself forcefully, loudly, and constantly." Time and again he had new ideas for a next book, wrote a number of prefaces in which he had full confidence for a day, and then rejected the whole idea and replaced it with new ones. His publishers, Simon and Schuster, had some thirty contracts for Van Loon books that never went beyond the idea stage.[12]

Women

Jan Greshoff in the obituary for the *Knickerbocker Weekly* described Van Loon as "a force of nature, an inexhaustible, violent spouting source of thoughts, feelings, and bright ideas." Not surprisingly, then, this man had no stable, monogamous love life. As mentioned above, in 1920 Van Loon divorced his first wife, Eliza Bowditch, and married Helen Criswell, better known as Jimmie. A Bryn Mawr College graduate, teacher, and owner of the popular Greenwich Village tearoom *The Mad Hatter*, Jimmie would remain Hendrik Willem's faithful partner for the rest of his life. She not only typed and edited his writings and gave him self-confidence by repeating that they were "darn good," she also many times suffered from his amorous whims. They divorced in 1927. In the fall of that year, Van Loon married the actress Frances Goodrich but early in the next year returned to Jimmie. Though they never officially remarried, she was both his second and fourth wife.[13]

Married or not, Van Loon constantly courted other women and bombarded them with letters and telegrams. Jimmie was very well aware of his romances and kept score: in a 1934 entry in her diary she noted, "Got warning of 24th [love affair]." Though this, of course, hurt her feelings, she knew that Hendrik Willem's fancies would never work and that in the end he would always return to her. The Dutch author Adriaan Van der Veen who in 1940 temporarily worked as Van Loon's secretary, wrote that the famous historian "like a puffing hippopotamus yearning for love" was chasing every woman who crossed his path – unsuccessfully. This observation was shared by Van Loon's eldest son, Henry, who said in an interview, "Hendrik loved other women. I'm afraid that pop had difficulty in having a full-blown sexual relationship with any girl. It didn't come to things. He would go from one to another." Van Loon himself had another perception of his "failures in dealing with the gentler sex." As he wrote in his *Report to Saint Peter*, "I never quite got over the feeling that all women lived on a sort of pedestal … and longed to be the heroines of one of those romantic periods which were common incidents in the lives of the medieval troubadours. It was only … at cost of terrific wear and tear upon my emotions and upon my bank account that I learned that the troubadour business had indeed gone out … and that all efforts made since then to revive the era of the chivalresque approach had been lamentable failures…. In spite of [his] many unhappy experiences, [he would] still cling to the ideals of the thirteenth century."[14]

Settling in Veere

After his short-lived relationship with Frances Goodrich, Van Loon left the United States for a few years to recover from his psychological wounds. With Jimmie as his companion he settled in the picturesque little town of Veere, in the Province of Zeeland, the Netherlands, and spent there from 1928-1932, as he later wrote, "the happiest years of [his] life." In the front room of his sixteenth century house "De Houtuin" overlooking the harbor, he wrote, among other things, his biography of Rembrandt and articles for Dutch weeklies and newspapers, such as the *Groene Amsterdammer, Algemeen Handelsblad*, and the *Middelburgsche Courant*. Also from his Dutch house he sent many letters to innumerable people all over the world and his stationary from then on until his death carried the silhouette of Veere. The town also served as the location for Van Loon's imagined encounters with such famous historical personalities as Plato, Confucius, Erasmus, William of Orange, Shakespeare, Leonardo da Vinci, Voltaire, George Washington, Thomas Jefferson, and many others in his 1942 bestseller *Van Loon's Lives*. Of course, it is the author, as mentioned above, who is the real hero in this mixture of fact and fiction. In the foreword to *Van Loon's Lives* he wrote that to the question, "Where can a civilized human being spend his days with the least possible minimum of irritation and the greatest possible maximum of inner satisfaction?" the only completely satisfactory answer was, "Veere." "The enchantment of that queer little paradise was such," he continued, "that we rarely felt the need of any contact with the rest of the world and we thought with infinite pity of our poor contemporaries, doomed to spend their days in such dull and unimaginative hamlets as London, Paris, New York, or Rio."[15]

For the inhabitants of the small community of Veere, the great big man and the frail, short-haired, always smoking (and often drinking!), small woman driving her two-seater across rural Walcheren, were an odd couple. Within a very short time, however, Van Loon made his mark on Veere and became a living legend – "a walking vacation," as Jan Greshoff once remarked. There are many stories about Van Loon's activities in Veere, such as the sailing race he organized for fishermen, for which he paid a considerable cash prize (in 1994 this sailing event was revitalized and has become an annual event called the Van Loon sailing day), the pancakes he baked for his fellow-"Veerenaren," the bicycle he had placed in front of his house that was available for all who needed it, the goblet he had offered for the winner of the locally famous tilting of the ring games in nearby Middelburg and which was bigger than the goblets offered by the city of Middelburg, the Province of Zeeland, and even bigger than the goblet offered by the queen. Van Loon, who loved publicity, was also able to lure to Veere the then-famous Australian ocean aviator Charles Kingsford Smith as well as Miss America. On both occasions Van Loon proved to be a master in public relations, instructing the many journalists and photographers who had come from afar. The telegraph and telephone employees of Walcheren were absolutely overwhelmed and exhausted by this unusual situation. Though Van Loon returned to the United States, he loved Veere as a temporary place of residence and continued to express his affection for the little town: both in his correspondence and in his books he very often referred to "that little paradise." In 1936 he donated his house in Veere to the local Reformed Church (*Nederlandse Hervormde Gemeente*), and he called his house in Old Greenwich, Connecticut "Nieuw Veere." Also in his book illustrations, the silhouette of Veere shows up frequently. No less than startling is it that in Van Loon's booklet *Christmas Carols* his illustrations of the town of Bethlehem have a striking resemblance with Veere![16]

Erasmus Reincarnated

In *Van Loon's Lives* Desiderius Erasmus plays a prominent role and with good reason. Not only was Van Loon a great admirer of the sixteenth century humanist, he also liked to think that he was the reincarnation of Erasmus. This opinion, as he explained to the *New Yorker*, was based upon a number of similarities between himself and the monk: both were born in Rotterdam and had spent a part of their school days in Gouda, both had had unhappy childhoods, both were brilliant conversationalists, both were hypochondriacs, both liked to draw, both hated professors, both liked catnaps, both were tolerant, both wore their spectacles on the ends of their long noses, and both were popularizers. To prove his point to a sceptical world, Van Loon in 1942 sponsored an exhibition at Holland House in Rockefeller Center, which included, among other things, a photograph of Van Loon's hands and a drawing of Erasmus' hands by Holbein, samples of the handwritings of both men, as well as self-portraits of Van Loon and contemporary portraits of Erasmus, all of which were identical and in Van Loon's opinion overwhelming proof that he was Erasmus reincarnated. When fans of his asked for a photo, he did not send a picture of his face but of his hands, the same hands as those of Erasmus. Often he signed letters with "Henricus Rotterodamus" and it comes as no surprise, then, that the 1942 English edition of Erasmus's *The Praise of Folly* was thoroughly introduced and illustrated by the twentieth century Erasmus, Hendrik Willem Van Loon.[17]

Fighting the Nazis

Just as in western Europe, the Nazi threat in the 1930s was hardly recognized in the United States. Van Loon, however, was convinced early on that the rising national-socialism in Germany would become a serious threat to democratic and humanistic principles all over the world. His reading of Adolf Hitler's *Mein Kampf* shocked him and was the incentive to start an anti-Hitler campaign. In 1938 Van Loon published *Our Battle*, "being one man's answer to *My Battle* by Adolf Hitler" which was, as the blurb expressed, "a ringing defense of democracy faced by the threat of fascism everywhere, … a clarion call to America to awake, to rearm, and to resist!" Van Loon saw Hitler as his personal enemy, especially when, after the publication of *Our Battle*, his books were forbidden in Germany. In another attempt to open his fellow Americans' eyes to the imminent danger of Nazism, he published the novel *Invasion*, "being an eyewitness account of the Nazi invasion of America." Also this book fell on deaf ears. In his struggle against Hitler he saw himself as an ally of Franklin Roosevelt whom he already knew from the days that Roosevelt had served as governor of New York State. A fervent Democrat, Van Loon was a faithful supporter of Roosevelt's political campaigns – he for instance contributed a biographical portrait of the president to *The Democratic Book of 1936* which was used at the National Democratic Convention in Philadelphia that year. And in the 1930s and 40s he was a regular visitor at the White House and at Hyde Park. The Franklin D. Roosevelt Library files of the correspondence between Van Loon and both Franklin and Eleanor Roosevelt testify to a mutually warm relationship.[18]

When in May 1940 the Netherlands were occupied by Nazi Germany, Van Loon immediately took action to support his native country: he helped organize the Queen Wilhelmina Fund that aimed to raise funds for Dutch war refugees, serving for months as its honorary chairman; he was also chair of the Netherlands Division of the National War Fund; as "Uncle Hank" over Station WRUL in Boston, he gave a great deal of his time and energy to short-wave broadcasts to Holland after the invasion, organizing and financing (!) these Dutch-language programs long before the Dutch government-in-exile assumed responsibility for them; he helped hundreds of refugees from Nazi-occupied countries, often personally giving them shelter, food, money, and getting jobs for them; and he did a great deal to provide Dutch seamen with a home in New York. Time and again he was asked for help and seldom turned a request down. The money he earned with his books was in no time spent on refugees and other war purposes. Jan Greshoff observed that Van Loon "was as generous as nature in the tropics" and that during World War II he "single-handedly achieved more for the Netherlands than all public relations efforts of civil servants combined." Of course, Van Loon did not forget the publicity around his many activities as a gigantic Santa Claus.[19]

Van Loon, who as a historian never forgot to remind President Roosevelt and his wife of their Dutch heritage, was instrumental in establishing contact between the president and Queen Wilhelmina and played a crucial role when the Dutch queen visited the United States in 1942 and 1943. That the exuberant Van Loon was neither able nor willing to act according to the rigid Dutch court protocol is not surprising. Reflecting on Queen Wilhelmina's visit to New York, he casually remarked, "Her Majesty is used to holding the floor in conversation. I showed her that that wasn't done in America." However, with Princess Juliana who during the war years stayed in Ottawa, Canada, Van Loon had a very warm relationship. To her and her children he sent many letters and drawings. And yet, also here he abhorred the court protocol. As he wrote to Greshoff, "I have done everything I could to help Dutchmen and thank God my position here [in the United States] is worth a whole army division. But those obedient men in Canada who serve the princess, still play court as in the days of William V at Wolfenbuettel. I have to let them go. It's a waste of time. For me there is only one goal now: the liberation of Holland. For that purpose I am prepared to give everything. But these old routine people are only a burden. Therefore, I will continue the struggle on my own!" In 1937 his literary activities had been honored with the title Officer in the Order of Orange Nassau. Now, in 1942, as a token of appreciation for his unrestrained efforts for the Dutch cause, Queen Wilhelmina decorated him on the occasion of his sixtieth birthday with the even more prestigious Order of the Netherlands Lion.[20]

Prince of Popularizers
Van Loon, who gave so much effort to help his native country and who had good reasons to be proud of the millions of books sold all over the world in many translations that had provided him the honorary title "prince of popularizers" in his adopted country, had never been able to accept the fact that he was not taken seriously as an author in the Netherlands. This explains his life-long love-hate relationship with his mother country. He was especially annoyed at the pedantic Dutch professors whom he described as "those despicable fossils from the university towns" who in his view had never produced anything but turds. If it were not for him, he was convinced, "millions of Americans would still think that Holland was some kind of tasteless cheese." Indeed, it was hard to deny that in the years 1920-1945 for many Americans the Netherlands and Van Loon were synonymous. "I put Holland on the map," Van Loon said, "and that's the simple truth."[21]

During the war years, Van Loon suffered from heart disease and his physician strongly recommended that he relax and reduce his activities. Van Loon was not the man to do so. His hyperactive lifestyle, combined with the long-standing bad food habit of eating too much too fast, proved to be fatal. In his living room Van Loon had a painting of Veere, covered with a black mourning cloth that was not to be removed until the end of the German occupation of the Netherlands. Hendrik Willem Van Loon did not live to be able to remove that black cloth. Just three months before D-Day, on 11 March 1944, he died of a heart attack. Without exaggeration one can claim, like Greshoff did, Van Loon was a victim of the war.[22]

Hendrik Willem Van Loon's passing away not only received extensive attention in the *New York Times* and *New York Herald Tribune*, but in a great many newspapers, journals, and periodicals across the United States. The *Knickerbocker Weekly* even published a "Hendrik Willem Van Loon Memorial Issue." Reflecting on Van Loon shortly after his death, Jan Greshoff thought that Van Loon was a world in himself with his own nationality. "He was no Americanized Dutchman, nor a Dutch-American. He could be both Dutch *and* American, because first and foremost he was Van Loon." Or, as Van Loon's youngest son once wrote about his father, "He remained till the day he died with one foot metaphorically on each side of the Atlantic, unable to make up his mind which way to throw his weight."[23]

To be sure, he was not a thorough scholar. But his strength was in bridging the gap between scholarship and the mass audience that admired him and that without his books, articles, radio talks, et cetera, would have had little or no contact with history and art. And he also served as a unique bridge between his native and adopted countries. As Adriaan Barnouw, Queen Wilhelmina Professor at Columbia University remarked, Van Loon had given himself wholeheartedly to America. "He spoke as an American to Americans and always found the catching phrase because he himself had been caught by the spell of America." The reason for his popularity in the United States, Barnouw explained, was due to the fact that "he did not produce the dead bones of scholarship but a recreation of the past from his imaginative brain." That was at the same time the very reason why Van Loon was not appreciated by the Dutch who in Barnouw's view "had no confidence in the knowledge he imparted because he offered it in a playful, waggish spirit. Dullness among them is the badge of true learning." But despite its coolness and misunderstanding, he continued, "Holland had in him her most eloquent spokesman in America after she herself had been gagged by Nazi tyranny. He championed her cause before countless listeners and readers, he heartened the people in the occupied homeland with his broadcasts over Station WRUL ... Holland may well be proud of having inspired such tenacity of love on one who had so completely identified himself with America."[24]

Reputation

After World War II a number of Van Loon's books were reprinted and even updated, such as *The Arts* and *The Story of Mankind*. When in 1959 Van Loon's *The Story of America*, originally published in 1927, was reprinted, historian Arthur M. Schlesinger, Jr. wrote in the Introduction, "In an age when knowledge grows increasingly specialized, the capacity to write about serious subjects in a lucid and arresting way becomes a necessity of civilized society. This was a gift which Hendrik Willem Van Loon possessed to a high and abundant degree.... *The Story of America* is a book which has brought the American past to life for thousands upon thousands of readers. It still has its juices, and I am glad that another generation has an opportunity to savor and enjoy its spirit."[25] Nowadays, however, few people in the United States or elsewhere are familiar with Van Loon's work. The popularity of Van Loon's books seems to have been buried with the author. The fact that in the post-World War II era many, many more people than in Van Loon's days had the opportunity to get a higher education has made the appetite for "outlines" somewhat obsolete. In addition, knowledge has become so specialized that the production of a synthesis of all knowledge has become more and more problematic.

And what about the post-war interest in Van Loon in the Netherlands? The editors of the *Knickerbocker Weekly* "Hendrik Willem Van Loon Memorial Issue" expected that Rotterdam or Veere after the war would have a Van Loon statue and that streets or squares in the Netherlands would be named after him. This did not happen. In Veere a Hendrik Willem Van Loon Foundation was established in 1956 aimed at raising sufficient funds to acquire Van Loon's house "De Houtuin" and turn it into a Van Loon museum. The effort failed and the foundation was dissolved in 1966. Over the years, now and then, reminiscences of contemporaries and short biographical articles have been published on Van Loon in Dutch newspapers, periodicals, and biographical dictionaries. Considering the prominent role he played in Dutch-American relations from the 1920s through 40s and the fact that no other Dutchman before or since has achieved such popularity in American cultural life, it is all the more astounding that this colorful personality has not yet been the subject of a thorough, scholarly biography. Granted, in 1972 Van Loon's son Gerard Willem published a well-written biography but used it to come to terms with his father whom he considered to be a capricious egomaniac, ignoring his father's charm and generosity. As his older brother Henry later observed about the book, "Willem was just bent on emptying the slops on his old man and he only filled his own pants in the effort."[26] It is unfortunate that he was unable to look at his subject with more distance and thus failed to analyze Van Loon's prolific writings. The author of this article is currently working on a biography of Van Loon, studying this multi-faceted "prince of popularizers" and twentieth century incarnation of Erasmus. Going through his voluminous correspondence and reading contemporary comments about him make it all the more apparent why Hendrik Willem Van Loon was America's most popular Dutchman.

Notes

1. Franklin D. Roosevelt to Mrs. Jimmie Van Loon, 11 March 1944, President's Personal File no. 2259, Folder Hendrik Willem Van Loon, 1940-1944, Franklin D. Roosevelt Papers, Franklin D. Roosevelt Library; Condolence telegrams and letters in Box 3, Folders 1-22, Hendrik Willem Van Loon Papers, Carl A. Kroch Library, Rare and Manuscript Collections, Cornell University.
2. *Knickerbocker Weekly*, 27 March 1944, 13-14; *New York Times*, 15 March 1944; Gerard Willem Van Loon, *The Story of Hendrik Willem Van Loon* (Philadelphia and New York: Lippincott, 1972), 374-375.
3. London *Times*, 14 March 1944.
4. Richard O. Boyer, "The Story of Everything," *New Yorker*, 20 March 1943, 24 and 3 April 1943, 24; Knickerbocker *Weekly*, 20 March 1944, 3 and 15; ibid., 27 March 1944, 10-11.
5. *Knickerbocker Weekly*, 27 March 1944, 10-11.
6. Ibid.; Hendrik Willem Van Loon, *The Fall of the Dutch Republic* (Boston and New York: Houghton Mifflin, 1913).
7. Van Loon's report on the shipwreck was frontpage news in the *New York Times*: Hendrik

Willem Van Loon, "Liner Noordam Hits Mine Off Holland But Stays Afloat, No Casualties Aboard," *New York Times*, 5 August 1917; G.W. Van Loon, *The Story*, 94-95.

8. Hendrik Willem Van Loon, *The Story of Mankind* (New York: Boni and Liveright, 1921); G.W. Van Loon, *The Story*, 128-129; Charles A. Beard, "The Story of Mankind," *New Republic* 29 (21 December 1921): 105; "Dr. Van Loon Gets Medal," *New York Times*, 28 June 1922; Hendrik Willem Van Loon, *Report to Saint Peter* (New York: Simon and Schuster, 1947), 190.

9. Johan Huizinga, "Aanleeren of afleeren?," *De Gids* 88.4 (April 1924): 130-137, reprinted in J. Huizinga, *Verzamelde Werken*, 9 vols. (Haarlem: Tjeenk Willink, 1948-1953), 7: 237-243; Hendrik Willem Van Loon, *The Story of the Bible* (New York: Boni and Liveright, 1923); "De Bijbelsche geschiedenis.... In 't Amerikaansch," *Algemeen Handelsblad*, 12 July 1924; See also Francis J. Wahlen, "Hendrik Van Loon and His Dutch Critics," *The Catholic World* 121 (July 1925): 499-502.

10. *New York Herald Tribune* obituary of Van Loon, 12 March 1944; Hendrik Willem Van Loon, "History," in Harold E. Stearns, ed., *Civilization in the United States: An Inquiry by Thirty Americans* (New York: Harcourt, Brace and Company, 1922), 297-308.

11. Van Loon was portrayed by Richard O. Boyer in three Profiles, "The Story of Everything," in the *New Yorker*: 20 March 1943, 24-31; 27 March 1943, 24-30; and 3 April 1943, 24-34; Hendrik Willem Van Loon, *The Arts* (New York: Simon and Schuster, 1937); "Arts and the Man," *Saturday Review of Literature* 16 (2 October 1937): 5-6; *New York Herald Tribune* obituary of Van Loon, 12 March 1944.

12. Hendrik Willem Van Loon, *R.v.R.: The Life and Times of Rembrandt Van Rijn* (New York: Horace Liveright, 1930); Hendrik Willem Van Loon, *Van Loon's Lives* (New York: Simon and Schuster, 1942), xviii; *New Yorker*, 20 March 1943, 24, 27, 31; ibid., 27 March 1943, 24; ibid., 3 April 1943, 24, 27-28; J. Greshoff, *Menagerie. Herinneringen en beschouwingen* ('s-Gravenhage: Stols, 1958), 147.

13. J. Greshoff, "Hendrik Willem Van Loon," *Knickerbocker Weekly*, 20 March 1944, 38; Adriaan Van der Veen, *Vriendelijke vreemdeling* (Amsterdam: Querido, 1969), 136; G.W. Van Loon, *The Story*, 163-171.

14. 17 November 1934 entry, Jimmie Criswell Van Loon Diaries, Box 64, Hendrik Willem Van Loon Papers, Carl A. Kroch Library, Rare and Manuscript Collections, Cornell University; Adriaan Van der Veen, "Strooi mijn as uit boven Zeeland," (review of G.W. Van Loon's *The Story of Hendrik Willem Van Loon*), *NRC Handelsblad*, 18 August 1972; Interview with Henry B. Van Loon, 8 January 1994, in author's collection; Van Loon, *Report to Saint Peter*, 208.

15. Van Loon, *Van Loon's Lives*, xvii-xviii.

16. A. Koch-de Waard, "A Veere Legend: Hendrik Willem Van Loon," *Knickerbocker International* 26.2 (February 1964): 36-39; J. Greshoff, *Het boek der vriendschap* (Amsterdam: Van Kampen, 1950), 334; "Hendrik Willem Van Loon. De wandelende vakantie Van Veere," *PZC*, 14 December 1968; Dirk L. Broeder, "Hendrik Willem Van Loon. Bohémien en kosmopoliet," *Elsevier*, 8 March 1969; Hendrik Willem Van Loon and Grace Castagnetta, *Christmas Carols* (New York: Simon and Schuster, 1937).

17. Boyer, "The Story of Everything," *New Yorker*, 3 April 1943, 33-34; In *Van Loon's Lives*, 5, the author does not refer to Hans Holbein's drawing of Erasmus's hands – as is mentioned in the *New Yorker* interview – but to Albrecht Dürer's drawing; Desiderius Erasmus, *The Praise of Folly*, introduced and illustrated by Hendrik Willem Van Loon (Roslyn, NY: Walter J. Black, 1942).

18. Hendrik Willem Van Loon, *Our Battle* (New York: Simon and Schuster, 1938); Hendrik Willem Van Loon, *Invasion* (New York: Harcourt, Brace and Company, 1940); Hendrik Willem Van Loon, "A Study in Backgrounds," *The Democratic Book 1936* (Philadelphia: The Democratic National Convention, 1936), 13-20; Hendrik Willem Van Loon files in President's Personal File no. 2259 and correspondence with Hendrik Willem Van Loon and Mrs. Hendrik Willem Van Loon in Eleanor Roosevelt Papers no. 100 Personal Letters, Franklin D. Roosevelt Library.

19. *Knickerbocker Weekly*, 27 March 1944, 12; Boyer, "The Story of Everything," *New Yorker*, 27 March 1943, 30; Greshoff, *Het boek der vriendschap*, 335-336; See also Van der Veen, *Vriendelijke vreemdeling*, 59, 122-126.

20. Boyer, "The Story of Everything," *New Yorker*, 3 April 1943, 30; Greshoff, *Het boek der vriendschap*, 337; The correspondence between Van Loon and Princess Juliana, 1940-1944, is located in the Archives of Her Royal Highness Princess Juliana at the Koninklijk Huisarchief, The Hague, and can only be studied after permission has been granted by or on behalf of Princess Juliana; The decisions to confer on Hendrik Willem Van Loon the Order of Orange Nassau and the Order of the Netherlands Lion were signed by Queen Wilhelmina on 28 May 1937 and 12 January 1942, respectively. In Archief Kabinet der Koningin, The Hague.

21. The literary critic and historian Van Wyck Brooks called Van Loon "prince of popularizers" and "a true belated man of the Renaissance," Van Wyck Brooks, *Days of the Phoenix: The Nineteen-Twenties I Remember* (New York: E.P. Dutton, 1957), 127; Van der Veen, *Vriendelijke vreemdeling*, 52, 54-55.

22. On Van Loon's food habits, see Gerard Willem Van Loon, "Father Liked His Food," *Town & Country*, December 1952, 107, 134-136, 141-142; Broeder, "Hendrik Willem Van Loon," 97; Greshoff, *Het boek der vriendschap*, 339.

23. *New York Times*, 12, 13, and 15 March 1944; *New York Herald Tribune*, 12 and 15 March 1944; *Knickerbocker Weekly*, 27 March 1944; Greshoff, "Hendrik Willem Van Loon," 38; G.W. Van Loon, "Father Liked His Food," 135.

24. Adriaan J. Barnouw, *Monthly Letters on the Culture and History of the Netherlands* (Assen: Van Gorcum, 1969), 241, 243.

25. Hendrik Willem Van Loon, *The Arts* (New York: Liveright, 1974), *The Story of Mankind* (New York: Liveright, 1999); Arthur M. Schlesinger, Jr., "Introduction," in Hendrik Willem Van Loon, *The Story of America* (New York: Fawcett World Library, 1959), vii, x.

26. "Champion of Tolerance," *Knickerbocker Weekly*, 27 March 1944, 3; Archives Stichting (Foundation) Hendrik Willem Van Loon in Gemeentearchief Veere; Two recent contributions on Van Loon were published by A. Lammers, *Uncle Sam en Jan Salie: Hoe Nederland Amerika ontdekte* (Amsterdam: Balans, 1989), 77-86 and C.A. van Minnen, "Een fenomeen herdacht: De terugkeer van Hendrik Willem van Loon in Veere," *Zeeuws Tijdschrift* 44 (1994): 184-193; G.W. Van Loon, *The Story*, passim, and review of the book by Van der Veen, "Strooi mijn as uit boven Zeeland"; Henry B. Van Loon to Dirk Van Loon, 13 February 1983, Dirk Van Loon Family Correspondence, in author's collection.

Notes on Contributors

Brian W. Beltman is an adjunct professor of American History at the University of South Carolina and a regulatory specialist with South Carolina Electric and Gas Co. He published several articles about Dutch immigration and wrote *Dutch Farmer in the Missouri Valley: The Life and Leters of Ulbe Eringa, 1866-1950* (1996).

James D. Bratt is director of the Calvin Center for Christian Scholarship at Calvin College, Grand Rapids, Michigan, and professor of history there, specializing in American cultural and religious history. His book *Dutch Calvinism in Modern America: A History of a Conservative Subculture* (1984) is a standard text on Dutch-American acculturation in the Midwest. He is currently working on a biography of Abraham Kuyper.

Janel M. Curry is Professor of Geography and Environmental Studies at Calvin College, Grand Rapids, Michigan, and assumes the position of Dean of Research and Scholarship at Calvin College in August of 2000. She published widely in the geography and natural resource management literature on connections among ethnicity, religious worldview, landownership patterns, and agricultural practice. She is co-author of an upcoming book, *Community, Nature, and the Public Good*.

Annemieke Galema is senior consultant of the Transfer & Liaison Group at the University of Groningen, the Netherlands. She edited the volumes, *Images of the Nation: Different Meanings of Dutchness* (1993) and *Van de ene en de andere kant. Noordnederlandse en Noorwestduitse migration naar de Verenigde Staten in de negentiende eeuw* (1993) a book about emigration from the Dutch-German border and her dissertation: *Frisians to America 1880-1914. With the Baggage of the Fatherland* (1996).

George Harinck is director of the Archives and Documentation Center of the Reformed Churches in the Netherlands in Kampen and staff member of the Historical Documentation Center for Dutch Protestantism at the Vrije Universiteit in Amsterdam. He has edited numerous volumes about Dutch church history and authored several monographs. He co-edited *Sharing the Reformed Tradition: The Dutch-North American Exchange, 1846-1996* (1996).

Richard H. Harms is curator of Archives of Calvin College and Theological Seminary, and archivist of the Christian Reformed Church. He is adjunct professor of History at the Grand Valley State University and lecturer at the Aquinas College Emeritus College. He is a former assistant City Historian at Grand Rapids Public Library.

Earl Wm. Kennedy is professor of religion, emeritus, Northwestern College, Orange City, Iowa, and a minister in the Reformed Church in America. He is the author of articles, papers, and reviews on various theological and church historical subjects, especially the 19th-century midwestern Dutch Reformed, and is currently writing a book about the Reformed and Christian Reformed in Orange City 1871-1921.

Hans Krabbendam is assistant director of the Roosevelt Study Center in Middelburg, the Netherlands. He wrote *The Model Man: A Life of Edward W. Bok* (1995) and co-edited several volumes on American-European relations: *Sharing the Reformed Tradition: The Dutch-North American Exchange, 1846-1996* (1996), *Social and Secure? Politics and Culture of the Welfare State* (1996), *Writing Lives* (1998), and *Through the Cultural Looking Glass* (1999) .

Donald A. Luidens is professor of sociology and chair of the department at Hope College. His research has focused on mainline Protestants, with special emphasis on the Reformed Church in America and the PresbyterianChurch. His co-authored book, *Vanishing Boundaries: The Religion of Mainline Protestant Baby Boomers* (1994) was the winner of the Book of the Year Award from the Society for the Scientific Study of Religion.

Cornelis A. van Minnen is Director of the Roosevelt Study Center in Middelburg, the Netherlands. He wrote *American Diplomats in the Netherlands, 1815-1850* (1994) and co-edited numerous volumes about European-American relations, most recently *Beat Culture* (1999) and *Religious and Secular Reform in America* (1999). He is currently working on a biography on Hendrik W. van Loon.

Roger J. Nemeth is professor of sociology at Hope College. His primary research interests are in comparative and historical sociology with an emphasis in religious organizations. He has co-authored numerous articles on the Reformed Church in America and is currently involved in a comparative study of the RCA and the Christian Reformed Church.

James C. Schaap, Professor of English at Dordt College, Sioux Center, Iowa, teaches writing and literature and writes fiction and non-fiction. His book *Our Family Album: The Unfinished History of the Christian Reformed Church* (1998), is a widely read popular history of the denomination to which he belongs. His fiction often tends to feature Dutch-Americans. His most recent book, *Romey's Place* (1999), a coming-of-age novel set in a small Dutch-American town in Wisconsin, is presently being translated into Dutch and will be published by Boekencentrum Uitgevers in Zoetermeer in 2000.

Yda Schreuder is Associate Professor of Geography at the University of Delaware, Newark, Delaware. She has conducted her PhD research in the Netherlands in the early 1980s and has published extensively on Dutch Catholic immigration to the United States. In 1989 her book *Dutch Catholic Immigrant Settlement in Wisconsin, 1850-1905* was published by Garland Publishing, Inc., New York.

Suzanne M. Sinke is Associate Professor of History at Clemson University, and for 1999-2000 is Fulbright Professor at the University of Tampere (Finland). She co-edited with Rudolph Vecoli *A Century of European Migrations, 1830-1930* (1991). She has published numerous articles on Dutch and German immigrant women as well as the forthcoming book *Dutch Immigrant Women in the United States, 1880-1920*.

Henk van Stekelenburg received his Ph.D. degree from the Catholic University Brabant at Tilburg in 1991. He published a trilogy about Noord-Brabant emigration to the U.S.: *Landverhuizing als regionaal verschijnsel, van Noord-Brabant naar Noord-Amerika, 1820-1880* (1991) and *"Hier is alles vooruitgang": Landverhuizing van Noord-Brabant naar Noord-Amerika, 1880-1920* (1994) and posthumously *De grote trek. Emigratie vanuit Noord-Brabant naar Noord-Amerika, 1940-1963* (2000).

Pieter R.D. Stokvis is affiliated with the Dutch Open University. He has written numerous articles about migration, both in English and Dutch. His Ph.D. dissertation about the early Dutch emigration movement (*De Nederlandse trek naar Amerika 1846-1847)* is a landmark book in Dutch emigration history.

Harry S. Stout is Jonathan Edwards Professor of American Christianity, Religious Studies and American History at Yale University and author of several books about American religion, among others about Jonathan Edwards, *The New England Soul: Preaching and Religious Culture in Colonial New England* and *The Divine Dramatist: George Whitefield and the Rise of Modern Evangelicalism* (1991) and co-editor of *New Directions in American Religious History* (1997), *Women and American Religion* (1999), and *Religion and the Civil War* (1999).

Larry J. Wagenaar is associate professor and director of the Joint Archives of Holland, Holland, Michigan on the campus of Hope College. He is the executive director of the Association for the Advancement of Dutch American Studies and co-author of *Albertus C. Van Raalte: Dutch Leader and American Patriot* (1996) among other Dutch-American titles.

Index